Word and Image in Japanese Cinema

Word and Image in Japanese Cinema examines the complex relationship between the temporal order of linguistic narrative and the spatiality of visual spectacle, a dynamic that has played an important role in much of Japanese film. The tension between the controlling order of words and the liberating fragmentation of images has been an important force that has shaped modern culture in Japan and that has also determined the evolution of its cinema. In exploring the rift between word and image, the essays in this volume clarify the cultural imperatives that Japanese cinema reflects, as well as the ways in which the dialectic of word and image has informed the understanding and critical reception of Japanese cinema in the West.

Dennis Washburn is associate professor of Japanese and Comparative Literature at Dartmouth College. He is the author of *The Dilemma of the Modern in Japanese Fiction* and translator of Ôoka Shôhei's *The Shade of Blossoms* and Yokomitsu Riichi's *Shanghai.* He has also co-edited two works with Alan Tansman: *Studies in Modern Japanese Literature* and the forthcoming translation of Isoda Kôichi's *Tokyo as an Idea.*

Carole Cavanaugh is assistant provost and director of the Center for Educational Technology at Middlebury College. She has published widely in the areas of Japanese literature and film. Her most recent work is a study of Mizoguchi's *Sansho Dayu* in the British Film Institute Film Classics Series.

Word and Image in Japanese Cinema

Edited by

DENNIS WASHBURN
Dartmouth College

CAROLE CAVANAUGH
Middlebury College

For Marge,
the dearest lover
of both words and
images!
Love
Carole

CAMBRIDGE UNIVERSITY PRESS
Cambridge, New York, Melbourne, Madrid, Cape Town, Singapore,
São Paulo, Delhi, Dubai, Tokyo

Cambridge University Press
The Edinburgh Building, Cambridge CB2 8RU, UK

Published in the United States of America by Cambridge University Press, New York

www.cambridge.org
Information on this title: www.cambridge.org/9780521777414

First published 2001
This digitally printed version 2010

A catalogue record for this publication is available from the British Library

ISBN 978-0-521-77182-5 Hardback
ISBN 978-0-521-77741-4 Paperback

Contents

Illustrations

Contributors

Carole Cavanaugh is assistant provost and director of the Center for Educational Technology at Middlebury College. She has published widely in the areas of Japanese literature and film. Her most recent work is a study of Mizoguchi's *Sansho Dayu* in the British Film Institute Film Classics Series.

Linda C. Ehrlich is associate professor at Case Western Reserve University. She has published numerous articles on the cinema and is the co-editor, with David Ehrlich, of *Cinematic Landscapes: Observations on the Visual Arts and Cinema of China and Japan*. In addition to her work on Asian cinema, she has written on Spanish cinema and has compiled an anthology *An Open Window: The Cinema of Victor Erice*.

Edward Fowler is the author of *The Rhetoric of Confession* and *San'ya Blues*. He teaches Japanese literature and film at the University of California, Irvine.

Kathe Geist has contributed numerous articles on Japanese cinema to periodicals and anthologies, most recently an article on "East Asian Cinema" for the BFI's 2nd edition of *The Cinema Book*. She lives and writes in Brookline, MA.

Aaron Gerow is associate professor in the International Student Center at Yokohama National University. His most recent work includes: "Consuming Asia, Consuming Japan" in the forthcoming anthology *History Revised: Citizenship, Education and War;* and "Zuzô to shite no *Sensôron*" in *Sekai* (1998.12).

Leger Grindon is professor and director of Film-Video Studies at Middlebury College. He is the author of *Shadows on the Past: Studies in the Historical Fiction Film*, and is currently writing a book on the boxer and boxing in Hollywood cinema.

Charles Shirô Inouye is author of *The Similitude of Blossoms, A Critical Biography of Izumi Kyôka (1873–1939), Japanese Novelist and Playwright* and translator of *Japanese Gothic Tales* by Izumi Kyôka. He is currently writing on visuality and the formation of modern consciousness in Japan. He teaches at Tufts University where he is dean of the College for Undergraduate Education.

Keiko I. McDonald is a professor in Japanese literature and cinema at the University of Pittsburgh. Her books include: *Cinema East: A Critical Study of Major Japanese Films; Mizoguchi; Japanese Classical Theater in Films;* and *From Book to Screen: Modern Japanese Literature in Films.* She has also co-edited, with Thomas Rimer, *Nara Encounters,* and is currently working on a book on the filmmaker Shimizu Hiroshi.

Susan J. Napier is associate professor in Japanese literature and culture at the University of Texas at Austin. She is the author of *Escape from the Wasteland: Romanticism and Realism in the Works of Mishima Yukio and Ôe Kenzaburô* and *The Fantastic in Modern Japanese Literature: The Subversion of Modernity.* She is currently at work on a study of Japanese animation.

Arthur Nolletti, Jr. is professor of Film and Literature at Framingham State College. He is co-editor, with David Desser, of *Reframing Japanese Cinema: Authorship, Genre, History* and editor of *The Films of Fred Zinneman: Critical Perspectives.*

Michael Raine is finishing a dissertation entitled *Youth, Body, and Subjectivity in 1950s Japanese Cinema* at the University of Iowa. He is currently visiting instructor in Film & Video and Asian Languages and Cultures at the University of Michigan.

Donald Richie is well known for his numerous writings on Japanese film. A resident of Japan since 1947, he has also written extensively on Japanese literature and culture, and is a regular contributor to the *Japan Times.* His recent works include: *The Honorable Visitors; Tokyo Nights; Lafcadio Hearn's Japan; Tokyo: A View of the City;* and, *Memoirs of the Warrior Kumagai: A Historical Novel.*

Antonio Santos is professor at the Chair of History and Aesthetics of Cinema in the University of Valladolid. His works include: *Kenji Mizoguchi* (Madrid: Cátedra, 1993); and *The Detective Plot in Film.* (Madrid : Cosema, 1995). At present he is engaged in research on the director Ozu Yasujirô.

Alan Tansman teaches Japanese and comparative literature at Georgetown University. He is author of *The Writings of Kôda Aya* and co-editor and co-translator with Dennis Washburn of *Studies in Modern Japanese Literature: Essays and Translation in Honor of Edwin McClellan* and the forthcoming *Tokyo as an Idea.*

Richard Torrance is associate professor of Japanese at Ohio State University. He is author of *Tokuda Shûsei and the Emergence of Japan's New Middle Class.*

Janet A. Walker is professor of Comparative Literature at Rutgers University. She is the co-editor, with Paul Schalow, of *The Woman's Hand: Gender and Theory in Japanese Women's Writing,* and the author of "The Russian Role in the Creation of the First Japanese Novel, Futabatei Shimei's *Ukigumo,*" in *A Hidden Fire: Russian and Japanese Cultural Encounters 1868–1926,* edited by Thomas Rimer.

Dennis Washburn is associate professor of Japanese and Comparative Literature at Dartmouth College. He is the author of *The Dilemma of the Modern in Japanese Fiction* and translator of Ôoka Shôhei's *The Shade of Blossoms* and Yokomitsu Riichi's *Shanghai.* He has also co-edited two works with Alan Tansman: *Studies in Modern Japanese Literature* and the forthcoming translation of Isoda Kôichi's *Tokyo as an Idea.*

Foreword

Outside Views of the Japanese Film

Donald Richie

All Western views of the Japanese film are, by definition, outside. What I want to do is to put them in some sort of order and show how the methodologies have varied, how the focus has shifted, and how reflexive these outside views have proved.

Sergei Eisenstein, in a 1945 essay quoted by James Monaco, devised an analogy for film scholarship. First, there is the long shot, which sees in films political or social implications; second, there is the medium shot, which focuses on the human scale of the film; and finally there is the close-up, which breaks down film into its elements, attempts to treat it as a language, and so on. Whether Eisenstein intended these stages to be read chronologically or not, his paradigm has proved fairly accurate – certainly so far as Western scholarship on Japanese film is concerned.

All of this scholarship is postwar, and its beginnings are in the 1950s with the work of Marcel Guiglaris, of Joseph L. Anderson, and of myself. These first works were very much of their time. They were all in long-shot, as it were.

Our methodology was also of its time. Both Anderson and I followed a main tradition of American criticism that was to see films not as products of authors, or of a structure approaching a language, but as evidence of social, cultural, and political movements. The model in our book was Lewis Jacobs: his work on the American cinema. Like him, we saw our field as culturally specific, yet our bias was toward synthesis rather than analysis, because we emphasized cultural values that Japan and America shared.

As Bela Balazs saw this is the basis of much early film appreciation. One perceives a common reality and this is judged as to its fidelity. The assumption is that film exists in the context of the world around it. It stems from reality.

Thus, whatever form cinema may take, it must obey the rule of its content. This is also an assumption of Siegfried Kracauer and it was widely shared by film scholars of the period. Film is not therefore a purely aesthetic object. Film is ruled by the reality it presents.

This was a view at the time accepted by a majority of film scholars, including those interesting themselves in Japanese cinema. Japanese reality was the source, and the virtue of the Japanese film lay in its fidelity. Ethics, and a resultant kind of humanism, became paramount to judgment. Later film theory was to considerably enlarge this notion.

J. Dudley Andrew has suggested this growth by indicating two categories that reflect the famous paradigm of the dichotomy between the early cinemas of the Lumière brothers on one hand and of Méliès on the other. Theories which celebrate the raw materials, what is seen, are essentially realist, and are for that reason *representational.* Theories which celebrate what is done with the materials are expressionist/impressionist, and are for that reason *presentational.*

A major contribution to film scholarship was an enlargement of the presentational idea and the assumptions of authorship as a means of codification. This perhaps marked the entry of Eisenstein's medium shot into the history of film theory – though he might have been surprised at the turn taken by his thoughts "on the human scale."

François Truffaut's *politique des auteurs* was the earliest and the most comprehensive indication that a different way of regarding film had evolved. Though André Bazin said that this theory consisted merely of choosing the personal in artistic creation as a standard and then assuming that it progressed, the theory did indicate that film was the product of an author, that it was not reality itself; nor was it an impression nor an expression of reality, but was rather the statement of an individual.

This was understood among scholars of the Japanese film as elsewhere and, since the move from the long shot to the medium shot seemed a natural one, there soon appeared a number of monographs on various directors, my own contributions included.

This also, in Japanese cinema studies as in all national-cinema studies, led to a strengthening of the idea of a pantheon, of a privileged few directors who best exemplified the ethics of this new theory. It also moved the discussion from the culture-specific to the person-specific.

The shortcomings of strict authorial theory also indicated one of the dilemmas of film theory in general. This is the contrast (noted earlier by many theorists) between the practical, which is film criticism, and the ideal, which is film theory. The former is descriptive in that it states what film is, and the latter is prescriptive since it indicates what film should be.

Descriptive writing on film is deductive; the writer examines and then draws conclusions. Prescriptive writing is inductive, the theorist deciding upon a system of values and then measuring the film against the system.

This is a dilemma because the dichotomy divides the field. At the same time, those who see in a divided field an answer to a further dialectic need not find this a dilemma at all. In any event, cinema was evolving a theory.

A question not often addressed is why it would want one. One theorist who asked this question was Christian Metz, who said that it was the function of theory to rescue film. If the cinema could support a system of theory, then it was just as respectable as the other arts, and indeed approached the theoretical ideal of a science. Such was necessary because cinema, the youngest art, suffered, said Metz, from an inferiority complex. With the explication of contemporary theory it need do so no longer. Prescriptive theory, though often needlessly elaborate and sometimes pretentious, served the need.

Models, linguistic and otherwise, were searched for and found, and film as language became an object for study. Eisenstein's close-up had been reached. Cinema was examined and its parts were analyzed. A system good enough for common use was discovered or constructed: structuralism provided the means for a study of the parts of film and their resulting whole.

The major approach in regard to Japanese film was that of Nöel Burch, though he considerably modified accepted structural theory in order to incorporate his own conclusions. His example also indicates the strengths of the structural approach. While remaining culturally specific he could still fit Japan into the frame of international cinema.

Basing his research upon the five information channels detailed by Metz – visual images, print or graphics, speech, music, and noise – he, in the first half of *To the Distant Observer,* defined Japanese cinema in a new and valid way. With Barthes as a pilot, he described a cinema that could be discussed in terms of signified and signifiers, of syntagma and paradigm, of the denotative and the connotative, and, at the same time, be seen as culturally specific, as Japanese.

And it is certainly true that in Japanese film the denotative quality causes no problem. A *torii* gateway is a *torii* gateway, recognizable. The connotative quality, however, is another matter. This is the meaning attached to the image. And it is often one that the foreigner cannot, for cultural reasons, decipher. The *torii* suggests a complex of associations not available to the foreign viewer without prior study.

Further, a point that Eisenstein himself brought up: a word is a word and a picture is a picture. Cinema may well have no language, but a *kanji,* a Chinese character, is still part word and part picture. In this sense it is what it means: in a way it is both signified and signifier.

Japanese film thus offers interesting challenges to the structuralist. Just as cinema was to be delivered from any indebtedness to sociology, anthropology, even history, now it could be seen as a closed system within itself – if the proper grids were used. In extreme cases what the film said was of small importance as compared to the way in which it said it. Content, which had been the major concern of earlier theory, was now sacrificed to the needs of form.

Of course, even to speak of form and content is to suggest a dichotomy that can barely be said to exist outside the Western world. (And even in this world as well, though David Bordwell has forever cleared up that matter by declaring – apropos of Ozu – that "the work's material [content] is what it is made out of; the form is the process and system of the making.")

Equally, to apply grids whether they are appropriate or not can falsify. In the Burch work, for example, both structuralist and Marxists grids were rigorously applied, though they eventually proved inappropriate to the connotations of the Japanese film.

One of the reasons is that the syntax of film is the result of its usage, not a determinant of it. Nothing is preordained. It evolves through use. And there are major differences that the rigors of an exact science may perhaps capture, but that an art cannot. Can then, the theorist must now ask, Western and Japanese syntaxes be profitably compared, and if so, to what extent?

There are difficulties and the largest is, perhaps, the one most ignored. Individuals take different approaches to Japan. These differences are due to disciplinary, personal, historical, and other factors. If we are creatures of our culture (as cultural anthropology tells us we are), then scholars of different cultural backgrounds manifest different ways of thinking that cause them to interpret differently.

Cultural forces shape scholarship on Japan through intellectual styles unique to the country and/or language area of the scholar. This is obviously true but there is a resistance on the part of academics to think of themselves as creatures of their culture. They like to think of themselves as free agents and to consider themselves to be above cultural restraints. Yet they are as much creatures of culture as everyone else.

To take but one example: the unnoticed impact of ideology. Russian-academic Japanese studies in general deal mainly with trade unions, labor movements, etc., topics important to the Marxist socialist approach and to the theory of historical materialism. American Japanese studies, on the other hand, stress the pragmatic, the democratic. The large number of monographic studies of rural communities is plainly the product of Anglo-American functionalism. It has, for example, never been fully adopted by French students of Japan. They are concerned with more theoretical and structured investigations. And so on.

In addition, scholarly endeavor often takes a further reflexive shape. The scholar looks at his subject as other – other, that is, than himself. Yet, taking Japan as the other really has less to do with who the other is than with the identity of the subject gazing at this other. The reason that otherness is an issue is that the viewed other is not an objective reality. Rather, it is an image, a perception that is subjectively constructed by the beholder on the basis of past background and experience rather than an objective account of any found reality.

A neglected writer on Japan, Helen Mears, underlined this in the title of her finest book, *Japan: Mirror for Americans.* When Anderson and I attempted to find ethical realism in Japan, and to define a democratic Japanese humanism, we were, despite our familiarity with Mears's work, drawing our own portraits as well as those of the Japanese filmmakers we wrote of.

One thus returns to definitions of reality, to questions pondered by Kracauer, by Bazin, by many other film theorists. The answers to these questions keep changing and this in part accounts for the richness of continuing film theory.

Godard, for example, feels that any language of film is debased by being manipulated into a false mirror of reality. It must be presentational rather than representational. It cannot, he holds, truly reproduce reality but it may be able to honestly reproduce itself.

This pregnant idea is quite applicable to such an overtly presentational cinema as that of the Japanese. As is Godard's later suggestion that the tension between mise-en-scène and montage is a major axis in the dialectic of film aesthetics. The one, as a modification of space, asks us questions we must answer. The other, as a modification of time, presents us with conclusions we must test. Together, they aim to discover, suggests Godard, a psychological reality that transcends physical, plastic reality.

Eisenstein would certainly have agreed since he held that it was necessary to destroy "realism" in order to approach reality. Film is not, he would have said, about the artist's relationship with his materials but about his relationship with his audience.

One finds these new concerns now in the works of several later writers on Japanese cinema, particularly the detailed and original work of David Bordwell, and especially his fine study of the poetics of Ozu. One also finds much else as well in these later writers on the Japanese cinema, and if I have not touched upon these further methodologies, it is because I have attempted to present this background in broad strokes, and to suggest directions that I feel have already been most beneficial to the study of Japanese cinema.

Nor have I touched upon theoretical writings by the Japanese themselves. For one thing, that is not my subject, and for another, this work, except for the occasional essay by Satō Tadao or by Hasumi Shigehiko, is not available to the general student of cinema.

Japanese film as an eminently presentational form of cinema is now being studied by a number of younger scholars. The culturally specific is being examined with a sharper focus than ever before as methodologies grow more subtle and more versatile. It is from this work that later general opinion will come, and through this new scholarship that the future audiences of Japanese film will be informed.

Introduction

Carole Cavanaugh and Dennis Washburn

> I was probably five or six when I saw a moving picture for the first time. I went with my father, if I remember rightly, to see this marvelous novelty at the Nishuro in Okawabata. The motion pictures were not projected on a large screen as they are nowadays. The size of the image was a rather small four-by-six feet or so. Also, they had no real story, nor were they as complex as films are these days. I remember, among the pictures that evening, one of a man fishing. He hooked a big one and then fell head over heels back into the water. He wore some kind of straw hat, and behind the long fishing pole he held in his hand were reeds and willows waving in the wind. Oddly enough, though my memory may be wrong, I fancy the man looked something like Admiral Nelson.
>
> – Akutagawa Ryûnosuke, *Tsuioku* (Memoirs, 1926)

In February 1897 both the Lumière brothers' Cinématographe and Edison's Vitascope arrived in Japan along with programs of short films. These moving pictures, generally no more than one minute long, were shown at venues like the Nishuro, halls for scientific displays, public meetings, and art exhibitions. Films were thus initially presented in Japan as a commercial spectacle, an educational experience, and a demonstration of the unprecedented capacity of technology to reproduce the real.

The near-simultaneity in the introductions of the cinema to Europe, the United States, and Japan was to have a marked effect on the generation that came of age in the 1910s and 1920s. Technology seemed to have neither owners nor antecedents, for the reality it represented boasted no genealogy and claimed no privileged cultural place. The fascination of

Japanese audiences for the apparatus of the motion picture, as much as for the images it projected, was not at all different from the curiosity of European spectators who checked for water or a mirroring device behind the screen after they viewed the Lumière film *A Boat Leaving Harbor.* Men and women of Akutagawa's day grew up with the sense that science and technology outpaced the traditions of Japan with little more speed than they did those of Europe.

The childhood memory of a writer whose work epitomizes the self-conscious, edgy attitude of Japanese artists in the early decades of this century provides an appropriate starting point for a consideration of the cultural importance of the cinema in Japan. Akutagawa's description of the program he viewed crystallizes not only a defining moment in his own psychological and artistic development, but a threshold experience for Japanese audiences at large. "Suddenly it was everywhere; it swept away all else," wrote Kubota Mantarô, and its sweep was not just geographical. Cinema was an index of the interpenetration of cultural forces that shaped the first wave of globalism a hundred years ago. The presence and availability of motion pictures transformed Tokyo into a city where the modes of presentation exchanged by popular and elitist art forms were redistributed as the new currency of modernity, a cultural movement that, unlike European modernisms, drew upon realism for its intellectual authority as well as for its mass appeal.

The privileging of cinematic realism over illusion resonates strongly in the way Akutagawa's memory ordered his recollection. In spite of his assertion that the film "had no story," he dwells on its narrativity. It is evident in his description that the film he remembered was a work of realistic narrative fiction, internally edited by a storytelling structure that ensured the coherence and temporal movement of its content. As others have noted, though the film consists of a single one-minute shot, the camera achieves narrativity through the editing choices it makes in where to begin, when to end, and what to record. In such short "realist" films the camera does not accidentally capture an actual event, but records a staged fictional sequence. Though simple, narrative is fully in place.

Narrative, however, is not the lone element at work. The short film Akutagawa remembers also commands his attention as spectacle, a novelty to be described not just for its content but for its surprising presence in the world. Without the procedures of editing that soon became standard – procedures that naturalized narrative at the expense of spectacle – the fishing film naively balances both story and the eye-catching power of the attraction in which it is contained. That equilibrium allows Akutagawa to relate the sequence of actions in the film while claiming that it has no story. The fishing film is both narration and spectacle, a phenomenon of early motion pictures Tom Gunning identifies as the cinema of attractions, preserved in Akutagawa's account as an interplay of word and image.

A key point in Akutagawa's recollection is that the film succeeded in disguising its fictionality from his view. He is impressed by the accumulation of quotidian details that surround and define the subject: the straw hat, the fishing pole, the hooked fish, the reeds and willows in the background. The technology responsible for the illusory wonder of the film is passed over in favor of its circumstantial realism. What Dai Vaughn terms the transcultural standard of pictorial representation is at work in Akutagawa's description; the natural incidentals that confirmed the reality of the scene arrested the wonder of viewers with equal force across divergent cultures. The response of the first film audiences confirms the cross-cultural power of mimetic aesthetics, a radically different form of performance and representation for the Japanese viewer. Film marshaled the natural and material world to project the subject within narrative as real, as no longer a construction in poetic words, masks, or theatrical make-up.

The authority of resemblance goes even further in its demand for subject identification. Akutagawa's recollection that the filmed man looks like Admiral Nelson demonstrates the mind's struggle to reconcile what it knows to be false with what it perceives to be real. Realism insists so strongly on identification that memory has not only supplied an identity, but it has also chosen a representative figure of Western imperial power. The mention of Nelson seems to concede that with film a foreign kind of vision, one that presents itself as natural and universal, has colonized the mind. Akutagawa was astonished not by the moving picture's power to deceive, but by its realistic transparency. He understands the film to be at once familiar and exotic, ordinary and marvelous, but not illusory as well as real, only real.

It is important to keep in mind that Akutagawa's remembered account is presented to us in the 1920s after many of the formal conventions of the Japanese cinema – especially the use of the *katsuben,* a film explainer or narrator – had been established. When Akutagawa claims that the film had no *hanashi,* he refers both to story and storyteller. The mediation of devices like the *katsuben* may be viewed historically as a continuation of earlier Japanese performance traditions (the storytelling practices of the *yoseba* or of the kabuki and bunraku theaters). But even if we acknowledge that continuity in performance practices, realistic narrative was ultimately privileged over either spectacle or presentational narrative as the dominant mode of film aesthetics. The relationship between word and image, their dynamic symbiosis, emerged in a way that subordinated elements of traditional narrative practice.

The effect of this newly perceived symbiosis was widespread. For example, Japanese fiction and its modes of (re)presentation were also transformed. Before the end of the nineteenth century very little fiction existed in Japan without some form of illustration. Realist modes banished pictures from fiction and exiled them to the Westernized sites of the museum and the movie house. Performance too was traditionally presented as commingled media; the bunraku theater, for example, is a mixture of puppets, realistic sets, music, and chanted text. The very notions of separating word and image, or of consciously bringing them together seamlessly in the realism of cinema, are alien to traditional Japanese aesthetics. And so perhaps the effort to negotiate the newly opened space between words and images, between narrative and spectacle, is more urgent in Japan than in other cultures, especially those of Europe where word and image had parted ways long before the advent of the technology of the motion picture.

The preoccupation with enunciating an aesthetic ideology that could occupy and exploit the space between word and image reached a peak in Japan in the 1920s. Artists at that moment were increasingly interested in film as the medium with the greatest potential to express the experiences of modern society. Literary artists turned to the unmediated power of the image as a way to recover for their words the authenticity and originality denied by the material culture of modernity. Numerous stories, essays, and manifestos published during this decade convey the depth of the interest of writers in the possibilities of film and of imagistic writing. The short story "Lemon" by Kajii Motojirô is representative of this interest.

"Lemon," published in 1925, is an autobiographical piece. The narrator is a young man who is poor, ill with tuberculosis, and chronically depressed. He takes to roaming the streets of Tokyo as a distraction from his suffering, and in his earliest perambulations he is drawn to places like the famous Maruzen bookstore, a site of exotic foreign goods, a marketplace of Taishô tastes, and a repository of literary culture. Over time, however, the fascination of Maruzen wears off and the place becomes oppressive as a reminder of his economic and cultural alienation. The narrator begins to wander the backstreets of Tokyo, where he finds not only traces of the old culture of Edo, but also a kind of exotic fascination in the déclassé objects of everyday life. He is especially drawn to a simple greengrocery, and after passing by it many times he finally stops in and buys a single lemon.

The lemon proves to have extraordinary restorative powers. It seems to cool his fever and transports him, in reverie, to far-off locales such as California. Liberated by the strange effects wrought by the lemon, the narrator walks on lost in thought until he finds himself in front of the Maruzen bookstore. He enters and goes to the art section, but instead of reading he uses some books to make a little castle. After looking at his work, he impulsively leaves his lemon on top of his castle:

> I felt strangely ticklish. "Should I leave, I wonder. Yes, let's get out of here," and I hurried out.
>
> The strangely ticklish feeling made me smile out on the street. How intriguing it would be if the mysterious villain who had come and planted that fearful bomb, shining yellow on a shelf in Maruzen, were I, and if, ten minutes later, there were an explosion with its epicenter at the Fine Arts Section.
>
> I intently pursued my daydream: "If that happened, then stuffy old Maruzen would be blown to bits."
>
> I went down to Kyôgoku, where the pictures on the movie billboards colored the streets with their strange appearance.[1]

The transformation of the narrator's physical and mental state is achieved through the agency of a simple natural object, which stands in contrast to the deliberate artifice of Maruzen. The sharp distinction between unmediated, authentic sensation, which finds its source in something as small as a lemon, and the mediating, alienating effect of the culture of words is the heart of this story. The contrast between the liberating effects of image and the constraining, structuring power of words is

[1] This passage from "Lemon" comes from Volume 1 of the *Kajii Motojirō Zenshū* (Complete works of Kajii Motojirō). Tokyo: Chikuma shobō, 1966. p. 13.

twisted by the narrative resolution in "Lemon" into a kind of double helix in which the simultaneous antagonism and mutual dependence of word and image entwine in a singular form. The imaginative leap at the end transports the narrator to a different realm of experience and, suggestively, to a different site of art represented by the garish billboards advertising their motion pictures.

With the possible exception of the locomotive, there have been few technologies so closely linked symbolically and materially with the aesthetics of modern culture in Japan as the motion picture. Taken as an abstract concept, film became a marker, a synecdoche for modernity. It is an art form whose very nature at once depends upon and reinforces the perception of a conflicted relationship between word and image, in which the need for authenticity and the drive for freedom are balanced against an aversion to the loss of tradition and a fear of chaos. The effort to resolve the divide between word and image is apparent in the impulse, so amusingly and beautifully depicted by Kajii, to overcome language itself by privileging a natural image – an image possessing the explosive potential to shatter the self-consciousness of modern culture that blocks the individual from experiencing the real.

And yet in Kajii's story the privileging of image relies, ultimately, upon the conjuring power of words to suggest the illusion of the transformation. Indeed, the word *lemon* itself is written in literary characters so difficult that they normally have to be glossed in order to be read. Kajii's (perhaps unconscious?) use of mediating characters for the imagistic title of his story points to the dual function of image and word that Chinese characters perform, and indicates why, as was noted previously, the separation of word and image was an alien notion in Japanese aesthetics before the late nineteenth century. However, given the theme of Kajii's story, its very title also points to a competing impulse to preserve the word, to maintain the stability of cultural meaning that contains the liberating transformation at the end of the story. The piquancy of "Lemon" is an effect created by the dialectic that operates between these contrary impulses.

This dialectic corresponds to the ontological dialectic of film, that of spectacle and narrative. Photographic realism challenges film's fascination with text by purportedly giving the as-is-ness of a world unmediated by language. The spatiality of motion pictures always works against the temporal movement of narrative. Film starts essentially as spectacle.

However, the temporality that characterizes language cannot be suppressed, and film inevitably appropriates the structures of narrative. In the economy of its production and distribution film brought about profound change as *the* medium of mass culture, but as an instrument of recording and shaping experience, film in Japan also became an elitist preserver of a textual tradition that paradoxically was no longer defined by the interdependence of word and image.

The essays in this volume explore in various ways the dialectic of word and image in the Japanese cinema. Although the methods and approaches taken by the contributors show considerable range, the common elements that run throughout the book originate in the fact that the essays all deal with the same fundamental historical developments. Moreover, in organizing this volume we included contributors equally from the academic disciplines of film studies and literary studies. We were motivated in part by a desire for an interdisciplinary collection, but more important, we wanted to highlight the space between word and image by exposing the ways in which that dialectic has informed the critical reception of the Japanese cinema outside Japan.

Our motivations are transparent in the structure of this volume. Part I, "Wording the Image/Imaging the Word," consists of essays that deal explicitly with the problem of the relationship between the motion picture and text, especially literary sources. The controlling order of words and the liberating fragmentation of images, the two forces that have largely determined the evolution of Japanese film, are the intensifying desires of modern culture: the desire for control, the impulse to totality that easily wipes away contradiction, and the desire for fragmentation that plays itself out in the politics of disaffection.

The irreconcilability of reality to representation in Japanese film often goes unacknowledged, or unrewarded. The essays in Part I take up this paradox and raise a number of critical questions. What does this historical paradox have to do with the rift between language and image? Is it on the line between the discursive and the visible that the tensions of Japanese modernity actually dissolve, or is it on that very boundary where they initiate their separate projects? These questions remind us again of the long history of Japanese art, in which the interdependence of text and pictures and a commingling of media were key features. That interdependence becomes especially complex for the motion picture.

Japanese film, though obviously wedded to pictorial representation, has tended to cling to the prestige of literary sources and to the authority of the scenario, especially during periods of intense censorship, than have most other national film traditions. This tendency characterizes the anxiety of other modern forms in Japan, such as the novel or contemporary drama, that originate as apparent disruptions with previous modes of expression and performance. The talent of the novel for telling its own story, an ability that counteracts the rewriting or retelling so prominent in traditional Japanese literature, is counteracted itself by the appropriation and re-visioning of earlier discourses that preoccupy the cinema.

We can consciously assume what Donald Richie calls "outside views" of the Japanese cinema in order to reflect objectively, or at least more modestly, the shimmering play of cultural lights and shadows. From such a vantage we can relate the representations that figure in Japanese film to the conditions that determined their production, and engage them in a dialogue with texts – sources, laws, or peripheral discourses – that are validated or resisted by the words and images linked together on the screen. Or we can experience the marginality of the films themselves, their oppositional relationship with the rhetorical structures that uphold them. Two broad tendencies emerge. The first is toward films that participate in Bazin's "myth of total cinema," a style that seduces the viewer into believing that it has recreated the world in its own image, which is collective, spatial, mythic. The essays in Part II, "Reflections of Identity," trace out this tendency in their analyses of works that either assume, or attempt to impose, certain shared images that define cultural identity in Japan. The second tendency is toward films that resist the arrogant realism that this kind of totalization implies; and the theme of resistance, both personal and political, is taken up in its various manifestations in the essays of Part III, "Outside the Frame of Culture."

To imagine a space between words and images in Japanese cinema is to prompt a larger question: Is there a rift in film, of all places, between the discursive and the visible? This question calls to mind a list of dualities that move the issue away from the autonomy of aesthetics toward the contingencies of history. The conceptual pairs we can make word and image stand for – representation and consciousness; the sensory immediacy of images and their mediation through language; the logical expectations of linguistic narrative and the mythic ambition of telling stories with pictures; the apparent affinity of the elite with the linguistic, and of the popular with the visual; a textual source and an adapted film; censorship and freedom of expression – all such pairs compel cinema to look for meaning outside the film frame itself, or the frame of structuralism that generates these dualities, and into their place in the struggles of Japanese modernity. In the space between word and image lie the historical imperatives that cinema reflects and recalculates. Stepping into that space is nonetheless an uncertain move for the critique of a cinema that comfortably envisions itself as representing the timeless content of culture demarked by the otherness that film in Japan attributes to its apparatus and mode. This collection of essays stakes its claim on the line or rift that runs between, where the domination invited by otherness is relinquished and where acquiescence to the authority of culture is postponed.

As with any collaborative work, this collection has come about through the efforts of many organizations and individuals whose assistance we would like to acknowledge. We want to sincerely thank Dudley Andrew, John Treat, David Desser, and Norma Field for making numerous invaluable suggestions that have improved the work. Aaron Gerow and Leger Grindon, besides contributing essays, also assisted us in organizing this project. We owe a special debt of gratitude to the Japan Foundation, the Toshiba Foundation, the Dickey Center at Dartmouth College, and the departments of Japanese, and of Theater, Dance and Film/Video at Middlebury College, for their financial support and their recognition of our endeavor.

PART ONE

WORDING THE IMAGE/ IMAGING THE WORD

CHAPTER ONE

The Word before the Image

Criticism, the Screenplay, and the Regulation of Meaning in Prewar Japanese Film Culture

Aaron Gerow

RENAMING THE UNNAMED

Despite the predominant tendency to term motion pictures an image medium both in the West and in Japan (where *eizô* [image] is in fact coming to supplant the word *eiga* [film] for many educational institutions offering film courses), the word both spoken and written has played a central role in the history of the art.[1] This is not simply due to the perfection of sound technology in bringing speech to the screen; there is also a long history of cinema inspiring, and in turn being inspired by, writing. The relationship between film and literature is certainly the most prominent example of such interaction between word and image, but it would be restricting to reduce our conception of such intercourse to only literary adaptation in cinema or to the "visuality" of the modern novel. Both inquiries assume a cinema-image/literature-word dichotomy that occludes the historical role writing and speaking about cinema has played in the constitution of the medium itself and of how it has operated in prewar Japanese film culture.

One could consider, for instance, the history of the importation and assimilation of cinema in Japan itself as the attempt to articulate a foreign object into the domestic language, of naming what had not yet been named. The creation of the medium's initial Japanese appellation, *katsudô shashin* (literally, "moving photographs"), or the lectures given by the first *benshi* (*benshi* is another term for "Katsuben" the film explainer or narrator whose words accompanied a film) to explain the newly arrived wonder, can be taken as manifestations of this discursive process of introducing audiences to an unknown technology. Words were essential in forming a conception of the medium itself, in making it accessible to audiences unfamiliar with its operations.

Yet it is clear that words did not simply supplement a preexisting, nonlinguistic object (e.g., the moving image) that needed a linguistic window to be seen. This is evident from the fact that the motion pictures did not arrive on Japan's shores completely unknown. Given that one of the early appellations for the movies was *jidô gentô* (self-moving magic lantern – an appropriation of the already existing name for the magic lantern), it is not surprising that some like Terada Torahiko saw it as merely a technologically more precise, yet aesthetically less interesting version of the popular lantern shows;[2] or that others like Kubota Utsubo could state, upon first entering a cinema hall, that motion pictures "were the most interesting of the *misemono* of *that kind*"[3] – as if both men were familiar with the medium before they had even seen it. Words used to name the medium were then not just articulating what was unknown, but redefining what had already been shaped by words.

This tension between the processes of naming the unnamed and renaming the already named is an example, I believe, of the shifting relationship between the image and the word in the prewar Japanese film world. Writing and speaking on the cinema were certainly essential in explaining a new, difficult-to-understand object, but that writing was, at the same time, already an essential part of the object itself. Discussions carried on in critical writings were not so much concerned with coming to grips with a static-object cinema as they were with transforming it precisely by altering the way words already operated in the cinema, primarily, as we shall see, through the establishment of film criticism and the screenplay as cinematic practices. In the end, the history of the word and the image in prewar Japanese cinema is less of a Manichean conflict between diametric opposites than of a struggle over the very nature of language and signification and its function in the social sphere. As will become evident later, by *word* and *image* I do not simply mean the types of signs used in writing and cinema, respectively: they are as much metaphors for different possibilities with regard to signification, figures at the center of a larger struggle in prewar Japan over the regulation of meaning itself.

A CHORUS OF VOICES: NOVELIZATION AND EARLY CINEMA

One of the dominant early models of the relationship between the cinema and the spoken or written word was that of explanation, of providing knowledge of the new medium to viewing audiences through printed matter or lectures. This function was not confined to the process of familiarizing the Japanese with a foreign medium, for it continued well after most urban Japanese were well aware of the moving pictures. Rather, it became part of the apparatus itself, becoming essential to how films operated and how spectators read their content. The example of the *benshi*'s role in narrating silent cinema is well known, but I would first like to focus here on a related phenomenon: the practice of novelizing films, carried out by a nascent film journalism.

The first film magazine in Japan, *Katsudô shashinkai* (Moving Picture World), listed, in its initial issue in June 1909, the three reasons it was being published:

> First, it is because interest in the moving pictures is growing ever greater. Their recent development and popularity is truly surprising: films span many fields and, needless to say, are becoming quite varied and complex. . . . Yet since they are shown one after the other in the space of two or three hours, there is no time to fully explain them. One can only sit back and gaze because there is no time to take them in as one switches to the next. Therefore, knowing or not knowing the story beforehand (or even after seeing it) may make a considerable difference in how deeply interested one is in the movies. For this reason, this magazine will compensate for the lack of explanation and offer knowledge necessary to enjoy watching the movies.
>
> Second, this will serve as a souvenir. There is no more convenient way of sharing the pleasures of the day than giving this as a souvenir to friends after the family goes out together to see the movies, or to those in the family who stayed home. Not only that, but is not reading the explanations and the summaries and narrating the scenes of the film one of the pleasures of a peaceful home?
>
> Third, it is a means of obtaining new knowledge about the world. As just mentioned, the moving pictures . . . are a means of equally and pleasurably injecting the freshest knowledge into people's minds. However, not even the smartest and most quick-thinking of persons, when viewing them only at a glance, could possibly taste and digest everything. Even if he could digest it, it would be difficult for him to remember it for long. Because of that, it is very necessary to put this information in a magazine to help viewers both understand and forever remember the world's new knowledge.[4]

Two of the above raisons d'être concern the role of film journalism in augmenting a lack in the signifying process of the cinematic apparatus. The presumption is that films, either through their formal style or mode of exhibition, cannot be understood as is. To alleviate this problem, *Katsudô shashinkai,* as well as its other fellow film magazines, concentrated on printing plot summaries and novelizations in order to help spectators either prepare themselves before the film or find out what they missed afterward. This in fact would become one of the major functions of Japanese film journalism up until the late 1910s (as was the case in other nations as well).

It is also evident that from early on, these plot summaries, or novelized versions of film stories, functioned as another important part of the film industry's apparatus: advertising. The very first film magazines, *Katsudô shashinkai, Katsudô shashin* (Moving Pictures), and *Katsudô shashin taimuzu* (Moving Picture Times), were operated by the motion picture companies themselves (Yoshizawa Shôten, M. Pathé, and Yokota Shôkai, respectively); novelizations functioned to announce the latest films, lure audiences to the theater, and prepare them to watch the movie. Summaries continued to dominate the pages of even the more independent film magazines produced by the commercial publishing industry that began appearing in the mid-1910s. These new magazines may have been owned by publishers structurally separate from the studios, but they were not free of the influence of their advertisers and supporters. Perhaps it was due to the fact that Tenkatsu studio founder Kobayashi Kisaburô helped finance *Katsudô no sekai* (The Movie World), a major proponent of reform, that the periodical was relatively favorable to (though not wholly uncritical of) his activities – as well as his company's films.

Novelizations did retain their function as advertising, but it would be inaccurate to claim that was their only role: one would suppose that making available a plot summary beforehand, complete with an exact explanation of the ending, would spoil the picture for many potential paying patrons.[5] Perhaps we do have to lend credibility to the statement by *Katsudô shashinkai* that novelizations were essential in helping spectators understand the film plot and access the often foreign world depicted therein. The discourse of novelization could be posited as one of the primary forms of cinematic knowledge in 1910s Japan, exemplifying how the motion pictures were defined, the process of meaning production, and the relationship between the image and the word.

Novelizations in the early film days in Japan were apparently not provided by the film company or based on the script, but rather composed by the magazine itself, which sent a reporter to the theater to watch the film several times and copy down the story.[6] Especially in the case of Japanese films, this was necessary because full-fledged film scripts were not yet in existence. The plot of a film was available only after being shown in the theater because the ultimate creation of narrative meaning still occurred in the sphere of exhibition, not production, especially given the role of the *benshi.* By being written following both production and exhibition, novelizations reflected the dominance of the latter in the creation of filmic meaning. Some plot summaries also bolstered the role of *benshi* by transcribing less the flow of filmic images than the rhetoric of their narration, sometimes word for word.[7]

Novelizations did, however, work against the localism of exhibition. When dependent upon a *benshi* for its final meaning, the same film could pose different effects according to where and with whom it was shown. By recording a version of what one *benshi* said, and distributing it to many locations via the print media, film magazines were helping to standardize the film text by creating a rendition of the plot that was supposed to hold true for all exhibition sites. Novelization also aided the process of shifting the load of cinematic meaning from the space of the theater to the filmic text itself, as well as centering the pleasures of cinema on the enjoyment of narrative, as opposed to less narrative thrills such as pure visual fascination and enjoying the *benshi's* playing with words.

The practice of novelization still presumed that even this more universal filmic text was dependent upon discourses external to itself. As evident in the logic of *Katsudô shashinkai,* it was assumed that means other than the film itself were needed after the production stage to assist viewers in understanding the text. One of these was the *benshi,* who explained what Japanese spectators were unfamiliar with or could not understand on their own. The other was novelization, which in many ways assumed the same function of the *benshi* in providing information to filmgoers. The analogy is important because even those novelizations that did not adopt the oratorical style of the *benshi* were considerably long and detailed, and, especially by the mid-1910s, sometimes reached ten pages in length. The presumed necessity of the *benshi* and of novelization was a declaration that the cinematic image on its own was insufficiently meaningful without the supplementary power of the word.

Yet the independence of the discourse of novelization rendered unclear the location of the source of narrative enunciation in motion pictures. It did not seem to reside either in the film, the magazine, or the sphere of production, reflecting the fact that movies in this era offered less a unified, univocal textual experience than a chorus of voices. Note that most of the novelizations were not only authorless, but they also rarely – especially in the case of Japanese films – cited any production information other than the film's title, genre, and studio. Interpenetrated by the words of the novelization, it was as if the film, somehow devolving from a production company, was in the end the product of a faceless amalgamation of discourses with no specific source. Never entirely the product of its producers, the *benshi,* or its novelization, the film text lacked self-sufficiency and depended upon the fact that any and all these various sources of enunciation would intertwine and mold the final cinematic meaning at the point the film was shown.

The cinematic text's lack of independence reflected on film journalism itself. The practice of novelization made film magazines one of the essential supplemental discourses, particularly in relation to the sphere of exhibition. It is important to note the similarity between film magazines and the programs distributed at some of the more high-class foreign-film theaters. Many of these free, four-page programs were in fact weekly periodical publications that, while centered on plot summaries and credit information for that week's program, also included articles and letters from film fans. Programs like the Teikokukan's *Daiichi shinbun* (Number One News, begun in March 1916) became an important center of debate on the cinema and, for some young critics like Iijima Tadashi, the first place to publish their thoughts on the medium.[8] The fact that the most important film journal in Japanese history, *Kinema junpô* (The Movie Times), started out as a four-page pamphlet with a layout similar to that of the theater programs indicates how closely early film journalism was tied to programs and the discourse of exhibition. Journalism was simply one facet of the cinematic apparatus, one of the means by which filmic meaning was transmitted to the audience.

That did not mean that the word was beholden to the operations of the image. Rather, the cinematic image, unable to transmit its meaning without the aid of such linguistic rhetors as the *benshi* and film magazines, was not defined as a mode of signification that was other to the word. Leaning on the shoulders of its older generic cousins like the novel and forms of oral storytelling such as *kôdan,* film was not yet constructed as an independent art possessing its own, unique forms of signification. Cinema had to rely on discourses outside itself because there was still no definition of what delineated the internal of the medium from the external. The word, even if it existed in an entirely different medium (e.g., the print medium), was still an essential element in how cinema operated and in how audiences understood it, so much so that *Katsudô gahô* (Movie Graphic) advertised its novelizations as the equivalent of the experience of going to the movies: "We believe that reading them in conjunction with the illustrations definitely produces a feeling similar to watching a moving picture."[9] The word was so central to the motion picture experience that seemingly the image itself was unnecessary; how the film presented its story, using formal devices defined as being particular to cinema, was less important. In the discourse of novelization, image and word were inseparable in creating an experience called the moving pictures, one that was itself difficult to distinguish as a signifying practice from other *misemono.*

REGULATING A NEW DISCOVERY: THE IMAGE

Another major discourse that initially treated the word as equivalent to the cinematic image was that of law. At first motion pictures were treated no differently from other *misemono* under censorship regulations, usually being covered by, but remaining unnamed within, old laws that covered fairground entertainments. Under these regulations, those wishing to present some form of entertainment publicly were required to obtain prior permission from the police station having jurisdiction over the area involved, a procedure that required submission of the names of those responsible, details about the performance space, and a summary of the entertainment itself.[10] Films were not viewed beforehand and were rarely, if ever, checked after opening. In the technology of censorship at the time, the written synopsis was considered sufficient for judging the film itself; it was the words that were the object of censorship because there was no conception of any form of meaning other than that.

This relation of the image and the word begins to change after 1908 when the film industry finally begins to regularize production and the medium itself experiences a boom, a change that is first apparent in how the state regulated the motion pictures. Right around that time, cinema became an object of concern for educators and regulators worried about film's corrupting influence on children, and it was these public leaders who started to form a discourse distinguishing film and its effects from those of other media. In this way, it was only by becoming a "bad object" that the motion pictures gained an identity.[11] As I have argued elsewhere, much of this transformation was symbolized in the debates over the immensely popular French film *Zigomar,* directed by Victorin Jasset.[12] In deciding to ban the film in October 1912, the police acknowledged a problem in the way they were censoring films:

> At police headquarters, looking at the original story of the French *Zigomar,* it was thought that there was nothing much to it. Even among works of this kind, if you inspect the moving picture license, you would think it is only a kind of child's play. That's why we approved it up until today thinking it had no effect on public morals. However, looking at the actual film, there is a world of difference from the explanation in both the scenery and the characters.[13]

The Tokyo police were admitting to a difference between the filmic text and its synopsis, in effect "discovering" the existence of the cinematic image: a semiotic experience apart from that offered in words, one accessible only through the "actual film" and its projection.

Yet the discovery was less that of a new, but stable form of signification, asserting its presence in the face of established ones, than that of an undefined force that itself posed a problem for the powers charged with regulating meaning in society. The influential newspaper *Tokyo asahi shinbun,* which campaigned first against the movies and then against *Zigomar,* had complained in general about the "unnaturalness" and incomprehensibility of such new film techniques as ellipses and cutting within the scene.[14] The cinematic image seemingly presented an experience that threatened the disintegration of meaning itself. As commentators also "discovered," this experience was not wholly a problem of the text, but also of the culture that surrounded it. Much of the criticism of *Zigomar* was devoted not to the film, but to a new culture of image consumption, of neon-lit entertainment districts and dark theaters that, it was feared, undermined the normal processes of reasoning and understanding and was antithetical to the established structures of meaning. New meanings could arise from this realm in the interaction of space, audience, *benshi,* and text, meanings that were not to be found in the summaries offered to police censors and that were thus difficult to regulate.

Through the discovery of cinema as a problem, police, educators, and other social leaders articulated definitions of cinema different from the one offered by the discourse of novelization. These mostly focused on film as image and as exhibition. Much of the history of the discourse on cinema in the 1910s centers on efforts to counter the threat of the filmic image by attempting to control the cinema depicted in these other definitions. Film as a product of the realm of exhibition became the object of study of such sociologists as Gonda Yasunosuke, while police and educators, in part using Gonda's findings, began to regulate the theatrical space with new laws such as Tokyo's 1917 Moving Picture Regulations. Some of these restricted film viewing by those, like children, who were deemed incapable of reading the image; others tried to reduce the cacophony of "voices" typical of entertainment districts (by regulating film theater billboards, for instance). Educators and the Ministry of Education also joined in this larger project of molding spectators whose reading strategies were socially responsible – that is, predictable and controllable – by recommending films (starting in 1916) or through banning film attendance by schoolchildren unless accompanied by a parent or a teacher on school outings.

Most efforts, however, centered on trying to stabilize and regulate the semiotic process of the image. This was first manifest in new requirements that films be prescreened as part of the censorship process, but it was also evident in strategies having recourse to the word. Central to the latter was the *benshi,* who still dominated both the exhibition space and the reading of the image. The *benshi's* presence was required at screenings in some localities,[15] and they were licensed (starting in 1917), tested (after 1920), and educated as part of the effort to make sure that proper knowledge was being transmitted to the audience. Told not to deviate from the summaries the police received, *benshi* were to act like novelizations – positing a universal text whose meanings did not deviate from theater to theater, or from police viewings to the paid screening. Fearing the lack of the importance of the word in the cinematic experience – its incomplete ability to regulate meaning – authorities often sought solutions that reinstituted the word as central to the act of watching cinema.

FILM CRITICISM AND THE INDEPENDENT TEXT

The difficulty confronting those in the 1910s who were concerned with the problem with cinema was that the dominant mode of writing on cinema, novelization, was clearly inadequate as a means of controlling the filmic image. Not only was it unable to grasp those other meanings emerging from the image and the theater, but it was also too much a part of the cinematic apparatus to fully act as its regulator. In a sense, this was the context behind the appearance of film criticism and, with it, the Pure Film Movement, in the 1910s. The Pure Film Movement, which was less a real movement than a general shift in the 1910s and the 1920s in how cinema was made and conceived, was an effort in criticism, and then in production, to first eliminate the "uncinematic" elements of Japanese film, such as the *onnagata,* and to then import filmic techniques such as close-ups and parallel editing so as to create a more purely "cinematic" Japanese film. At first glance, it would seem odd to locate such pure film reformers as Kaeriyama Norimasa and Shigeno Yukiyoshi in the effort to reword the image: their call for a pure film, starting as it did with the argument to eliminate the *benshi,* demanded a cinema centered on the image, not on the word. Their proposal was for a filmic text that was sufficient in itself, that could enunciate its meaning on its own without the intervention of the supplementary word.

Yet in spite of Kaeriyama's forays into film production (starting with *The Glow of Life* ["Sei no kagayaki," produced in 1918, released in 1919]), the Pure Film Movement was first and foremost a development in film criticism, centered on determining what constituted good cinema and how to write about it. How they staked out a territory for writing on film reiterated the primacy of the word in the film image. The definition of criticism became an issue with the first film magazines as young film aficionados took to task such older critics as Yoshiyama Kyokkô (usually cited as the first film critic[16]) for their relative sympathy to the "canned-theater" style, which dominated Japanese productions. The September 1910 issue of *Katsudô shashinkai* included a piece written by Higashiyama Gaishi that signaled a transition toward different standards for critical writing. Setting the stage for much later criticism in coterie magazines, Higashiyama called for an impressionist style of criticism and for more criticism written by fans. Yet his emphasis on the space of exhibition is revealed in the matters he lists for critics to discuss:

1. Evaluation of the script
2. The actor's performance methods (costumes, expressions)
3. Scene selection (scenery, lighting)
4. Photography (lightness/darkness, linking)
5. Projection (electric power, shaking of the machine, size of the screen)
6. Skill of the *benshi*
7. Use of music[17]

While Higashiyama's prayer for the appearance of "true moving picture critics" helped set the stage for later developments, his attention to the *benshi* and the projector reveals that his film criticism was not significantly different from the evaluation of a live theater performance.

The critics that were gathering around such reformist journals as *Kinema rekôdo* (started in 1914) began postulating a definition of film criticism as an independent mode of discourse. On an economic level, this independence was represented by the creation of coterie magazines less reliant upon industry support. *Kinema rekôdo* and *Kinema junpô* (started in 1919) were both the equivalents of college literary magazines, the brainchildren of groups of young friends who started publishing on their own. Not begun as commercial ventures, these journals brandished their independence from the industry and rigorously lambasted Japanese films for their lack of cinematic essence. With their success, many others followed in their path. According to Makino Mamoru's monumental, soon-to-be-published index of prewar film periodicals, while there were only seven magazines listed as having published articles on film in 1918, there were a total of sixty-seven in 1924, a significant number of which were coterie magazines.[18] While the boom also coincided with the rise of mass journalism, it also reflected the grass-roots nature of criticism within the Pure Film Movement. Criticism was to be written by dedicated members of the audience who had no connection to the industry, whose role, in fact, was to communicate the ideas of the audience of film producers. As such, criticism was a kind of "idealistic amateurism."[19]

Reformist critics also sought independence on the level of their mode of discourse, positing a mode of evaluation specific to the screen. Writing under one of his pseudonyms, Kaeriyama asserted that there were two meanings of the phrase "a good film": "One is 'value as a work of art' and another is 'value as a photographic picture.'" While the latter criterion was mostly centered on technique, the former he defined as "the value when looked at from the pure standpoint of the moving pictures."[20] The central tenet of the new criticism was to judge film as film, not just as a story or a performance, and emphasize whatever cinematic modes of signification were used to transmit that narrative. As the critic and film censor Tachibana Takahiro argued, "Photoplays possess their own terminology. Those who cannot read those terms I ask to think about the act of viewing and criticizing a photoplay. To put it bluntly, I want them to cut all relationships with the stage and see photoplays as photoplays."[21]

In discussing how to evaluate Japanese films, *Kinema rekôdo's* Shigeno Yukiyoshi countered Yoshiyama Kyokkô by arguing that the standard of cinema was universal and specific to the medium: "Judging

'Japanese pictures as Japanese pictures,' as Yoshiyama urges, may be appropriate for discussing drama, but . . . to criticize moving picture technique, one must first compare it to foreign works in general."[22] To reformers like Shigeno, Yoshiyama's call to compare Japanese films with one another was equivalent to making theatricality the standard for cinema; to them, cinema could only be judged as cinema by comparing Japanese films to works that represented a more universal standard of cinema, that is, foreign films.

The critic, then, had to be knowledgeable of these universal standards, but it was such knowledge that qualified the critical populism of the Pure Film Movement. The prominent critic Mori Iwao castigated some of his colleagues for lacking qualifications. Critics, he charged, "do not seem to have even thought about what the moving pictures are. . . . One can say there is not one who criticizes and appraises the entirety of the film from the standpoint of moving picture 'art.'"[23] Becoming a film critic, in Mori's mind, required a special relationship with the medium, a love and deep appreciation of its unique beauty and charms; it demanded a particular form of spectatorship able to enter the world created by the film, yet serious and studied enough to pronounce judgment on the work's quality. As *Kinema junpô* argued: "While an article of criticism is nothing but the expression in words of the comments in the mind of the critic – who himself is no different from a mature spectator – we hope that the critic's attitude is very serious."[24] Critics had a grave responsibility toward other spectators and the cinema. "Critics are people who lead; they cannot be led," wrote Tachibana. "Their responsibility is considerable."[25]

If there was one individual who was not allowed to criticize the film, it was the *benshi*. Judging from complaints at the time, it was not unheard of for *benshi* to insert critical commentary into their narration of a film, a practice for which they were roundly condemned by reformers. Ishii Meika, editor of *Katsudô gahô,* added, "Since explanation is neither a lecture nor a speech, it should not in the least separate itself from the film and mix in subjective criticism or arguments."[26] In such comments, one sees an attempt to eliminate the very "fragmentation of the signifier" that Noël Burch claims as a central facet of the *benshi* phenomenon.[27] As I have argued elsewhere,[28] much of reformist discourse on the *benshi* was directed at creating a cinematic text that was whole and self-sufficient, which narrated itself without the need of such supplementary discourses as the *benshi* or novelizations. This involved tying the *benshi* to the text as an enunciative tool subservient to the transmission of the text's unified meaning, in effect inserting the *benshi's* narrative enunciation into the text and eliding the *benshi's* presence in order that the text could speak for itself.

The creation of the self-sufficient cinematic text and the founding of film criticism are not unrelated. Restricting the *benshi's* explanation to serving the film was in many ways a precondition for founding film criticism as an authoritative institution, allowing reformist critics to monopolize the right to speak on the text. Recall that under the discourse of novelization, journalism was the printed equivalent of the *benshi,* functioning as part of the cinematic apparatus in ensuring the transmission of filmic meaning. By negating the double of its former self, film criticism then asserted both the particularity of its discourse and its own independence from the textual apparatus. While an uncritical *benshi* was not to stray from the film, criticism could firmly assert its distance from the process of narration. To reform Japanese cinema, progressive critics created a form of discourse capable of aiming not at the furtherance of narrative comprehension, but at the negation of certain modes of narration altogether.

THE PURE, WORDLESS IMAGE

Asserting the independence of criticism was an important step in declaring the liberation of the image from the word. If the first conceptions of the moving pictures failed to distinguish between the filmic image and the word as modes of meaning production, the rejection of certain forms of speaking as parts of the cinematic experience (e.g., the critical *benshi*) postulated a difference between word and image (in which the former could harm the effect of the latter) at the same time that it asserted the primacy of the image in filmic signification. Establishing criticism as the legitimate arena for speaking on cinema completed this division between word and image by in effect removing the word from the process of cinematic signification and depositing it in the critical field. Film journalism was to be separate from the cinematic apparatus, earning its independence both because the image was now considered self-sufficient, and because that self-sufficiency established film journalism as a legitimate mode of writing distinct from other forms of art criticism.

Film criticism in effect depended on the conception of the image as pure. Much of the discourse of the Pure Film Movement was deeply concerned with distinguishing the cinema as an inherently silent visual medium that produced meaning through pantomime, its silence and visuality distinguishing it from other arts such as the theater. Even while positing the screenplay as the centerpiece of reform, *Kinema rekôdo* argued that screenwriting must be pursued "without leaving the limits of pantomime" and went on to cite *The Student of Prague* as a particularly commendable example of honoring the uniqueness of the image: "This is what only the moving pictures can represent. Although it is words that express in the theater, it is certainly difficult to know such things as [that film's] form [through words]. It is only the moving pictures, creating titles with words when pantomime is insufficient, . . . only such a composite form of moving picture that has the greatest value as a photoplay."[29] Many recognized that pantomime was occasionally insufficient to communicate narrative meaning and they thus acknowledged the supplementary role intertitles must play. Yet Kaeriyama, in his *How To Produce and Photograph Moving Picture Dramas* ("Katsudô shashingeki no sôsaku to satsueihô") took pains in his chapter on the screenplay to counsel his readers on the need to keep titles to a minimum by using parallel editing and other cinematic devices. Also cautioning against making the script too literary, he maintained a clear distinction between the cinema and its more literary cousins like theater and the novel.[30]

The early 1920s featured several debates on the legitimacy of using intertitles in the film. Fans joined in, and one reader, in countering the argument of a fellow magazine contributor, offered a succinct summary of the reasons for eliminating titles and the *benshi:*

> The photoplay itself is essentially a silent drama. Silent drama does not need words or writing. Therefore, in place of the words of the theater, it emphasizes skillful expression and a clever attitude and makes use of liberal editing, close-ups, and cutbacks which are understood by all. If, as you claim, the *benshi* is useful, then how can you argue with a straight face that close-ups and cutbacks are necessary? . . . By concretely expressing any kind of event, the photoplay occupies a completely different field than the stage. The more you watch a film and apply your imagination, the more the value of a photoplay appears. Therefore, words and titles, which are unnatural and greatly damage the true value of cinema, should naturally be eliminated.[31]

Film purists understood the lack of words as the basis for cinema's development of a unique mode of signification. Adding words to the film in any manner, either through the *benshi,* the titles, or elements in the diegesis, was seen as preventing filmmakers from seeking out more filmic solutions to narrative problems. While admitting that it was inevitable that the name, for instance, of a train station would appear within the frame, Midorikawa Harunosuke, for one, went to the extreme of arguing that "it is absolutely unforgivable for that station name to offer some kind of explanation of the plot."[32] In defining the cinema as pure and unique, it appears that for some it was intolerable to supplement the filmic text with any linguistic signs. This attitude was not uncommon in world cinema in the silent era – movements such as French Impressionism (Germaine Dulac's *The Smiling Madame Beudet* in 1922) and German Expressionism (F. W. Murnau's *The Last Laugh* in 1924) featured efforts to produce titleless films – but the Pure Film Movement was more influenced by early American attempts in this direction.[33] Cinema was defined by the pure image, which itself was seen as inherently devoid of the influence of words.

ANTERIOR CRITICISM, OR THE WORD AS CINEMA'S SUPEREGO

With journalism and the operations of the word now divorced from the cinematic apparatus, the question of what role was left for writing to play in the filmic experience remained. If the pure motion picture text was supposedly complete in itself, without need for linguistic explanation, writing on cinema could no longer play the part novelization did. Nevertheless, in the authority concomitant to reformist discourse, criticism found a role for itself that reversed the hierarchy it forced upon the *benshi* (in which the *benshi's* words could only serve the image) and reestablished writing as cinema's leader. Reformers like Mori portrayed the role of criticism as analogous to that of a loving adult raising an infant through education and punishment.[34] A *Kinema junpô* editorial, summarizing the duties of critics, declared that "one of their most important missions" is to "explain the impressions given to them by the film and prompt self-examination on the part of all those involved in that film: the producers, exhibitors, *benshi,* and spectators."[35] "The function of film criticism," another critic added, "lies in both judging the value of produced pictures as well as in correcting and aiding films and filmmakers, offering the driving force for reconstruction."[36] In this manner, film journalism shed its role of transmitting narrative meaning and presented itself as a guide for cinema.

Reformist journals were peppered with comments on how their critical activities had prompted changes within the Japanese industry. Criticism had presumably inspired such transformations not only through the power of its specific judgments, but also through offering itself as a model for practical action; as a form of practice, it became the mold into which cinema would be poured. Film production and distribution were asked to do as film journalism did: if film criticism was independent and foregrounded the uniqueness of its discourse, so should film practice; if criticism shed the requirements of commercialism to pursue film art, so should the motion picture industry. Ultimately, if criticism was to act as a driving force in the production of the image, it was through postulating an authorial source for its meaning. Early cinema in the era of novelization was the product of no specific individual but rather of a faceless amalgam of intersecting genres and discourses. Reform, however, required a subject responsible for the film if the critic were to lay blame on individuals who should act differently in the future. The very act of criticism made no sense if there were no author accountable for making the film incorrectly.

The model for this necessary subjectivity was to be found in criticism itself. In the narrative of reform, critics first had to assume an independent position and bear responsibility for their own role in bettering the motion pictures. As in the case of Mori Iwao's writing, criticism of film criticism became an important activity for journals like *Kinema rekôdo* and *Kinema junpô,* which castigated film critics for lacking knowledge of cinema and for not realizing the gravity of their role in raising an infant cinema. The two magazines thus made a point of attaching the author's name to most of their printed film criticism.[37] Dissenting with Hugo Freedburg's assertion that it was the task of fans and film authors to lead the cinema, Mori argued that such people could not be trusted: "The author is, if anything, a person who, excused as an insider, tends toward mistakes by waving around art, art, and art, and fans are conceited, smug, and irresponsible. In the end, I think both the cool intelligence which correctly penetrates the truth of things and the authority to work for complete progress cannot be had without critics."[38]

While clearly it was film producers who had to change their practices to realize reform, Mori's statement implied that the reformist subjectivity that bore "intelligence" and "authority" had to originate in critics first. The authorial subject in production would, in a sense, only inherit the responsibility for proper cinematic creation from the critic. In understanding the transformations in early Japanese cinema, it is crucial to see how the birth of criticism was not only antecedent to, but a necessary condition for, the development of the ideologies of the film auteur or the film star. Authorship had to be injected into cinema from without. This may seem like the bravado spouted by any critic, but criticism's central role in Japanese film history is best exemplified by the large number of critics and writers who entered the film industry to put into practice their newfound reformist agency, individuals such as Kaeriyama Norimasa; Mori Iwao (who later became vice president of Tôhô); Midorikawa Harunosuke (Noda Kôgo); Furukawa Roppa; Takada Tamotsu (a *Katsudô kurabu* [Movie Club] reporter who later became a prominent film and theater director and essayist); Kishi Matsuo (a *Kinema junpô* writer who later joined Tôhô as a scriptwriter and director); and even Tanizaki Jun'ichirô (who supported film reform and became an adviser and screenwriter at Taikatsu) – to name just a few.[39]

The assertion of the reformist authority of the word in effect transformed the temporal relationship between writing and the image. In novelization, word and image may have functioned in parallel to produce what in the end was a narrative deemed equivalent to a written story, but the linguistically composed text was always somewhat temporally behind the film. With no real script having been written before the film was produced (or a script unavailable in the case of foreign films), the actual transcription of the film into words or its explanation by the *benshi* took place afterward. In criticism, with its supposition that adding words after the fact could do nothing to change a completed film (except, of course, damage it), writing that took place after the film's completion was in some sense redirected toward a point theoretically before cinematic meaning was created. This was paralleled by the assertion that cinematic meaning was established not postproduction, in the sphere of exhibition, but in the temporal space, before the film was completed, where those authors responsible for the film acted. Film journalism directed its focus toward those subjects – the filmmakers, exhibitors, and spectators – who played a role in producing cinematic meaning. The film was fait accompli, but if it was lacking in artistic quality, the castigation of past acts would provide the rules by which future films would be made. Superlative films were to be praised, but in the dominant critical discourse of the time, usually termed "impressionist" criticism, this did not involve offering explanations of hidden meanings or helping readers further understand the text, but rather evoking the critic's impressions of the text's cinematic excellence. Since nothing could be added to the text, criticism merely focused on indicating how such texts exemplified "cinema" itself, again as a guide to future films.

Criticizing the past in order to direct the future, the words of criticism were to assume centrality in the film world. Film producers (or even spectators) were supposed to read film criticism to learn what they had done wrong and to keep those lessons in mind when approaching their next film. Criticism and the warnings of the word then found residence inside the minds of producers, acting as the superego that would regulate their future desires. In creating authorial subjects responsible for cinematic meaning, film reformers also carved out an internality to themselves complete with a conscience that would correct and censor the creation of the image. While pronouncing the self-sufficiency of the image, reformers always presumed that the word would act as the symbolic warden regulating the cinematic imaginary.

THE IMAGE AS CODE

This conclusion should prompt us to look again at the Pure Film Movement's effort to separate word and image and to make the latter the definition of a pure cinema. Reformers' criticisms were directed at a *misemono* brand of cinema that made the *benshi,* novelization, and the film itself all indistinguishable elements in the production of cinematic meaning. Radically separating the image text from the other written or spoken texts was intended to distinguish cinema as a unique art, but not, it must be stressed, in the way police censors sensed was occurring with *Zigomar.* There, amid a chorus of different voices, police noticed an image text that was operating on its own, dangerously out of control and seemingly beyond reach of the confining influence of words. Reformers may have desired an independent image text, but as can be seen from their discourse on intertitles, it was not one to be unrestricted and undefined.

Purists' complaints against the existing Japanese fare were often centered on the fact that they were narratively unclear or hard to understand. While critics like Midorikawa flatly rejected the use of intertitles in the early 1920s, it is important to note that at the beginning of the Pure Film Movement, intertitles were something Japanese cinema was faulted for *not* having. In listing the deficiencies in the Japanese product, a 1916 article in *Kinema rekôdo* charged: "The titles are far too simple and there is a great need to write them more carefully so that viewers can understand the plot . ."[40] Intertitles in Japanese films in the mid-1910s were faulted for failing to assist the film in communicating narrative meaning; they were more properly subheadings, largely confined to announcing the titles of each scene. The reformers' emphasis on intertitles and the narration contained therein transformed the *benshi*'s relation to the film text. The illustrious *benshi* Somei Saburô noted how early *benshi* for foreign film, without good translations of the intertitles, would often simply "look at the image and give an explanation that roughly fit." Advances in both cinematic form and spectator knowledge rendered such practices untenable. *Benshi* now, he claimed, use better title translations and "correlate them with the film as a framework, adding appropriate accompaniment and explanation as a form of coloration."[41] Explanation was not just of the image, but of the titles, in effect treating the film as a narration embodied in linguistic enunciations.[42]

The effort to eliminate titles should not be seen as a rejection of this process of adding intertitles, but as its extension. Midorikawa wrote, in upholding the silent, titleless film, that "even if silence is meaningless, . . . the silent drama of pantomime is meaningful. At times, it possesses much deeper meaning than a drama with dialogue."[43] The image in a pure film without titles represented not a return to the narratively ambiguous image of early Japanese cinema, the semiotically undefined text that concerned censors, but rather the complete internalization of narrative enunciation within the text. Titles were to be eliminated only insofar as the image could equally or better handle the same narrative load, and had assumed the same certainty of signification as writing or speech. As such, the titleless film was not allowed to be ambiguous or open to different spectator readings. The metaphor *Katsudô no sekai* used to describe the meaning uniquely expressed by cinema was, in the end, "the words of the moving pictures" *(katsudô shashin no kotoba),* defined as the "words which substitute for the words of theater."[44] The definition of the cinematic sign was, in the end, to be found in an analogy with the word.[45]

The vision of a pure cinema in the 1910s was always one in which meaning was stable, univocal, and understandable. Kaeriyama stressed that the filmmaker must have a reason or an opinion behind every shot: "Even in shooting a scenic picture, the producer must approach the creation of each and every scene with a viewpoint and judgment: Does this have value as an image? What is the relationship between the mood on the spot and the status of film's color or image?"[46] In the film theory of the reformers, each and every shot must bear a meaning or intention founded in the choice and judgment of the filmmaker. Even a titleless film has to carry the burden of meaning, yet to be as univocally meaningful as reformers desired, it must obey a strict and unified semiotic code that centrally grounds meaning. One can say that progressive critics objected to existing Japanese cinema precisely because it lacked such a code; or, more specifically, because it featured a hodgepodge of codes and voices (which enabled the pleasure of experiencing their conflict, as, for instance, when *benshi* criticized the film they were explaining). Neither reformers nor film censors countenanced a film with multiple meanings. As purists, reformers demanded the separation of these codes according to media and type of sign (image, speech, music) but never gave up the conception of the code as the systematic reduction of potential meaning down to single decisions for each semiotic situation.

The word may have been divorced from the image, but the image was to be coded like the word. It should be evident that here I am not using *word* to simply refer to written signs of language, but to refer also to a code modeled on the form of language in which signs are ideally regulated, univocal, and unambiguous. The image was to be freed of signs of speech and writing only at the price of the image internalizing a code as "linguistic" as writing and speech, something similar to the narrator system Tom Gunning outlines.[47] The externalization of the word from the image made possible a code other than that of the word, but it was nevertheless a code, and one in which meaning took precedence over the image. This is evident from the fact that many reformers still allowed for the use of intertitles if the image could not sufficiently narrate by itself, since such narrational devices ensured that the image properly operated as part of a unified code and that there were no ambiguities in its reading. The advantage the coded image had over the previous cacophony of Japanese cinema was that narration could now emerge from within the text; whereas one once had the *benshi* narrating the text from without, the film image was now narrating itself from within, but only by reinternalizing the word *as code* to function as the linguistic center of semiotic control.

KURUTTA ICHIPEIJI AND THE HYBRID IMAGE

Tensions did exist, however, between the valorization of the image and the concomitant emphasis on univocal meaning. These surfaced at times, particularly in the 1920s when the ideals of the Pure Film Movement merged with theories about cinema imported from France, Germany, and later the Soviet Union. The movement, while declaring as its goal the attainment of a pure cinema, should not be confused with the experimentalism of French film purists like Louis Delluc and Léon Moussinac. Especially in the 1910s, reformers were focused largely on a commercial and narrative cinema, one that made understanding central. But in the 1920s, when the ideas of Delluc started entering Japan along with the films of Marcel L'Herbier and of Abel Gance, and news arrived of the German absolute films, some critics began asserting a purity of the image that rejected not only the word, but narrative and the restrictions of reason as well. They were not in the majority, however, and this growing split within the critical establishment surfaced, in particular, in the debates over Kinugasa Teinosuke's 1926 film *Kurutta ichipeiji,* or *A Page of Madness.*[48]

Influenced by both German Expressionism and French Impressionism, Kinugasa's film went without intertitles and was thus hailed by some critics like Iwasaki Akira as "the first film-like film born in Japan."[49] Its non-narrativity itself was the object of celebration. The emphasis on the film's purity led many to denigrate the contribution Kawabata Yasunari and the Shinkankaku modernist literary group made to the film. This finally was cinema, not literature. But in spite of this praise, many critics complained of the difficulty in understanding the film. If it was a pure film, they argued, one should be able to comprehend it without the explanation of the *benshi* or the help of intertitles. *A Page of Madness,* however, was shown with the *benshi* present and its reliance on them for narrative assistance was severely criticized by such critics as Naoki Sanjugô. Even Iwasaki acknowledged this as a sign of the film's imperfect purity.[50]

A Page of Madness represented an experiment in new forms of both cinematic and literary signification, but the primary expectation that greeted it was that it must, even without intertitles, operate like a complete and efficient semiotic system that ensured the univocality of meaning. Even the Shinkankaku writers, supposedly engaged in a "war of utter rebellion against language," in Yokomitsu Riichi's words, failed to question this view of a strict film language as a means of controlling meaning and readership.

Kataoka Teppei, for instance, when announcing his own intention to produce a titleless film, described what to him constituted cinematic syntax: "The filmmaker or artist emphasizes seeing this part or that, and gives the order, 'You must look at these parts.' The selection of those parts from the entirety of a certain event, their arrangement in order, and the addition of a continuity are what constitute an artistic progression."[51]

This use of close-ups and editing to analyze space and vision, arranging those sections to narrativize the visual field, was certainly attractive to many 1920s novelists interested in new forms of writing and signification, in escaping traditional structures bound in words through a popular art that spoke in pictures. But the fascination exhibited here was not with the subversion of language, but rather with controlling sight so as to produce a new linguistic syntax that, while not using words, still preserved the fundamental structures and order of meaning and understanding. Their literary revolution did not undermine the basic centrality of language based in a unified subject, or the rational word holding sway over the irrational image.

However, what the debates on *A Page of Madness* did reveal was a strong undercurrent in the late 1920s that saw alternatives to this order of language. Writers for the Nagoya film-coterie magazine *Chûkyô kinema,* for instance, defended Kinugasa's film for its nonnarrative aspects, but came down hard on it for what they, in the end, considered its fundamentally literary nature: its refusal to completely do away with story and its subjection of filmic technique to semiotic effect. Cinema, they declared, need not be understood. The statements of these avant-garde cinephiles reveal the contradiction in pure film discourse between its demands for both visual purity and comprehensible narrative. What ultimately suppressed this contradiction, and with it the hope for visual experimentation divorced from semiotic motivation, was the evolution of the screenplay as the realization of the linguistic core ultimately desired by the Pure Film Movement, the word which would finally serve to regulate and contain the image text

FROM NOVELIZATION TO SCREENPLAY: THE LITERARY DEFINITION OF FILM

The development of the motion picture script was seen as the most crucial aspect of the pure film reforms.[52] Kaeriyama began his chapter on film scenarios in his *How to Produce and Photograph Moving Picture Dramas* with the following statement: "The moving picture script is the blueprint for the production of moving picture dramas. The value of the drama is largely decided by the scenario because the director determines the actions of the actors and all facets of the work according to it."[53] A similar emphasis on the screenplay was visible in the development of the classical Hollywood system and reflects one of the major influences of American practices on Japanese reformers who did read the cinema how-to books in English. I would, however, like to focus on how the scenario was articulated in the Japanese discursive sphere.

It was due to the script's central role in deciding the meaning and quality of the film that Kaeriyama and others repeatedly stressed a difference from its theatrical counterpart, one embodying the visual and pantomimic qualities unique to cinema they demanded the writer be aware of.[54] The script itself was the starting point for cinematic creation, but as such it was only a brief sketch with no value of its own until filmed. When Mori stressed that "a screenplay is not literature,"[55] it was understood that cinema was to be the creative art, not screenwriting. Nevertheless, the role of the screenplay in producing the final product was considered immense. At a time when the function of the director was still ill-defined and the concept of editing rudimentary (this was true in the United States as well), the scenario writer was largely assigned the role of planning out the film, from the story and titles to the editing and image composition. This is why early attempts by film reformers to describe authorship in the cinema usually focused on the screenwriter.

The need for authorial writers was, at the same time, related to the requirement to restrict cinematic meaning and control the image.[56] This is evident in how the history of censorship draws a clear line of progression from written summaries to the screenplay as technologies for regulating the cinema. As mentioned previously, most localities required exhibitors to submit a plot summary or *benshi* script when applying for permission to show a film. The *Zigomar* incident may have exposed the inadequacy of such a policy if it did not include a prescreening of the film itself, but it did not lead to the abandonment of the procedure itself. If there was a change in regulations, it was from requiring submission of the explanation *(setsumeisho)* to demanding the plot summary *(sujigaki)*. Very early regulations tended to require either one (in Ôsaka in 1911) or just the explanation (in Shizuoka in 1912; in Aomori in 1914), but toward the end of the decade, the plot summary became the written form of choice (for instance, in Tokyo in 1917, or in Ôsaka in 1921).[57]

Despite the increased emphasis on prescreenings, regulations, far from ignoring the plot summary, actually placed increased emphasis on it. Most regulations treated it as an authorized record of the film. The codes for Hyôgô (issued in 1911 and revised in 1918) demanded that each page of the summary bear the official stamp of the prefectural police. Article 61, Section 10, of the 1921 Tokyo Performance and Performance Site Regulations obligated exhibitors to keep an approved copy of the summary at the theater for the police officer stationed in the theater to consult,[58] a requirement also found in the 1921 Ôsaka codes, among others. Since such a summary was presumably to be used by the officer to check if the content of the *benshi*'s narration or the film matched the approved written version, it is evident that censorship codes responded to the problems posed by *Zigomar* not simply by paying more attention to the image, but also by attempting to reassert the accountability of the filmic text to the word. While moving picture regulations reduced the definition of individual films to a content summary in part out of bureaucratic necessity, authorities, confronted with a semiotically unpredictable visual medium, could also be seen as attempting to constrain that through the word. The centrality of the word is exemplified by the rather curious requirement found in many regulations demanding that exhibitors reapply for permission to show a film even if they only made changes in the plot summary.[59] Even if the celluloid remained untouched, one change in the synopsis was enough to obligate reapproval since it had been designated the official version of the text's meaning. Censorship codes thus reduced film to a literary text, in effect offering a literary definition of the cinema.

Censorship regulations did evince an increased interest in the screenplay as an extension of plot summaries. Hiroshima's Moving Picture Regulations of 1920 demanded that a plot summary accompany applications, but stated that a script was also acceptable. A glance at regulations like those of Tokyo (1921), Hyôgô, and Fukushima (from 1917), which covered both film and stage, reveals how the synopsis was treated as the equivalent of the theater script and subject to the same approval and reapproval procedures, an equivalence which represented increased attention to the possibility of film scenarios at a time when the practice of screenwriting had not yet been established. Calls for script censorship were voiced in film magazines early on, but these would not be answered until the 1939 Film Law, which instituted preproduction censorship as a cornerstone of thorough state intervention in the industry.[60]

Before then, a major change in censorship procedures was represented by the Moving Picture Film Inspection Regulations issued in May 1925, which finally nationalized film censorship under the jurisdiction of the Home Ministry.[61] These codes required submission of the *benshi* script for approval, but within the structure of the new censorship procedures, this took on a meaning different from regulations fifteen years before. The regulations were remarkably short – only fifteen articles – since clauses concerning the theater, the audience, and the *benshi* that dominated local film codes had all been eliminated. The 1925 censorship codes were the first in Japan to truly define the moving picture text as separate from the realm of exhibition, the regulation of which would now be left up to local police. National censorship in effect declared exhibition irrelevant in judging the meaning of the film; the *benshi* script was taken as an authentic representation of the content of the film text that was the same no matter which *benshi* read it and where. The locus of meaning had significantly shifted from the *benshi* at the site of exhibition to the film and the realm of production. Although the codes themselves did not require that *benshi* keep to the approved version of the film's meaning, Home Ministry officials made clear their desire to local officials that prefectural laws should ensure that *benshi* did not engage in "explanation" that differed from the script.[62] The *benshi* script was then assumed to be a reflection of the film's intention as it was produced, approximating in many ways what would become the film scenario.

The gradual progression from the plot summary to the screenplay is also visible in film journalism. One could say that magazines never abandoned novelization because they simply switched from synopses to scenarios in offering reading matter for their buyers. *Katsudô shashin zasshi* ("Moving Picture Magazine"), which in its first year in 1915 was mostly devoted to novelizations, was also printing original, unproduced screenplays as if they were merely another form of novelization. By the mid-1920s it became quite common for magazines to regularly print the screenplays of actual films just as they were being released. When famous writers like Tanizaki and Kawabata started trying their hand at penning scripts for production,[63] the film scenario itself began to acquire literary status, and some novelists like Akutagawa Ryûnosuke tried writing them with no intention that they be filmed.[64] In the 1930s, journals entirely devoted to publishing screenplays, like *Shinario* (Scenario) and *Shinario kenkyû* (Scenario Research), began appearing, laying the institutional foundation for what would be called *shinario bungaku* or "scenario literature."

When a six-volume series entitled *Shinario bungaku zenshû* (Complete Works of Scenario Literature) was published in 1937, the prominent critic Iijima Tadashi declared: "With us unable to be pleased at Japanese cinema, it has become necessary for us to try cinematic creation through the printed word. While planning the artistic establishment of Japanese film though 'scenario literature' may seem like a rather long road, from the standpoint of those appreciating cinema, it is necessary for us to take these measures."[65] Nearly twenty years had passed since Mori Iwao had declared that the screenplay was not literature and now the literariness of the film's blueprint was deemed necessary to render Japanese cinema more artistic. Iijima felt that writing in the form of the scenario was necessary for film reform. But as a leading reformist critic since the early 1920s, he did try to distinguish the cinematic aspects (camera, editing, etc.) from the literary aspects (mainly focusing on dialogue) in the scenario. The former, developed to their fullest in the silent film script, would actually be harmed, he argued, if written in too literary a fashion since their destiny was properly in the hands of the director, not the screenwriter. The coming of sound, however, opened up an avenue for the cinematic pursuit of literature in the form of dialogue. The split between dialogue and cinematic form allowed Iijima, in his post-talkie theorization of motion picture art, to claim for film both cinematicity and literariness without having to question their distinction or advocate their mixture.

It is important to note that in describing the need for literature in cinema, Iijima ultimately shifted his focus to the issue of the permanence and control of meaning. In complaining about contemporary film production, he argued: "Strangely, it seems that the literary value of dialogue is the most neglected aspect in Japanese talkies. This is because the words on screen disappear after an instant and do not possess the quality of permanence. In this regard, one cannot but recognize the superiority of literature composed in written words" (SBJ, 10–11). Literature possessed permanence, a "privilege" and condition for artistic greatness that Iijima felt had long escaped cinema. To him, the promise of scenario literature lay precisely in its ability to finally make the motion pictures eternal and thus art. But in saying so, Iijima was only articulating the sense immanent to the discourse of most intellectual critics that cinema could only be artistic and socially respectable if it became literary.[66] This permanence also reflected on the issue of cinematic meaning: "The talkie scenario possesses a central element which will never differ from that of the film made from it, no matter who reads it. It is the dialogue that, just as on screen, will be read by us when printed in the scenario as written words which do not vary whatever the conditions may be" (SBJ, 20). This was not simply an issue of printed dialogue: even when spoken on screen, words to Iijima promised to finally give cinema that self-contained textuality, that unchanging and univocal meaning that pure film reformers had desired since the 1910s. The scenario thus became the ground of meaning that rendered the conditions of reception irrelevant to signification, reasserting certainty to the transmission and control of cinematic meaning.

Iijima was writing only of the dialogue when he said that it permanently expressed the will of the author and "could not be changed in any way by any foreign element" (SBJ, 23), but the existence of the talkie scenario clearly changed cinematic textuality as a whole. While to Iijima one could only "imagine" *(sôzô)* a silent film from reading its script, with a talkie screenplay one could "make presumptions *(oshihakaru)* to a considerable degree about the film itself" (SBJ, 21). Despite his efforts to distinguish literary from cinematic elements in the scenario, Iijima, in his desire for a permanent cinematic text, rendered the script largely equivalent to the moving picture, perhaps not in the signifiers used, but in the experience they both shape – a conclusion that recalls *Katsudô gahô*'s boast that reading its novelizations was much like going to the movies.

CONCLUSION: FILM IN THE IMAGE OF THE WORD

Much had changed from the time *Katsudô shashinkai* could claim its synopses were sufficient for those who had not seen the film to when Iijima praised the talkie scenario as a way to "presume" what the final film was like. In the former case, novelizations could be said to record the cinematic experience because that experience made no distinctions between word and image. The sense remained, however, underlined by the *Zigomar* incident, that there was something about that experience that escaped the words written about the cinema. The problem, after that point, facing those concerned about the motion pictures was then one of rethinking how the word can relate to the filmic image.

As I have shown here, the process was twofold. First, there was the necessity to recognize the problem, to cite the cinematic image as different from the word and articulate its uniqueness by arguing that writing and speech had no part in its operations. This process of divorcing the image from the word had the effect, however, of realigning the word with the image precisely because cinema now became a unique object of knowledge in written discourses such as film criticism. The word had been reshaped to accommodate the image. Reformers may have celebrated the image as different, but that distinction itself made cinema a better object of regulation. Once known, cinema was now subject to prescriptions and proscriptions, its future form beholden to the advice of the word.

This leads to the second aspect of the process: the effort to rework the image for the word. From censors to sympathetic film reformers, many writing on cinema saw it as an object of correction. The problem was precisely the lack of control over film meaning (by either film censors, filmmakers, or critics) and the solution was continually sought in the word. Cinema was to be reshaped in the model of the word: it was to have an autonomous, self-sufficient textuality that spoke for itself; a univocal mode of signification that approximated that of the written language; an author who would produce meaning that spectators would only passively receive. The screenplay became the pivot of this quest to reform cinema and perhaps the fact that it became so central to Japanese film culture indicates how effective this reform was, creating a hegemony in film culture that lasted until the end of the 1950s. By the time Iijima was writing in the late 1930s, the screenplay was in many ways the film – not only because meaning was now produced in the realm of production via the script, but also because the image had been remade in the image of the word.

One need not recall the fact that this equivalence between screenplay and film was the necessary condition for the institution of script censorship in 1939 to realize that the issue of the relation of the word and the image is not merely confined to the motion pictures. My discussions here of the shifting relations between word and image in prewar Japanese film culture point to larger transformations that encompass not only cinema, but also literature, art, and other media as well. At the center was a conflict over the definition of meaning and signification, one that was often complex but which, as we have seen here, could often be characterized as that between the conception of language as bearing an unambiguous, plentiful sign that can enforce its own meaning within a certain semiotic structure, and the vision of the sign as fundamentally ambiguous, countering the order of meaning and reason through a radical decentering of semiosis. Discussing debates over the cinema in twentieth-century Japan, I would contend, illuminates a much larger issue: the struggle over meaning and language in the modern emperor system.

NOTES

1. This essay was originally a chapter in my doctoral dissertation, "Writing a Pure Cinema: Articulations of Early Japanese Film" (University of Iowa, 1996), and at that stage it benefited greatly from the comments of my committee, composed of Dudley Andrew, Mitsuhiro Yoshimoto, Lauren Rabinowitz, Stephen Vlastos, and Kathleen Newman. I then considerably rewrote the text after receiving feedback from many of the "Wording the Image" conference participants (at Dartmouth in September 1997), particularly the organizers, Carole Cavanaugh and Dennis Washburn, and my respondent, David Desser.
2. See his essay "Eiga jidai," found in the collection published under his pseudonym: Yoshimura Fuyuhiko: *Zoku Fuyuhiko shû* (Tôkyô: Iwanami Shoten, 1932): 284.
3. Kubota Utsubo, "Hajimete katsudô shashin o mini itta hi," *Shumi* 4.8 (August 1909): 10; the emphasis is mine. *Misemono* are the Japanese equivalent of fairground entertainments. This and all other translations from the Japanese, unless otherwise noted, are my own.
4. Hakkô no shui," *Katsudô shashinkai* 1 (June 1909): 1.
5. The danger that giving the audience an excessive amount of explanation before the film might "kill the picture" had already been cited earlier by Eda Fushiki, who wrote a series of essays on the dos and don'ts of *benshi* narration in *Katsudô shashinkai.* See, in particular, his "Katsudô shashin eishahô: zoku," *Katsudô shashinkai* 9 (May 1910): 5–6.
6. See Imamura Miyoo's account of *Katsudô shashin zasshi:* Imamura Miyoo, *Nihon eiga bunkenshi* (Tôkyô: Kagamiura Shobô, 1967): 182–83.
7. Makino Mamoru offers the novelizations printed in *Katsudô shashin zasshi* as one of the sole surviving records of the style of *benshi* oration from that time: Makino Mamoru, "Katsudô shashinban: 'Ametsuchi no majiwarishi koro,'" *Nihon eiga shoki shiryô shûsei 1: "Katsudô shashin zasshi,"* vol. 1 (Tôkyô: San'ichi Shobô, 1990): 10. *Katsudô shashin zasshi* was the journal most oriented toward giving novelizations in *benshi* form, going as far in some cases as including the *maesetsu,* the explanation before the film started.

8. For more on the theater programs and their relation to the history of film criticism in Japan, see Makino Mamoru, "*Kinema junpô* to eiga hihyô no seiritsu," *Kinema junpô fokkukuban,* vol. 13 (Tôkyô: Yûshôdô, 1995): 19–37. Makino gives a list of some of the critics who got their first chance working as editors with these programs.
9. "*Katsudô gahô* no go daitokushoku," *Katsudô gahô* 1.1 (January 1917): n.p.
10. See Okudaira Yasuhiro's short history on prewar censorship: "Eiga to ken'etsu," *Kôza Nihon eiga,* ed. Imamura Shôhei, et al. (Tôkyô: Iwanami Shoten, 1985–6): vol. 2: 302–18.
11. For a detailed account of this process, see my dissertation, "Writing a Pure Cinema: Articulations of Early Japanese Film."
12. See my essay, "Swarming Ants and Elusive Villains: *Zigomar* and the Problem of Cinema," *CineMagiziNet!* (Autumn 1996), available on the net at http:www.cmn.hs.h.kyoto-u.ac.jp/backIssue/no1/Subject1/ziogomar.htm, or the slightly revised Japanese version, "*Jigoma* to eiga no 'hakken': Nihon eiga gensetsushi josetsu," *Eizôgaku* 58 (1997): 34–50.
13. "*Jigoma* no katsudô shashin kinshi to naru," *Tôkyô nichi nichi shinbun,* 10 October 1912: 7.
14. "Katsudô shashin to jidô (ni): jidô no ukuru hirô," *Tôkyô asahi shinbun,* 7 February 1912: 6.
15. A reason Furukawa Roppa cites as an obstacle to efforts by reformers to eliminate the *benshi:* "Setsumeisha no kenkyû: yon," *Katsudô gahô* 5.12 (December 1921): 95.
16. See, for example, Iwamoto Kenji's brief history of film criticism in Japan: "Film Criticism and the Study of Cinema in Japan: A Historical Survey," *Iconics* 1 (1987): 129–46.
17. Higashiyama Gaishi, "Katsudô shashin gekihyôka," *Katsudô shashinkai* 13 (September 1910): 3.
18. Makino Mamoru, ed., *Nihon eiga bunken kômoku sôran* (Tokyo: Yûshôdô [forthcoming]). The list does not cover the many magazines for which copies no longer exist and also includes more general magazines like *Kaizô* that, with the increased popularity and respectability of cinema, began devoting more pages to its presence.
19. To paraphrase Makino on the mood at *Kinema junpô:* "*Kinema junpô* to eiga hihyô no seiritsu": 33.
20. Mizusawa Takehiko, "Yoi shashin to wa ikan?," *Kinema rekôdo* 50 (October 1917): 31.
21. Tachibana Takahiro, "Eiga hyôron no hyôron," *Kage'e no kuni* (Tôkyô: Shûhôkaku, 1925): 114–15.
22. Shigeno Yukiyoshi, "Nihon shashin o hyôsuru koto," *Kinema rekôdo* 14 (August 1914): 2.
23. Mori Iwao, "Dai-hachi geijutsu hintôroku jûyon: Gendai eiga hihyôka kishitsu 1," *Kinema junpô* 128 (March 21, 1923): 13.
24. "Eiga hihyô to iu koto," *Kinema junpô* 4 (August 11, 1919): 1.
25. Tachibana Takahiro, "Eiga hyôron no hyôron": 119.
26. Ishii Meika, "Eiga setsumeisha hissuron," *Katsudô gahô* 6.2 (February 1922): 29.

27. Noël Burch, *To the Distant Observer: Form and Meaning in the Japanese Cinema,* rev. and ed. Annette Michelson (Berkeley: University of California Press, 1979): 84.
28. See my "The Benshi's New Face: Defining Cinema in Taishô Japan," *Iconics* 3 (1994): 69–86.
29. "Katsudô shashingeki kyakuhonjô no kenkyû: dai-ikkai," *Kinema rekôdo* 27 (September 1915): 2.
30. See Kaeriyama Norimasa, *Katsudô shashingeki no sôsaku to satsueihô* (Tôkyô: Hikôsha, 1917): 41–88.
31. Nagai Toshirô, "Arakawa-shi no setsumei yûyôron o bakusu," *Katsudô gahô* 5.7 (1921): 96.
32. Midorikawa Harunosuke, "Jimaku zakkan," *Katsudô kurabu* 4.7 (July 1921): 41. Midorikawa later came to fame as Noda Kôgo, Ozu's main screenwriter.
33. Eileen Bowser notes that the American efforts began very early, around 1911. See Bowser, *The Transformation of Cinema: 1907–1915* (Berkeley: University of California Press, 1990): 140. Midorikawa's example is *The Old Swimmin' Hole* (De Grasse, 1920).
34. Mori, "Gendai eiga hihyôka kishitsu 1": 13.
35. "Eiga hihyô to iu koto," *Kinema junpô* 5 (August 21, 1919): 1.
36. Izumi Haruki, "Eiga hihyô no hyôjun: ichi," *Katsudô kurabu* 4.6 (June 1921): 20–21.
37. According to Makino, *Kinema junpô,* which originally did not run authored criticisms, began doing so in order to underline who was "responsible" for the piece. The policy, however, met with stiff objections from readers and was abandoned until May 1923, when it was reinstituted for good. Makino, "*Kinema junpô* to eiga hihyô no seiritsu": 34.
38. Mori Iwao, "Dai-hachi geijutsu hintôroku jûgo: Gendai eiga hihyôka kishitsu 2," *Kinema junpô* 129 (April 1, 1923): 14.
39. Others include Murakami Tokusaburô (a *Katsudô kurabu* writer turned scenarist); Oda Takashi (first a reporter for *Katsudô kurabu* and then a scriptwriter for Shôchiku and Nikkatsu); and Kisaragi Bin (one of the more avid amateur critics who went on to write scenarios at Nikkatsu).
40. "Gujin no gugo ka, arui wa Nihon eiga no ketten ka," *Kinema rekôdo* 40 (October 1916): 427.
41. Somei Saburô, "Jimaku to setsumei: Setsumeisha no tachiba," *Katsudô no sekai* 2.6 (June 1917): 62.
42. The *benshi* style proposed by many reformers was one in which explanation was restricted to merely reading or translating the intertitles of foreign films.
43. Midorikawa, "Jimaku zakkan," *Katsudô kurabu* 4.7: 41.
44. "Kenkyû: Eigageki to butaigeki: Katsudô shashin no kotoba ni tsuite," *Katsudô no sekai* 2.6 (June 1917): 13.
45. This could also be found in later Soviet montage theory, which emphasized an analogy between the shot inserted in a montage sequence and the word in a sentence. Japanese reformers, however, were more concerned with how to contain the threat of polyphony in the image through what was seen as a more stable semiotic element, the word.

46. Kaeriyama Norimasa, "Katsudô shashin no shakaiteki chii oyobi sekimu," *Kinema rekôdo* 42 (December 1916): 537.
47. Tom Gunning, *D. W. Griffith and the Origins of American Narrative Film* (Urbana: University of Illinois Press, 1991).
48. For more on these debates and on the context surrounding the production of Kinugasa's film, see my *A Page of Madness* (Flicks Books, forthcoming), or my "Eiga no ta no kanôsei," *Gengo bunka (Meiji Gakuin Daigaku Gengo Bunka Kenkyûjo)* 15 (1998): 66–80.
49. Iwasaki Akira, "Kurutta ichipeiji," *Kinema junpô* 243 (October 21, 1926): 48.
50. Ibid.
51. Kataoka Teppei, "*Kurutta ichipeiji* ni tsuite," *Engeki eiga* 1.7 (July 1926): 33–34.
52. In *Katsudô no sekai*'s words: "How can we make films that represent true Japanese civilization? Needless to say, it is through a screenplay that represents true Japanese civilization": "Eigageki to butaigeki: Kurubeki Nihon eiga," *Katsudô no sekai* 2.9 (September 1917): 40.
53. Kaeriyama, *Katsudô shashingeki:* 41.
54. For other articles on screenwriting at the time, see Tsubouchi Shikô, "Kyakuhonka no kushinsubeki ten," *Katsudô no sekai* 1.5 (May 1916): 24–28; Ikeda Daigo, "Katsudô shashin to Chikamatsu no fukkatsu," *Katsudô no sekai* 1.5 (May 1916): 28–30; Matsui Shôyô, "Tensai no shutsugen o matsu," *Katsudô no sekai* 1.5 (May 1916): 30–32; Kôda Rohan, "Kyakuhon sakusha ni tsuite," *Katsudô no sekai* 1.10 (October 1916): 2–4; Ide Tetsujo, "Eiga kyakuhonka no yobi chishiki," *Katsudô no sekai* 2.7 (July 1917): 2–4; Akita Ujaku, "Butai kyakuhon to eiga kyakuhon no shimei," *Katsudô no sekai* 2.7 (July 1917): 5–8; and Okamoto Kidô, "Katsudô shashingeki no kyakuhon," *Katsudô no sekai* 2.7 (July 1917): 10–13. It is interesting that most of these were written by established playwrights or novelists.
55. Mori Iwao and Tomonari Yôzô, "Katsudô shashin taikan," *Nihon eigashi sôkô,* ed. Okabe Ryû (Tôkyô: Film Library Council, 1976–1978): supplementary volume 2, p. 65; quoted in Joanne Bernardi, "The Early Development of the *Gendaigeki* Screenplay: Kaeriyama Norimasa, Kurihara Tômas, Tanizaki Jun'ichirô and the Pure Film Movement" (Ph.D. diss., Columbia University, 1992): 95.
56. Bernardi writes that, in Kaeriyama's mind, "the best way for a director to realize such a well-rounded narrative was to make the film according to a plan, the screenplay, which would give him greater control over the finished product." Bernardi 47.
57. Many of these regulations are reproduced in Monbushô Futsû Gakumukyoku, *Zenkoku ni okeru katsudô shashin jôkyô chôsa* (Tôkyô: Monbushô, 1921): apps. 1–35. The 1911 and 1921 Ôsaka codes are available in Terakawa Shin, *Eiga oyobi eigageki* (Ôsaka: Ôsaka Mainichi Shinbunsha, 1925): 230–48.
58. In a holdover from established modes of theater censorship, most motion picture regulations in the 1910s and 1920s required that a seat or box be set up at the back of the theater for police officers. Since the officer was often

charged with checking the *benshi*'s narration and maintaining order in the theater (enforcing seating regulations separating men and women, for instance), the regulation still maintains a vision of cinema as a live performance.

59. See, for instance, Article 16 of the 1920 Hiroshima codes, or Article 13, Section 3, of the 1918 Hyôgô regulations.
60. For more on the Film Law, see Gregory J. Kasza, *The State and the Mass Media in Japan, 1918–1945* (Berkeley: University of California Press, 1988): 232–51.
61. The regulations are reprinted in *Katsudô shashin "firumu" ken'etsu jihô* 1 (1925): furoku 1–2.
62. See the record of a meeting between local and Home Ministry officials reproduced in *Katsudô shashin "firumu" ken'etsu jihô* 1 (1925): furoku 11–14.
63. For more on Tanizaki and on Kawabata's relation to film, see my "Celluloid Masks: The Cinematic Image and the Image of Japan," *Iris* 16 (Spring 1993): 23–36. Bernardi also discusses Tanizaki's scripts for Taikatsu in some detail: Bernardi 176–87, 251–95.
64. I have discussed Akutagawa's two film scenarios, "Yûwaku" ("Temptation") and "Asakusa Kôen" ("Asakusa Park"), in my "The Self Seen as Other: Akutagawa and Film," *Literature/Film Quarterly* 23.3 (1995): 197–203.
65. Iijima Tadashi, "Shinario bungakuron josetsu," *Shinario bungaku zenshû 1: Shinario taikei* (Tôkyô: Kawade Shobô, 1937): 6; hereafter referred to as SBJ in the text.
66. Iijima himself later cited these tendencies in the Pure Film Movement as one reason Japanese silent film was "literary": Iijima Tadashi, "Nihon eiga no reimei: Jun'eigageki no shûhen," *Kôza Nihon eiga* 1: 126.

CHAPTER TWO

The Cinematic Art of Higuchi Ichiyô's *Takekurabe* (Comparing Heights, 1895–1896)

Janet A. Walker

In Section 3 of her master work, *Takekurabe,* Higuchi Ichiyô (1872–96) has one of her adolescent characters, Shôta, suggest to another, Midori, that they put on, as their contribution to the forthcoming neighborhood Otori Festival, a magic lantern *(gentô)* show. He goes on to suggest that they ask another character, Sangorô, who is talented as a street-hawker and can make people laugh with his chatter, to do a running narration *(kôjô)* to accompany the performance.[1] Regrettably, this magic-lantern performance never takes place – but the mention of it places Ichiyô's story firmly in the historical context of the mid-Meiji introduction from Europe of popular entertainments anticipating the cinema. The magic lantern *(gentô),* or stereopticon, was "introduced into Japan in 1874 as a toy."[2] "Lantern-slide shows had been touring Japan from 1886, and as early as 1893 an Italian had brought something called a 'kinematograph' show to Nagasaki," which was accompanied by 'live narration.'"[3]

By the time Ichiyô wrote *Takekurabe* in 1895–1896, home magic-lantern performances of the sort planned by Shôta and Midori had become a common form of entertainment for bourgeois families such as Shôta's. It is significant that Shôta's and Midori's plans include two

In revising this essay, which was presented, in a much different form, as a paper at the "Wording the Image" symposium at Dartmouth in September 1997, I have benefited greatly from the comments of David Desser, Arthur Nolletti, Jr., Aaron Gerow, and Keiko I. McDonald. I am especially indebted to David Desser for his ongoing encouragement of my work as well as for his help in formulating some of my ideas on cinema.

aspects of what was later to become cinema: projection of images to an audience watching in the dark, and explanation and commentary *(kôjô)* by a live narrator – who would, in cinema, be called a *benshi* (narrator/commentator). Thus, Ichiyô connects the world of her adolescent characters on the verge of adulthood with the medium of cinema on the verge of being born.

Ichiyô's completed story was published in book form, significantly, in 1896, the same year in which moving pictures were introduced into Japan. It was in 1896 that the Japanese imported the Kinetoscope, a one-man moving-picture machine, from America; in 1897 came the Cinématographe Lumière from France, and the Edison Vitascope, again from America, both of which used a several-man crew to "project moving pictures on a screen."[4] Ichiyô, dying prematurely of tuberculosis in 1896, did not live to see the introduction, much less the proliferation, of moving pictures in her country, but it is my thesis in this essay that she anticipated certain techniques of cinema in *Takekurabe.* In one particular scene, the climatic scene of the work, the action flows forward visually in ways typical of mature cinematic narration. In addition, Ichiyô presents emotions visually in terms that later became typical of cinema: by focusing on concrete objects that have subjective meaning for the protagonist and also communicate meaning to the viewer.

Ichiyô's narrative technique in this scene from *Takekurabe* anticipates techniques of narration that cinema would utilize only decades later. James Monaco notes how film, as it developed from the late nineteenth century from a primitive visual medium to a sophisticated art form, replicated the "complex systems of the novel,"[5] including both "narrative form"[6] itself and narrative devices such as metaphor, metonymy, and the trope.[7] What Ichiyô's text shows us is the kind of fictional narrative techniques that cinema could and did draw from in order to become a complex narrative form. In this essay I shall demonstrate how Ichiyô reworked techniques of visual narration from the traditional Japanese theater and visual imagery from the lyric and narrative traditions, combining them with the Western Symbolist technique, used in short narratives and dramas, of structuring narration around a complex image. In the course of my analysis I will indicate how cinema later utilized these techniques.

I first thought of Ichiyô's *Takekurabe* in cinematic terms years ago, when I read it for the first time. By *cinematic,* I mean that I recalled it as if I were recalling a movie; another way of saying this is that it seemed to me that the mode of reading *Takekurabe* was typical of cinematic modes of "reading" narrative. There was a visuality and movement about the work that affected me strongly. Having said this, I should note that I associated cinematic qualities with only one vivid scene from the work – the scene where Midori, the thirteen-year-old apprentice geisha, hurls a piece of brightly colored cloth toward her undeclared and unwilling sweetheart, the fourteen-year-old priest-to-be, Shinnyo (the latter character is referred to in both the Seidensticker and the Danly translations as Nobu, the name by which he is addressed). Midori gives him the red piece of cloth in order to help him repair his sandal, whose cord had broken as he was passing in front of her house, leaving him stranded and helpless in heavy autumn rain. This, the climactic scene of the work, clearly stands out from the other sections of the work; it is the only scene narrated in such a visual, protocinematic style.

The work is characterized by at least three modes of narration, which, woven together expertly, give this penultimate story of Ichiyô's the narrative complexity and brilliance that make of it her acknowledged masterpiece. Briefly, some sections are sketches, descriptive and evocative of the area around the Yoshiwara, where the action of the story takes place. These sections are narrated by a narrator who has a deep and extensive knowledge of the social realities of the quarter and who moralizes about the fates of the people in it in the manner of the late-seventeenth-century fiction writer Saikaku, but with a distinctively modern narrative point of view.[8] These sections are the "objective" sections, using David Bordwell's terminology developed in regard to filmic narration.[9] Some of the short sections of the work (there are sixteen in all) are exclusively objective, and some pass smoothly from the objective to the subjective, providing "explicit signals for the transitions between objectivity and subjectivity."[10] (I use Bordwell's terms invented for cinematic narration deliberately here to emphasize that the work as a whole can be read as both a film and a story.) Other sections of the work are oriented around the depiction of major events, for example, the planning for the Otori Festival; the attack on Midori and Sangorô by the "side-street" gang led by Chôkichi; and the climactic scene of the work, in which Midori throws the scrap of silk to the stranded Nobu. There are also some sections where the narrator focuses almost exclusively on the revelation of the subjectivities of her characters.

The scene that I am interested in is unique in that it both narrates an important action in a dramatic way, and sheds significant light on the emotions, and subjectivities, of the characters Midori and Nobu. The narrator here is not the narrator of the sketch sections, but a narrator who is able to create a highly dramatic, visual scene that has unusual (for the work as a whole) expanse and movement. The scene takes up two sections – Sections 12 and 13 – and amounts to four to five pages, which is about one-eighth of the work; reading it, one has the sense of the narrative suddenly slowing down, intensifying, and expanding visually, as if the scene were being performed on a stage or on a movie screen. Rhetorically, this scene communicates a great deal of emotion; it moves the reader more than any other in *Takekurabe,* which is probably why I remembered it alone out of all the scenes in the work.

The scene in question, in Sections 12 and 13, is a climactic moment in the evolving drama of the budding love between Midori, soon to become a geisha, and Nobu, soon to become a priest. *Takekurabe,* as is well known, focuses on a group of adolescents coming to adulthood in the Daionji quarter just outside the Yoshiwara, the major pleasure quarter in Tokyo.[11] Out of the five characters depicted – Nobu, Midori, Chôkichi, Shôta, and Sangorô – two (Shôta and Sangorô) remain stationary in their roles, Shôta as the highest-class, and wealthiest character, and Sangorô as the lowest-class, and least powerful character. The other three cross a liminal area of free childhood into the fixed roles of adulthood during the course of the story. Of the three, Chôkichi, the pugnacious son of a fireman who disrupts Shôta's and Midori's plans for the Otori Festival, preventing the magic-lantern show, seems, by the end of this scene (Section 13), to have acquired some of the power whose lack had frustrated him earlier, leading him to engage in fighting and harassment; at the end of the scene, he is shown dressed elegantly, if somewhat ostentatiously, and he graciously offers the stranded Nobu his sandals.

It is Nobu and Midori who undergo the most dramatic transformations. While at the beginning of the work they are brought together in the temporary, egalitarian place of childhood, by the end they occupy positions at opposite ends of the spectrum with regard to the activities of the pleasure quarter that is the central symbolic locus of the work. Midori, the future geisha, is tied forever to the quarter, while Nobu, the future priest, must (equally) forever shun its sexual attractions. The potential love between the two provides the most powerful example of emotional drives that must come to some expression, of emotional conflicts that must come to some resolution, so that it is no accident that the climactic scene focuses on the interaction of these two characters.[12] The scene expands and slows down precisely to accommodate, and express, the powerful emotions generated by the two characters; by its conclusion it has provided a site of resolution of the conflict generated by their opposing drives. I will give a summary of plot details that one needs to know to understand the meanings of the climactic scene, but my summary will include only the plot line of the love between Midori and Nobu, and the related threads of plot that one needs to know to understand what happens in the climactic scene of Sections 12 and 13.

At the Otori Festival on the twentieth of August, Chôkichi, the fifteen-year-old son of the fire chief of the neighborhood and the self-appointed leader of the "side-street gang" *(yokochô-gumi),* had come to harass the children of the "main street" *(omotemachi):* Shôta, the twelve-year-old son of the local moneylender and thirteen-year-old Midori, sister of a popular courtesan at the Daikokuya. On this yearly occasion when the two groups of adolescents would try to outdo each other in their elaborate plans for the festival, Chôkichi decided to try to win the competition through intimidation and force, and had brought his gang to where he thought Shôta, the leader of the other group, would be, hoping to pick a fight with him. He was emboldened in this effort by having obtained the support of Nobu, the priest's son. Not finding Shôta, however, Chôkichi and his group had beaten up Sangorô, a fifteen-year-old boy from the "side-street" area who had joined with Shôta and Midori to arrange their contribution to the festival. When Midori intervened in Sangorô's defense, Chôkichi had thrown his muddy sandal at her, striking her in the forehead.

The relationship between Midori and Nobu goes back even further than the August Otori Festival: to April of that year, when Midori had made friendly overtures to Nobu at an athletic meet at the school they both attended. Noticing that Nobu had tripped over the root of a tree and had fallen down, muddying his jacket, Midori had spontaneously offered him a red silk handkerchief to wipe it. For Nobu this overture was anything but innocent; he had taken the handkerchief she offered him, but when he noticed that someone had seen them talking and had started to spread rumors about a possible match between them, he began to turn away from Midori, treating her coldly. On another occasion, when she had asked Nobu to pick a flower for her from a branch she could not reach, he had done it, but in a cold manner, almost throwing the flower at her. As a future priest, he was determined not to be gossiped about by the people of the quarter.

The naturally friendly and outgoing Midori was surprised and dismayed by Nobu's coldness toward her. When he continued to shy away from her, she was hurt. And when she suspected that Nobu, who she knew had been won over by Chôkichi for his gang at the time of the August Otori Festival, might have been involved in the attack (meant for Shôta) on Sangorô, she became angry at Nobu as well. As time passes, Midori's unconscious attraction to Nobu becomes covered over with anger and hurt; and Nobu valiantly covers his forbidden (to a future priest) attraction to Midori with coldness and reserve. It is in the midst of these ambivalent, conflicted emotions that the two meet in the climactic scene, set in autumn of the same year. Here is the scene:

12

Nobu could have gone to his sister's some other way, but when he took the short-cut he had to pass it: a latticed gate and inside it a stone lantern, a low fence, autumn shrubs, all disposed with a certain quiet charm. Reed blinds fluttered over the verandah, and one could almost imagine that behind the sliding doors a latter-day widow of the Azechi no Dainagon would be saying her beads, that a young Murasaki would appear with her hair cut in the childish bob of long ago. It was the home of the gentleman who owned the Daikokuya.

Rain yesterday, rain again today. The winter under-kimono his sister had asked for was ready, and Nobu's mother was eager for her to have it at the earliest possible moment. "Even if you have to hurry a little, couldn't you take it to her on your way to school? She'll be waiting for it, I know."

Nobu was never able to refuse. He slipped into a pair of rain clogs and hurried off with the bundle in his arm and an umbrella over his shoulder.

He turned at the corner of the moat and started down the lane he always took. At the Daikokuya gate a gust of wind lifted his umbrella. This would never do. He planted his feet and pulled back, and the thong of one of his clogs gave way. And it had seemed sound enough when he left home. His foot slipped into the mud – this was a far more serious problem than the umbrella.

There was no help for it. He bit his lip in annoyance. Laying the umbrella against the gate, he moved in out of the rain and turned to the job of repairing the thong. But what to do? He was a young gentleman, not used to working with his hands, and no matter how he hurried the repairing seemed no nearer finished. Hurry, hurry. He took out some foolscap he had drafted a composition on and tried twisting a strip of it into a paper cord. The perverse wind came up again and the umbrella sailed off into the mud. Damn it, damn it. As he reached to catch the umbrella O-hana's kimono rolled weakly off his knee. The wrapping was filthy, even his sleeve was splashed with mud.

Sad it is to be out in the rain without an umbrella, and incomparably sad to break one's sandal along the way. Midori saw it from afar through the door and the gate.

"Can I give him something to tie it with, Mother?" She rummaged through a drawer of the sewing table and snatched up a bit of printed silk. Almost too impatient to slip into her sandals, hardly bothering to take up an umbrella, she dashed out along the garden flagstones.

Her face turned scarlet as she came near enough to see who it was. Her heart pounded. Would anyone be watching? – she edged fearfully up to the gate. Nobu shot a quick glance over his shoulder. Cold sweat ran down his sides, and he felt a sudden urge to run off barefoot.

The Midori we have known would have pointed a teasing finger – look at him, would you. Just look at him. She would have laughed herself sick. She would have poured out all the abuse that came to her. It was good of you to see that they broke up our party the other night, and all because you were out to get Shôta. You had them beat up Sangorô, and what did he ever do to you? You were behind it, you were lording it over all of them. Do you say you're sorry? You were the one that had the likes of Chôkichi call me dirty names. What if I am like my sister? What's wrong with that? I don't owe you a thing, not a single cent. I have my mother and my father and the gentleman at the Daikokuya and my sister, and I don't need to ask favors of any broken-down priest. So let's not have any more of it. If you have anything to say to me say it out in the open, don't go talking behind my back. I'm here, any time you want to fight. Well, what about it?

She would have clutched at his sleeve and attacked with a violence that would have cut him low. But here she was, shrinking back in the shadow of the gate. Not a word out of her. And still she stood there squirming, unable to open her mouth and unable to walk off and leave him. This was indeed a different Midori.

13

Nobu always approached the Daikokuya gate with mounting terror, and he looked neither to the right nor to the left as he marched past. But the unlucky rain, the unlucky wind, and now this bungle. He stood under the gate trying to twist the paper cord. Already miserable enough, he felt as though someone had dashed ice water on him when he heard those steps. He trembled violently, his face changed color. Even without looking he knew it was Midori. He turned his back to her and pretended to be engrossed in the broken thong, but he was in such a panic that it was hard to see when the clog would be ready to wear again.

Midori stood watching. How clumsy he is! How does he expect to get it done that way? See, it comes undone even before he's finished twisting. And now he puts straw in. What good will that do? Doesn't he see he's getting muddy? There goes his umbrella. Why doesn't he shut it? Midori could hardly restrain herself. And yet she was silent. You can tie it with this – but something kept her from calling out to him. She stood in the shadow of the gate, heedless of the rain that wet her sleeves.

From the house came the voice of her mother, who could not see what was happening. "Midori, the fire for the iron is ready. Where is the child? Now what are you doing out there in the rain? You'll catch another cold, and you've just gotten over one."

"I'll be right in," Midori called back, wishing that somehow she could keep Nobu from hearing. Her heart raced. She could not open the gate, and yet she could not ignore the unfortunate. Turning over all the possibilities in her mind, she finally thrust her hand out through the lattice and tossed the cloth over to him. He ignored it. Ah, he's the same as ever. All Midori's resentment gathered in her eyes, tears of annoyance welled up. What does he have against me? Why doesn't he come out with it? There are plenty of things I would like to say too. He's impossible.

But there was her mother calling again. Midori took a step or two back from the gate, then collected herself with a start – what could she be thinking of, demeaning herself so – and marched firmly into the house.

Nobu was suddenly lonesome. He turned toward the gate. The tatter of silk, its red maple leaves shining in the rain, lay on the ground near his feet. He looked fondly at it in spite of himself, and yet, miserable though he was, he could not bring himself to reach over for it.

Clearly he was getting nowhere. He took the cord from his cloak and passed it several times around the clogs and over his instep in a most unpromising makeshift. That might do – he started out, but it was virtually impossible to walk. Could he ever get as far as Tamachi? No help for it. He started out again, the package at his side. He let his eye wander back to the maples on that bit of silk.

"What's the matter? Broke it, did you?" Someone came up behind him. "You won't get far that way."

It was the pugnacious Chôkichi, evidently on his way home from the quarter. His sash was tied low on his hips in that swaggering manner he affected. He had on a brand-new cloak and carried a figured umbrella on his shoulder, and the shining lacquer on his rain clogs suggested that they had come from a shop case but that morning. A dashing figure indeed.

"I broke it and I can't think of anything to do," Nobu said weakly.

"I'll bet. You wouldn't know what to do. But it's all right. You can take mine. You won't break these."

"What will you do?"

"I'm used to going barefoot. Here we go." Chôkichi hitched up his kimono skirt with aplomb and stepped out of his clogs. "You won't get anywhere with those."

"You're going barefoot? But I couldn't. . ."

"It's all right, I'm used to it. You'd cut your feet up, but mine are tough. Here, put 'em on." The beetle brows were pulled into a frown, but the words were remarkably friendly coming from one about as popular as the god of plagues himself. "Here, I'll toss yours in at your kitchen door. That'll do it. Come on, let's have 'em." The good turn done, Chôkichi held out his hand for the broken clogs. "There you go. See you at school."

The one set out for his sister's, the other turned toward home, and the red maple leaves, a store of regrets, lay abandoned by the gate.[13]

Nobu, passing by the Daikokuya on the way to his sister's, breaks the cord of one of his sandals. Midori, from inside the Daikokuya, sees what has happened; not knowing it is Nobu, but simply moved by the plight of someone breaking the cord of his sandal in the midst of a storm, "she grabbed a scrap of Yûzen crepe silk from out of the drawer of the sewing box,"[14] and rushed out the door with it, intending to offer it to the stranger as something to repair his sandal with. When she sees that the person is Nobu, however, she is overwhelmed by her conflicting feelings: hesitant love and compassion for Nobu are nearly squelched by hurt for what she believes is his dismissal of her feelings; and also anger toward him for what she believes (erroneously) is his major role in Chôkichi's attack during the Otori Festival a few months earlier. As she sees Nobu struggling ineffectually to mend his sandal, she wants to call out to him to offer him the scrap of silk. When her mother calls out to ask why she doesn't come in out of the rain, Midori, after a moment of wrenching indecision, hurriedly throws the scrap of cloth at Nobu. As before, when she had handed Nobu the red silk handkerchief, he doesn't respond, and Midori turns to go inside, her overtures to him having again been rebuffed and her feelings frustrated.

Nobu, on his part, also had mixed feelings about seeing Midori. He could have avoided going past the Daikokuya on his way to his sister's place, if he had wished to avoid seeing Midori, but that he did take that route indicates his interest in seeing her. His trembling and virtual panic when he recognizes Midori clearly demonstrate his attraction to her; yet his refusal to look at her or talk to her shows that he will do everything in his power to avoid expressing this attraction and to keep it from showing. It is only when Midori has turned around and gone into the house, after throwing Nobu the piece of silk cloth, that Nobu can allow himself to look at the scrap of red cloth that has become for him a metonymy for Midori. Here Ichiyô elaborates on the piece of red cloth as she focuses on Nobu's feelings: As Midori clattered over the stepping-stones, Nobu now looked back over his shoulder at her forlornly. The red silk, in a pattern of autumn leaves, was wet with rain. It was beautiful and lay scattered near his foot. Somehow he was drawn to it – but he couldn't pick it up. Gazing at it futilely, he felt miserable.[15] This is the climactic moment of the whole two-section scene, for it is here that Nobu renounces his affection for Midori, leaving the freedom and possibility of childhood behind. Midori's moment of renunciation of childhood freedom comes later, in Section 15, when she sobs quietly in her room after what is possibly her first sexual encounter with a customer. It is a quiet, introverted scene, taking place in an interior, without the visually dramatic qualities of the much longer scene between Nobu and Midori. It lacks the action, the kinetic qualities, of the two-section scene that narrates the last meeting, and parting, of Nobu and Midori.

One can view this scene just as if one were viewing a movie. One can imagine a film camera recording Nobu hesitantly and fearfully passing by the gate of the Daikokuya in the rain, and then bracing himself against the strong wind, at which point he suddenly crouches on the ground to look at his broken sandal. Then the camera would zoom in on Nobu as he tries to fashion a substitute paper cord out of a piece of twisted paper from his school notebook. Leaving Nobu, the camera would go inside the house to focus on Midori watching the ill-fated traveler from the window. The camera would zoom in on her as she takes a scrap of printed red silk from out of her mother's sewing-table drawer, allowing the viewer to perceive the redness, but probably not yet the pattern of the cloth. That will come later, at the point when Nobu turns to gaze carefully at it as it lies in the mud.

As Midori, now standing in the entrance of the house, looks out at Nobu, the camera would focus long on her face – first at the moment when she recognizes Nobu, and then more intensely on her face and gestures as she stands in the rain, unable to decide whether or not to offer the piece of cloth to a person toward whom she harbored powerful feelings of anger and resentment mixed with love. Then the camera would show her hesitating, as she hears her mother's call to come in out of the rain, and struggling once more to decide what to do; and finally, it would show her hurling the cloth through the lattice at him. It would follow her as she takes a tentative step toward Nobu, and then as she turns around, once and for all, and retreats into the house.

The camera has recorded action and emotion up to this point, but now it would focus on an object that will arouse emotions in one of the actors, Nobu, as well as in the viewers. This is the scrap of Yûzen crepe with its stylized *momiji* (red autumn leaves) pattern in brilliant red, which was barely glimpsed when Midori grabbed it out of the sewing-table drawer, but which now is fleshed out in visual and metaphorical detail. The camera, adopting Nobu's viewpoint now, would focus on the beautiful red piece of cloth lying in the mud, allowing, indeed inviting – but in the camera's wordless way – the viewer to contemplate the implications of the scrap of cloth's being hurled in mixed anger and love by the woman, and gazed at fondly but left untouched by the man. One of these implications is surely that, where the two had been children before, in this rite of courtship they are acting as adults. The viewer would perceive the scrap of bright red cloth, abandoned in the mud, as emblematic of the failure of communication, of the relationship between the two could-have-been lovers, Midori's initial outgoing affection having turned to anger and frustration, and Nobu's timid interest in her having been frozen out by his concern for his priestly self. Then the camera would move away from the bright-colored scrap of cloth (which nevertheless remains in the viewer's mind as an important symbolic object) to focus once more on Nobu's efforts to mend the cord of his sandal.

In this climactic scene, there are lengthy interior monologues in which Midori's conflicting thoughts and feelings are expressed, but there are no equivalent monologues for Nobu. The camera has a chance to linger on Midori as she acts, gestures, and emotes; but with Nobu the camera would mainly zoom in on the piece of cloth that is a repository for Nobu's emotions, not much on Nobu's emoting. There would only be the brief focus on Nobu as he looks back at the retreating Midori and then turns to gaze forlornly at the red cloth lying in the mud. Then, after he rises to go on his way, the camera would again rest briefly on Nobu as he allows his eyes to wander one last time to the bit of red cloth: His eyes lingered on the red leaves of the Yûzen – he could hardly bear to go off and leave them. He turned to look at them with regret. . . .[16] The text makes it clear that Nobu has come to a final resolve to leave behind Midori, and all that she represents, but also that this resolve is only achieved with a tremendous effort at self-discipline, and not without clearly felt regret at what he has lost.

For Nobu, the bright red leaves on the scrap of cloth reflect the emotional brightness and color of Midori, as well as of the world of the pleasure quarter, from which he, as a priest, will be forever banned. Visually, his resolve to leave behind Midori, and the glitter of life itself, to become a priest, is shown by his leaving, a bit later, the scene without looking back. For the viewer, meaning here the Japanese viewer, or, better, the viewer aware of long-standing Japanese associations of emotions with seasons, the *momiji* are not only a metaphor for the brightness and liveliness of Midori, and the pleasure quarter, but also communicate a sadness traditionally associated with the end of the annual natural cycle, and, by extension, with the end of a love affair. These are some of the associations that hover over the brightly colored scrap of cloth as the camera focuses on it.

The camera would then cut to Chôkichi, the erstwhile pugnacious fireman's son, who enters the scene dressed to the teeth, having reached a stage in his life where he wishes to attract women and having, in fact, just come from the pleasure quarter. His entrance offers a comic relief from the intensity of the Midori – Nobu encounter. Evidently wishing to make amends for having involved Nobu in the disgrace of the attack on the "main street" children at the Otori Festival earlier in the year, he now lends Nobu his own fancy sandals in a grandly debonair gesture. As the two young men go off, each in a different direction, the camera would linger a final time on the red scrap of cloth: The two parted, Nobu going toward his sister in Tamachi's place and Chôkichi going in the direction of his home. The red Yûzen, where (so many) feelings still remained, left behind a pitiful appearance as it lay uselessly outside the lattice gate.[17] All the human beings who had anything to do with the scrap of red cloth have left the scene; and the camera now would view it one last time, objectively and from a distance, as a "useless" and "pitiful" object, the symbol of a possible love definitively and finally rejected.

In the climactic scene of *Takekurabe* in Sections 12 and 13, Ichiyô anticipates cinematic techniques in two major ways. First, in structuring and presenting this scene, Ichiyô's "camera" is an artist of decoupage, dividing the scene into small pieces or moments ("shots"), then arranging them carefully into a continuity of images that guides the viewer/reader spatially and dramatically to an emotional climax and then to a resolution of the conflict posed.[18] This technique of decoupage suggests the mode of presentation and the mode of arrangement of scenes of a dramatic spectacle – indeed, the terms "climax" and "resolution of the conflict" seem to evoke Western drama, in particular. In her structuring of the scenes of *Takekurabe* toward a resolution of a conflict, Ichiyô might well have learned from Ibsen's plays, some of which might have been known to her in text and/or in performance. Or she might have learned from plots of European short stories or novels organized according to Aristotelian demands.

But Ichiyô's mode of presentation and organization of scenes or "shots" owes more to the indigenous tradition of kabuki, the most popular form of theater from the 1700s on, and the form of theater that influenced Japanese writers of fiction well into the Meiji period, even after their encounter with Western poetics.[19] Ichiyô's method of organizing the movement in her climactic scene is similar to that in kabuki. Kabuki as a form of theater involves organized movement (gesture and dance) as well as spectacle – both visual elements – in addition to its verbal display and its plot. Ichiyô's scene shows a mastery of choreographed movement and spectacle that allows the reader to visualize the action dramatically, as if watching a play. She provides the viewer with dramatic, intense gestures and movements: Nobu's struggle with his umbrella against the rain and wind, his digging his foot into the mud to balance himself, and the slipping of his foot into the mud despite his efforts, provide a visualizable, choreographed dance or, at the very least, a sequence of gestures that, in its kinetic interest, evokes the dance sequences of kabuki. The "dance" or gesture of the rainy wind, which had tried to tear away Nobu's umbrella, is then repeated in a more muted sequence of movement, in which the wind succeeds in sweeping the umbrella into the mud, at which point the package that Nobu is taking to his older sister rolls off his lap into the mud.

Midori's gestural and dance sequence is her dashing out of the house with the scrap of Yûzen silk to give Nobu, her edging fearfully up to the gate (where he has knelt to try to repair his sandal), then her squirming hesitation as she tries to decide whether to give him the cloth – then her tossing him the cloth, her hesitation again (as he does not take it up), and, as the conclusion of her dance, her "marching firmly into the house." Ichiyô, as kabuki director, also provides her audience here with sharp contrasts between movement and quiescence: thus Nobu's little dance and Midori's flinging the piece of silk crepe toward Nobu, then suddenly rushing inside her house, contrast with still shots where the characters do not move visibly but engage in intense interior monologues. The action on Ichiyô's "stage" is carefully blocked, in terms of contrasting moods of movement and stasis, as a series of steps toward an emotional climax. From here it is not far to, using David Desser's formulation, cinema's arrangement of moments or "shots" into a continuity of images that guides the viewer to an emotional climax.[20]

Donald Richie points out that early cinema in Japan "was regarded as an extension of the stage, and not, as in the West, a new kind of photography."[21] And Keiko I. McDonald argues that "early Japanese cinema was greatly indebted to formal properties of the classical stage, especially Kabuki, and also to the Kabuki/Bunraku repertoire."[22] Ichiyô, in this scene from her fictional narrative, in her conveyance of a sense of movement and emotionality, mediates between the narrative style of her theatrical tradition and the cinematic narrative style of the future. This was the narrative style of a medium that Lewis Jacobs argues would provide a "confluence of senses: visual, aural, kinesthetic, spacial, temporal," as well as create the "illusion of movement."[23] Ichiyô's scene could not recreate the aural sense of theater or cinema – this possibility, and its combination with visuality and movement, were only fully realized in cinema. But the ways in which she uses visuality and movement in decoupage anticipate cinematic practice.

Besides conveying a cinematic sense of movement, Ichiyô used the concrete object in a way that anticipates the way objects are used in the cinema, evoking the particular power that objects have in that medium. I am thinking here of the piece of red Yûzen silk that, appearing at several junctures of the plot of *Takekurabe,* functions as perhaps the most important communicator of meaning in the work. *Takekurabe* has other concrete objects that play a role in the creation of narrative meaning – the red handkerchief that Midori hands Nobu early in the work, so that he can clean mud off his hand; the unusual-looking flower that Nobu picks for Midori; the sandal, including both the sandal of Nobu, whose thong so fatefully breaks in front of Midori's house, and the fancy sandals that Chôkichi lends Nobu so that he can go on his way; and the paper narcissus that Nobu leaves at Midori's gate at the end of the work. But the piece of red silk is clearly the most important nexus of threads of meaning.

David Desser points out that film, lacking the capacity to "show" abstract states of mind and thoughts, must rely on the concrete, on what can be "seen," to communicate meaning.[24] Film can reproduce concrete objects but more often it uses objects as metaphors and symbols to evoke "wide-reaching associations and implications."[25] A particularly sophisticated use of a concrete object in a film is as an organizing symbol to communicate meaning. Orson Welles structures his film *Citizen Kane* (1941), for example, around the symbol of the sled, whose meaning the viewer only realizes at the end of the film, when it is identified with the mysterious name "Rosebud" that Kane utters at his death. The first view of the sled is a long focus in the first flashback scene of the film; here, the sled, abandoned in the snow as the child Kane is forcibly taken from his parental home to live with the wealthy but unloving rich man, serves as a symbol of the parental love that he lost in childhood. The first view links up with the last view of the sled, this time with the name "Rosebud" visible on it, when it lies, again abandoned, but this time as a result of Kane's death, in a large warehouse containing Kane's many possessions. The camera moves leisurely over the horrifying sea of abandoned objects, eventually coming to rest on the sled. But before the viewer has a chance to dwell on it, a workman hurls it into a large fire that has been lit to destroy the unwanted objects. The viewer has only a brief opportunity to catch the word "Rosebud" written on the front end of the upright sled before the object goes up in flames. The sled, as a concrete object symbolizing Kane's lost ability to love, thus unites the film's, and Kane's beginning and end, in a powerful arc of meaning.[26] Cinema is particularly adept at utilizing objects as symbols because of the direct visuality of the medium. But literature, especially drama and fiction, can also use concrete objects to convey meaning, visualizing them through words.

Ichiyô's use of the scrap of red Yûzen silk as a symbol to communicate meaning can be historically grounded in an emphasis on visuality in European culture in general, as well as in the literary movement of Symbolism that dominated European fiction and drama in the late nineteenth century. It is no accident that film and its antecedents developed in a period when vision – what Martin Jay calls the "master sense of the modern era"[27] – was becoming dominant. Literature demonstrates visuality precisely in the increasing reliance on concrete objects, rather than on ideas, to communicate meaning. The beginnings of literary visuality, in the sense of a focus on concrete objects, are found in Baudelaire's poetry. By the late nineteenth century, visuality in this sense began to dominate the two European literary forms closest to lyric poetry in their brevity: the short story and the drama.

Rey Chow rightly views the short story, which came to prominence in the late nineteenth century in the West, accompanying the disappearance of the mid-century four-decker novels, as the literary form most demonstrative of the characteristics of the emergent dominant visuality. She singles out the condensed nature of the short story, its "quick capturing of life with minimal background detail within a frozen span of time" and its tendency to "become a picture," as aspects of its visuality.[28] But I would add to these characteristics the short story's frequent organization of meaning around a concrete object, a visual image. Short stories such as Edgar Allen Poe's "The Black Cat", written in the 1840s, were precursors of this tendency, but the late nineteenth century abounds in short stories that communicate their major meaning through a concrete object.

One thinks here of Maupassant's famous story "La Parure" (The Necklace), written in the 1880s, in which the major meaning of the story is tied up in a concrete object. This kind of short story, in which meaning involving a concrete object is suddenly revealed at the end, the article becoming "symbolic of the basic situation,"[29] is probably the model for Herman J. Mankiewicz's "Rosebud" symbol in *Citizen Kane.*

Drama of the time also offers examples in which a concrete object becomes a dominant mode of textual organization. Like the short story probably obtaining its trust in the visual image from French Symbolist poetry, and, like the short story relying on shortness for an effect of intensity impossible to achieve in the four-decker novel, drama used concrete objects as symbols in order to organize and communicate meaning. One thinks here of Ibsen's *The Wild Duck* (*Vildanden,* 1884) or *Hedda Gabler* (1890) – both of which Ichiyô could have known or known of. In both of these plays, concrete objects – the wild duck in the play of the same name, and the pistols of General Gabler in *Hedda Gabler* – are utilized as the major devices to communicate meaning. In the latter play, in particular, the pistols go beyond their function in structuring the plot (i.e., they transcend the kind of detective-story function of the necklace in Maupassant's story), serving as well to communicate, in a poignant and intense manner, the emotional reality of the main character. As Rolf Fjelde puts it, a sense that concrete objects are able to "liberate and implement the personalities and vital energies of the characters," a sense of "the individual as a field of force entering into and appropriating certain personally expressive objects to fulfill its ends, appears to be the principle underlying much of the use of symbols in the plays."[30]

Ichiyô's careful organization of her story around the concrete object of the scrap of red Yûzen silk[31] is comparable in its complexity and skill to that of Ibsen. What Ibsen does not communicate, however, is the visuality of the objects – apparently the wild duck is not simulated on stage by an actual object but is merely referred to,[32] the verbal level winning out over the visual. But in Ichiyô's *Takekurabe* the piece of red silk is carefully visualized – in words, to be sure – but it is made palpable and physical in ways not achieved in Western Symbolist drama, and achieved in the Western short story (the stories of D. H. Lawrence, for example) only after the Japanese-influenced Imagist poetics had made its mark on European poetry. Ichiyô's capacity to use verbal language to create a powerful visual image out of a concrete object – a visual image that, in cinema, would be literally visual – stems from a lengthy tradition of lyric poetry that validates the concrete object to an extent unknown in other poetic traditions.

Reaching its first period of greatness during the Heian period (795–1185), the lyric tradition of *waka* utilized a number of concrete objects, mainly natural phenomena, in order to communicate emotional, moral, and intellectual meaning. But concrete objects turned, through poetic language, into poetic images could be visualized, or heard, or smelled by the reader or listener of *waka* as well. It is common knowledge that Ichiyô in her early years was a member of a female poetic coterie that attempted to imitate Heian *waka,* and that she used devices from Heian *waka* in her works.[33] In addition, the very title of *Takekurabe* was suggested by the Heian collection of *waka* accompanied by prose, the *uta-monogatari* (poem-tale) *Ise monogatari* (The Tales of Ise, ca. the first half of the tenth century) – in particular, by section 23, in which a boy, in love with a girl, writes her a poem referring to how his height *(take)* has increased since he last saw her.[34] It is my opinion that Ichiyô was able to give her visual image of the scrap of red silk such power because she was able to tap into the visuality of the Japanese *waka* tradition. I would like to discuss the scrap of red silk as a reworking of a cluster of Heian images.

When the reader/viewer (I am imagining the reader of *Takekurabe* seeing the concrete object visually, as in film, as he/she reads the text) first sees the scrap of red silk, as Midori hurriedly grabs it out of her mother's sewing box, it is described merely objectively as "a scrap of Yûzen crepe silk" *(yûzen-chirimen no kirehashi).* It is not made visible to the reader/viewer through any mention of color or pattern, so that one learns nothing of its cultural meaning. One can only speculate on its social meaning, at this point, and here the reader/viewer might imagine that the scrap of silk came from the kimono of one of the female inhabitants of the Daikokuya. Since Yûzen crepe silk was used for very fine kimonos, the kimono the scrap came from was probably that of a high-ranking geisha. So that what Midori rushes out to hand the stranger in distress is probably a scrap from a geisha's silk kimono. That the stranger turns out to be Nobu, the soon-to-become priest, means that the mention of the kind of fabric brings home, to a reader/viewer alert to the implications of the scrap of silk in terms of gender and profession, the opposition between the geisha world of Midori and the priestly world of Nobu.

Rey Chow points out that the visual images of film "do not have possibilities of interiorization and abstraction that are typical of the written word."[35] Verbal texts gain part of their power from this ability to interiorize and abstract, but Ichiyô renounces this ability and instead presents a powerful image that the reader/viewer must decode by viewing it and drawing conclusions as to its meaning. She thickens the meaning of her visual image – the scrap of Yûzen silk – the next time it is referred to: when the camera zooms in on it after Midori has thrown it down near Nobu and run toward the house. The text presents it as a powerful visual image: "the pattern of autumn leaves on the red silk wet with rain" *(beniiri yûzen no ame nurete momiji no kata),* as if the camera alone were gazing at it, but the sentence then goes on to allow for the pattern of wet red leaves to be perceived, and found beautiful, by Nobu *(beniiri yûzen no ame nurete momiji no kata no uruwashiki).* The text goes on to state that something is "scattered near my foot" *(wa ga ashi chikaku chiriboitaru),* and the subject of the verb *scattered* can only be the autumn leaves *(momiji).* Literally, the text began by mentioning the pattern of autumn leaves on the red silk, but the leaves, through poetic license, have now separated themselves from the cloth and become real leaves that have been scattered by the autumn wind.

What Ichiyô has done here by verbal means is to evoke, in the mind of the Japanese reader/viewer, a visual image of autumn leaves *(momiji)* that have scattered during an autumn rain – an image that is at the same time visual and the catalyst for a flood of poetic associations and meanings. For the Japanese reader, the person familiar with the *waka* tradition, the words *autumn leaves* – actually *red autumn leaves (momiji)* – *wind (kaze), autumn* (*aki* – autumn shrubs are mentioned as part of the setting at the start of Section 12) and *scatter (chiru)* are well-known poetic images in poems dealing with autumn, for example, poems in the two *Autumn* books of the early tenth-century poetic anthology *Kokinwakashû* (Collection of Poems Ancient and Modern). As has been pointed out by Jin'ichi Konishi, the poems of the imperial poetic anthologies were arranged according to linked principles of association and progression.[36] Thus, poems on all four topics (as well as on other autumnal topics) occur generally in the order that the phenomena they represent would occur in nature.

Book 1 of the *Autumn* poems announces all four topics, but in Book 2 the topics tend to occur in clusters. In number 256, for example, *momiji* occurs with *akikaze;* in number 281 *momiji* occurs with *chiru;* in number 284 *shigure* (autumn rain) occurs with *momiji,* but *chiru* is implied; in number 285 *akikaze, momiji,* and *chiru* again occur in a cluster. In number 286 the speaker of the poem says he is as helpless as the *momiji* being scattered by the wind; number 287 mentions fallen leaves; and number 290 contains autumn, wind, and scattered.[37] Together these *waka* create, through visual imagery, a moment in late autumn when the brightly colored autumn leaves are scattered by the autumn wind and (sometimes) rain. Bringing several of the images together in one *waka,* or in several *waka,* one after the other, heightens the intensity of the season. In addition, human action and emotion are related to the natural phenomena in *waka* number 286, where the speaker compares his helplessness to that of the autumn leaves scattered by the wind.

In her Sections 12 and 13, Ichiyô has created a comparable moment of intensity, where the cluster of autumn, wind, rain, and scattered leaves – encapsulated in the *momiji* on the scrap of Yûzen silk – enhances the emotion of the characters and expresses verbally, and visually, their unspoken emotions. The color red *(beniire)* that Ichiyô mentions several times (and that is not mentioned in the poetic image of red autumn leaves – *momiji*) calls the attention of the reader/viewer to color in a way that technicolor cinema would, so that in her emphasis on the color red she anticipates color film. If the scene were filmed in technicolor, the viewer would see the red silk cloth in reality; but Ichiyô enables the reader/viewer to see the red both by her reference to *beniiri* and by her evocation of (red) *momiji* and their dense poetic associations.

While the *waka* both individually and in a cluster link humankind to the world of nature in the muted Buddhist mood of transience, Ichiyô's cluster of *waka*-derived images, which are located in the one intense image of the red, *momiji*-patterned scrap of silk cloth, evokes in Nobu a more intense and conflicted mood. As he looks one last time at the red leaves on the cloth lying in the mud, he can hardly bear to leave them, and turns his back on them with real regret. For a moment Ichiyô allows a modern, individualistic sense of moral choice to enter the experiential world of her story, and the concrete object is still vital, part of nature. But the narrator, in her last reference to the concrete object that is the main carrier of meaning in the story, returns it to the status it had when the reader/viewer first glimpsed it in Midori's hand: a piece of silk *(beniiri yûzen)* with only social meaning. At the last mention of it, the narrator imbues it with a subdued mood of sadness and evanescence.[38]

In conclusion, Ichiyô, in the climactic scene of *Takekurabe,* both in the visuality and movement of her decoupage and in her use of a powerful visual image as a dominant mode of textual organization, anticipated cinematic practice. Ichiyô probably owed to the Western short story, and to the Symbolist drama contemporaneous with it, the narrative strategy of using an image or a symbol to unify the various strands of a fictional narrative. But it was her own tradition of kabuki theater that suggested modes of managing visuality and kinesis in decoupage. Finally, Ichiyô's writing rests on long, indigenous lyric and narrative traditions of utilizing concrete phenomena as carriers of human emotion. Ichiyô devised ways of turning the literary image into a highly visual and kinetic one, creating a visual narrative technique that formed a transition between literary and cinematic narrative. Her capacity as a Japanese writer to create a narrative that was visual and kinetic suggests the aesthetic possibilities in the Japanese narrative tradition that allowed it to develop a major tradition of cinematic narrative.

NOTES

1. Higuchi Ichiyô, *Takekurabe,* in *Higuchi Ichiyô shu.* ed. Wada Yoshie, *Nihon Kindaibungaku Taikei* 8 (Tokyo: Kadokawa Shoten, 1983), 233–34. Henceforth I shall refer to this work as *Takekurabe.* For English translations, see "Growing Up," trans. Edward Seidensticker, in Donald Keene, ed., *Modern Japanese Literature* (New York: Grove Press, 1956), 70–110; and "Child's Play," trans. Robert Lyons Danly, in Robert Lyons Danly, *In the Shade of Spring Leaves: The Life and Writings of Higuchi Ichiyô, a Woman of Letters in Meiji Japan* (New Haven: Yale University Press, 1981), 254–87.
2. A magic-lantern show of the sort that Shôta and Midori were planning to put on would probably have consisted of the projection, to an audience watching in the dark, of still images with color and shading that were drawn on glass slides *(taneita).* Professional performances would have involved moving images, making the *gentô* a kind of protocinematic form. For my understanding of the *gentô* and its significance, I am indebted to Aaron Gerow, E-mail communication, 23 October 1997.
3. Joseph L. Anderson and Donald Richie, *The Japanese Film: Art and Industry* (New York: Grove Press, 1960), 23.
4. Ibid., 22.
5. James Monaco, *How to Read a Film,* rev. ed. (New York: Oxford University Press, 1981), 20.

6. David Bordwell and Kristin Thompson, *Film Art: An Introduction* (Reading, Mass.: Addison-Wesley, 1980), 292.
7. Monaco, *How to Read a Film,* 134–40.
8. For a comprehensive discussion of Ichiyô's debt to Saikaku, see Robert Danly, *In the Shade of Spring Leaves,* 109–32.
9. David Bordwell, *Narration and the Fiction Film* (Madison: University of Wisconsin Press, 1985), 152.
10. Bordwell, *Narration and the Fiction Film,* 152.
11. For a moving essay on *Takekurabe* that emphasizes the power of the story to bring the reader to experience nostalgia for his/her own childhood, see Maida Ai, "Kodomotachi no jikan – 'Takekurabe' shikiron," in Maeda, *Higuchi Ichiyô no sekai* (Tokyo: Heibonsha, 1978), 250–93.
12. Yamane Kenkichi argues convincingly that Nobu and Midori share the stage as the hero of the work, linked by their powerful *tairitsukan* (feelings of opposition). See Yamane, *Higuchi Ichiyô no bungaku* (Tokyo: Ôfusha, 1976), 108.
13. Edward Seidensticker, "Growing Up," in Keene, *Modern Japanese Literature,* 100–4.
14. *Haribako no hikidashi kara yûzen-chirimen no kirehashi o tsukamidashi. . . . Takekurabe,* 257.
15. *(Midori) katakatato tobiishi o tsutaiyuku ni, Shinnyo wa ima zo sabishiu mikaereba, beniiri yûzen no ame nurete momiji no kata no uruwashiki ga wa ga ashi chikaku chiriboitaru, sozoro ni yukashiki omoi wa aredomo, te ni toriaguru koto o mo sezu, munashiu nagamete uki omoi ari. Takekurabe,* 259.
16. *Yûzen no momiji me ni nokorite, sutete suguru ni shinobigataku, kokoronokori shite mikaereba . . . Takekurabe,* 260.
17. *Shinnyo wa tamachi no ane no moto e, Chôkichi wa wagayado no kata e to yukiwakareru ni, omoi no todomaru beniire no yûzen wa, ijirashiki sugata o munashiku koshimon no soto ni todomenu. Takekurabe,* 260.
18. For the formulation of this idea in cinematic terms, I am indebted to David Desser, E-mail communication, 8 December 1997.
19. It is well known that kabuki theater, in particular, as the most popular form of theater in the Edo period, exerted an influence on late-Edo fiction in the form of a reliance on dialogue as the major mode of narration (see Tamenaga Shunsui's *Shunshoku umegoyomi,* ca. 1832). And fiction-writers' reliance on dialogue as a major mode of narration continued into the Meiji period (see Part II of Futabatei Shimei's *Ukigumo* – The Floating Cloud, 1889). Robert Danly argues that Ichiyô's mastery of dialogue (in illustration of this, he quotes and analyzes a passage from "Jûsan'ya" – The Thirteenth Night, 1895) "suggests the makings of a playwright." *In the Shade of Spring Leaves,* 143–45. Ichiyô's expert capacity to create lively dialogue is in evidence in a number of chapters of *Takekurabe,* but in this climactic scene it is the movement and visuality that demonstrate her debt to kabuki.
20. David Desser, E-mail communication, 8 December, 1997.
21. Donald Richie, *Japanese Cinema: An Introduction* (Hong Kong and New York: Oxford University Press, 1989), 8.
22. Keiko I. McDonald, *Japanese Classical Theater in Film* (Rutherford, N.J.:

Fairleigh Dickinson University Press, 1994), 9. See her discussion of this early period in Chapters 1 and 2. See also Hiroshi Komatsu's discussion of the influence of kabuki on early Japanese film in "Some Characteristics of Japanese Cinema Before World War I," in *Reframing Japanese Cinema: Authorship, Genre, History,* ed. Arthur Nolletti, Jr., and David Desser (Bloomington and Indianapolis: Indiana University Press, 1992), 229–58.

23. Lewis Jacobs, "The Nature of Film Expression." In *The Movies as Medium,* ed. Lewis Jacobs (New York: Farrar, Straus and Giroux, 1970), 16.
24. David Desser, E-mail communication, 15 December, 1997.
25. John Harrington, *The Rhetoric of Film* (New York: Holt, Rinehart and Winston, 1973), 147.
26. Robert L. Carringer considers the Rosebud symbol "a rather shameless piece of melodramatic gimmickry." But his objection is that, as a plot device, Rosebud is "presumed to be the key to everything"; thus, the symbol is torn away from Kane's personal traits and forced to play the major role in a detective-story plot. The idea of using the Rosebud symbol was not Welles's but that of the credited co-author of the *Kane* screenplay, Herman J. Mankiewicz. Carringer's grudging acceptance of the Rosebud symbol ("it is arguably a more effective narrative device than Welles's original idea of making the object of mystery something literary, such as a line from a Romantic poem") argues for the effectiveness of a concrete object in creating important meaning in a film. *The Making of "Citizen Kane,"* rev. ed. (Berkeley: University of California Press, 1996), 19.
27. Martin Jay, "Scopic Regimes of Modernity," in *Vision and Visuality,* ed. Hal Foster (Seattle: Bay Press, 1988), 3.
28. Rey Chow, *Primitive Passions: Visuality, Sexuality, Ethnography, and Contemporary Chinese Cinema* (New York: Columbia University Press, 1995), 15.
29. My analysis of the characteristics of Maupassant's story is derived from Ian Reid, *The Short Story.* The Critical Idiom 37 (London: Methuen, 1977), 61.
30. Rolf Fjelde, Foreword, *Ibsen: Four Major Plays* (New York: New American Library, 1965), xvii–xviii.
31. In my discussion I speak of one concrete object that communicates meaning in Ichiyô's story – the scrap of red Yûzen silk – and one concrete object that communicates meaning in Orson Welles's *Citizen Kane,* the sled named "Rosebud." But in both works there are more concrete objects than one that work symbolically to communicate meaning: in *Takekurabe* flowers work in tandem with the scrap of red silk to create a complex structure of symbolic meaning, as the sled operates with the glass snow scene ball to communicate complex interlocking meanings in the Welles film. This use of interlocking symbols is also typical of Ibsen's *Hedda Gabler,* where the concrete objects hair, slippers, and a book manuscript interact with the pistols to produce a complex network of meaning. But in this essay I wish to concentrate on the concrete object per se and how it operates in the short story in a way that anticipates its operation in film, so I will not take up the use of interlocking symbols.

32. David Desser, commentary on my paper, "The Cinematic Art of Higuchi Ichiyô: Visuality in *Takekurabe*." Presented at "Wording the Image: A Symposium on Japanese Film and Narrative," Dartmouth College, 25–28, September 1997.
33. For discussions of Ichiyô's relation to Heian literature, see Danly, *In the Shade of Spring Leaves,* in passim.
34. The situation of a boy and girl of marriageable age, as potential marriage partners, that is expressed by the poetic exchange in the beginning of episode 23 of the *Ise monogatari* probably shaped Ichiyô's making Nobu and Midori a potential married couple in her story. For a translation of the episode, see Helen McCullough, trans. *Tales of Ise: Lyrical Episodes from Tenth-Century Japan* (Stanford: Stanford University Press, 1968), 88.
35. Rey Chow, *Primitive Passions, 7.*
36. See Jin'ichi Konishi, "Association and Progression: Principles of Integration in Anthologies and Sequences of Japanese Court Poetry, A.D. 900–1350," trans. Robert H. Brower and Earl Miner. *Harvard Journal of Asiatic Studies* 21 (1958), 67–127.
37. For a translation of the *Kokinwakashû* see Helen McCullough, *Kokin Wakashu: The First Imperial Anthology of Japanese Poetry* (Stanford: Stanford University Press, 1985).
38. A black and white film was made of *Takekurabe* by Gosho Heinosuke in 1955. Because of the absence of color, Gosho was unable to re-create the image of the red silk scrap of cloth, and he has Midori throw Nobu a white or light-colored cloth instead. The effect of this substitution is that the dense meaning of the *momiji*-patterned scrap of silk is lost. Furthermore, the red scrap of silk in Ichiyô's story had conveyed a mood of sad resignation and a feeling of transience that were typical of the story as a whole. By contrast, Gosho's film, through its harsher characterization, achieves a mood of tragedy. As is always the case, the filmed version differs greatly from the literary text on which it is based. But *Takekurabe* is a great film in its own right, and I am indebted to Arthur Nolletti, Jr., for making a print of the film available to me.

CHAPTER THREE

Once More and Gosho's Romanticism in the Early Occupation Period

Arthur Nolletti, Jr.

A demobilized soldier in his early thirties stands on a street corner outside a Tokyo museum, waiting for someone. At his feet is a suitcase with the name Nogami Tetsuya on it. His face is tense, anxious. Suddenly, he sees a woman walking across the street, but she neither stops nor looks his way. Moments later he sees another woman, but she too passes by. Deep in thought, he paces back and forth for awhile. Then, from his breast pocket, he takes out a woman's wristwatch. Holding it tenderly, he thinks to himself, "I came back to the designated place. . . . I wanted to see her once again . . . but in vain." As his thoughts continue, the scene dissolves into another. Once again he waits at the same place. However, he is no longer in uniform, and the day, which before was sunny, is now rainy and dreary. "Did she forget her promise?" he wonders. "She said if she were alive, we'd meet again. Is she alive? Couldn't she survive the war?" Her words then come back to him: "Let's meet again," she says, almost pleadingly. "Remember, every Sunday at 10:00 in the morning."

Thus begins *Ima hitotabino* (Once More, 1947), the first film Gosho Heinosuke made after the war, and the first of two films he directed for the Toho Studio. Based on the novel by Takami Jun and told in flashback, *Once More* is a sweet, unabashedly sentimental love story with political overtones. It focuses on the relationship between Nogami (Ryûzaki Ichirô), a doctor who devotes himself to caring for the poor, and Tozuki

I wish to thank my friend and colleague, Sachiko Fujii Beck, for her translation of the articles by Gosho, Horie Hideo, and Uekusa Keinosuke, without which this essay would not have been possible.

Akiko (Takamine Mieko), a sheltered woman from a wealthy bourgeois family who finds herself drawn to him and his humanitarian ideals. The couple first meet when Nogami goes to a play that is directed by his friend Kambara (Kitazawa Hyo) and stars Akiko. Over a ten-year period, beginning in 1936 when Japan is at war in China, the couple continue to meet, only to be separated by various obstacles. These include their arrest because of their political beliefs and antiwar activities, Akiko's enforced marriage to a fiancé whom she no longer loves (Tanaka Haruo), and Nogami's conscription. Indeed, as fate would have it, Nogami receives his draft card the same night that Akiko and he have reunited after years of separation. Since he is ordered to depart the next day, the couple have only a few hours together. But during that time, they pledge to meet after the war at the same place and at the same time: Sunday morning at 10:00 A.M.. Once again, circumstances intervene, but in the end they are reunited forever.

Although enormously popular and highly acclaimed in its day – it ranked third in the *Kinema Jumpo* "Best Ten" poll of 1947 – *Once More* is all but forgotten today. This is unfortunate, for the film not only has undeniable historical and aesthetic significance but is also one of Gosho's major works. This essay focuses on how the film exemplifies Gosho's "romanticism," a term that had particular relevance in the early years of the American Occupation. Section I provides a brief overview of Gosho's career up to the making of *Once More*. Section II situates the film in its historical context, paying special attention to the Toho labor strikes, which greatly affected it. Section III explains Gosho's concept of romanticism in detail. And the final section offers a close analysis of the film, in particular, how it expresses Gosho's notion of romanticism both thematically and stylistically. This last section also comments on Gosho's collaboration with scriptwriter Uekusa Keinosuke, and on the film's relation to its source and its indebtedness to foreign and Japanese films.

I.

By the time Gosho made *Once More* in 1946, he had already directed seventy films, having made his directorial debut in 1925 with *Nantōno haru* (Spring in Southern Islands). In a career spanning over forty years, he would direct twenty-nine more films, his last being a feature-length puppet film, *Meiji haru aki* (Seasons of the Meiji Period) in 1968. Gosho, however, never considered himself retired. Nor did he lose his passion for filmmaking. Even when he was hospitalized in 1981 and anticipating his death, he was planning his 100th film, *Oku no hosomichi,* which is the title of one of Bashō's poetic journals.[1]

The director of Japan's first successful "talkie," *Madamu to nyôbô* (The Neighbor's Wife and Mine, 1931), Gosho is best known as a leading exponent of the *shomin-geki* (dramas about the everyday life of the common people). Yet his work is much broader and more varied than many critics claim.[2] Apart from working in a wide range of genres, including nonsense comedy, melodrama, and the *jidai-geki* (period films), he was instrumental in the development of the *junbungaku* movement that began in the 1930s – adaptations of "pure" (i.e., serious, often classical) literature as opposed to commercial literature. In fact, one of his greatest successes was his adaptation of Kawabata Yasunari's novel, *Izu no Odoriko* (Dancing Girl of Izu, 1933), a bittersweet tale of doomed love. It was this film that established Gosho as a master of lyrical love stories. It also demonstrated his ability to depict the plight of the poor and the oppressed of society, especially women.

As for Gosho's visual style, it remained remarkably consistent throughout his career. Known as "the director who uses three shots where others use one," he favored a form of piecemeal montage, which he said owed much to Ernst Lubitsch (i.e., cutting together numerous shots, some often very short in duration, to reveal the texture of his characters' lives and convey their innermost feelings). He also often used "short, probing camera movements to fill in the perspective of a scene."[3]

No less consistent than Gosho's style, and even more important, was his basic philosophy in life and art: a deep and abiding belief in humanistic values. As he once said, "The purpose of a film director's life is to describe the real life around him and create works which express the true feelings of human beings. . . . All films, as all works of art, must touch the emotions of the audience and touch them deeply. . . . Only if we love our fellow human beings can we create. From this love of humanity streams all creativity."[4] Although this statement may sound banal, and although Gosho's films may occasionally slip into sentimentality, they are grounded in keenly focused observation and are as forceful in their moral acuity as they are compassionate in their understanding of the human heart. As Mark Le Fanu has observed, "Gosho knows what we are put here on earth for, and can communicate that knowledge transparently."[5] Gosho also knows, and shows time and again, that human individuality is the most precious thing in life and that when it is threatened the result is tragedy.[6]

Given Gosho's convictions, it is not surprising that he declined to make "national policy" films, which the authorities demanded during the war. In fact, under the Motion Picture Law (1939), which put the film industry under direct government control, not only were finished films subject to censorship, but all scripts, prior to shooting, were also required to be submitted for "preproduction censorship."[7] Most of Gosho's scripts were rejected, and "those that were filmed were hardly to the liking of the Ministry of Information."[8] *Shinsetsu* (Fresh Snow, 1942), which starred the popular Takarazuka actress Tsukioka Umeji, emerged as a melodrama, its propaganda elements few and far between. Then there were his two works in the *junbungaku* movement. The first *Mokuseki* (Wooden Head, 1940), from the novel by Funabashi Seiichi, intended by the authorities as a *haha mono* ("mother film") with national policy overtones,[9] but in Gosho's hands it became a rich psychological study of an unmarried woman doctor whose life is dedicated to her work in viral medicine and to her daughter, whom society believes is illegitimate. Nicknamed "Mokuseki" by her staff because she is stubborn – i.e., strong-willed – she is such an unusual female character for the period that Sato Tadao considers the film to be about the emerging independence of women,[10] a theme that cannot have pleased the authorities. Gosho's second work in the movement *Gojû no tô* (The Five-Storied Pagoda, 1944), based on the celebrated novel by Kōda Rohan, tells the story of a brilliantly gifted journeyman carpenter who defies all odds to build a pagoda of unparalleled beauty and magnificence. Although his determination and rectitude could be regarded as an example for the Japanese people to emulate, especially during the latter days of the war, Gosho's two principal themes – the glorification of individuality and the human will, and the belief in art as immortal and indestructible – are actually quite antithetical to the spirit of the time.

Gosho's resistance to making propaganda films, of course, came at a price. Between 1931 and 1936 he had made twenty-seven films, but during 1940–45 when militaristic strictures were at their most severe, he completed only three films. A fourth, *Izu no musumetachi* (The Girls of Izu, 1945), he finished after the war. He was even replaced as the director on one film, *Kakute kamikaze wa fuku* (Thus Blows the Divine Wind,

1944), when the army found out that he intended to turn it into a love story.[11] To be sure, Gosho was not the only director whose output decreased during the war, a period in which the studios likewise experienced a decline in film production. Nevertheless, he made little or no attempt to conceal his resistance, and that in itself was sufficient to irk officialdom. What protected Gosho from censure or worse was his poor health. He had contracted tuberculosis in 1937 and had nearly died. During the three years that it took for him to recover, he made no films, and for the rest of his life he suffered recurrent bouts of the disease.

II.

In October 1946 Gosho began filming *Once More* at the Toho Studio. Japan had surrendered in August 1945, and now the American Occupation force was busy implementing its main goal for the country: democratization. As Kyoko Hirano has pointed out, this ironically meant that the film industry was once again subject to censorship.[12] Themes that were considered feudalistic, militaristic, or antisocial were forbidden, while those that dramatized the struggles of antiwar activists during the war or the new status of women (in keeping with Japan's 1947 Constitution) were approved and encouraged. As might be expected, the censors tended to see things from the American, not the Japanese, point of view, to say nothing of the fact that at times their objections could be petty, even absurd. For instance, in the case of *Once More,* they demanded the following changes: that the death of Akiko's artist-husband should be an accident instead of a suicide, the latter presumably smacking of the kamikaze spirit; and that the lovers should rendezvous at a building with Western-style architecture, not Russian-style architecture, the latter being "communist-looking."[13] For the most part the Japanese film industry willingly complied with the recommendations of the CIE (Civil Information and Education section) of the SCAP (Supreme Commander of Allied Powers), and made "democratization films." At Toho these films were the staple product during the first few years of the postwar period, and were welcomed by a moviegoing public exhausted by fifteen years of war, beset by harsh economic times, and eager to sample the new democratic freedoms.[14]

Critics and historians alike have described the atmosphere of these days as complex, heady, and confusing. On the one hand, there was grinding poverty, rampant unemployment, and a feeling of numbness after Japan's defeat; on the other hand, there was a palpable sense of excitement and expectation regarding the prospect of freedom. Film historian Fujita Motohiko, for example, in describing the latter, writes: "People were able to see clearly and vividly a return to idealism . . . after a political period of suffocating fascism and war. . . . It was a rare period when people's single-minded devotion and purity were able to exist without any logical reason."[15]

The situation at Toho, which mirrored the national scene and was no less confusing, impacted the shooting of *Once More*. According to Kakehi Masanori, Gosho's first assistant director on the film, material shortages after the war left raw film in short supply; therefore, the amount of negative film a director could use was severely restricted. Since Gosho favored numerous short shots and since the amount of raw film he had been allocated was far too little, Kakehi visited other production units and got them to donate a few feet of film.[16] This problem, however, was inconsequential next to the union strike, which closed down all productions.

As part of the democratic process, the Occupation authorities initially encouraged trade unions, but later changed their minds when they saw former Marxist and Communist leaders assume leadership positions.[17] Between March 1946 and August 1948 the labor union at Toho struck three times, gaining important concessions, such as salary hikes and a voice in the decision-making process, in the first and second strikes.[18] (However, the union suffered defeat during the third and final strike.) It was during the second strike – which lasted fifty-one days from October through December of 1946 – that shooting on *Once More* was brought to a halt until the following year. Both Kakehi and Horie Hideo, one of the film's second assistant directors, give vivid accounts of what the shooting was like. According to Kakehi, the atmosphere was tense and emotional because cast and crew were sharply divided over whether to stay with the union or join those who now opposed the strike and left to form "Shin Toho" (New Toho). Under the circumstances, Kakehi came to see his task as trying to keep harmony on the set so that the film could be completed.[19] There was also, of course, no small irony in the fact that life was imitating art, that a film about political struggle and dissent was being made in precisely that environment. Horie relates yet another complication, one that occurred when production was resumed:

Gosho pushed himself too hard in order to make up for lost time, and became ill. In order to get back on schedule, we were forced to work harder and to stay all night almost every day until the production was close to the end. Gosho's doctor advised him not to work but to have absolute rest; however, he stubbornly continued to work. In fact, he asked us to bring a portable bed from studio storage, and then he directed from his bed. I remember vividly Hasebe [Keiji, the other second assistant director] shouting out directions while he translated Gosho's hand gestures. Since Gosho was not able to use his voice, he used hand gestures to give us directions. For example, he moved his right hand to show the position of props and his left hand to indicate the blocking of the actors.[20]

As ill as he was, Gosho refused to confine himself only to directing. He was also determined to fulfill his responsibilities as an active union member. Therefore, he not only attended meetings after work but also collected funds for the strike, even traveling to outlying districts to do some of the collecting.[21] During the third and final strike, he became even more involved in the union. "I couldn't stand seeing people who had faithfully helped me to make films get fired," he explained. "I was no communist, but I couldn't reject my friends' plight."[22] On August 19, 1948, he participated in the much-written-about sit-in that was broken up by the American military armed with tanks, machine guns, and even aircraft. The next day, a photograph of Gosho and other strikers appeared on the front page of the papers, with the caption, "The Red Fighters." Soon after, his contract at Toho was cancelled.

III.

While filming *Once More,* Gosho wrote an article for the journal *Eiga Tenbô* (Film Review), entitled "Romanshugi no igi enshitsuka no tachibakara" (The significance of romanticism in movies – from the director's point of view). In it he states that his purpose is to explore his thoughts on "romanticism." He also states that these thoughts are directly relevant to *Once More,* for in this film he means "to depict the value of 'affection' which exalts and uplifts the human mind."[23]

After declaring that he believes romanticism to be the foundation for moviemaking as an art, Gosho says, "I don't intend to write about the past at this moment, but no one can deny that one of the main thoughts of the literary arts in Japan has been romanticism, which has never faded away from the feelings of the Japanese people."[24] Here Gosho is referring to the specific literary movement in Japan that began around 1890, lasted for about fifteen years, and came to be chiefly associated with Kitamura Tôkoku (1868–94). Although Gosho does not go into details about this movement per se – he seems to assume that his readers are familiar with it – we need to do so briefly.

The Japanese Romantics of the 1890s looked both to the Japanese past and to European literature, especially the poetry of Shelley, Wordsworth, Byron, and Keats. As Donald Keene has noted, "Not only was the emotional side of human feelings stressed, but the importance of the individual and of freedom was a prominent theme."[25] There was also "a special reverence for 'platonic' love, transcending desire, [which] was definitely not in the Japanese tradition."[26] In fact, in "Ensei shika to josei" (The pessimist-poet and womanhood, 1892) Tôkoku began his essay by proclaiming the supreme importance of love: Love is the secret key to life. Only after love came into being did human society exist. If love were taken away, what color or flavor would life possess?[27] These words stirred Tôkoku's readers greatly, for they enabled love "to be recognized as the motivating force behind much of life, and [to be] no longer mocked as a kind of malady that temporarily robs people of their senses."[28]

By now it should be apparent that this concept of romanticism is congruent with Gosho's own philosophy of art, life, and filmmaking. As such, it animates *Once More* and is the origin of, and the motivating force for, Nogami's political activism and his love for Akiko. However, when he tries to explain to one of his friends that his love for her also causes him pain and suffering, the response he gets is not surprising: he is urged to cure himself, as if love were a malady. Nogami's friend, in fact, is guilty of the very thing that Gosho considers inimical to romantic belief: excessive intelligence, that is, an imbalance between reason and feeling. In this regard Gosho cites three novelists, Hori Tatsuo, Dazai Osamu, and Kawabata Yasunari, whose characters' search for peace of mind is exacerbated by this flaw. For Gosho these writers are proof positive that not only is romanticism still alive in the arts, but also that all art is based on the expression of feelings. Hence he states unequivocally, "I want to advocate that artistic activity is based on the human being's fervent desire for nostalgia and growth."[29] While what he means by "nostalgia" is somewhat vague, its basic meaning seems clear enough: the attainment of love, the achievement of peace of mind.

Thus far in his essay, Gosho has spoken of romanticism pretty much as an end in itself. But he also sees it as a means to an end, as a way for film to give expression to something even more lofty and significant: "Humanitarianism is the main goal of film, and concerns all human nature and spirituality. Especially in this current social situation, to accomplish our mission we must reconstruct humanity and free ourselves from feudal mentality. Therefore, humanitarianism is an absolutely essential concept for contemporary society. . ."[30]

As examples of films that successfully achieve this goal, Gosho cites Chaplin's *The Gold Rush* (1925), which looks at American society with a satiric but compassionate eye; and John Stahl's *The Keys of the Kingdom* (1944), which he had seen recently, and about which he has this to say: "It plainly depicts that the hero [a missionary played by Gregory Peck] overcomes all hardships to attain philanthropy and belief in his own faith. This movie appeals very much to us because of its theme, the rediscovery of humanity."[31] Interestingly, Gosho's comments on Stahl's film might well serve to describe *Once More* and its two main characters.

In the latter half of the essay Gosho focuses on the question, "How should a director realize his concept of romanticism in a film?" His answer is that "the completion of an artistic and literary script is absolutely vital to successful filmmaking. Based on the scenario, a director is responsible for the synthesis of the six elements in filmmaking: scenario, camera techniques, setting, acting, music, and sound effects. Along with the results of this synthesis, a director composes the complete artistic effect and atmosphere, and creates a harmony between audience and film."[32] To illustrate this concept of romanticism, Gosho looks to French films of the 1930s – in particular, Julien Duvivier's *Le Paquebot "Tenacity"* (The Packet-Boat "Tenacity," 1933). He praises Duvivier for creating "a lyrical poem" in which the setting is not only "perfect" for the theme but also "glorifies" it, the theme having to do with an innocent, jobless couple who somehow manage to hold on to their belief in the future.[33] Gosho cites "the port harbor in Northern France, the cobblestone pavement in the backstreets, and the shabby hotel," singling out Duvivier's use of the whistle from a ship as "an important element in intensifying the romantic atmosphere of the love story."[34] But what doubtless impresses Gosho most of all in this and other French films (including René Clair's *Sous les Toits de Paris* [Under the Roofs of Paris, 1929]) is that they are about the life of ordinary people, yet the power of beauty emerges, thanks to the directors' romanticism.[35] In other words, their theme is that of humanitarianism, that is, the rediscovery of humanity. While, strictly speaking, Gosho is describing the above mentioned films, in actuality he is also describing the one film that is certainly foremost in his mind at this time, *Once More*. In the next section of this essay, we will examine how Gosho's romanticism manifests itself both thematically and stylistically. But first we need to comment on Gosho's collaboration with writer Uekusa Keinosuke, and on the film's relation to its source and to Kurosawa.

IV.

In his essay Gosho was sensitive to the fact that some readers might find talking about romanticism out of place, "especially after the war when towns were burnt to the ground."[36] He plainly knew that a love story, no matter how lyrical, tender, or touching, could not be simply a retreat into escapism or nostalgia. To be sure, it could eulogize the beauty of love, which indeed *Once More* does, but it must also tap into the mood of the time, the feeling of freedom and liberation mentioned earlier, to help the Japanese make the transition from the militarist past to the postwar era.[37] In this respect, one of the primary reasons Gosho made the film was to correct the misconception, held by young people, that there had been no opposition to the militarists.[38] Gosho realized that the "black valley" – what many Japanese writers have called the period from the early 1930s to the end of the war – had to be confronted, understood, and come to terms with before the Japanese could rightly rediscover their humanity.

Knowing the unique importance that Gosho assigned a film's script, we can well understand that it was imperative for him to find a writer who shared his feelings about romanticism. In Uekusa Keinosuke, he found such a writer. Best known for his screenplays for Kurosawa's *Subarashiki nichiyôbi* (One Wonderful Sunday, 1947) and *Yoidore tenshi* (Drunken Angel, 1948), Uekusa, like Gosho, had participated in the Toho strikes and was deeply pained by the union's eventual defeat. Nevertheless, as he explains in his memoir, *Keredo yoake ni: waga seishun no Kurosawa Akira* (After dawn: Memories of Kurosawa Akira in my youth), he also felt that the entire strike experience gave those who fought for their rights confidence and spiritual hope: "It was a period in which it seemed as if they could gain back their youth, which had been barren for fifteen years. The heart of youth came back to everyone. It was a new beginning, and it brought them back to human feelings."[39] It is precisely this kind of idealism, this romanticism, that Gosho and Uekusa sought to convey in *Once More* by means of the love story.

With this goal in mind, they made major changes in Takami Jun's novel, on which the film is based. Takami's novel was essentially political in theme and realistic in style, with the relationship between the hero and heroine underscoring the fact that life in totalitarian Japan was so intolerable that even an apolitical woman was prompted to join a leftist movement. Gosho and Uekusa retained this notion, but obviously "romanticized" the relationship. They also changed Nogami from a Marxist law student to a medical student in order to give his commitment to socialist ideas and humanitarianism concrete form, and no doubt greater warmth. Finally, they gave the lovers, and the audience, a happy ending. Takami, like many politically committed intellectuals, had been forced to recant his leftist beliefs during the war. Consequently, he wanted to emphasize not only the suffering and sense of frustration that he and others had endured, but the continuing legacy of that experience even after the war. The way he sought to do this was to have Nogami return from the war alive, but being forced to leave the woman he loves forever. Needless to say, when Takami saw Gosho's film, he felt, quite correctly, that it was entirely different from his novel.[40]

Takami's novel, however, was not the only important source that Gosho and Uekusa drew on. According to Fujita Motohiko, they were clearly influenced by Kurosawa's *Waga seishun ni kuinashi* (No Regrets for Our Youth, 1946), which Toho made the year before *Once More*.[41] First of all, the historical period and the narrative structure are much the same in both films. That is, both begin in the present, right after the war, then flash back ten years earlier as memories of their protagonists. Second, the atmosphere and the social and political conditions of the time, as well as the harassment that the characters suffer at the hands of the police, are conveyed mainly through the use of newspaper headlines. Third, both films deal not only with idealistic youth, but also with a well-off bourgeois heroine who, seeking the meaning of life, falls in love with a man and follows him. Finally, both films tend to be vague about the political ideologies that their characters embrace.[42]

Three points need to be made. While Fujita is correct about the presence of a heroine who undergoes a personal and political transformation, Kurosawa's heroine, Yukie (Hara Setsuko), is clearly the central protagonist in the film, whereas Akiko, Gosho's heroine, is one of two main protagonists, the story arguably belonging more to Nogami than to her, since it is his memory. Also, Akiko is much more traditional than Yukie, whose characterization was fiercely attacked by critics as "extreme and unnatural."[43] Quite possibly, Gosho and Uekusa were aware of this criticism and wished to avoid it.

Fujita is also correct in claiming that *Once More* is vague when it comes to the exact nature of Nogami's and Akiko's political beliefs. In fact, the most extended account of these beliefs is Nogami's lecture on socialism. "It's not just an idea," he explains. "We must face reality and tell the truth. Gaze into the face of poverty. Real society is filled with injustice. Just take a look at people around you and at the settlement. They are poor and unhappy." Clearly, these words are so general that they could be appropriated by any number of ideologies. But that is the point, for Gosho and Uekusa are not interested in political ideologies per se but in humanitarianism as the goal and motivating force of all ideologies.

Finally, although *Once More* and *No Regrets for Our Youth* may be classified as melodramas, they are worlds apart in tone, mood, and style – the former a sumptuously mounted love story; the latter, a woman's rite of progress.

As mentioned at the outset of this essay, *Once More* is a love story with political overtones. This is not to imply that the political theme is unimportant or merely tacked on as colorful historical background. Quite the contrary, it is an intricate part of the love story, for Nogami and Akiko's love for one another becomes political in that it compels them to search for the truth and take a stand against the oppressive military state.

Following the opening two scenes, in which Nogami waits for Akiko at the place that they have vowed to meet after the war, *Once More* moves into an extended flashback. The first scene of this flashback establishes Nogami's idealism and the political theme.

The time is 1936. The setting is Tokyo University. In the background the bells of the campus tower ring out, complemented by the sonorous voices of an unseen male choir – evocations of memory and halcyon college days. Nogami, who is soon to graduate, is talking with several classmates who ask why he has turned down the offer of a prestigious position at the university. When he says that he wants to work as a doctor at a settlement (i.e., a clinic) for the poor, one of his classmates scoffs, "Not that same old socialist doctrine." Only his two friends, Tanaka (Kôno Akitake) and Kambara, respect his choice and share his political convictions. Later that afternoon, the three sit together on a hill directly beneath the bell tower, the sound of the male choir still filling the air. The setting may be idyllic, but it cannot prevent the three from being troubled by news that war in Manchuria is imminent. Agreeing to oppose the war, they also agree to serve the poor. As their discussion comes to an end, the bells ring out the hour. "Farewell to the campus trees, farewell to the town tower," Kambara remarks, half-playfully, half-ruefully. The time has come to put their ideals into practice. The carefree days of youth are over.

Throughout the film, Tanaka and Kambara serve as foils for Nogami. All three start out with strong convictions and the desire to change Japanese society, but each has a different opinion on how to bring about that change. Nogami, as we have seen, dedicates himself to serving the poor; Tanaka believes in political agitation leading to revolution; and Kambara puts his energies into theater. Here he can help subsidize Tanaka's campaign to unite workers in Yokohama, stage classical and political works, and form study groups to educate his acting company about social conditions. At one point he even invites Nogami to deliver a lecture on the subject, a lecture that deeply affects Akiko, who is among the listeners. However, when the government begins crushing all political opposition, Tanaka and Kambara see that their beliefs have been compromised and have come to naught. The former, like Nogami, is imprisoned; the latter is defeated and demoralized. "The world has changed," Kambara tells Nogami, who has just been released from prison. "Tanaka predicted this war, and now we're fighting China. . . . All of our dreams are gone." Only Nogami manages to hold on to those dreams.

Also serving as a foil for Nogami is Sakon, Akiko's fiancé. Born of an aristocratic family, he plays Hamlet in Kambara's production and has aspirations as a painter. However, soon after his marriage to Akiko, he becomes obsessed by the idea that he is losing his talent as a painter and blames her. He knows that she was forced into marrying him, he knows that she tries to be a good wife, but he also knows that it is Nogami whom she loves. In short, he sees his inadequacies reflected in her eyes and he grows to hate her. Unlike Nogami, he has no inner resources on which to draw. Indeed, he is trapped by the imbalance between reason and feeling that Gosho sees as anathema to the artist. Concerned only with himself, Sakon cannot grow either as an artist or a human being. He is a product of his class, which is smug and complacent, and wholly uninterested in the world outside. Thus, when Akiko's birthday party is interrupted by a workers' strike at the factory that her brother owns, her guests' reaction is at first one of confusion, then of irritation. "I hate the poor," one of them blurts out. Their lack of compassion not only adds to the harshness and brutality of the time, but also leaves those among them, like Sakon, who have talent and, under different circumstances, might have made a contribution to society, defenseless and, in the end, believing in nothing.

What stands in greatest contrast to the harshness of the time is Nogami and Akiko's love. Their love in fact is the moral center of *Once More,* and everything that takes place is in relation to it. Indeed, their love not only represents a sublime faith and purity that ultimately transcends time and space, but it also underscores the theme that only through faith or belief in something outside oneself can one escape cynicism and despair in the world, and achieve a true sense of self. This is the lesson Nogami teaches Akiko as he awakens her soul; it is also the lesson she teaches him anew.

Nogami's commitment to love is as intense and complete as is his commitment to serving the poor. Having fallen in love with Akiko at first sight, he confides to Kambara that he is in agony because her wealthy background is an impossible barrier to overcome. When Kambara, somewhat cynically quoting Goethe, says that it is possible for a man to love ten women, Nogami replies, "I believe that true love means loving only one woman purely, spiritually, and totally."

There is no question that Akiko shares this feeling. Indeed, she is drawn to Nogami the first time she sees him, on the evening of the performance of *The Marriage of Ophelia.* Before the show, he accidentally enters her dressing room while she is going over her lines as Ophelia. After the performance, he waits in the auditorium for Kambara, who is on the stage with his cast to pose for a picture and to celebrate. All the while Akiko watches Nogami as he stands awkwardly, stiffly – like a pole, as she will later tell him. He does not know what to do with himself because he feels her eyes are on him, and because he cannot help looking back. "Is that your friend?" she asks Kambara. "Won't he come on up?" "He's strange," Kambara answers. Still, she keeps looking his way. She almost certainly sees something that Nogami does that night in the auditorium, something that gives her a sense of his character. At one point a cleaning woman passes by him, dropping one of her rags. Although he has been watching Akiko as intently as she has been watching him, and is clearly smitten with her, he bends over to pick up the rag and hands it to the woman. Clearly not expecting such kindness, she bows gratefully in return. In one sense, of course, it is a purely insignificant act, this picking up of a cleaning woman's rag. But in another sense it is far from insignificant, for it shows his genuine concern for people, even at this intensely emotional moment in his life. Later, when everyone has gone, Nogami stays behind and secretly retrieves one of the white roses from Akiko's bouquet that was tossed aside during the celebration. Taking it back to the settlement as a keepsake, he feasts his eyes on its beauty. "I want to see her," he says.

Akiko, of course, sees none of this business with the rose, but she gets an even closer look at Nogami a few days later when Kambara formally introduces them. Once again, she sees his shyness and reserve, and, more important, his selfless and compassionate nature. Stealing a few quick glances at his clothes – first, his shirt sleeves, which are too long for his jacket, and next, his scuffed and worn shoes – she smiles gently: she knows this man.

She also trusts and respects him, and realizes that he is the one to help her overcome the feelings of guilt and emptiness she has in living a privileged, sheltered life – a life that in her case directly exploits the poor. Thus, following the lecture that Nogami delivers to Kambara's acting troupe on socialism and the desperate situation of the poor in Japan, she goes off on her own to read as much as she can. Determined to pursue the idealism of the man she loves, she begins to take an activist position. When Kambara spends the profits from his show, which he promised Nogami for Tanaka's campaign, she takes money from her own pocket, allowing Nogami to think that it comes from Kambara. (To his credit, Kambara tells Nogami where the money really came from.) Shortly thereafter, she shows up at Nogami's settlement to see firsthand the nature of his work and to plead with him to help her understand the issues she is grappling with. "The rich and poor live in the same society," she says. "There are so many contradictions. Show me the way." At first Nogami, not wanting to love her because of her class, which he sees as callous and arrogant, tries to rebuff her. "This is not a place for a rich lady's curiosity," he says, his turmoil being given requisite melodramatic expression by the raging rainstorm that is going on. But the combination of his love for her and her obvious sincerity leads him to soften. When he sees her off, he warns her about the danger of the political path she is about to take, but she is resolved. "Don't worry," she assures him, having found strength in his love and support, "Now I can face anything that comes."

From this point on, the lovers experience increasingly difficult obstacles that test their love to the limit. Akiko becomes more involved in political activities (we hear about these but are not shown them). These include her work in the slums that leads not only to her arrest, but also to her being branded a "Red Lady" by the newspapers and being put under surveillance by the police after her release. When she flees from her estranged family to work in the country as a nurse, she writes Nogami to ask him to meet her, but he is arrested and imprisoned for several years. Alone and defenseless, Akiko is brought back to Tokyo by her family and forced to marry Sakon. However, Nogami remains in her thoughts, just as she does in his – a fact that Gosho visualizes by superimposing images of her over Nogami's sitting figure in prison. Having fallen back into her old life, she feels wholly unworthy of Nogami's love, a feeling that only intensifies when she sees him briefly after his release from prison. "I'm ashamed of myself. I was weak," she confesses. "I took the wrong way." Disappointed but determined to keep their love pure, Nogami urges her to be happy with Sakon, and leaves for a clinic at a dam site in northern Japan.

Their love, however, like all great loves, has a spiritual quality that defies even time and space; they cannot truly be separated. Thus, one night as Nogami stands at the dam, he reads a letter from Akiko, hearing her voice in his mind. Pausing, he shouts her name out longingly across the rushing waters, whereupon the scene cuts to a shot of her, as if she were only a few feet away. Later in the film, Gosho once again reaffirms this idea of mystic communion between the lovers. Akiko must come to the dam site for Sakon's belongings after his accidental death there. (Half-mad because of his inability to paint, Sakon had come to confront Nogami about Akiko.) Following a phone call from Nogami, who reports the news of what has happened, she prepares to leave. However, the sound of Nogami's voice continues over the visuals as he explains that out of respect for Sakon, it is better that they not see each other. As Nogami's voice carries over into the next scene, we see Akiko arrive. The implication is unmistakable: Nogami's words have been in her thoughts ever since he spoke to her. True to his word, he is nowhere to be found. But he has left her a white rose, the symbol of their love.

Although Nogami and Akiko preserve their love as a thing of beauty, doing so ironically denies them happiness. In fact, by this point in the film their very integrity has become a flaw – albeit a noble flaw. Kambara says as much when he brings them together one evening. "Let me give you a piece of advice," he tells them frankly. "Have more courage to be happy. Fight for it. Be hungry for it." These are exactly the words the audience wants to hear, for the couple's integrity has come to mean only continued self-sacrifice. Taking Kambara's words to heart, Nogami and Akiko finally talk openly in a way that they have never had the chance to do before. And the next day, even though Nogami has been drafted and must report for duty, the couple enjoy their longest and happiest time together. Sharing a picnic lunch in the outer garden of the Meiji Shrine of the Museum of Fine Arts, they reminisce, talk of their future, and hope for the war to end soon. She even gently teases him about how stiffly he stood the first night they met. When it comes time for them to separate, she promises to commit herself once more to their shared political ideals. Finally, they exchange watches as keepsakes and vow to rendezvous at the same place on Sunday at 10:00 A.M., after the war ends.

On that first Sunday, she does not appear, but Nogami returns on each Sunday thereafter in the hope – and belief – that she cannot be lost to him. His faith is not in vain. He learns that during the war she worked as a nurse and that she has not met him because she is ill. Shortly after, they are poignantly reunited.

Takami's original ending notwithstanding, Nogami and Akiko's final, happy reunion is the only possible ending imaginable – at least in Gosho's world. Their reunion, however, is not simply the fulfillment of a vow, or even the triumph of love over all earthly adversities. Rather, it is the triumph over reason and credibility itself; as such, it is as incontrovertible and emotionally right as the reunion of two other lovers in screen history: Chico (Charles Farrell) and Diane (Janet Gaynor) in Frank Borzage's *Seventh Heaven* (1927). This time, however, unlike in Borzage's film, it is not the man who comes back from the dead, as it were, but the woman. Thus, in the final scene when Nogami awakens the sleeping Akiko, it is as if he were bringing her back to life – not just symbolically but literally – for she is barely able to speak, her strength being so depleted. What has earned the lovers this rebirth, this second chance, is their deep and abiding faith in love not just as a thing of flesh and blood but as a platonic ideal.

However, it is not just the lovers who believe – it is also, and preeminently, Gosho himself. To *Once More* he brings a total and unwavering belief in not only love but also melodrama itself – one that is without apology or condescension. It is easy to dismiss Gosho's conviction as naive, even quaint, and the film itself as sentimental, even banal melodrama, but that is to fall into the trap of the cynics and the demoralized characters in the film and to miss the enormous skill and delicacy Gosho brings to the material. In the paragraph above I referred to Borzage's *Seventh Heaven*. There is no way of knowing if Gosho was influenced by the film, or even saw it. Nor does he mention it in his essay on romanticism. Even so, as Sato Tadao has pointed out, it was one of a half-dozen American films on which Japanese films were modeled until the late 1940s.[44] Certainly there are few films closer in theme and spirit to *Once More* than Borzage's.[45]

Although Gosho is deeply committed to the love story for its own sake, he is no less interested in it as a metaphor for Japan's postwar recovery. Specifically, he fervently believed that the country's recovery could not simply be political or economic in nature; it must also be moral and spiritual, and must entail what he calls the "rediscovery of humanity." Thus regarded, *Once More* becomes an allegory, in which the two lovers serve as models for the new social and ethical order that Japan must establish, an order that is based on humanitarianism. Or, as Gosho himself said, in *Once More* he wanted "to depict the value of 'affection' which exalts and uplifts the human mind."

In the remainder of this essay we will concentrate on the visual form that Gosho's romanticism takes and the synthesis of six elements that it depends on: scenario, camera techniques, setting, acting, music, and sound effects. (For our purposes here, "camera techniques" will also include the editing by Nagazawa Yoshiki.) To examine this synthesis, we will focus on the sequence in which Nogami and Akiko first meet. Consisting of sixty-one shots in six minutes and thirty seconds, this sequence is made up of four scenes:

1. Nogami's first sight of Akiko before the performance of *The Marriage of Ophelia* (forty-eight seconds; eleven shots).
2. The performance itself (two minutes, two seconds; twenty-three shots).
3. The cast party immediately afterward (two minutes, twenty-five seconds; twenty shots).

4. Nogami's return to the settlement (fifty-four seconds; seven shots).

The two stylistic elements that one immediately notices in the sequence – and in the film as a whole – are the editing and photography. Gosho's piecemeal editing – that is, his use of three shots where other directors use one – makes for an often fast tempo, one that keeps the narrative moving. Thus, while the average shot length in the sequence is 6.1 seconds, thirty-four of the sixty-one shots (i.e., 56 percent) are four seconds or less. This editing strategy has the distinct advantage of enabling Gosho to focus in tightly on emotion and achieve an intensity of effect by linking the audience to the two main characters' every gesture, mood, and response.

No less important is Miura Mitsuo's rich black-and-white photography. It not only captures the complete spectrum of shades but uses both shallow focus and deep focus perspectives, along with a wide range of optical devices (including double-exposures, rack focus, wipes, and dissolves). A longtime collaborator of Gosho – he shot his first film – Miura gives the visuals a luminous glow befitting romantic love. (He is ably assisted by Onuma Masaki's lighting.) This was exactly the look Gosho wanted, for his aim was to make *Once More* sumptuous in every way so as to improve the quality of Japanese film, which he felt had been compromised by cheap and poorly made love stories since the end of the war.[46]

The first scene establishes the sequence's basic dramatic action – Nogami and Akiko's immediate attraction to each other – and fundamental editing strategy, the shot/reaction shot. This strategy is used in six of the scene's eleven shots (shots three to nine), beginning with Nogami's stepping into Akiko's dressing room by mistake. In shot four Akiko, in costume as Ophelia, is seated at her dressing table, rehearsing her lines in front of the mirror and reflected in it. Shot five shows Nogami, frozen in place at the doorway, stunned by her beauty. Shot six offers a close-up of Akiko, whose sweet pleas for Hamlet's love are interrupted by the sight of Nogami in her mirror. Startled, she turns around. Nogami, however, seems wholly unaware that she has seen him, and in shot seven continues staring at her. In shot eight she rises, and in shot nine – the only two-shot in the scene – takes a few steps to get a better look at him. Clearly intrigued, she self-consciously touches her hair and waits for him to say something (Figure 1), but he stammers, attempting an apology, and rushes off.

1. Akiko's dressing room; Gosho Heinosuke, *Once More* (1947).

Like most of the sequence, this scene privileges Nogami's point of view, allowing us to see Akiko through his eyes. However – albeit to a lesser degree – we also see Nogami through her eyes. Thus, while he gets a good first look at her, in return she gets a more than adequate first look at him, their faces appropriately laved by softly diffused light.

The second scene is in many ways not only the heart of the sequence but the richest example of Gosho's synthesis of formal elements. In this scene we see the opening of the play, Akiko's entrance, and, most important, her exchange of glances with Nogami, who is in the audience.

The scene begins with the camera tilting down from a close-up of the auditorium ceiling to a long shot of the stage as the curtain rises to the sound of applause. At the same time, we hear the first notes of the melody that plays throughout the scene and serves as Nogami and Akiko's love theme in the film. At first we assume that this melody is nondiegetic music, that it is simply part of Hattori Ryoichi's background score for the scene, but the last shot – a close-up of a phonograph record playing in the wings – shows that this is not the case. As it turns out, this is the first example of the playfulness that Gosho brings to the sequence as a whole.

After the introductory shot of the stage, the next two shots provide a closer look at Matsuyama Takashi's set. The perfect embodiment of idyllic love and romance, this tranquil garden setting is mounted on a platform two steps high, and is decorated with arched trellises that are covered with white roses. The overhead and borders consist of netting strewn with leaves that have a silver sheen under the lights, and the cyclorama is painted in a pale hue to give the effect of a soft and gentle evening sky. Hamlet is seen dozing on what appears to be a Victorian love seat.

At this point Akiko enters in full costume, slowly crosses to center stage, and pauses momentarily. Illuminated by a pool of light, she looks directly out, as it were, into the house. Then she resumes walking, but more slowly and deliberately than before. A striking reverse shot in deep-focus shows her from behind as she moves from right to left, and beyond her we see the audience. All eyes are on her. Now the scene moves into a series of shots/reaction shots (shots eight to thirteen). The first of these is a medium shot of Nogami, who is completely rapt by the vision of Akiko and singled out in the audience by key lighting (Figure 2). The cut from this shot to the next, in which Akiko continues her walk across stage, bathed in soft-focus, is an eyeline match between Nogami and her

2. Nogami watches Akiko onstage; Gosho Heinosuke, *Once More* (1947).

(Figure 3). Although we cannot be perfectly sure that she is looking at him, and him alone, the effect of the match cut is to create just this impression – and, in the process, to suggest that the real drama at hand is not the public performance of Hamlet and Ophelia on stage but the private communion of Nogami and Akiko. At the end of this shot, Akiko lowers her eyes demurely, momentarily breaking the eyeline match. Shots ten and eleven resume these matches, and as she continues walking, the camera moves into an even closer view of her, revealing a lovely, but somewhat melancholic expression on her face.

It is not insignificant that Ophelia is the role Akiko plays. As Shakespearean scholar Elaine Showalter points out, Ophelia's behavior, appearance, gestures, costumes, and props are "freighted with emblematic significance, and for many generations of Shakespearean critics her part has seemed to be primarily iconographic. Ophelia's symbolic meanings, moreover, are specifically feminine."[47] That is to say, she represents the woman who feels too much and consequently is doomed to suffer disappointment in love – a victim of love-melancholy.[48] In Hazlitt's words, she is "almost too exquisitely touching to be dwelt upon."[49] Akiko's costume, props, and deportment clearly convey this image of Ophelia, which is as familiar as it is inherently pictorial. Thus, she is

3. Akiko as Ophelia; Gosho Heinosuke, *Once More* (1947).

dressed in a long, flowing white gown with full sleeves, a cinched waist, and a pale-colored shoulder cape. A pearl necklace and earrings serve as accessories, and white roses adorn her hair and make up the wreath bouquet that she carries. For Akiko, however, Ophelia is less a role in a play than a means to define her own character: a woman who also feels too much and will suffer disappointments in love, but whose end will not be tragedy. If she is and is not Ophelia – if, in other words, she is enacting her own dream – she is also the embodiment of Nogami's dreams as the nonpareil of sensibility and loveliness. Indeed, this portion of the scene, in which she crosses the stage, even feels like a dream because of the look on her face, the soft-focus photography, and the gliding, floating motion of her walk.

By contrast, shot twelve seems at first a rather conventional, even gratuitous shot, as Gosho cuts to two women in the audience who remark on Akiko's beauty. But what justifies this shot and makes it highly unusual is that Gosho suddenly, unexpectedly pans from the women to Nogami, as if to reinforce the fact that he is the narrative's chief interest. Shot thirteen is a companion shot to shot twelve. In it, Akiko, who is seen in extreme long shot, no sooner completes her walk than Gosho once again quickly pans, this time from her to Nogami. Since it is by now unmistakably clear that Nogami is enamored of Akiko, these two back-to-back moving camera shots imply that Gosho is interested in more than simply telling the story. He means to reproduce the sense of exhilaration that Nogami feels – the cinematic equivalent of his rising heartbeat, the first excitement of falling in love. Still, one suspects that there is yet another reason for Gosho's moving camera strategy: the sheer pleasure he takes in filmmaking itself. Indeed, the unexpected nature of the editing and camera movement in shots twelve and thirteen have a beauty and elan that remind one of what Robert Bresson once said about editing, that it is "a door through which the poetry enters."[50] Such is Gosho's poetry.

This poetry is no less evident in shots fourteen and fifteen, only here it is the use of sound that is noteworthy and playful. In shot fourteen, we are given a frontal medium close-up of Nogami, who looks more mesmerized than ever. Several seconds into the shot we hear a sigh, "Oh," followed by a direct cut to shot fifteen, where the source of the sound is identified as Hamlet. Greeting Ophelia, he rhapsodizes: "Listen, Ophelia, I had a dream just now about our wedding. I was so happy. . . . Are you happy?" In these two shots the sound cut precedes the picture cut by some eight or nine frames. This practice is, of course, quite common today, but in 1946 it was not. What Gosho in effect does by using this sound bridge is to take advantage of the viewer's expectation established by synchronized sound. Simply put, Gosho gives voice to Nogami's feelings about Akiko by putting a "word" in his mouth, a strategy that is also witty since the voice actually belongs to Sakon, Nogami's rival for Akiko, and since Nogami is in no position at the moment to speak for himself.

Apart from the above example, sound in the scene is confined to the love theme, a few patches of dialogue, and a smattering of applause. This does not mean, however, that Gosho's use of sound elsewhere in the film is without interest. For instance, in the two opening scenes we see cars go by, rain strike the pavement, and people with umbrellas scurry past Nogami, but there is a scrupulous avoidance of natural sounds. We hear only Nogami's thoughts in voice-over and Hattori's musical score. Here the absence of expected diegetic sound constitutes a negation of external reality and a privileging of Nogami's subjectivity, that is, his and Akiko's world. Even when natural sounds are heard or are dominant – as the raging water at the dam site – they frequently are pathetic fallacies in the world of romance, an externalization of the protagonists' emotions. In short, Gosho's use of sound is often complex.

Scene three of the sequence, which occurs immediately after the play, is almost totally devoted to Nogami's and Akiko's interaction. It opens with yet another of Gosho's deliberately playful shots: a rack focus shot that gradually comes into focus with its image inverted – which is to say that we are watching a picture being taken, in this instance, the cast picture. When this is done, while the cast celebrates – which we hear rather than see (a piano playing, the buzz of talking, occasional outbursts of laughter) – Gosho foregrounds the series of shots/reaction shots between Nogami and Akiko. Lit in lustrous high key, she is seated on the apron of the stage, looking directly into the house at Nogami, who is standing in the rear. Too shy to join the party, he waits for Kambara, but also feels the attraction of Akiko's unspoken invitation. Clearly, she wants him to come up on the stage. Gosho positions Akiko in close-up and situates the camera slightly below her face, underscoring her unapologetic staring. This is an Ophelia of a different order. By contrast, it is Nogami who is vulnerable and unsure of himself; indeed, he is touchingly boyish. Not only do the medium and long shots that Gosho gives him further this impression, so too does his body language. In shot four, he sways back and forth in place as he stands in the aisle; in shot seven, not knowing what to do with his hands, he twists the rim of his hat; in shot nine he sits on the armrest of the aisle seat, only to decide seconds later that he does not want to sit at all; then he takes out his cigarettes, which, in shot eleven, he decides he does not want; finally, in shot thirteen, he sits down again. During all of this, he tries not to look at Akiko, and at times even turns away, but not for long. As for her, she takes her eyes off him only for a moment or two at most, when she is handed a soft drink or asks Kambara who Nogami is. Of course, while Nogami is too shy to act on the attraction he feels, he is also unwilling to leave or stop looking. Realizing this, she does everything she can – short of taking the final, unthinkable step and actually speaking. It is at once a tender and amusing scene.

A word about the acting. As Nogami, Ryûzaki is appropriately stolid in a role that the Japanese call *tateyaku,* a man of honor, courage, strength, and purity of heart who typically is more comfortable with duty than with romantic love.[51] Hence Nogami's anguish and confusion, awkwardness and discomfort – his standing as stiffly as a pole, to quote Akiko. Ryûzaki conveys all of this admirably, while also showing us the man Nogami truly is: one of sensitivity and feeling who even allows himself to weep, something no self-respecting *tateyaku* would ever do. Takamine brings to the part of Akiko a most poignant combination of strength and vulnerability. In this she is helped enormously by her remarkably expressive face and the look of sadness, pain, and yearning that almost always seems to be in her eyes, a quality that reminds one of Gail Russell, an American actress of the 1940s. Indeed, Takamine's face becomes the site of the drama, and manages emotional shadings even when Akiko is unutterably happy and smiling radiantly.[52]

The fourth and final scene provides an apt coda for the sequence. As the sounds of the cast party fade, suggesting that it is over, the camera locates one white rose on the floor, then dollies to yet another one. As a hand enters the frame to claim this discarded rose, the love theme starts up softly. The shot dissolves to Nogami back at the settlement as he places the rose in a glass beaker and fills it with water. He then sits down at his lab table and admires the rose. The next shot, representing his point of view, is quintessential Gosho in its sweetness and sentimentality: a close-up of the rose with a superimposed multiple image of Akiko dressed as Ophelia and looking up and smiling before fading away very slowly. In strictly narrative terms, this elaborate shot is hardly necessary since both Nogami's thoughts and the association of the rose with Akiko are perfectly clear. But once again, Gosho's interest is not simply in telling a story but in delving into the texture of romance itself, and in creating for the audience the secret emotional life – the fantasies, dreams, and desires – that each of us has but often refuses to admit.

In concluding our discussion of the synthesis of cinematic elements necessary for Gosho's romanticism, we need to comment briefly on one last element: scenario. We have already talked about Uekusa's adaptation of Takami's novel. Here we wish to take note of the way in which Uekusa accommodates Gosho's visual style. The sequence just analyzed provides an excellent example. It not only depends almost entirely on visuals but – as must be obvious by now – it makes its basic story point early on. Yet there is no feeling of attenuation or redundancy, in part because Nogami's and Akiko's characterizations deepen throughout the sequence, but also because the filmmaking itself is so fluid and elegant. To be sure, there are scenes in the film that rely as much on dialogue as on visuals. According to some critics, there are even scenes in the first half that are "didactic and stiff,"[53] presumably because the dialogue is burdened with political exposition. However that may be, Uekusa plainly understood that Gosho was the kind of director who "thought" through the formal elements of film and required his scriptwriter to do the same. In this respect Gosho clearly demonstrates that his roots are in silent film.

After the success of *Once More,* Gosho made a second film for Toho, *Omokage* (A Visage to Remember, 1948), about the relationship between an elderly professor, his young wife, and a friend and former student who is attracted to the wife. In it, Gosho retained some of the romantic elements of *Once More,* primarily in the photography and production values. But the theme and material were quite different, and with the film, Gosho "made a decisive move in the direction of art cinema."[54]

Gosho would go on to make other love stories, his last being *Utage* (Rebellion of Japan, 1967), which deals with a married woman's frustrated love for an officer caught up in a coup d'état against the 1930s militarist government. But never again would he make a film like *Once More.* Born out of a confluence of his personal vision, the tenor of the times, and the long-standing tradition of romanticism in Japanese literature, the film had a purity and an innocence that could not be duplicated.

On the surface, it was a paean to love – love as spiritual redemption – but underneath, it was an allegory about the need for postwar Japan to rediscover its humanity. In one sense of course this was much the same humanistic theme that Gosho had held from the outset of his career, but the war and the Occupation gave it new urgency and meaning. Like the American and French films that Gosho singles out for praise in his essay, *Once More* is a film whose themes are glorified by the power of beauty that the director brings to his images. But Gosho's romanticism is not merely a matter of style or theme; as we have seen, it is also a philosophy of art and life and a means to an even loftier and more noble end: humanitarianism. The cornerstone of Gosho's cinema, humanitarianism gave his films a wisdom and sublimity, warmth and compassion, that not only enriched Japanese film as a whole but introduced a new word into the language: "Goshoism."

NOTES

1. Horie Hideo, "Gosho Heinosuke to sono kaiwai: Ikiru koto wa hitosuji ga yoshi." *Gosho Heinosuke tokushû*. Eiga kozo. ("Gosho Heinosuke and His Milieu: Living One's Life to the Fullest." Special Issue on Gosho Heinosuke. Film Lecture.) (Tokyo: Gendai Engeki Kyodai Foundation, March 1987), 28.
2. See, e.g., Mark Le Fanu, "To Love is to Suffer: Reflections on the Later Films of Heinosuke Gosho," *Sight and Sound* 55, no. 3 (Summer 1986), 198; and especially Horie, who says, "He was a prolific director and his works are categorized in a wide range of genres. . . . He was described as 'The Master of Women's Pictures,' 'The Master of Lyrical Films,' and 'The Master of *Shomingeki*' in advertising catch-phrases. Each title, however, merely describes one side of Gosho; none captures his essence as a director" (29).
3. John Gillett, "#607: Heinosuke Gosho," *Film Dope* (April 1980), 31.
4. Joseph L. Anderson and Donald Richie, "The Films of Heinosuke Gosho," *Sight and Sound* 26, no. 2 (Autumn 1956), 77,80.
5. Le Fanu, 198.
6. Anderson and Richie, *The Japanese Film: Art and Industry,* expanded ed. (Princeton: Princeton University Press, 1982), 356.
7. Shimizu Akira, "War and Cinema in Japan," *Media Wars Then and Now: Pearl Harbor 50th Anniversary.* ("Nihon ni okeru sensô to eiga," *Nichibei eiga sen: Paru Haba gojûshûnen*). Yamagata International Documentary Festival '91, October 7–10 (Tokyo: Cinematrix, 1991), 5–50. The essays in this informative anthology are published in Japanese and English. Also see *Japan/America Film Wars: WWII Propaganda and Its Cultural Contexts,* ed. Abe Mark Nornes and Fukushima Yukio (New York: Harwood, 1994), 7–58.
8. "Heinosuke Gosho," *World Film Directors: Volume One – 1890–1945,* ed. John Wakeman (New York: H.W. Wilson Co., 1987), 403.

9. Ibid.
10. Sato Tadao, interview by the author, National Film Center, Tokyo, April 15, 1985.
11. Kakehi Masanori, "Gosho Heinosuke no sekai: Gosho Heinosuke no entotsu no mieru basho o megutte (The world of Gosho Heinosuke: About his work *Where Chimneys are Seen*). In *Nihon eiga o yomu: paionia tachi no isan* (Reading Japanese film: Heritage of the pioneers) (Tokyo: Dagereo Shuppan, 1984), 133.
12. Kyoko Hirano, "Japan," *World Cinema Since 1945,* ed. William Luhr (New York: Ungar Co., 1987), 380.
13. Kyoko Hirano, *Mr. Smith Goes to Tokyo: Japanese Cinema Under the American Occupation, 1945–1952* (Washington, D.C., and London: Smithsonian Institution Press, 1992), 75, 242.
14. For further discussion of the immediate postwar period, see W. Scott Morton, *Japan: Its History and Culture* (New York: McGraw-Hill, 1984), 201–9.
15. Fujita Motohiko, *Nihon eiga gendai-shi: Shôwa '20s* (Modern history of Japanese cinema II: 1945–1955) (Tokyo: Kashin-sha, 1977), 47–48.
16. Kakehi, 120.
17. Morton, 205.
18. Hirano, *World Cinema,* 382.
19. Kakehi, 133.
20. Horie, 29.
21. Kakehi, 133.
22. Wakeman, 403.
23. Gosho Heinosuke, "Romanshugi no igi enshitsuka no tachibakara" ("The significance of romanticism in movies – from the director's point of view"), *Eiga Tenbô* (Film Review) 11, no.3 (1946), 33.
24. Ibid., 32.
25. Donald Keene, *Dawn to the West: Japanese Literature of the Modern Era – Fiction.* (New York: Holt, Rinehart, and Winston, 1984), 186.
26. Ibid., 187.
27. Quoted in Keene, 195. For analyses of Tôkoku's ideas on social and spiritual harmony, see Francis Mathy, "Kitamura Tôkoku: Essays on the Inner Life," *Monumenta Nipponica* 19, nos. 1–2 (1964): 66–110, and Janet A. Walker, *The Japanese Novel of the Meiji Period and the Idea of Individualism* (Princeton: Princeton University Press, 1979), 69–74.
28. Ibid., 199.
29. Gosho, 32.
30. Ibid., 32.
31. Ibid., 32.
32. Ibid., 33.
33. Ibid., 33.
34. Ibid., 33.
35. Ibid., 33.
36. Ibid., 32.
37. "200 Classics of Japanese Cinema," *Heinosuke Gosho.* Tenth Hong Kong International Film Festival, presented by the Urban Council, 1986, 27.

38. Ibid., 27.
39. Uekusa Keinosuke, *Keredo yoake ni – Waga seishun no Kurosawa Akira* (After dawn – Memories of Kurosawa Akira in My Youth) (Tokyo: Bungeishunju Publishers, 1985), 7–12.
40. "200 Classics of Japanese Cinema," 27. For an overview of Takami's work, see Keene, 871–878.
41. Fujita, 50.
42. Ibid., 49–51. *No Regrets for Our Youth* is based on the 1933 incident in which Prof. Takigawa Yukitoki was forced to resign from Kyoto University because of his alleged Communist thought. For detailed discussions of the film, see Donald Richie, *The Films of Akira Kurosawa* (Berkeley and Los Angeles: University of California Press, 1970), 36–42, and Kyoko Hirano, *Mr. Smith Goes to Tokyo,* 179–204.
43. Hirano, *Mr. Smith Goes to Tokyo,* 194.
44. *Currents in Japanese Cinema,* trans. Gregory Barrett (Tokyo: Kodansha International, 1982), 32. The extent of *Seventh Heaven's* influence on Japanese film is well detailed by Yamamoto Kikuo in *Nihon eiga ni okeru gaikoku eiga no eikyô* (The influence of foreign films on Japanese cinema) (Tokyo: Waseda Daigaku shuppan, 1983), 460–67. Yamamoto cites reviews of the film, in the October 21, 1927, issue of *Kinema Jumpo,* that highly recommend it, praising its script, art direction, soft-focus photography, and use of the moving camera. The scene of Chico's going off to war is singled out as particularly memorable; it is noted that audiences were deeply touched throughout the film, and that they laughed and cried. As an example of the film's influence, Yamamoto cites specific allusions to Chico and Diane in the Japanese silent film, *Hafu no minato.* At one point the heroine talks about the "Chico type." Later, another character remarks, "I wonder where Janet Gaynor is," only to be answered in an intertitle: "Here's Janet Gaynor" (462).

    Even Ozu paid homage to the Borzage film. See David Bordwell, *Ozu and the Poetics of Cinema* (Princeton: Princeton University Press, 1988), 72.
45. However, two other American films with which *Once More* has points in common are McCarey's *Love Affair* (1939) and LeRoy's *Waterloo Bridge* (1940). In fact, LeRoy's film, like *Once More,* opens with its male protagonist returning to the spot where he and his love met before the war, then proceeds into an extended flashback. Anderson and Richie note that LeRoy's film was an influence on Shochiku's postwar smash hit, *Kimi no na wa* (What is Your Name? 1953) (*The Japanese Film,* 260–261), but I have not been able to find anything that suggests it was an influence on Gosho.

    Once More echoes other films and filmmakers, although this does not necessarily mean that any influence is involved. For instance, *Once More* evokes the lush, virtuoso lighting and photography of 1940 Cukor melodramas like *A Woman's Face* (1941) and *Keeper of the Flame* (1942). A notable example is Nogami and Akiko's meeting at the gallery where Sakon's paintings are on exhibit. Here the two characters, both dressed in black, are at times basically silhouetted against the background or only back-lit or side-lit. At other times – as in close-ups that reveal the feelings they are trying to hide – they are lit by a soft key light, their faces partly in shadow, like Joan

Crawford's scarred face in Cukor's 1941 film. Occasionally, *Once More* also reminds one of Sirk. A case in point is Sakon's visit to Nogami at the dam site. As Sakon grows more and more distraught, he becomes convinced that he can paint again, and rushes out to the dam's narrow walkway, calling out Akiko's name. Low-angle shots and the acceleration of the cutting tempo convey his out-of-control behavior – he races to the forefront of the frame, shot after shot, as if he will plunge either off the screen or, as it turns out, to his death. Here melodramatic excess is the perfect objective correlative for the character's loss of control. Gosho may not be as baroque as Sirk – we need only think of Marylee's frenetic dance during her father's heart attack in *Written on the Wind* (1956) – but he too understands the kind of excess that melodrama sometimes requires.

46. "The Significance of Romanticism in Movies," 33.
47. Elaine Showalter, "Representing Ophelia: Women, Madness, and the Responsibilities of Feminist Criticism," *Hamlet,* by William Shakespeare, ed. Susanne L. Wofford (Boston and New York: Bedford Books/St. Martin's Press, 1994), 224.
48. Ibid., 225, 228.
49. Quoted in Showalter, 228.
50. Robert Bresson, "Appendix: Interview," by Ian Cameron, *The Films of Robert Bresson* (New York: Praeger, 1969), 135.
51. For a discussion of the *tateyaku,* see Sato, *Currents in Japanese Cinema,* 15–30.
52. Uekusa told me in an April 16, 1985, interview, at the National Film Center in Tokyo, that Hara Setsuko was originally chosen to play Akiko, but she did not do it because of the Toho strike. Takamine, who had first gained attention in Yoshimura's *Danryû* (Warm Current, 1939), was therefore borrowed from Shochiku. According to Uekusa, both he and Gosho were a bit in love with her throughout the shooting.
53. "200 Classics of Japanese Cinema," 27.
54. *"A Visage to Remember (Omokage)," Heinosuke Gosho,* The Tenth Hong Kong International Film Festival, 29.

CHAPTER FOUR

The Taunt of the Gods

Reflections on *Woman in the Dunes*

Linda C. Ehrlich and Antonio Santos

> Things made of clay are easily broken. When a piece is on the point of being broken and yet retains its integrity – this is the point at which it is beautiful.[1]
>
> – Teshigahara (quoted in Ashton, 1997)

When first released, in 1964, *Woman in the Dunes* – an independent production made on a limited budget (about $100,000) – achieved a kind of cult status in the West.[2] In the film, and in the novel by Abe Kôbô on which it was based, we can recognize an updated version of the myth of Sisyphus – the man imprisoned in the Absurd and tormented by the need to find a meaning to his circumstances – as an allegory of our time.[3] The pit and the desert are represented as places of synthesis, based on a dynamism of opposition and of merging rules. These are the qualities that make this film both accessible and obscure, universal and specific.

Woman in the Dunes is a meditation on identity. This is made explicit by Teshigahara, the director, from the opening credit scene in which a mass of *hanko* (name-seals) fills the screen. The woman is never named and the man's proper name – Junpei Niki – is given only at the end of the film. The entomologist is first introduced as a character tied to identity cards that are his social credentials. The novel, divided into two parts, opens with the statement "One day in August a man disappeared" and closes with the man's decision that "there was no particular need to hurry about escaping." A simple "Notification of Missing Persons," dated seven years hence, follows.

The urban society in which the man was constrained is sharply replaced by another social environment, as rigid as the original one. In the city he is called by his proper name; in the pit he is not. Paradoxically, this loss will allow him to find a new identity, which in turn will permit him to discover a deeper meaning to his life, even under the tyranny of an absurd fate.

Teshigahara revels in, even indulges in, the need of experimentation intrinsic to the New Wave, through the use of such devices as the hand-held camera, disjunctive editing, nondiegetic sound, as well as elegant sweeping shots.[4] He is a master of montage, particularly of a montage of qualitatively linked patterns. As art historian Dore Ashton noted:

> Teshigahara's *Woman in the Dunes* is saturated with techniques common to the visual plastic arts. His close-ups of sand, grain by grain, recalls Miro's blade-by-blade close-ups of grass. His way of focusing on an insect, so that it takes up the whole screen and transforms itself into an attenuated, hardly identifiable object, is similar to many approaches in metamorphic or organic abstraction – that of Arshile Gorky for instance.[5]

As viewers, we are pulled inside the director's subjective universe, in the same way the man is pulled into the woman's universe. We start to relinquish our will over the compelling and sensuous visual images, but our critical mind might notice moments in the film that are overly self-conscious, hence artificial. At times we are denied the privilege of sight as the screen is bathed in a murky darkness. Language enters after a long initial sequence of images at the opening of the film, reminding the viewer that the story line is but one entryway into this film.

At first it seems that *Woman in the Dunes* will be a film of stark contrasts: poor villager versus intellectual, man versus woman, dry versus wet, entrapment versus freedom. As the film progresses, however, shades of gray enter, and these seeming dichotomies are revealed to be less absolute than they seemed at first. One way to follow this engagement with ambiguities is to trace the pattern of the relationship between the man and the woman – at once realistic and metaphorical – that serves as the focal point of this highly symbolic work.

FIRST MEETINGS

We are first introduced to the woman through her voice and through a point-of-view shot that can only be hers. Then the camera focuses on a close-up of her feet. She is, at this stage, nothing more than an element in the environment, like the sparse furnishings of her house. Details are to be added, one by one, like the piling up of sand. The patterns of her life are echoed in the patterns of her simple clothing and dwelling, and in the ever-changing patterns of the sand.

The man is at first filled with arrogance toward the unexpected environment in which he finds himself. Unable to "capture" it as he does the insects he plans to study, he experiences increasing frustration. Again the director first presents the character's involvement in this new relationship by focusing on the feet – in this case, the man's feet as he descends the ladder into the pit where the woman dwells. During this entire introductory sequence between the man and the woman, the woman's point of view predominates as *she* examines *him*. We hear only the sound of the ladder creaking and the groans of the man as he struggles down. In contrast, the woman's voice is soft, inviting, as she beckons him inside.

With only one lamp for illumination, the conversation between the man and the woman assumes a quick sense of intimacy. As she scoops out rice for his evening meal, a deep-focus shot connects them both in a sudden domesticity. After engaging in what appears to be small talk, the woman abruptly (and seemingly innocently) introduces the topic of insects. Insisting that the insect eating away at the newly thatched roof of her house is a "ki-kui-mushi," the man (assuming her ignorance) tries to correct her by calling it by more common names: termite, saw-beetle. As she describes it further, however, we become aware of her keen powers of observation and of her pragmatism. It is indeed a "ki-kui-mushi."

While the man is eating, the camera at first remains still and then moves in closer, almost imperceptibly. It is obvious that what to the man is only an adventure is something more to the woman. While engaged in what is basically a polite conversation, full of stereotypical phrases, the man also ridicules the woman's assertion that sand might cause moisture. Despite his show of arrogance, it is obvious that she is the active one, and that he is the one being acted upon. This long sequence is followed by a sudden cut, and then by a close-up of the man preparing an insect for the specimen box. We now begin to wonder, however, who is the master and who the victim in this new universe. Both insects and their hunters share a world with boundaries, and both will fall into analogous traps. The pit in which the man is confined looks like those traps made by certain kinds of insects and spiders to camouflage their nests and confine their victims.

Extreme depth-of-focus shots allow us to see the human figures as small against the vast universe of sand. Rarely in the film are we privileged by shots that reveal the entire house and its surroundings. When this occurs, as when the man first tries to leave the hut after resting there one night, we experience a momentary sense of shock. His shadow appears large against the sand as he frantically tries to dig his way out.

GROWING INTIMACY/ESCAPE

Soon the man learns of the villagers' scheme to keep him in the pit, and of the woman's compliance. The man does all he can to show animosity toward the woman, including overpowering her and tying her hands. None of these obvious means help him in his immediate goal: to escape, and to return to a more familiar world.

The first clear signs of sexual attraction appear when the man and the woman struggle as he tries to break down the walls of her house to make a ladder. He loses his balance and ends up lying on top of her as sand from the porous rooftop cascades all around them. Somewhat taken aback, they rise and adjust their clothing. The woman retreats behind a translucent screen. On the other side of the screen, the man asks her, in a surprisingly tender voice: "Shall I brush the sand off?" Her reply is as startling as the sharp cuts and visual montage sequences frequently employed in this film: "Aren't all city women beautiful?"

In an extreme close-up, we watch as he wipes the sand off of her body and gradually undresses her. The camera reveals her body in gentle, unpredictable directions: a close-up of her feet gripping the sand, later followed by a close-up of her hand against his shoulder, and then patterns of sand eddying *down* the cliff. The music on the sound track maintains one long sustained note, a kind of drone, gradually growing louder. In this stylized lovemaking, the concentration is always on the woman's face. Again, the man is the agent, but not the central actor. We see only his back and his hair.

As if to remind us of the metaphoric connections between parts of this strange universe, the director suddenly cuts to a shot of one bird flying away along with the slow movement of the sands as the camera pans slowly past the woman, now lying alone, asleep. The man is sleeping at some distance from her. Next, we see an insect crawling back into a dark corner. Then the man awakens and sees the door open, in a shot taken from a markedly skewed angle, as a blinding light streams inside. An image of sand flows in ripples just outside the open door. What is this bird, this insect, this sand? On one level, they are obvious symbols of freedom, mundane existence, change. But is this their entire significance?

From the very first images onward, sand is identified by its never-ceasing movement, as well as by the continuous succession of days and nights. (Note the shifts from a close-up of a watch, to eyes dissolving to become a woman's recumbent form, to waves of sand, spokes of an umbrella, a woman's nude body.) The flow of sand is shown in a dual, and essentially ambiguous, form. It represents elements of life and death, torment and pleasure, work and desire. Sand is also seen as water, a maternal symbol linked with sexual desire (*nureba,* or erotic scenes; literally, "wet scenes"). Streams of sands sliding over smooth surfaces provide a very obvious sexual analogy. As the man's sexual interest in the woman increases, a shot shows us the naked body of the woman dissolving into the dunes.

When passion breaks out, the couple lies frantically in the sand. The wedding ritual consists of cleaning out the sand from the lover's body. Sweaty bodies are tied together, but also cut into bits, by the work of editing, calling to mind the first images of Alain Resnais's *Hiroshima, Mon Amour* (1959), also starring the actor Okada Eiji.[6] In the French film, however, the bodies of the couple were strictly anonymous; they belonged to abstractions whose faces it was impossible to discern. In *Woman in the Dunes,* both man and woman are perfectly identified by their faces, and the scientific way of shooting their reactions demands the identification of both as specimens.

As the man climbs over the roof, a steady camera shows him viewed from a distance. Whose point of view is this? Someone standing in a watchtower? Our own? The wind blows around him furiously, deafening him and impeding his progress. The camera moves behind the man for a moment, followed by a series of rapid crosscuts. The sound of the wind grows louder as he reaches the top of the cliff. To one sustained note on the sound track, the newly freed man races across the sand. (At this point, the cinematographer shoots directly into the sun.) While we hear the sound of the man running, we (paradoxically) also see him standing still. A montage of images that cross spatial and temporal boundaries seems appropriate to this new universe with its uncertain boundaries.

From his first appearance, it is possible to notice analogies between the trapped man and the myth of Sisyphus. In the continuous climbing and descending of the entomologist, we can recognize a common loss of direction. The frequent transgressions of the visual raccord during the walk of the man across the desert give us an insight into his sense of being astray. This mechanism, employed from the beginning of the film, will be repeated with even greater intensity in the course of his failed escape. The man becomes trapped in a sand bog and needs the help of others to pull him out. As he gives up, a blot of water forms across the camera lens. Now we see another close-up of feet – the rough shoes of one of the villagers. They lower the man back down into the pit in the dunes as we are shown a close-up of insects on a board. The man moves to the right in one shot, and to the left in the following shot. In this way, one movement contradicts the others.[7]

Interspersed throughout the film, a series of dreamlike, unreal images rhetorically corroborate the man's confused wandering. Initially, we see a boat lost in the desert, covered with sand. Lost in the dunes, the walker relinquishes his urban credentials. Some time later a woman appears, as if in a dream. Maybe she is a fleeting reminiscence of his cast-off urban life. This will be his only explicit evocation of his past, because the exile in the pit will imply a radical renunciation of that part of his life. The evocation will be fleeting. There is no communication between the man and that briefly glimpsed woman, nor are they even able to see each other. She fades away without leaving any trace, confirming in this way the voluntary repudiation by the man of some essential patterns of social coexistence: partnership, marriage, or family.

Sisyphus, the most crafty of men, was condemned for his sins to a cruel punishment. Carrying a mighty boulder, he had to climb to the very top of a mountain, but every time he was at the point of reaching its summit, the large rock would tumble down to the bottom, where he would begin the climb again. In such a way, he had to toil forever and ever.[8] In *Woman in the Dunes,* we witness the vain efforts of the prisoner to climb up the pit on different occasions. Everything is useless because inevitably he finishes by rolling down its sandy walls. Links with the legendary Greek malefactor are quite evident.

Albert Camus proclaimed Sisyphus a champion of the absurd, as much for his passions as for the torment he suffered. In the words of the French writer, there is no more terrible punishment than useless, hopeless work. Sisyphus is considered a proletarian of the gods whose face has turned to stone. He is a tragic character because of his awareness of the nonsense of his existence. As happiness and the absurd are sons of the same land, Sisyphus's joy will be born from the acceptance of his fate.

Sand is elsewhere an analogous word to rock, which renders the experiences of both prisoners interchangeable. Like Sisyphus (in Camus's interpretation), the man will be spiritually reborn when he realizes that his real identity is buried in the depth of his prison. Only then, when faced with the need to recognize his own absurdity, will a paradoxical and resigned sense of well-being enter his soul.

RESIGNATION

Three months later – the man is now transformed in appearance and demeanor. Garbed in rough-spun traditional Japanese clothing and sporting a beard and mustache, he is shown hunched over, "entrapped" by the laundry the woman is hanging out to dry. She appears more youthful and complacent in her new domesticity, while his face has become lined, older, weathered. The hut seems to have a somewhat warmer and more comfortable air about it than in the earlier sequences.

We are surprised to hear the formerly assertive man beg the villager who brings supplies for even a few minutes "on top" to see the sea. Seen from the villager's point-of-view on the top of the cliff, the man appears stunted and diminished. Around the woman, however, he remains arrogant and aggressive. While the woman is patient, long-suffering, resilient, the man is impulsive and temperamental.

Later the camera follows the man as he suddenly rushes angrily outside the hut, muttering, "I won't die." A crow passes by. In an extreme close-up shot, we see the woman's hand as she patiently strings beads to earn money for the radio she feels would make the man happy. In a fit of anger at his situation, the man flings the box of beads she is working on into the sand. Stooping to pick them up, she admits how frightened she is that she will be left alone again. In a high-angle shot we see the man stooping as well to pick up the beads. As we gaze at a close-up shot of the beads and sand in a sieve, we hear the man's voice musing, without his earlier scientific detachment: "Perhaps tomorrow there is a chance that things will change." His tone of voice softens as he suddenly hands her his specimen box for the beads, and she looks up in surprise. The sequence ends with a close-up of his insect-specimens burning on the fire, and thus with the end of the man's plans to be remembered for posterity by having an insect bear his name.

In this universe, everything is placed in a new perspective. Even the positive value placed on work is brought into question when the man learns from the woman that the villagers are involved in selling inferior sand to construction companies. The woman is aware that it could cause buildings to collapse, but also, in a self-preserving way, she knows that she will not be there to see the collapse. Since she never leaves the pit, she knows that the buildings will never fall on her.

During the course of the film, the peasants often make jokes with their victims. They compare the man to a turnip, a commonplace vegetable that like the captive, is firmly rooted in the earth. The woman, moreover, is treated like an animal, and her extrauterine pregnancy is detected, thanks to one peasant's experience with cattle. The "hangmen" constantly prove their power over their victims – depriving them of water and food, and making fun of their pain and anxiety. As a reminder of their inferiority, the couple receives a humiliating comic strip (drawn by the Spanish artist Conti) in which a man, run over by a steamroller, politely begs his aggressor for forgiveness.

RITUAL AND THEATER

In this central part of the film, Teshigahara resorts to a highly theatrical presentation to show the spiritual depths to which the man has descended. The villagers promise the man a chance to see the sea if he will make love to the woman before their eyes. They shine a spotlight on the man, to the sound of increasingly frenzied drumrolls. We note that the villagers disguise their appearance with scarves, goggles, and the masks of animals (dog, monkey, insect), thus emphasizing the bestiality of the scene. With dancing spotlights, flaming torches, and rapid cutting between shots, we are placed in the uncomfortable position of seeing what is not meant to be seen in the open.

4. A staged rape; Teshigahara Hiroshi, *Woman in the Dunes* (1964).

The woman warns the man to ignore the villagers and not to act the fool. He refuses to heed her and urges her to pretend (see Figure 4). Again the man and the woman struggle, as in the earlier scene when he tried to break down the house. In this voyeuristic scene, however, the woman is fighting – not for her possessions and means of survival – but for her basic dignity.

The masks with which the peasants cover their faces replace their daily personality with a pitiless and hieratic one. From the prisoners' perspective, imprisoned in sand, the hunters have acquired a different nature, as mighty as it is unattainable. Beyond their human condition, the "hangmen" display attributes usually reserved for gods in pantheistic cults (see Figure 5).

Dances with percussive instruments link this scene with Shinto liturgical rites, and, more precisely, with the *kagura* ritual, which evokes, from ancient times, the invocations of the Sun Goddess hidden inside a cave.[9] The celebrants dance masked, dressed in white, in time to the rhythm of percussion and cymbals. They supplant the liturgical function of the gods with the hope of attracting for themselves the land's prosperity and fecundity. The noise of the drum sounds like thunder, showing its affinity to

5. Masked villager; Teshigahara Hiroshi, *Woman in the Dunes* (1964).

rain and water. It points out a synesthetic trope that brings together the tactile ("like water") and the acoustic (the noise of the thunder). Its cosmic nature is applicable to the sides of the well themselves. The well's cylindrical form, covered with the vault of heaven, is a replica of the shape of the drum itself.

The drum has a double dramatic function: the first is a bellicose and punitive one; the other possible meaning is a beneficial one. The cosmic drum produces a regenerative element that, at the end of the tale, will fertilize the captive's soul. Takemitsu Toru's original sound track emphatically insists on percussion, and indeed the music renders both symbolic functions reconcilable.[10]

Thanks to a calculated imposture, the peasants assume the high position of the gods in the *satokagura* ritual.[11] All they wish to do is humiliate the man and achieve their own preeminence. Nevertheless, as we shall see, such a masquerade will anticipate a double mechanism of fertilization.

The perception of the hunters that is received by the captive is a double one: if, from an objective point of view (the one that the omniscient narrator shares with the spectator), they are nothing but cruel, depraved peasants, from the prisoners' perspective, these peasants have achieved the rank of gods, being the providers of life and death. The position they adopt toward the victim is the same as that of the gods when they tormented Sisyphus.

In order to highlight this circumstance, the two dramatic functions played by the guards are never seen together in the same shot. They are seen either as peasants or covered up with ritual masks. In the same way, the confrontation between the space of the prisoners and that of the persecutors is visually resolved through an opposition of angles. The high-angle shots correspond to the semi-gods' point of view, while the low-angle shots reflect their victims' perspective inside the well. Through this device, the insurmountable distance separating each is emphasized.

Between the captives and the peasants a mechanism of reciprocal representations is established. The well suddenly loses its confining function and becomes a stage. The spectators are placed at the top of this improvised stage, in a semicircular auditorium that looks like the *cavea* in the ancient Greek theater. Lanterns carried by the peasants converge on the stage as if they were spotlights.

One of the persecutors, covered up with a mask, moves his head in a three-quarter movement from right to left. In the following shot, the prisoner is seen in a position similar to that of a masked peasant. Immediately afterward, he turns his head and shoulder in the same manner and direction as that of the masked guard. The prisoner's gesture is thus a prolongation of that of the masked guard.

While it is true that this sequence could be viewed as a ritual, it is important to remember, however, that true rituals can have no spectators.[12] What remains, when there are inquisitive spectators, is sanctified drama, or secularized ritual, but not a religious ritual per se. Another way of interpreting this disturbing sequence is that the woman is like the pot referred to by Teshigahara – something that is pushed to the edge but that retains its integrity and does not break.

When the masquerade is finished, one of the spectators – disappointed by such a pathetic peep show – throws a handful of sand into the well where the humiliated man is lying. This gesture allows us to recognize not only the disapproval of those present at the top of the well, but also a forewarning of an irrevocable punishment: the victim is buried in sand, sealing his fate. The act reminds us of Shinto ceremonies, where celebrants throw handfuls of salt on the ground as an arid substitute for water. The sand thrown into the well advances, in a metaphoric way, the discovery of water within its own entrails.

CRISIS

In addition to the images of barrenness and dryness in the film, surprising images of fecundity arise that, paradoxically, are most effective in black and white. Water is found in an arid wasteland. The woman becomes pregnant. But even these seemingly positive events reveal their opposite: the pregnancy appears to be an ectopic one. As the woman moans in pain in the hut, the man rushes outside to try to get the attention of someone in the village. He waves a flaming torch – an echo of the earlier voyeuristic scene – except that now the man is the main agent, albeit a weak one.

As the village men come to take the woman away to the hospital, they casually hand the man the radio he had been hoping for. He turns it on to the sound of lyrical Western classical music that is at once soothing and jarring in contrast to the visual image. The man stands rather impassively, with his hands at his side. He starts to tell one of the villagers about the water in the trap but thinks better of it. The director cuts between shots of the woman's agonized face and the sound of the pulley being turned as the village men laboriously lift her to the land above. She cries out in distress as she is being taken from the safety of her home.

In the final scene, the man, dressed now in traditional Japanese-style attire that sports a wave pattern, climbs the rope to "freedom." He is a black figure outlined against white sand. There is another close-up of feet, but this time it is a shot of the man's rough straw sandals on the ladder. The camera assumes dizzying angles as the man climbs to the top. In a medium close-up shot we see his upper body outlined against the landscape of the ridge, with inviting waves in the background. We feel as disoriented as the man feels after so much time spent below in the pit.

In one of the film's most abrupt transitions, the next thing we see are footsteps in the sand and then the man walking, yet again, in the pit. He takes off the cover of the trap, and his face and the landscape are reflected distortingly in the water collected in the hole. As he looks up, a little boy peers over the ledge. Who is this child, and what has this man become? An inner monologue informs us of the man's thoughts: "There's no need to run away yet. If not today, maybe tomorrow." In a repeat of earlier close-up shots, we are aware of the man's hand in the water and a close-up of his eye, like the eye of the crow shown earlier.

The camera pans down the print on his jacket, and suddenly we see the official Missing Person Report (with letters moving upward), bringing to a full cycle the man's initial musing about the role of documents in our lives. This simple epilogue reveals the real social name of the missing citizen. Nevertheless, this identity has long since been relinquished by its owner, precisely when he accepted an absurd fate. At the very last moment of the film the Chinese character (Kanji) that means "The End" appears as a stark black word placed asymmetrically against a seemingly endless white background.

The Water Inside the Rock

Throughout this tale, sand receives a treatment usually reserved for the liquid element. The woman washes up dishes with sand. Both the woman and the man are living inside a well-like space, that is, a place from which people usually take water. At the top, the peasants pull the sand out with a bucket and pulley, just as if they were extracting water. Both elements are visually mixed, together with fire, through oneiric dissolves.

The great ontological problem that the man creates for himself at the end of the story is how to extract water from the rock. It is possible to note a parabolic question: this lost man, prisoner of the absurd, must fertilize his own soul in order to obtain fresh water from his personal desert. Even though this discovery might not allow him to achieve happiness, at least he will succeed in conquering a state of resignation that will give peace to his thirsty mind.

The small trap he invents for hunting crows is meaningfully called "hope." From its entrails, like a miracle, water springs out. Its renewed flow clarifies the process of self-knowledge. In a meaningful sequence, the prisoner burns the dissected insects that, like himself, were trapped by a mightier being.

The discovery of water is preceded by images of crows. This bird, often associated with an unpredictable fate and death, could also be regarded as a messenger of the gods. In the film, crows adopt the position and perspective that, in the former scene, were withheld for the "peasant-gods": long high-angle shots from a bird's-eye view. We could imagine that the gods are metamorphosed into crows, or that these black birds replace those higher beings. The low flight of the crows directs the captive's sight toward the trap dug in the sand, just in the center of his pit. This is an instrument designed to entice some bird into the well, with the purpose of sending out a message for help. The unfortunate man finally goes toward the trap, only to discover the same daily disillusionment: no animal has fallen inside. Nevertheless, when the paper covering its surface is moved away, the man's eyes open in surprise: the container buried in the sand is half filled with water, although there has been no rain in the last weeks (see Figure 6).

The prisoner's first impulse is eloquent. He looks at his face in the water; he recognizes himself; he refreshes his hands in the liquid. His scientific mind attempts to provide a rational explanation for the miracle. He tries to measure it, and to reduce it back to comprehensible events. It is difficult to find any explanation that justifies this mysterious wonder.

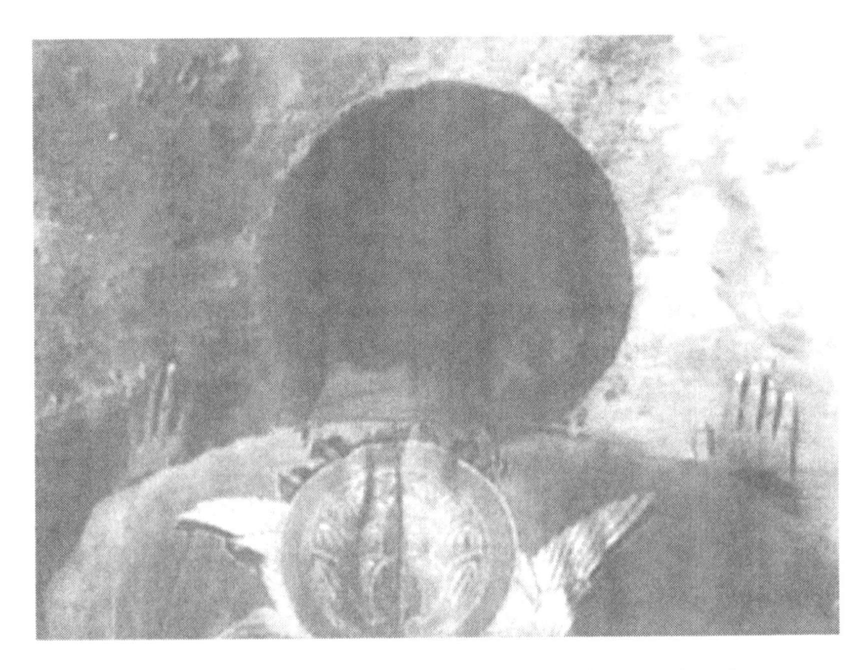

6. Junpei discovers water; Teshigahara Hiroshi, *Woman in the Dunes* (1964).

The man's first consideration is to assimilate that wonder, as well as to increase its efficiency, by trying to turn it to more use. He proposes to tame, through scientific reasoning, a symbolic fact.

The buried water metaphorically represents the man's spiritual strength, conquered by the prisoner, who finally becomes reconciled with himself and with the space he must inhabit. Together with this surprising discovery, the recognition of his new strength now puts him on the same level with the other villagers. The cylindrical form of the barrel, now containing water, corresponds with the drum beaten by the semi-gods in the previous scene. This drumbeat was identified with thunder and with water. After noticing his surprising ability to obtain water, the prisoner, drunk with joy, beats the air as if it were a drum.

Now he knows he is master of his own fate inside the well. He will not need to depend on outer supplies anymore. As owner of a new physical and spiritual strength, he ranks himself equal to his persecutors' power.

The man has fertilized two feminine elements: the woman and the land (from which he extracts water). Yet fertility is not an unqualified motive for joy, since the prisoner has helped initiate life and, at the same time, death. Man's spiritual progress cannot be redeemed without some compensation, since the price of his liberation must be pain. Appropriating a device often used in Japanese cinema and literature, his rising corresponds to her fall. Her departure from the well also leads to her narrative annulment and, possibly, to her death. Nevertheless, before this happens, she will give the man a last chance for choice.

The rudimentary rope marks a fragile boundary linking two opposed worlds: the realm of the gods as opposed to the purgatory of the submitted people. The purpose of reaching its top by climbing its rungs suggests, symbolically, the path toward self-improvement upon which, unconsciously, the captive has decided. In the same way, the *kagura* celebration uses a ritual rope (often painted or represented in the curtain) to delimit a sacred space, separated from the ordinary world. In the film, the rope-ladder marks the border between two different worlds that share a common instinctive law: that of survival.

Without demonstrating much enthusiasm when he is conscious of the possibility of escape, the man slowly climbs the rungs. Freedom, for which he has longed, comes when it is not necessary anymore. Gods and men are now linked by what separates them: sand. Once on the outside, the man suffers the same feeling of misplacement he had endured at the beginning. He wanders without finding his bearings; he goes up and down the dunes, hesitantly, echoing the same situation that had connected him with the tormented Sisyphus.

Immediately, the opposition between outer water (the degraded sea) and inner water (the one buried in the well, fresh and clear) becomes apparent. Unconsciously, his steps drive him toward the well. Both the film and the novel present his return through ellipsis. The trap becomes a sanctuary, and he is transformed into its guardian. The proletarian of the gods is reborn in the guise of an anchorite priest. In this way, he progressively breaks all his links with his outer ties.

It could be considered that the well renews its condition as a maternal uterus. After his experience of change, the lost man decides to become one with the telluric haven where he has experienced his rebirth. Once again, he looks at himself in the water, where he is now reflected as a child who watches out from the top of the sandy walls. This image is highly expressive, because it explicitly elucidates a process of regeneration, as well as a triumph over anxiety and worry.

CONCLUDING REMARKS

In Teshigahara's adaptation of Abe Kôbô's novel, a sense of timelessness is located in what seems to be historical space, and the sculptural and the ephemeral are constantly interchanged. One wonders if now, at the millennium, it would be possible to present a sense of alienation in such an aesthetically lush manner.[13]

Movement serves as the main narrative impulse in this story that is told through a kind of associational montage of patterns: the movement of the man from city to the desert, of the woman from the desert to the hospital in the city; the movement of the sands, of the water. The man's feelings move from disregard of the woman, to antagonism, to contempt, and then to concern and even caring. The woman's stance is a more steady one, but she too shifts from viewing the man as a utilitarian object (for work, for sexual pleasure) to having a desire for a more dignified union. At first he appears the more intellectually engaging character, while the woman appears primarily corporeal and pragmatic. As the film progresses, however, viewers may find themselves oddly "trapped" by the implications of the woman's worldview. What at first appeared absurd slowly seems to develop its own logic, like the efforts of an insect that patiently builds a home for itself in the sand. The woman emerges as the one who both creates and maintains tradition, while the man moves from a stance of "knowingness" to what might be regarded as a more enlightened sense of "unknowing."

On the surface, *Woman in the Dunes* might appear an exercise in negative thinking. What else could one expect of a film full of images of entrapment, ridicule, and voyeurism, a film in which the majority of scenes are either claustrophobic or disorienting? And yet, by its end, this film conveys a sense of belonging, purpose, and commitment. At what point does such a radical change occur? Or is it a mistake to look for a single moment of peripeteia, as in classical Western drama? Teshigahara and Abe set up a sense of hopelessness and repetition that makes the small "turning points" more noticeable, even shocking. In the seeming absurdity of the situation in which the man finds himself, there are familiar, and even redeeming, qualities. Are these nothing but extensions of what all of us experience daily, in the many encounters in which we find ourselves?

In an interview with Joan Mellen, the director denies that *Woman in the Dunes* deals with a conflict between a sense of civilization and a sense of the primitive in contemporary life.[14] Teshigahara equates the digging in the sand with the way people use custom and duty to structure their lives. He equates the voyeuristic scene of the villagers, watching the couple make love, with the process of an outsider becoming an insider, of exposing vulnerabilities. He stresses the emphasis in the film on the problem of communication between people, and the international aspect of the story: "You could find such a sandpit in New York or San Francisco, or anywhere in the world."[15]

NOTES

1. Dore Ashton, *The Delicate Thread: Teshigahara's Life in Art* (Tokyo: Kodansha, 1997), 130.

   Teshigahara Hiroshi (b. 1927) was trained as a painter and was the son of a famous *ikebana* master of the Sogetsu school. Along with his achievements as a filmmaker, he is also known for his skill as a ceramist and *ikebana* master.
2. The film won a Special Jury Prize at Cannes in 1964 and was also nominated for an Academy Award for best foreign-language film.
3. *Suna no onna* (Woman in the Dunes, 1962), by Abe Kôbô, was translated by E. Dale Saunders (New York: Random House, 1972).

Abe (1924–93) received his inspiration for the setting of *Woman in the Dunes* from the sand dunes of Sakata, but he made no effort to identify the locale in the novel. Teshigahara re-created this scene in Hamamatsu by specially constructing towering cliffs of sand.

Abe himself had grown up in Manchuria, a desert environment. Inspired by writers like Philip Roth, Bernard Malamud, Poe, Nietzsche, Beckett, and Kafka, and by detective novels, Abe wrote novels and plays focusing on the dilemmas presented by modern life, and by the human conflict between dream and reality.

4. The Japanese New Wave developed in the late 1950s and early 1960s through the efforts of directors like Oshima Nagisa, Yoshida Yoshishige, and Shinoda Masahiro, among others. It was inspired in part by French Nouvelle Vague directors like Francois Truffaut and Jean-Luc Godard.
5. Ashton, *The Delicate Thread,* 96.
6. After studying economics at Keio University, Okada (1920–96) joined the Shinkyo Theater Group. In 1950 he made his screen debut in the first "kissing film," *Until the Day We Meet Again (Mata au hi made),* by director Imai Tadashi. He also starred as the rebel leader in *The Ugly American.*

   In the planning of *Woman in the Dunes,* there had been some discussion about having a non-Japanese actor play the role of the man. This plan was abandoned because of scheduling difficulties.
7. Transgressions of the raccord rules are not limited to the directionless walk of the man in the desert. We can also observe them in the treatment the woman receives inside the pit. When she drinks, we notice that in one shot she looks to the right, and in the following, to the left.
8. The cinema has approached the myth of Sisyphus on different occasions, especially in gangster films, where criminals who climb from the base to the top of society, only to fall to the depths as Sisyphus did, are frequent. This is the case with Bull Weeds, whose slogan is "The city is yours" in *Underworld* (von Sternberg, 1927); with Tony Camonte ("world in your hands") in *Scarface* (Hawks, 1932); and with Cody Jarrett ("the top of the world") in *White Heat* (Raoul Walsh, 1949). Even more explicit is the final scene of *The Prowler* (Joseph Losey, 1951), where a fugitive (Van Heflin) tries to escape from the police by climbing to the top of a hill, tumbling over and over before being killed by his persecutors.

   More recently, there is the character played by Robert De Niro in *The Mission* (Roland Joffe, 1986) – a mercenary who, to expiate his sins, must load his weapons on his back and climb with them to the top of Iguazu Falls. His load falls with ominous insistence, forcing the convict to suffer considerable torment.
9. *Kagura,* etymologically, means "god" and "music." Invocation to light is the equivalent of the search for knowledge, the fertile rebirth of the cycles of life. After the celebration of the gods, day and light are recovered. This process also occurs in the film. Oppressive darkness gives way to a sunnier scene in which the prisoner finds water. After the prolonged period of sterility, both the Earth and the Woman are fertilized.

10. Takemitsu Toru (1930–1995) gained an international reputation for his innovative musical compositions, blending influences from Japan and the West. In 1963 he won the International Modern Music Conference Prize in Paris, and he has held professorships at Yale University (in 1975) and at the University of California at San Diego (in 1981). He founded an annual international contemporary music festival in Japan called "Music Today."

    An associate of artists like John Cage, Seiji Ozawa, and Peter Serkin, he was also highly influenced by the music of earlier composers like Claude Debussy and Olivier Messiaen. Takemitsu composed over forty works for orchestra, over twenty works for chamber ensemble, thirty instrumental pieces, five choral works, and more than eighty film scores (including the score for *Kwaidan* [1964, directed by Kobayashi Masaki]; for *Silence* [*Chinmoku,* 1971]; for *Double Suicide [Shinju ten no amijima,* 1969], directed by Shinoda Masahiro; for two films directed by Kurosawa Akira [*Dodeskaden,* 1970, and *Ran,* 1985]; as well as scores for *The Ceremony* [*Gishiki,* 1971] and for *The Phantom of Love* [*Ai no borei,* 1978], by Oshima Nagisa).

    For more information on this unique artist, see Noriko Ohtake, *Creative Sources for the Music of Toru Takemitsu,* (Aldershot, Eng.: Scolar Press, 1993).
11. The ancient *kagura* dances were performed by hermit monks who lived in the mountains. Here we find a new parallelism with the peasants, whose isolated society occupies the upper spaces of the community. Mountains are, elsewhere, sacred spaces in Japan, usually reserved as a dwelling place for gods (*yama no kami,* in the Japanese tradition).
12. David George, "Ritual Drama: Between Mysticism and Magic," *Asian Theater Journal* 4:2 (fall 1987): 127–65.
13. We thank Professor Norma Field for this suggestion.
14. Joan Mellen, *Voices from the Japanese Cinema* (New York: Liveright, 1975), 176–77.
15. Ibid, 176.

CHAPTER FIVE

Adapting *The Makioka Sisters*

Kathe Geist

Ichikawa Kon claims he wanted to adapt Tanizaki Jun'ichirô's *Makioka Sisters (Sasameyuki)* in 1948, when the novel first appeared and he was still an assistant director. The dream faded, particularly when others adapted the book for the screen, first in 1950 and later in 1959, but was revived when a Toho producer asked him, in the early 1980s, to direct a new version of the literary classic. A large budget was assigned to the consequently lavish production, whose release was scheduled to coincide with Toho's fiftieth anniversary in 1983. Despite a budget that could have accommodated the necessary special effects, Ichikawa's version is stately and quiet and omits the most dramatic occurrence in the novel: the Kobe flood of 1938. Nevertheless, the film preserves the ethos of the novel, essentially an upper-middle-class "home drama," and in spite of the inevitable condensation required to adapt a 500-page novel to film,[1] the story, characters, and even minute events from the novel are clearly recognizable. There are, however, minor changes as well as obvious omissions that subtly rework the novel's ideology. Tanizaki's paean to a lost world of leisurely and refined, upper-middle-class culture becomes, in Ichikawa's hands, not only a tribute to an earlier style of filmmaking, but also an exercise in traditionalism, intended to affirm Japanese identity at a time when Japan was reemerging as a major commercial and industrial power.

Tanizaki's novel covers five years in the lives of the four Makioka sisters, daughters of an old, respected, and once-wealthy merchant family in Osaka, Japan's traditional center of bourgeois culture. The story focuses on the attempts of the two older, married sisters to find suitable matches for their younger siblings. The plot is constructed around five *miai* (marriage interviews) for Yukiko, the most conservative and the most "Japanese" of the four. Amid these are woven the misadventures of the youngest sister, Taeko, a modern, independent girl with questionable morals. The story is seen mostly through the eyes of Sachiko, the second sister, whose house in the suburb of Ashiya attracts the two younger sisters more than does the family home in the old merchant quarters of Osaka. Tsuruko, the eldest sister, charged with maintaining the family's integrity, finds herself thwarted in this endeavor on two grounds. First, the younger sisters prefer Sachiko's home in Ashiya and spend most of their time there, where Sachiko and her husband Teinosuke are less strict and tradition-bound than are Tsuruko and her husband Tatsuo. (Both husbands are *yoshi,* who have been adopted into the Makioka family and have taken the family name.) Second, less than a year into the story, Tatsuo's bank transfers him to Tokyo. With the old Makioka store and most of the wealth gone, the adopted husbands must work in modern businesses to support their wives. Once in Tokyo, Tsuruko has even less control over the three younger sisters, and, with no need to maintain the Makioka name in a city where no one knows them, she and Tatsuo live rather shabbily in an attempt to save money. Unlike Sachiko, who has managed to bear only one child, Tsuruko has six children to support.

The book, whose Japanese name means "a light snowfall," the kind that disappears as soon as the sun comes out, is Tanizaki's elegy to a lost culture – that of bourgeois Kansai – one that he, a Tokyoite, had embraced after his second marriage in 1935, only six years before he began writing the novel in 1941. Completed after the war in 1948, the novel is filled with that peculiarly Japanese nostalgia for passing things, but its central irony is that while the Makioka sisters mourn the changes that come with the passing of time, in terms of both traditional seasonal change and in various personal losses,[2] outside forces, which seem distant from cozy Ashiya, are moving quickly to obliterate their entire way of life. That irony is underscored, for example, toward the end of the novel, when Sachiko receives a letter from her German friend and former neighbor, who, writing of wartime hardships, adds, "We are both young nations fighting our way up, and it is not easy to win a place in the sun. And yet I do believe that we will win in the end" (*The Makioka Sisters,* 465).

In creating a structure for his film, Ichikawa reduced the novel's five-year time span to one year, neatly framed by the sisters' annual *hanami* (flower viewing) pilgrimage to Kyoto, but retained most of Yukiko's *miai.*[3] Between the *miai,* he interwove Taeko's story, some of which has occurred before the plot begins. Five or six years in the past, Taeko ran away with her boyfriend Okubata, son of a jewelry merchant, an incident that got into the newspapers and created a scandal. Too young to marry, and obliged in any case to wait until Yukiko married, Taeko was forbidden to continue seeing Okubata. She turned to doll-making, a hobby she has parlayed into a small business, for which she maintains her own studio. She has continued to see Okubata, however, and the plot concerns her romantic involvement with him, his friend Itakura, once an apprentice in the Okubata business, and a bartender named Miyoshi.

In the film, Taeko's past is told in black-and-white flashbacks. The black and white is emblematic of the newspaper stories that recorded the scandal; it is also reminiscent of Japanese *taiyôzoku* (rebellious youth, literally, "sun tribe") films of the 1950s and 1960s, many of which were shot in grainy black and white. To a large extent, in fact, the film's Taeko resembles the emotional, rebellious teenagers from 1960s films more than she does Tanizaki's sophisticated, self-contained *moga* (modern girl) from the 1930s.[4]

As in most adaptations from novel to film, many of the modifications condense the story, make it easier to follow, and make characters easier to identify. For example, Yukiko's groom in the book is the son of a viscount's concubine, in other words, a bastard. Ichikawa simply made him a second son and therefore, like his counterpart in the book, not the viscount's heir. He also changed the man's name from Mimaki to Higashidani.

A more important example is the postponement of Tsuruko's move to Tokyo, which occurs in the first third of the novel and allows various themes to develop: the exacerbation of tensions between the two older sisters over the residence and behavior of the two younger sisters; Sachiko's dismay over her sister's lack of decorum in her Tokyo residence; and an unfavorable comparison between Tokyo and Osaka that testifies to Tanizaki's infatuation with Kansai. To give the film greater unity, Ichikawa kept the four sisters together throughout the film and postponed Tsuruko's move until the end, where it neatly pairs with Yukiko's impending marriage to signal the breaking up of the old family, the parting of the four sisters, and, given the soldiers we see in the station, the eventual disappearance of their whole way of life.

This farewell scene is only the second time we glimpse any of Tsuruko's children. Although she has six in the book and claims, in the film, to have a lot (we never see more than three), they are heard off-screen only once and seen only twice. In the book the children's noisy presence is frequently remarked on, particularly in the small Tokyo house, and they are, in fact, the main reason Tsuruko and Tatsuo try to live so cheaply in Tokyo. When Sachiko visits her sister in Tokyo she is appalled: "The wild disorder, . . . the clutter that left hardly a place to stand, was far worse than she had imagined; . . . the whole house shook when one of the children ran up or down stairs" (195). In the film, Kishi Keiko's regal bearing as Tsuruko is never undermined by the presence of unruly children, nor is Ichikawa's quiet, stately mise-en-scène disrupted by them.

Modeled on the quiescent home dramas of directors like Ozu, the film omits the book's few highly dramatic episodes: the Kobe flood, Taeko's battle with dysentery, Itakura's operation and death scene, and Taeko's pregnancy and the delivery and death of her illegitimate child. While most of Ichikawa's changes were necessarily subtractive, one plot device in particular was added to the original story – Teinosuke's infatuation with Yukiko. Passages such as the following suggest this infatuation, but nowhere in the book is it made explicit:

> With Yukiko back, the Ashiya house was gay and noisy again. Yukiko, so inarticulate that one hardly knew she was about, added little to the noise, but one could see from the difference she made that something bright was hidden behind that apparent melancholy and reserve. And it was like a spring breeze to have all the sisters under one roof. The mood would be broken if one of them were to go. (257)

Tanizaki attributes these sentiments to no one in particular, but since Sachiko's consciousness is the one most present in the book, these thoughts could well be hers. In reality, they are Tanizaki's, who also had his wife's sisters living in his house and was particularly fond of one of them.[5]

Ichikawa took passages like this, added what was known of Tanizaki's own inclinations and the obsessiveness he so often wrote about in other works, and created for Teinosuke, who tends to float along in the background of the novel, a quiet obsession with Yukiko. However, scenes like the one in which he steals a kiss while helping her dress, and later fights with Sachiko about it, are entirely absent from the book. The scene in which he comes upon Yukiko and Taeko chatting in their room, in which Yukiko seductively pulls her kimono over her leg while gazing at him, is based on the passage in the book in which Teinosuke, fearing that Taeko and Yukiko have alienated one another, finds Taeko clipping Yukiko's toenails: "Yukiko quietly pulled her bare feet out of sight and took a more lady-like posture. As he closed the door, Teinosuke saw Taeko kneel to gather up the shiny parings. It was only a glimpse, and yet there was a beauty in the scene, sister with sister, that left a deep impression on him" (258).

Yukiko's action and Teinosuke's feelings here are more innocent and more diffuse than those presented in the film.[6] Moreover, the film develops a theme around the difficulties of being a *yoshi* (adopted husband), which is absent from the book. In one plot development, the elegant Tsuruko refuses at first to accompany her husband Tatsuo to Tokyo and only relents toward the end of the film. In a scene with the matchmaker Itani, which has no counterpart in the book, Teinosuke says, "A rich merchant's daughter and a clerk's son can never agree." Markus Nornes discusses at length both the "masochism," the pain Tanizaki's men enjoy at the hands of women, that is, Teinosuke's obsession with Yukiko, and the abasement of the *yoshi* as it appears in the Ichikawa film version of *The Makioka Sisters.* Neither theme is pursued in the book.[7]

The scene at the end of the film, in which Teinosuke, distraught over Yukiko's impending marriage, drinks sake alone and remarks to the waitress (after she tells him that sake without food is poison) that "poison will do fine," is a nod to Ozu and has no counterpart in the book. It recalls the Ozu fathers who drink alone after their daughters marry, particularly the father in *An Autumn Afternoon* (*Samma no aji,* 1962), who, when asked by the barmaid if he has just come from a funeral, says, "Something like that."

Another substantial change from book to film is in the character of Taeko. The book's Taeko is the model of a 30s *moga;* she is sophisticated, unemotional, has short hair, and smokes. The only similarity here to Ichikawa's Taeko is the smoking. While his costumers put Taeko into something resembling 1930s fashions, they left her hair long and wavy to satisfy contemporary standards of beauty. More important, however, is the difference in her personality. While both characters have very youthful faces, Ichikawa's Taeko *acts* childishly, throwing temper tantrums and storming out of the house at times. In contrast, Tanizaki's Taeko simply does what she wants to do, breezing in and out of the household, entertaining the family with her friends, her stories, and her passion for traditional Japanese dancing, then disappearing for days at a time whenever the family registers disapproval of her actions. True, she once slams the front door so hard the house shakes, but this is the only indication she gives of being angry. When Itakura dies, the film's Taeko throws herself on the floor and then into Sachiko's arms, distraught. Although the book's Taeko regularly visits Itakura's grave, she shows little emotion when he dies. "She spoke with the usual calm," Tanizaki says of Taeko when she tells Sachiko she is pregnant (*The Makioka Sisters,* 443).

The degree of Taeko's moral lassitude also changes from book to film. The book's Taeko has not only eloped unsuccessfully with Okubata as a young girl, but she also continues to see him, takes money from him, and apparently realizes that he is stealing from his family in order to give her presents. She becomes involved with his friend Itakura, a photographer who was once an apprentice in the Okubata family's jewelry business, and, after he dies, lives with Okubata, who has by now been disowned by his family for stealing from them. At this point, the Makiokas semi-disown Taeko, forbidding her to live at home anymore. Increasingly bored with Okubata, Taeko becomes involved with a bartender named Miyoshi and becomes pregnant. Hoping to avoid a scandal, the Makiokas ship her off to Arima Springs and bring her back only shortly before the birth of her daughter. In delivering the baby, who is no longer in the right position, the doctor's hand slips, and the infant dies. Not only does the Makioka family take Taeko's transgressions seriously enough to disinherit her, Tanizaki parallels the corrupt streak in Taeko with revolting descriptions of her battle with dysentery, Itakura's death from gangrene, and the difficult delivery of her child. Although Sachiko has a miscarriage and both she and her daughter Etsuko become ill at various times, only those illnesses associated with Taeko are described so graphically and horrifically.[8]

Although Ichikawa was faithful to the outlines of Taeko's story, he toned down her transgressions, omitting the most dramatic and compromising, and generally presenting Taeko in a more innocent light. Okubata threatens to blackmail the Makiokas with tales of Taeko's misdeeds, but these are never made explicit, and she never lives with

Okubata, nor becomes pregnant by Miyoshi, although she moves in with him at the end of the film. She lies to Yukiko about the source of some jewelry and a camel-hair coat she has recently acquired but is apparently unaware that Okubata has stolen to give them to her. Toward the end of the film she explains that she became involved with all these men because she was jealous of the family's preoccupation with Yukiko. In other words, she is a rebellious teenager trying to get some attention. When Sachiko visits her at the end of the film, she is the image of a proper Japanese wife: her hair is tied back in a braid, she wears a kimono, serves tea, and is generally demure and self-effacing. There is some precedent for this in the book: Taeko takes up a modest life with Miyoshi after the baby's death, but we never see her within the context of this life, nor do we find out what she thinks about it. The last portrait Tanizaki gives us of Taeko is of her weeping bitterly, along with Sachiko and Miyoshi, at the death of her child after the harrowing delivery. If there is a sense of repentance here, it is for real sins, whereas Ichikawa's Taeko has simply "settled down" after a rebellious youth.

Taeko's relationships with men of a lower social class beg an issue that is fundamental in both book and film, but it is treated differently in each. The film makes a point of the family's callousness toward its servants. Taeko, for example, is deliberately rude to the young servant Oharu when Oharu tries to console her; Tatsuo yells at his servant when in truth he's angry at his family. As soon as the old man, who agrees to live in the family house while Tsuruko and Tatsuo are in Tokyo, finishes his short speech of acceptance, the family ignores him. The most moving of these scenes is that involving Tsuruko's maid Ohisa, who has just learned of her brother's death in the war. Tsuruko has hung out Yukiko's kimonos and against this background mentions to her husband that the maid Ohisa is crying because she has lost her brother. He responds, "We must console her. He died for the country. Send money to his parents." Then they talk about the kimonos, and Tsuruko comments, "We couldn't get such good ones now we're at war." There is a cut to Ohisa in the dark kitchen washing the tears from her face, and we see clearly what the war means, at this juncture anyway, to the Makiokas as opposed to what it means for the lower classes, whose peasant sons and brothers made up the backbone of the Imperial Army.[9]

This obviously critical view of master/servant relationships does not exist in the book, where the relationship between the Makiokas and their servants is close, even affectionate, and their superiority is simply taken for granted. While Sachiko takes great pains to keep her servants from hearing matters she fears they will gossip about, she is, at times, forced to rely heavily on her maid Oharu, who deals with sensitive matters and keeps family secrets. At one point she describes her feelings about Oharu in great detail to her sister Tsuruko. A bumptious, slovenly girl with irrepressibly good spirits, Oharu, who dislikes washing, offends the other maids with her bad smell, and only the pleadings of her parents, who find her too difficult to keep at home, have persuaded Sachiko to retain her. Yet Sachiko muses, "After five years I almost think of her as my daughter. She may be a little tricky at times, but . . . she does have her good points. Even when she is more trouble than she is worth, I can never be really angry with her" (209). Something of this relationship is suggested in the film in a scene in which Sachiko gives Oharu a koto lesson, but for the most part, the servants are used in the film to illustrate the barrier between the Makiokas and the lower classes.

Markus Nornes has written an insightful analysis of class in the film in terms of the Japanese concept of *uchi* (inside) and *soto* (outside) or "us and them." In his analysis, the servants as well as Taeko's lower-class lovers, Itakura and Miyoshi, are *soto.*[10] In the book, however, the servants are clearly part of the family, therefore *uchi,* but Itakura and Miyoshi are not, and the Makiokas react strongly against Itakura, in particular. Ken Ito has suggested that "Tanizaki purchased the smoothly ordered world of *Sasameyuki* at the expense of his previous insights into class and power. . . . The illnesses that strike down first Itakura and later Taeko leave the impression that Sachiko's values are those of the novel itself."[11] On the contrary, as stated earlier, these illnesses, as symbolic devices, are connected to Taeko's moral impurity rather than her breach of class barriers. Interestingly, Taeko's relationship with Itakura, rather than with the bartender Miyoshi, is always the issue in the book, in part because, by the time Miyoshi arrives on the scene, Taeko has already slipped beyond the pale socially, but also because Itakura is a social climber and consequently a much more complex and problematic character. In portraying Itakura and the Makioka's response to him, Tanizaki candidly exposes their cruelty when he records Sachiko's reaction to Itakura's fatal illness: "To be honest, Sachiko could not keep back a certain feeling of relief now that the possibility of Taeko's marriage to a man of no family had been eliminated by natural and wholly unforeseen circumstances. It made her a little uncomfortable, a little unhappy with herself, to think that somewhere deep in her heart she could hope for a man's death, but there was the truth" (286). Moreover, Itakura's fate makes an angry case for the fact that inferior medical care is the lot of those lacking the money and sophistication of the upper middle class.

In the film Itakura is lumped with the servants to illustrate the Makiokas' exclusivity, and he is made to resemble them. The book's Itakura has lived in America, acquired egalitarian ways, and is something of a swashbuckling hero when he saves Taeko from the flood, but he strikes the other Makiokas as presumptuous and insincere. By contrast, the film's Itakura is a deferential country bumpkin, who always hangs his head in Taeko's presence.

Ichikawa has long had a reputation as a social critic and his identifying Itakura with the servants and both as subject to the Makiokas' slights is an unsubtle criticism of class barriers, one which champions a democratized Japan. Nornes insists, however, that the film's structure and ideology reinforce an *uchi/soto* dichotomy that is very much at the heart of how the Japanese see themselves in relation to the rest of the world, and that the film therefore unconsciously legitimizes the myth of Japanese homogeneity and the exclusivity this myth implies.[12]

Within the film's conscious, liberal agenda, there is also the implied criticism of the characters' obliviousness to the coming war. The film makes reference to the war several times, in addition to the scene where Ohisa mourns her fallen brother; twice we see soldiers boarding or riding on trains and once we are shown the headline of a windblown newspaper, "Japanese Army Occupies Canton." The sound of a soldiers' farewell party heard from a room next to one of Yukiko's *miai* initiates the characters' only discussion of the war, which quickly turns back to a discussion of fish – those found in Wuhan. The characters also refer at times to wartime shortages. Tsuruko and Tatsuo use the war as an excuse to save money on their parents' memorial service: "It's wartime, and we mustn't have big parties." This comment summarizes those made frequently in the book to the effect that all manner of fun, frivolity, and display must be reined in because the government is exhorting austerity and self-sacrifice.

The book's Makiokas have more of an awareness of the developing war and what it may mean for them as they watch the war develop in Europe. Sachiko has written to her former neighbor, Mrs. Stolz, that "the Makiokas were well, although with the China Incident dragging on they were gloomy at the thought that they too might soon find themselves in a real war; they could not but be astonished at how the world had changed since the days when the Stolzes were next door, and they wondered wistfully if such happy times would ever come again. . ." (411).

Besides suggesting that the Makiokas, while not politically sophisticated, do not welcome the prospect of war, the passage is part of an ever-present ethos of ephemerality that runs through the book. Whether it's the Stolzes moving, the war clouding the horizon, the cherry blossoms falling, the Hirado lilies fading, or the Kabuki ending its Osaka run, Sachiko is always acutely aware of passing time and its tolls: "The tall white hagi shedding its blossoms in the garden made Sachiko think of that garden at Minoo and the day her mother had died" (336).

The film evokes this sense of ephemerality through its many references to season and climate: cherry blossoms at the beginning, autumn leaves in connection with Yukiko's last two *miai,* snow in the final scenes. At times Ichikawa borrows from Ozu, whose films foreground ephemerality and transience.[13] A shot of clouds bridging scenes of Taeko at Sachiko's house and Taeko in her studio is reminiscent of Ozu, as are the boat and train whistles that occur from time to time, first at the beginning and the end of the *miai* with Nomura. These seem to refer particularly to Teinosuke's unrequited love for Yukiko, for in each instance the sound is over a shot of him looking at her. The singing from a soldier's farewell party in a neighboring room is also one of these signs of transience or nostalgia, for it is Yukiko who will soon be leaving. (As in the book, the cosmic shifts brought on by the war evoke a more narrowly personal sense of nostalgia in the Makiokas' world.) Boat whistles also occur in connection with Taeko and Miyoshi – when we first see her in his bar and the first time Sachiko visits Taeko after she has gone to live with Miyoshi. The whistles are, of course, part of the working-class, waterfront milieu Taeko has consigned herself to, but given their occurrence earlier in the film, they also suggest the loss of Taeko to the family.

One hardly needs Ozu as a referent to understand the meaning of the train whistle or the close-ups of the whistle blowing and the wheels turning as Tsuruko leaves for Tokyo; the second whistle, however, sounds over a close-up of Yukiko watching the train leave with tears in her eyes, and refers not simply to the parting with Tsuruko, but again to Teinosuke's loss of Yukiko, for he is shown watching her in the background.

More than an evocation of transience is apparent, however, in Ichikawa's nature footage. The opening sequence, extra long because it contains the credits, unfolds as follows. A shot of the rounded hills of Arashiyama in the rain cuts to an extreme long shot of the Togetsu bridge, an Arashiyama landmark, where tiny figures carry umbrellas. A close-up of branches with cherry blossoms, dripping with rain, is followed by a closer shot of a single branch. After an interior sequence with the family, there is another long shot of Arashiyama with petals fluttering down, followed by another close-up of a branch of blossoms, and then an extreme close-up of a single cluster. We watch the kimono-clad women, framed in the shoji doorway, watching the blossoms, and then a montage sequence of the family wandering under the sun-drenched blossoms next to Osawa Pond. This is followed by shots of the Heian shrine. The family enters the last of these, and four shots of weeping cherries, deep pink in bright sunshine, follow. Then we see a telephoto sequence of family members through the blossoms, which appear as a screen of pink blurs. Eleven more shots of the weeping cherries follow, allowing the credits to play out, and these include a two-shot sequence of schoolchildren walking beneath the cherries, a row of cherry trees reflected in a pond, and a close traveling shot over individual branches and blossoms. A sunset signals the day's end. We return to the family and Tsuruko pointing, not at the sunset, but at a last spectacular view of weeping cherries. Aspects of this long sequence suggest melancholy, nostalgia and transience: the rain, the petals fluttering down, the schoolchildren, the sunset. There is, throughout, a dreamlike quality, which suggests the fragility of all that we see. Nevertheless, these sequences, often shot from below or in close-up, burst out of the wide screen with such brilliant color that they create a celebratory mood more than a nostalgic one.

The same treatment, though shortened, is given to the maple-viewing at Minô during Yukiko's third *miai.* The sequence begins with a traveling shot down a waterfall with brilliant maples beside it, cuts to water splashing over rocks at the bottom of the waterfall, then to a long shot of people on a bridge viewing the waterfall. A closer shot of the *miai* party walking under the maples is interrupted by a sequence of Taeko taking a bath back in Ashiya. Returning to Minô, we see a branch of maple leaves followed by two close-ups, after which the *miai* narrative resumes.

Not only does the landscape receive this celebratory treatment, but so do all the aspects of traditional culture that the film includes. The inn sequence that comes between the many shots of cherry blossoms at the beginning contains a close-up of Yukiko placing a tiny dish on her exquisitely arranged tea tray. Tsuruko joins the party late, and, as she takes off her *haori,* a close-up of her back reveals her elegant obi. In a later sequence in which Tsuruko tries on several different obi, the camera, accompanied by traditional string music, travels down her green silk kimono and over the half-dozen obi lying on the tatami floor.

The "old Japan" motifs coalesce in Yukiko's last *miai,* which takes place at Viscount Higashidani's villa near Arashiyama. A temple bell tolls over shots of the Togetsu Bridge and again as the family walks toward the villa. Teinosuke comments on the wintry landscape, but the leaves are still a brilliant orange. The camera dwells lovingly on the architecture of the old villa. There is another disrobing shot in which a close-up of the Makioka crest on Sachiko's *haori* reveals her brocaded kimono as she takes the outer garment off. Inside the villa there is a close-up of the kettle used in boiling water for a tea ceremony. Two more shots of autumn leaves punctuate the *miai* sequences, but "old Japan" is just beginning to build to its crescendo. The *miai* sequence is followed by four shots of lanterns from a festival, which come toward the camera, blurring as they get very close. These are followed by a ten-shot kimono montage:

- A long shot of a blue kimono with cranes on a kimono rack
- A closer shot of the same kimono in which the camera travels up the kimono
- A close-up of cranes on the same kimono
- A close-up of a single crane on the kimono
- A gold kimono fluttering in front of the camera
- A traveling shot toward a beige kimono with wisteria
- A traveling shot toward a gold and white kimono
- red kimono fluttering
- Part of a maroon kimono with a cherry blossom motif
- long shot of silver brocade kimono on a rack to the right of Tatsuo, who is reading a map.

It turns out that *all* of these kimonos belong to Yukiko, and Tsuruko is airing them in anticipation of Yukiko's eventual marriage. The sequence thus has a narrative rationale, but it doesn't fit easily into the diegesis because we have to wonder who or what made them flutter. Certainly not Tatsuo, and Tsuruko comes into the room only after Tatsuo has put away his map. Existing somewhat outside the narrative, the sequence is pure celebration.[14]

That the kimonos are Yukiko's is important, for this celebration of old Japan devolves particularly on her, since, in looks and habits, she is the most old-fashioned of the sisters. The book also emphasizes this. Teinosuke's loss of her – and the film's thematic justification for his obsession with her – is our loss of old Japan. In this sense the film, unlike the book, concentrates not on the loss of a particular era, the era of gracious living between the world wars, but on the loss of traditional Japanese culture generally.

This change is most clearly seen in the film's neglect of another aspect of the book: the constant presence of either Western friends or Western culture, which characterized the 1920s and 1930s in Japan. In the book, the house next to Sachiko's has been built for foreigners and, through the first half of the book, is occupied by the Stolzes, who become good friends. Taeko has befriended a White Russian family, the Kyrilenkos, with whom the rest of the Ashiya Makiokas become acquainted. References to Western books, films, music, as well as to Western-style restaurants, abound in the book, reminding us how much prewar Japan took Western culture for granted. Donald Keene comments, "The military authorities were right when they decided in 1943 that *The Makioka Sisters* was subversive, for in this novel Tanizaki indicates that Western elements had become precious parts of the lives of cultivated Japanese and were no longer merely affectations or passing crazes as in the days of Tanizaki's youth."[15]

Ichikawa is true to this aspect of the novel in several instances. For example, some of the characters, particularly Taeko, wear Western clothes. Sachiko has some Western-style rooms in her house, and the beautician/go-between Itani has a sign on her beauty salon that reads "Itani Beauty Shop," which hangs over the picture of a Western-coiffed woman. (This detail is actually at odds with the book, where Itani is teased because she *never* wears Western clothes. That she is teased, however, indicates how much Western dress was taken for granted at the time.) The *miai* with Nomura takes place in a Chinese restaurant, which, ironically, becomes the locale of the characters' only discussion of the war in China. Beyond these instances, however, the film makes little reference to an international scene. Moreover, the Makiokas themselves, apart from Taeko's dress and Sachiko's Western parlor, seem little touched by things foreign. Yukiko's final, successful *miai* is the all-Japanese one. (Although this meeting in Arashiyama with the groom's family takes place in the book, the initial *miai* has taken place in a more informal, Westernized setting.) When, in the film, Tsuruko remonstrates against the move to Tokyo, Tatsuo counters, "It isn't a foreign country or the remote mountains." No foreigners appear in the film, and only the report that Miyoshi wants to "open a big club for foreigners in Kobe" acknowledges that such beings exist. One could argue that adding the foreign characters from the novel to the film would have made the already complex story too complicated; but Ichikawa could have created more of Tanizaki's international ethos through the dialogue or the mise-en-scène, much as Ozu did in all but his wartime films. That Ichikawa did not suggests that his focus lay more on traditional culture generally than on the particular culture of the 1930s.

No elegy, therefore, for the lost Japan of the 1930s, the film goes beyond nostalgia to an actual celebration of traditional Japan as seen in the overpowering fullness, brightness, beauty, and abundance of the shots in the "old Japan" sequences. The culture on the screen seems not lost, but newly found – as in some sense it was for its 1983 audience. Not that they didn't know about cherry blossoms and maple leaves – seasonal fetishism has a long and present history in Japan – but to see them celebrated so gloriously was no doubt reassuring to Japanese reemerging for the first time since the war as major players on the world's stage. With the outside world both more demanding and more accessible, there was a renewed interest in rediscovering Japanese identity.[16] The film thus dispenses "traditionalism" in the anthropological sense, meaning the way in which cultures create new traditions or adapt old ones to accommodate new developments.[17] According to Theodore Bestor, traditionalism seeks "to legitimate contemporary social realities by imbuing them with a patina of venerable historicity," and is "a common Japanese cultural device for managing or responding to social change."[18] While a *jidai-geki* would remind Japanese of their traditional culture, *The Makioka Sisters* served the particular purpose of legitimating the new affluence of the 1980s by associating it with a traditional context. Rich, urban, and middle class, the Makiokas hail from the last great era of urban wealth in Japan. In a contemporary world where few youngsters sit regularly on tatami or know the features of a traditional house, where few women wear a kimono and fewer still can afford to own one,[19] the film presents an image of urban, middle-class people enveloped by tradition – literally, if one thinks of the extent to which the film dwells on the kimono – and invites audience members to identify with these people and reinvent their own Japaneseness.

To this end, the inclusion of 1930s foreigners would serve no purpose. With so many Westernized aspects integrated into the contemporary Japanese lifestyle and so many traditional habits lost (how to walk in a kimono, how to sit on one's knees for hours at a time), reminding audiences that Western influences were already pervasive in the 1930s would hardly be reassuring. For all that the film is politically liberal with respect to social class and war-guilt, it fully indulges the "myth of Japanese uniqueness,"[20] by creating a full-blown, all-Japanese fantasy world in many of its sequences.

Nornes's observation that the film structures itself around concepts of *uchi* and *soto* and thus reinforces the sense of Japanese homogeneity, in which everything non-Japanese is *soto,* is relevant here because this dichotomy likewise fulfilled a need for Japanese to be reassured of their particular identity as a people at a time when Japan was once again becoming more fully involved in world politics and economics.

A particular internal social change *The Makioka Sisters* attempts to mediate is the growing trend toward liberation among Japanese women. The film's insistence on the tenuous position of the *yoshi,* absent in the novel, suggests a new insecurity on the part of Japanese men, who may feel more at the mercy of women now than in the past.

At a time when Japanese women were just beginning to enter the workforce and seek careers, the film celebrated the physical, couturial, and behavioral perfection of traditional Japanese women, and this accounts for many of the major changes from novel to film. The modification of Tanizaki's Taeko, for example, was necessary in order to keep her appearance and character more in line with those of the other sisters. She was thus conceived of as more misguided than corrupt and shown as fully restored by the end of the film: a meek and subservient Japanese wife, serving tea. The film closes with the four Makioka sisters, perfect Japanese women all, under the cherry trees – Teinosuke's memory of the previous year's *hanami* – and any doubts we may have had of Taeko fitting this model have, by this time, been assuaged.[21] Teinosuke's obsession with Yukiko, also absent from the novel, underscores the film's dedication to the perfect Japanese woman, Yukiko being touted as the most traditional and old-fashioned of the sisters in both novel and film. Even the change in Yukiko's bridegroom's birthright, from bastard to legitimate son, while simplifying the story, also serves to keep Yukiko unsullied (something Tanizaki's sense of irony would not permit, for the novel ends with the observation that Yukiko's premarital jitters resulted in diarrhea).

As noted before, Tanizaki's Tsuruko, burdened with children, economizing, vainly trying to exert some authority over her sisters, and reduced to tears when they snub her at one point near the end of the novel, is transformed in the film into a regal princess with real power over both her sisters and her husband. While the book's harried Tsuruko never considers an alternative to following her husband to Tokyo, the film's Tsuruko rebels against his decision, and this becomes one of the major conflicts the plot must resolve. Her eventual repentance and Tatsuo's moving gratitude for it suggest that women with freedom and choices should nevertheless choose to support their husbands.[22]

Evoking Ozu in the closing scene where Teinosuke is mourning Yukiko's marriage, Ichikawa weds one kind of traditionalism to another – tears for the perfect woman and a salute to Japanese cinema's Golden Age. Ozu, who was more Westernized and more liberal than most scholars and critics will acknowledge, is nevertheless still mythologized as the "most Japanese" of Japanese directors. It was fitting, therefore, for Ichikawa to close with a scene-long tribute to Ozu, who, if not really the "most Japanese" of directors was probably the one most obsessed by those "most Japanese" notions of transience and nostalgia. In fulfilling its nostalgic mission of saluting 50 years of Toho, the film also performed the important feat of reconnecting contemporary Japanese to their past, celebrating it, and disavowing certain uncomfortable present tendencies, freer women and greater internationalization.

NOTES

1. While in Japanese, the novel is over 1,000 pages, the English translation runs around 500 pages. The version quoted throughout this essay is Edward G. Seidensticker's 1957 translation, ed. New York: Alfred A. Knopf, 1975).
2. See Reiko Tsukimura, "The Sense of Loss in *The Makioka Sisters,*" in Kinya Tsuruta and Thomas E. Swann (eds.), *Approaches to the Modern Japanese Novel* (Tokyo: Kawata Press [Sophia University], 1976), 231–40.

3. Although Ichikawa stated in an interview (R5/S8 publicity notes) that he had retained all five of Yukiko's *miai,* only four are actually staged in the film, those with Nomura, Hashidera, and Higashidani (the book's Mimaki), and a man from Toyohashi. The *miai* with Segoshi, whose mother is discovered to be mentally ill, has taken place before the film begins, although it is alluded to in the first scene. The *miai* with Sawazaki (which involves the firefly hunt) is omitted. In the book a *miai* with a Mr. Saigusa from Toyohashi has taken place some ten years before the plot begins.
4. Ichikawa had, in fact, contributed to the *taiyôzoku* genre with *Punishment Room* (*Shokei no heya,* 1956) and would make two subsequent films dealing with the problems/viewpoints of young people, *A Crowded Streetcar* (*Mannin densha,* 1957) and *Conflagration* (*Enjo,* 1958). See David Desser, *Eros Plus Massacre: An Introduction to the Japanese New Wave Cinema,* (Bloomington: Indiana University Press, 1988) 41–42.
5. Tanizaki had, in fact, had a serious love affair with the sister of his first wife, one reason that his marriage ended in divorce.
6. Tanizaki was famous for having a "foot fetish"; thus anyone familiar with his work could easily read far more into this passage than Tanizaki actually wrote. See Donald Keene, *Appreciations of Japanese Culture* (New York: Kodansha International, 1971), 172f. Nevertheless, Tanizaki is explicit about Teinosuke's devotion to Sachiko and a paragraph that begins, "The most eager of all to keep Yukiko a little longer was Teinosuke," ends with the explanation that "his real motive" was to provide a distraction for Sachiko, who was still mourning over her miscarriage (*The Makioka Sisters,* 134).
7. "Context and *The Makioka Sisters," East-West Film Journal* 5:2 (July 1991), 46–68. Nornes, perhaps inadvertently, implies that the relationship Ichikawa creates between Teinosuke and Yukiko originates in the novel, but it does not. Although Nornes has cultural evidence for male disdain of the *yoshi*'s position (55), Tanizaki did not write it into the book, perhaps because the relationship between Sachiko and Teinosuke is based on Tanizaki's relationship with his second wife, Matsuko, and Tanizaki was not a *yoshi.* Ironically, his own father was one, and this apparently did cause problems in the parents' marriage.
8. For a discussion of the relationship in Japanese minds between illness and impurity, see Emiko Ohnuki-Tierney, *Illness and Culture in Contemporary Japan* (New York: Cambridge University Press, 1984), 34–35 ff; also see William Johnson, *The Modern Epidemic: A History of Tuberculosis in Japan* (Cambridge: Council on East Asian Studies, Harvard, 1997).
9. See Edwin O. Reischauer, *Japan: Past and Present* 3d ed. (New York: Knopf, 1969), 159–60.
10. "Context and *The Makioka Sisters,"* 58f.
11. *Visions of Desire: Tanizaki's Fictional Worlds* (Stanford, Calif.: Standford University Press, 1991), 205–6.
12. "Context and *The Makioka Sisters,"* 60.
13. See Kathe Geist, "Narrative Strategies in Ozu's Late Films," in Arthur Nolletti, Jr. and David Desser (eds.), *Reframing Japanese Cinema: Authorship, Genre, History* (Bloomington: Indiana University Press, 1992), 92–111.

14. The celebration was literal as well as figurative, for the company that supplied the kimonos for the film was also celebrating its fiftieth anniversary.
15. *Appreciations,* 178.
16. Ross Mouer and Yoshio Sugimoto, *Images of Japanese Society* (London: Routledge & Kegan Paul, 1986), 389.
17. See Eric Hobsbawm and Terence Ranger, *The Invention of Tradition* (New York: Cambridge University Press,) 4f.
18. Theodore Bester, *Neighborhood Tokyo* (Stanford, Calif.: Stanford University Press, 1989), 10.
19. At least one well-heeled father I know of let his daughter choose between a formal kimono and a trip to Europe for her college graduation present; the cost for each is about the same.
20. Peter Dale has written extensively and quite polemically on Japanese self-mythologizing in *The Myth of Japanese Uniqueness* (Oxford: Oxford University Press, 1986). Hiroshi Minami discusses the sudden reemergence of a Japanese obsession with Japaneseness in the early 1970s in "The Interpretation Boom," *Japan Interpreter* 8(2): 159–73.
21. It has been argued that the film's women, even Yukiko, are all very strong-minded and rule the men in the film. True enough, but always within the home sphere. These kimono-clad beauties, with the exception of Taeko, do not work outside the home. Home and work, women's and men's worlds, are so completely separated in Japan that spouses are never invited to work-sponsored social events and business associates are not entertained at home. The particular threat that present-day women pose is precisely that of entering men's work world and shattering this carefully preserved distance; thus the importance of Taeko's new domesticity at the end of the film.
22. In fact, Japanese women today often stay behind when their husbands are transferred, not for themselves, but because their children cannot change schools easily. Tsuruko's decision to accompany Tatsuo creates a comforting fantasy for men while the fact of her acquiescence is an admonition to women to support their men, however they may. This, on a larger scale, is precisely the decision Crown Princess Masako made in giving up her career to serve her country's traditionalism and save her prince from eternal bachelordom.

CHAPTER SIX

In the Show House of Modernity

Exhaustive Listing in Itami Jûzô's *Tanpopo*

Charles Shirô Inouye

Within a context of continuous interaction between the visible and invisible elements of artistic expression, within the give-and-take between the graphemic and phonemic elements of the sign, the development of the motion picture (*katsudô shashin*) in Japan represents yet another attempt by the visual to adapt to the growing dominance of the phonetic in modern culture.[1] Other earlier reactions to the phonocentrism of modernity would include the talking penis- and vagina-heads of Utagawa Kunisada and their counterparts in the genitalia-centered texts of Santô Kyôden, where visual signs seek to become sources of speech.[2] Another would be the brief collaboration, and subsequent failure, of Takizawa Bakin and Katsushika Hokusai as they attempted to produce *gôkan* (lengthy texts of illustrated fiction) together. The seeds of cinema were planted here in this failure.

Both Bakin, the writer, and Hokusai, the painter, sought and accomplished *narrative* brilliance, despite the fact that one specialized in words and the other in pictures. Hokusai's use of two-dimensional figures to tell stories gives us an important insight as to the general semiotic formation of modern consciousness. The movement toward narrativity reflected and emphasized earlier narrative uses of the image, such as *etoki* (narration of pictures), *emaki* (narrative picture scrolls), *Nara ehon* (picture books), and *otogizôshi* (illustrated narratives), though Hokusai moved significantly further in this direction than earlier visual artists. Needless to say, he readily proved his ability to narrate with pictures; and it was precisely this brilliant success that made Bakin reject him and seek out a less capable illustrator. Bakin himself was better at writing *yomihon* (reading books) than *gôkan* because his imagination was totalizing and modern. As the one who Tsubouchi Shôyô later had to discredit in order to carry out his Eurocentric literary reforms, Bakin set a course with his strongly fictional, word-centered work that contributed to the separation of literature and visual art that occurred in the nineteenth century. It was in this state of divorcement that *katsudô shashin* brought word and picture together again.

Motion pictures did this in a new way, one that went beyond the narrative potential of *gôkan* illustrations. In what Walter Benjamin has called the "age of mechanical reproduction," projecting a series of pictures in rapid succession accomplished an illusion of connection, one picture joined seamlessly to the next. Through this process, the (static) image became more intimately (or, should we say, realistically?) tied to time. With the creation of motion pictures, the syntactic "becoming" of narration and the paratactic "being" of the image merged in a powerful combination. With the invention of film, it became possible for the temporal orientation of the phoneme (sound existing in time) and the spatial presence of the grapheme (matter existing in space) to join together in near-perfect collaboration.

Of course, this almost miraculous symbiosis, represented by the oxymoronic term *motion picture,* did not happen overnight. Consider how, in early showings, the mechanics of projection were as interesting to the Japanese audience as the projected images themselves – the viewers sitting at right angles to the projected images, directly facing the projectionist and the assistant. Eventually all traces of production, including the narrator *(benshi)* who once sat or stood by the screen and gave voice to the flickering images, became invisible. As motion pictures developed, the projectionists, the narrator, even the existence of other viewers of the film, eventually became hidden away in the darkness of the modern show house. With this vanishing of everything outside the moving images on the screen, motion pictures gained their own internal voice. They began, in modern fashion, to speak for themselves, which is, after all, the principal aim of modernity.

When viewed within the interplay between these two formal components of the sign, grapheme and phoneme, it becomes clear that the distinguishing feature of motion pictures was motion rather than pictures. That is to say, the innovative and in this sense modern, improving, and essential feature of movies was narrative and temporal. We have only to look at *gôkan* texts to see the beginnings of this transformation. Sharing the space of the printed page, *gôkan* illustrations established a visual story that supported (and sometimes competed with) the one being told by words. Although these pictures were frequently metamorphic, belying their lineage to the visual exaggerations of *bakemono* (monstrosities) that flourished in, especially, the graphemic resurgence of the eighteenth century, these more "textual" pictures were more clearly committed to the longevity (and absolute length) of the story. Length was essentially a commercial concern, which was aided by examples of Chinese colloquial fiction, especially *The Outlaws of the Marsh (Shui-hu chuan),* which was tremendously influential in the development of modern fiction in Japan. But the social and intellectual consequences of this developing market for reading materials were also profound. The desire for length and continuity prepared the way for the more seamless union of word and picture that was later made possible by cinematic realism.

With the advent of motion pictures, metamorphosis took on a new, mostly negative meaning. Change was made to happen in real time, to seem actual rather than imagined. Indeed, the rapid projection of images onto a screen attempted to establish the very lack of monstrosity or radical ontological change.[3] To begin with, the coherence of motion pictures was not to be questioned. By mechanical means, the change from one picture to the next occurred with such speed and with such unflagging determination that the resulting flow of images established nothing less than the mimetic reality of the modern. Motion pictures (even more so than photography) established a reality that moved rapidly forward, even when it flashed back to remember the past. It electrically generated a kind of progress that spoke for itself, as the advocates of the Pure Film Movement would have motion pictures do. In this, the camera and the projector created a new rhetoric of plausibility that helped to establish the hegemonic nature of modern ideology itself. That is to say, one scene followed the preceding scene in a consciously determined manner that was nevertheless natural and plausible. As we watch such productions, we are made to think, "What could be more obvious than such order?" Or, perhaps stated more accurately, we are made not to think, not to question the reality of what we are seeing. This deception and its anesthetizing of the critical will become a necessary condition of "true stories," whether that truth is Mizoguchi's fictional *Taki no Shiraito* or Leni Riefenstahl's famous "documentary,"

Triumph of the Will.[4] These are narratives that supposedly transcribe or document events.

In short, plausibility was a primary goal of both the modern film, which embraced figurality in order to discipline its power, and the modern novel *(kindai shôsetsu)*, which shunned it by substituting another, more abstract form of visuality. In Japan, plausibility was not accomplished without great difficulty, however; and it is important to understand why. A close look at how both filmic and novelistic techniques developed reveals the many problems involved in establishing such a natural logic of realistic narrative. Indeed, the first attempts to establish a plausible linearity in Japan were at best half-hearted. We know, for instance, that early films were spliced together with little or no concern about linear order, just as the novels and short stories of Natsume Sôseki, Shimazaki Tôson, and many other modern writers displayed curious breaks in their narrative flow, as if the flow of plot was never a preeminent concern. Some might be surprised to learn that when a section of a film had become worn out, it was sometimes replaced with footage from a completely different movie, with little regard given to the details of continuity. In the early stages, this seemingly arbitrary method of establishing order was not viewed as an insuperable problem. As long as the *benshi* could supply the necessary ligatures, the implausible narrativity of the film – that is, the rupture of its realistic linearity – could be patched over by external narration. With the development of talkies, and as the voice of the cinematic image became internalized and the celluloid images came to be endowed with speech, the *benshi* lost their prominence and function. And as this happened, the correlation between image and word became precise and fixed, and the freedom of discontinuity or rupture was greatly diminished. In other words, the increasingly linear nature of modern narrative came to require a precise correspondence between phoneme and grapheme. As talkies became increasingly sophisticated, as intertitles disappeared, the illusion of an actor actually mouthing the words heard by the audience was finally accomplished. Again, the goal of modernity is to gain a distinct voice.

This correspondence between word and picture, sound and body, marked an important moment in the semiotic development of modern consciousness. It changed the meaning of truth by making true replication *(shashin)* a matter of activity *(katsudô)*. That is to say, it made true life a process of progress rather than a static isolation. Re-presence, the constant realignment of reality and ideology, became a higher priority than presence; and the representation of the truth came to be seen (and simultaneously heard) as an inevitable sweep of time and process. Needless to say, the effects of this development were stunning. More than ever before, the world could be taken down and taken in. Life could be documented, more truly on film than on paper. For the first time, both the sound and sight of reality could be captured and controlled – not as a disordered collection of impressions, not even as someone's best discursive opinion, but as a continuous stream of true experience, of actual events, whether collected on the battlefield or within the movie studio. The energy for this new reality emerged here in the melding of the strengths of the phoneme and grapheme: "what could become" actually formed the modern sense of "what actually is." The development of the modern world happened as if it were inevitable, a manifest destiny.

When speaking of signs and their significance, it is hard to determine what precedes and what follows, what is cause and what is effect. One thing we can surely say, however, is that the extraordinary attempts that have been made to document even the most hideous atrocities and private secrets of the modern period followed from a desire for completeness that was conditioned by motion pictures themselves. This passion for improvement (and violence) through integration served to satisfy each viewer, one at a time, as a modern individual. And yet this service to privacy occurred within a roomful of other viewers held in a common darkness that could grant only a partial illusion of the private. The show house, this strange, new public-yet-private space, appropriately expressed and produced the required atomization of human life as the modern individual gave himself up to larger, inclusive, and even comprehensive ideological systems – nationalism, capitalism, communism, fascism, and so forth. The show house provides us, then, with a useful metaphor for modernity, this self-aggrandizing posture that seduces and even requires the individual to give himself up *in order to have and to belong to* a privileged view of life in progress. Before the spectacle of the integrated grapheme and phoneme, the viewer in the darkened room, surrounded by the shadows of other viewers, found a new pleasure of surrender to this utterly confident and forceful plausibility.

We still have not come to a state of complete honesty or clarity about the role that mass culture plays in the role of mass murder. Perhaps it is because we are convinced that both developments were (and will continue to be) necessary. What those who persist in clinging nostalgically and uncritically to the modern do not understand, however, is that even though we might wish to continue to benefit from the improvements of modernity, the continued interaction of the grapheme and the phoneme (as propelled by modern institutions such as the show house) will necessarily reconfigure the semiotic field in ways that will eventually make a modern view untenable, or at least not as persuasive as it once was. I would argue that it has already done this in postindustrial societies. Specifically speaking, motion pictures have done so by doing what they do best: pushing the features of motion so far ahead that narrativity collapses, leaving us in a state of disorder as to plot. As a supreme irony of modern life, such progress leaves us in a state of confusion that somehow makes sense. A new discontinuous and even fragmented visual regime returns us to a heightened mythical awareness of narrativity. Even more to the point, it leads us to a yearning for presence, even at the price of disconnection, even at the risk of modernity's demise and the end of the truth of improvement.

This readjustment of narratively deployed signs inevitably took place within the development of motion pictures, as the medium progressed from silent film, to talkies, to films such as Itami Jûzô's *Dandelion (Tanpopo,* 1986), with its mix of syntactic and paratactic narrative styles. If the birth of *katsudô shashin* is a reactive attempt by the grapheme to secure an alliance with the powers of the phoneme, the further development of motion pictures toward visual discontinuity seems to suggest that the grapheme, in its relationship to the phoneme, has become equally important and perhaps even the dominant member of this union. To be sure, the spatial, associative powers of the picture were always appealing, even as they gained motion in the process of coming into synchronization with oral (and written) narrative patterns. Considerations of cinematic editing as a process of "montage" by Eisenstein and Pudovkin in the 1920s, for instance, mark an early assertion of the ability of pictures to speak for themselves in a way that does not privilege the phoneme and its narrative regime. In postwar Japan, the surrealist novelist and playwright Abe Kōbō spoke to the issue of the grapheme's power by noting the success of pictures in forming their own structures of coherence: "The cinematic language called montage was discovered in the search for expression outside the framework of the story [sutôri], and I think it is because of this discovery that film was destined to become the champion of modern art."[5]

By "modern art," Abe, Japan's most prominent proponent of the avant-garde, more precisely meant what I would call modern*ism,* or that international and visually oriented rebellion that occurred within (and as an important part of) the realm of an essentially phonocentric modern development. The corrosive desire to find a mode of expression "outside the framework of the story," an impulse that is apparent in Abe's highly visual and often nonsensical novels and plays, becomes a part of mass culture by way of, for instance, Teshigahara's cinematic version of Abe's *Woman in the Dunes* (*Suna no onna,* 1962), in which the spareness of the script is balanced by the eloquence of sand and the human body. Surely, the constraints of "story" are felt here in this evocative and slowly paced film, which spends as much time going nowhere as possible. In this narrative of entrapment, the press of scientific inquiry and of progress is interrupted by the lyricism of space.

The daring, experimental attempts of "modern art" to critique the press of modernity have not remained on the margin but have penetrated through to the center of contemporary culture. We might wish to see this as a shift from one ideology to another – from a militaristic emperor worship to a pacifistic reign of democracy, for instance. But the magnitude of change that has taken place might indicate a different attitude toward ideology in general. Present-day Japan is, as Masao Miyoshi has lamented in his discussions of Murakami Haruki and other present-day writers, an age of the surface, an age of nothing but style.[6] In truth, as the phonocentric thrust of print culture is weakened by the prevalence of the new videographic culture of television, cinema, anime, and the World Wide Web, a new logic of "style" and "playfulness" asserts itself in ways that are reminiscent of the early-modern period and of a time prior to the promises of mass ideology. Depth is no longer a pressing issue since visibility, rather than invisibility, has come to reign. Even if we are still sitting in the darkened show house, the private invisibility of our seeing is being seen.

The ongoing negotiation between word and picture, phoneme and grapheme, seems to have robbed the viewer of anonymity, without which, modern power dwindles like a colony. The mystique of modern consciousness – the self-negating yet aggrandizing will to give oneself up in order to become an empowered and necessary part of the comprehensive whole – has been illuminated for what it is: a choice of narrative possibilities, an investment, the buying of a certain reality. From the very start of Itami's *Tanpopo,* we are made to think critically of the private-yet-public show house. We see a gangster and his lover settling in to watch a film; and immediately the gangster, peering directly into the camera, sees us seeing him, "Ah, so you're in a movie theater, too" (see Figure 7). Everything and everywhere has become a movie, including the kaleidoscopic one that supposedly flashes before our eyes at the moment of death. That final movie, *"ningen saigo no eiga,"* will be seen by the gangster as he dies of gunshot wounds in the final moments of the film. Within this all-too-conscious symmetry, this blatant assertion of "style," we realize that vision is not ours alone but is available to anyone who pays the price of admission. We understand that the motion picture is a framed pleasure that we pay for. As such, it is not to be disturbed by any unpaid-for and out-of-frame intrusions. When the gangster threatens a noisy potato-chip-eating moviegoer who shares the space of the same show house, he threatens him with violence: "Make that noise during the show and I'll kill you!" And when he warns his lover not to disturb the final movie that will surely come at his moment of death, we are reminded of (and reduced to?) life's evanescence, now measured by our ability, pathetic, enamored of violence, and limited as it is, to get our money's worth.

Perhaps it is not man but man's money that is really the measure of all things. Created at the peak of Japan's so-called economic miracle, just

7. Viewing the viewer; Itami Jûzô, *Tanpopo* (1986).

prior to the collapse of stock and real estate prices and the bursting of that nation's economic bubble in 1990, Itami's work critiques Japanese society with a warm and understanding humor that places us both within and without the capitalist structure of profitability. As expressed by the main narrative line of the film, the unambiguous goal of the protagonist is success. Tanpopo struggles to make a go of the noodle shop that her deceased husband has left to her. On a dark and stormy night, she meets Goro, a truck driver passing through, and becomes inspired to turn her shop into "the real thing" *(honmono).* To this end, all energy is expended, all necessary outlays of capital are made, all knowledge is utilized, all tactics are employed. In the 1980s, an era of *karôshi,* or "death by overwork," Itami's characters are willing to give their all to this cause. On beyond Goro and his younger partner Gan, there is Piskin (Tanpopo's childhood friend), Sensei (a failed physician turned spiritual leader of the homeless), and Shôhei (now a chauffeur but at one time a practiced cook). Everyone gives their best effort. Everyone contributes so that, in the end, Tanpopo realizes the capitalist dream of establishing a profitable business.

This single-minded intensity of all participants is a joke, of course. The comic point in this improbability – why should all these people help her? – is that this ramen shop and the world that both contests and supports it are *majime* (serious) to the point of being humorous. (Figure 8 shows Tanpopo's single-minded dedication to success.) Itami relies on exaggeration, broadness of comedic action, and a plot that is incessantly focused on one thing and one thing only. Consequently, issues of non-work-related desire cannot have an obvious part in Tanpopo's relationship to either Goro or Piskin. Romance, which is intimated throughout the main narrative, is pushed off to the side. Piskin, the least sympathetic of Tanpopo's two possible suitors, actually raises the question of love. Following his second fistfight with Goro, a manly one-on-one that allows these two to become partners in their attempt to help Tanpopo, he asks, "Are you in love with Tanpopo?" To this, Goro replies, "I just want to make her shop into the real thing. That's all." Being *majime,* they cannot let another (i.e., a non-ramen-related) desire interfere. *Majime* rejects play, or, perhaps better stated, it abhors any form of play that is not equally *majime,* whether overtly sexual or not.

But, as I mentioned, this plot-driven narrativity is only a part of the whole. While the issue of erotic distraction is pushed out of the main

8. Tanpopo's single-minded dedication to success; Itami Jûzô, *Tanpopo* (1986).

story, it is openly revealed in three *renga*-like (or linked verse) sequences of vignettes that accumulate around the linearity of business-as-usual. In the first, for instance, a group of businessmen pass by Goro and Tanpopo, who are in the middle of physical exercises, getting in shape for the challenge ahead. The camera follows the group (thus leaving the main story behind) to a French restaurant in which the *kaban-mochi,* the lowest man on the company pole, performs a comic inversion by embarrassing his superiors with his superior (though frightfully tactless) knowledge of French cuisine. After his betters all unimaginatively order the same meal of flounder, he chooses from the menu like a connoisseur. The camera follows the waiter to another part of the restaurant, in which a *mana kyôshitsu,* a finishing school, is in progress. Another inversion occurs as a middle-aged Japanese woman, an expert on Western manners, is undercut by the eagerness of a real Westerner to prove that he can eat noodles the Japanese way. Through this scene, a hotel worker passes; and the camera follows him to the next vignette, where, in the secrecy of their hotel room, the white-clad mobster and his lover, introduced to us in the film's initial scene, use the food brought to them by room service to heighten their pleasure in lovemaking (see Figure 9).

This motion picture has a dual structure, by which the strongly teleological motivation of Tanpopo, Goro, and company, is subsumed (and thereby amplified) within a larger contemplation of seriousness that is

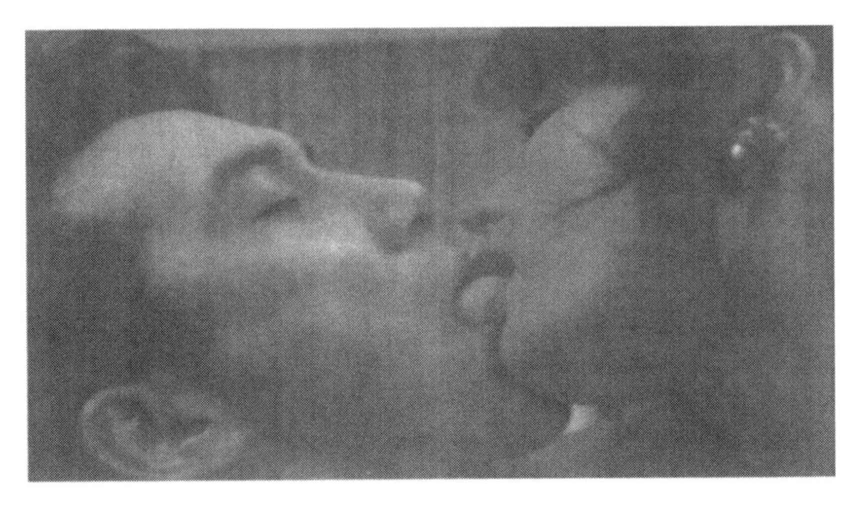

9. Food heightens pleasure; Itami Jûzô, *Tanpopo* (1986).

made possible by these extra scenes. (Already, by calling them "extra," I have given away my own lingering modern orientation.) They are like charms added to a bracelet, like moments of play and festivity that punctuate the routine of economic production. Evocative and vivid, they create a lyrical rupture in the otherwise dedicated tale. Their structural function is to produce a widening of the main story so that, in the end, even the story of capitalism seems to be contained within a context of seemingly endless, arbitrarily discovered performances.

From another vantage point, we could say that, in a way, these vignettes form their own narratives, not in a linear fashion but in an associative manner that is reminiscent of much Edo-period writing. The logic of these outbursts of play is not causal and syntactic but associational and paratactic. Their poetic nature reminds us of narrative methods used by earlier modern writers such as Ihara Saikaku, who was first a *haikai no renga* (comic-linked-verse) poet and later a story writer; or Santô Kyôden, who, as a visual artist, writer, and entrepreneur, was one of many multifaceted eighteenth-century artists who were similarly influenced by the associational and highly visual linking techniques of communal poetry.

Of course, the accumulation of scenes in *Tanpopo* is also reflective of technologies that did not exist in the early modern era. Its own brand of *nioi-zuke,* a traditional *renga* (linked verse) term for "link by fragrance" (or mental association), is filmic in the way the materiality (and seeming arbitrariness) of the camera, moving from scene to scene, are heightened, thus sharpening the sense that food fascination, in its conjunction with the thematic of *majime,* is impressively omnipresent. Itami gives the impression that he could have sent the camera anywhere, and it would have found scenes of the same inexhaustible fascination for food. In the end, in the late stages of capitalist development, the massiveness of culture, generated by the essentially maniacal productivity of mechanical production, has established a state of uniformity that develops from an earlier condition of difference. That is to say, it has accomplished this satisfying arbitrariness in a paradoxical (but all too familiar) way: as the result of progress and by way of a model of economic and social development that begins to establish modernity or a sense of comprehensiveness by way of knowable and measurable differences – progressive and traditional, high culture and low culture, urban and rural, domestic and foreign, and so on. In short, with the development of modernity comes the emergence of mass culture. And in a state of mass-produced culture, the important differences between things eventually become blurred.

These vignettes are alike in that they express an appropriately undying interest in food – curry-flavored potato chips, sole meunière, whipped-cream-dipped breasts, turtle soup, Peking duck, raw oysters, and on and on. From the first scene to the fifty-seventh, we are bombarded with things to eat, so that we might say that all the scenes in *Tanpopo* are about food, even though it does not follow that they all clearly support the plot of the main narrative. Some viewers might be bothered because everything in *Tanpopo* is not plot-centered, not contributing to the progression of the main story. When I show this film to my students, some are genuinely confused by it. By now, however, theirs is becoming a familiar and useful confusion that, like the emergence of character that occurred at the dawn of the modern era, is forming its own patterns of signification and comprehensibility. The popularity of Quentin Tarantino's *Pulp Fiction* provides a marker of how the associational, paratactic logic of the image is disrupting the linear, syntactic logic of the story in an appealing way. The same might be said of television advertisements, music videos, and such, with their quick enumeration of sometimes not-so-obviously connected visual clues.

To reinforce an earlier point, the confluence of *Tanpopo*'s two narrative styles is an inevitable development in the ongoing play between phoneme and grapheme. It marks a reassertion of pictocentrism that emerges by way of the grapheme's eventual dominance over the phoneme within the evolution of the motion picture. Even within the span of the modern period – from the beginnings of urban life in the 1500s to the onset of videographic culture in the 1970s – the give-and-take has occurred in constant reaction to developing technologies. Here, the seamless flow of reality that was accomplished by the confluence of motion and pictures has finally led to the sort of associational discourse that happens to lie outside the realm of story, to use Abe's words. Abe would probably view this emergence of the visual as a progressive force. Yet the point that must not be lost in our appreciation of the cutting edge is that the narrative structure of *Tanpopo*'s most experimental portions echoes a well-established narrative pattern.

As a rhetorical device, it was called *-zukushi.* This term, a gerund for *tsukusu* (to use up, to exhaust), refers to one of the ways in which linkage *(tsukeai)* was accomplished in the writing of *haikai no renga. -Zukushi* is an exhaustive listing, where one thing is presented many times, in each case from a slightly different angle. The connections between one example and the next are made loosely through their commonality, rather than by a more linear orientation of cause and effect. *Tanpopo* might be, for instance, an example of *tabemono-zukushi,* where an exhaustive repetition of food produces the appropriate narrative effect.

Needless to say, the looseness of this sort of linkage disrupts the more seamless logic of plot. In works where *-zukushi* plays an important part, a generic blurring of the difference between lyric (spatial) and epic (temporal) elements occurs. It would not be an exaggeration to say that within the Japanese tradition such mixing of poetry and prose is common, perhaps even characteristic.[7] In a work such as Saikaku's *A Woman Who Loved Love* (*Kôshoku ichidai onna,* 1686), which is not usually seen by Japanese scholars as an example of *-zukushi,* we can nevertheless clearly detect his background as a *haikai* poet in both the visually rich texture of his style and in the structure of this narrative. This work is a character study *(katagi),* an early attempt to answer the quintessential modern question: What is a human being? It is made up of an exhaustive recounting of the amorous encounters of one woman's life, and is a *-zukushi* in this expanded sense of a list.[8] Other works, such as *The Man Who Loved Love* (*Kôshoku ichidai otoko,* 1686), *Five Women Who Loved Love* (*Kôshoku gonin onna,* 1686), and *Japan's Eternal Storehouse* (*Nihon eitaigura,* 1688), share similar qualities of listing. While we might be tempted to call these works episodic in nature, these units do not always build, one upon the next, as episodes do. Their manner of organization is not necessarily concerned with continuity and with the plausibility of epiclike connection.

Clearer examples of *-zukushi* are found in the puppet plays of Chikamatsu Monzaemon. Consider how the play *Love Suicides at Sonezaki* (*Sonezaki shinjû,* 1703) begins with an extensive listing of thirty-three temples, delivered (orally, by the narrator) in a rhythmical, almost trancelike fashion. The naming of these temples by the narrator establishes the emotional tone of the play. It also establishes an appropriate imaginative space.[9] As suggested by Donald Keene's omission of this opening portion from his translation of the original text, this lyrical moment, "virtually unrelated to the remainder of the play," is not absolutely crucial, although it would be hard to argue that its presence does not matter.[10] In another play, *Love Suicides at Amijima* (*Shinjû ten no Amijima,* 1721), we encounter an exhaustive listing that occurs within the body of the play; and in this case, the rupture that is caused in the forward movement of the work is clear. Having made the decision to kill themselves, Jihei and Koharu make their way through the city of Osaka to their place of death by way of an exhaustive listing of bridges. There are twelve bridges in all: Tenjin-bashi, Umeda-bashi, Midori-bashi, Sakura-bashi, Shijimi-bashi, Ôe-bashi, Naniwa-bashi, Funairi-bashi, Horikawa-bashi, Tenma-bashi, Kyô-bashi, and Onari-bashi. By way of this *hashi-zukushi,* which supposedly marks a physical movement toward a place, we are allowed to dwell upon the impending suicide of two lovers and to consider the contrasting bustle of life and activity that these bridges express. More than simply marking their physical trip to the water where they will die, this list is meant to heighten the intensity of emotion and our ability to sympathize with the doomed lovers by placing ourselves into the same emotional space. In this function, *-zukushi* is not so unlike the *mie* that takes place on the kabuki stage, where a visual summing up and an arresting of forward movement also occur.

The importance of the oral component in this sort of exhaustive listing supplies an important point of contrast with what happens centuries later in a film like *Tanpopo.* In Itami's *tabemono-zukushi,* a similar kind of lyrical rupture is established through exhaustive listing; but it is accomplished more visually. That is, the intended effect is produced by providing images of different (or should we say similar?) items, by concatenations of vignettes that slow the forward movement of the main story in three places. While the audience of a puppet play is left to imagine the listed images, a list of temples or bridges in a motion picture can actually be shown on the movie screen. This development toward the use of pictures, to accomplish what was once done by the human voice, marks a significant challenge to the modern reign of the phoneme. In Chikamatsu's day, the sound of a name and its connection to one's knowledge of a particular temple or bridge might have been enough to carry the day; but in the Japan of the 1980s, the space of Tokyo is established with panoramic shots of the city, and with these related food scenes that take place in parks, apartments, stores, and so on.

Of course, there is no way to understand the visual listing that distinguishes a film like *Tanpopo* without considering its precedents in both the puppet theater and in pictures that did *not* move. Before motion pictures came into being, there were woodblock prints, which were not placed into motion, yet were similarly developed, within a culture of the cliché or mass printing.[11] Motion pictures, woodblock prints, and printed books all have, as a basis for their existence, the mechanical production of sameness. Given the tendency toward exhaustive listing in the works of playwrights such as Chikamatsu, we should not be surprised to find that the technique of *-zukushi* was also prevalent in early-modern woodblock prints as well. For both artistic and commercial reasons, visual artists often made series of similar images that centered on one object or subject. In this form of organization, the modern concern for alterity is continued with reference to that which is similar. For instance, series of beautiful women *(bijin-zukushi),* series of views of Mt. Fuji, or series of domestic workers indicate a widespread and sustained interest in seeking subtle differences among things that are alike.

This movement from a base of sameness toward examples of difference represents an important paradigm of modernity that has not often been discussed since its importance has been hidden by the phonocentrism of modern discourse, which has a converse logic. That is to say, modernity is usually envisioned as a movement from difference toward sameness, as in *E pluribus unum,* where unanimity emerges by way of various pluralities, and where discovery eventually leads to the assimilation of the Other.[12] Within this regime of discovery, tribes come together as folk, regionalisms become covered over by nationalisms, dialects disappear into a state of standard language, newly discovered lands become appropriated as colonies of larger empires, and so forth, so that the newly discovered plenitude of the modern world is unified by ideological systems that place each element of the whole in relationship to all others. This is, of course, precisely the function of the darkened show house, which gives to each customer the empowered position of the viewer, the perspective for which plurality becomes one. As we sit before the flickering screen, the opportunity is there for us to consider the possibility that numerous viewers are seeing the same thing, and that their identity as members of a group that has paid to see is similarly ensured by their common purchase. We join in laughter and tears, signaling our collective humanity to each other. We are fans. And yet, in the dark, we just as easily forget about anybody but ourselves – ourselves and the screen.[13]

In an age of mechanical reproduction, the printing of books and visual images, along with the development of motion pictures, usher in a time which eventually, like Itami's white-clad mobster, makes us see ourselves seeing the Other. The printer's cliché, the physical form by which visual plenitude of the modern age is pounded out as an identical series, eventually poses a threat to the ideology of sameness-through-difference by divulging the mechanics of modernity, and by producing a state of mass culture. It shows, in other words, how, as an extension of the finding-and-conquering logic of discovery, the new Other reality eventually becomes a sameness. Following from the plenitude of mechanical reproduction – the stamping out of steel automobile fenders, the printing of posters, the developing of photographs – the uniformity and even banality of modern life (as highlighted by the repeated soup cans of Andy Warhol) emerges as an inevitable awareness of the artificial and forced nature of perspectival systems. In the end, it is our atomized monotony, just as much as the grandness of imperialistic or fascistic splendor, that becomes the focus of the artist. Here we arrive at Abe's sense of the "modern" and the importance of motion pictures to an attempt to get outside narrativity. Eventually, the wholeness and plausibility of modernity becomes fractured; and the linear, plot-oriented narrative becomes subject to disruption. The very notion of the "real" comes into question. Reality is framed by quotation marks, now implicated as false by the processes of truth that made reality possible in the first place.

Sameness-from-difference (as in the realm of the modern state, with its engulfing and unifying vision) gives way to the kind of difference that comes from sameness (in what, for example, Miyoshi deems the lamentable realm of style).[14] Depth vanishes, and all becomes a matter of surface – a change of clothes, a consumerist choice of multiple options. Which drink? Which candy? Will the popcorn be buttered or plain? As we become aware of ourselves watching Itami's film, we ourselves become framed by the framing function of the motion picture itself – this mechanical listing of the same-yet-changing object and its deep logic of -*zukushi*. We become framed as viewers when we gain awareness of the means of production by which the illusion of reality, which must always include us, is created. This framing, this rupture in the motion of the motion picture, finds a metaphor in the mechanical breakdown that interrupts the free flow of images. The lights of the show house are brought up to bright. We look at each other awkwardly, almost embarrassed by being caught in the act of watching.

At whatever level, this new awareness of the constructed nature of what we are seeing comes poststructurally – following a challenge to the authority of the author, and after an intense focus on form, on the function of narrative, and on the materiality of expression. In other words, postmodern vision comes only after a new awareness of production takes hold. Consequently, a new consciousness of materiality – the integrity of line, and light – must occur, along with a novel awareness of the artificiality of art. These two points – materiality and artificiality – are never long forgotten by those who actually make works of art. For this reason, the deconstructive enlightenment of poststructuralist critics remains largely unimpressive to those who have understood all along that the truth has been, and will always be, a choice of possibilities. After all, a necessary condition for the making of reality is not having to be always in the dark.

But if we can return to the particular historical moment of Itami's film, it is not an accident that this enlightenment came at a time when Japan had the economic power to reconsider its relationship to the world and to review its own success. Precisely because of its ability to frame the viewer and to disrupt the otherwise seamless flow of cinematic illusion, *Tanpopo* effectively narrated both the semiotic and thematic complexities of Japan in the 1980s. This was a time when the grapheme began to reassert its position by way of this form of narrative that began with its suppression, and it was also the time for Japan to emerge victoriously as a participant in a "universal" capitalist narrative of postwar recovery and economic growth. In other words, by 1980, the raison d'être of the motion picture had moved from motion to the picture; just as a transition occurred from a discourse of catching up with the West to one of the so-called theories of Japaneseness *(Nihonjinron)* and their obsession with cultural essences. At the same time, the sophistication of Japan's cinematic production led us to a situation where the motion picture could begin to point to its own constructed, not necessarily linear, nature.

These changes mark profound social transformations. By the 1980s, the success of consumerism, driven by an almost manic dedication to increased production, generated a culture of affluence in which practically all Japanese could not only participate but from which they could also take their identity as members of a prosperous, ethically undisturbed middle class.[15] Economic success engendered an aura of cultural sameness, a superiority that sought multiplicity from a common base of experience and value and established itself with a flurry of *Nihonjinron,* or theories of Japaneseness. While "foreign" influences continued to be naturalized by this Japaneseness, they were also exalted as components of another life of play, a field of avocational pursuits that were pursued with equally ardent attention. From a newly configured base of globally gathered common culture, the pursuit of difference appeared as a fragmentation or, to use Ueno Chizuko's words, "differentiation within equalization," supposedly a (welcome) mark of postmodern culture.[16]

In summary, I have argued that the motion picture emerged within the sweep of the phonocentric modern era. It did so by employing mechanical means to make pictures acceptably narrative, which is to say, intimately allied with the passing of time. In this sense, the essence of motion pictures was motion rather than pictures. The greater purpose and effect of this new semiotic configuration was to make modernity seem even more possible and plausible than even the novel was able to do. By way of the motion picture, a sense of reality was established through a seamless continuity, and as the natural working out of various ideological formations that encouraged progress toward various goals, such as capitalism, communism, imperialism, and so forth. One common end of these modern systems was the assimilation of difference by first discovering and then engulfing it. But within this utterly believable discourse of progress, the grapheme eventually reasserted its spatial powers of presence to disrupt this progress. It did so partly because of the way in which modernity was actually successful in producing a state of similarity: by presenting numerous copies or near copies of the same things. By slowing the speed of this construction of reality, or by disrupting continuity with less gradual (and therefore less plausible) transitions or connections, we have become aware of the motion picture's constituent frames and of the constructed nature of the narrative that is actually comprised of nothing more than an exhaustive listing of pictures. With this process of bringing space back into the motion picture, that is, making pictures less plausibly tied to time, we even become aware of the space of viewing: the show house and its specialized function of making the private individual a part of the public community. The show house is a central metaphor for the nature of modernity itself, for it bestows a sense of self while placing that self within a much larger atomizing system. It hides both the viewer and the mechanics of the motion picture in a totalizing darkness. At the moment when we become aware of this darkened space, as is inevitable when watching a motion picture such as Itami's *Tanpopo,* we are no longer alone in the darkness, but are aware of ourselves and of others, who might be seeing the same things differently, rather than seeing different things in the same way.

Perhaps what we should call postmodern is not simply the emergence of fragmentation and the end of linearity. More precisely, the decline of modernity seems to be marked by the coexistence and obvious clash of syntactic and paratactic regimes of expression in which the tensions between "from many comes one" and "from one comes many" are allowed to play themselves out at many semiotic levels. Surely, the incompatibilities do not get resolved as often as they simply get renamed. The anxieties of Japan in the 1980s are still very much alive today. They are encapsulated in familiar chains of paradox: without the individual there is no state, and without such a system of uniformity there can be no individual freedom; the abundance created by industrialization has created a poverty of choice, but only by way of this affluent poverty comes a true sense of spiritual abundance; and on and on. Seen at its best, the world of *Tanpopo* represents an inclusion of the homeless and the wealthy, the female and the male. It is about cooperation, accomplishing good deeds, and the softening of hearts. Seen at its worst, it is about a fiercely competitive world of success at all costs, disrupted by occasional fits of irrelevant, excessive behavior that decorate the chain of work as it rules within one of the most productive societies on earth. However we choose to understand the themes of this film, what we can no longer easily disagree upon is the way we have been seen as seers in the show house of modernity. Like the characters in *Tanpopo,* with its exhaustive listing of food, the "we" of modern consciousness has been framed.

NOTES

1. Here, *grapheme* refers to the visible, material component of the sign, such as a line. *Phoneme* refers to the invisible sound of the sign, such as the pronunciation of the word *sound.* My larger concern is to try to trace the development of modern consciousness by examining the way sign systems change over time, especially as measured in the changing mix of graphemic and phonemic elements. Modernity is phonocentric in the sense that, for instance, modern writing becomes less calligraphic and more uniformly transcriptive of colloquial speech. As I have argued elsewhere, this phonocentrism is antifigural, rejecting both illustration and classical figures of speech.
2. For more on Kunisada and Kyôden, see "Modern Japanese Literature on its Own Terms," *Revisionism in Japanese Literary Studies: Proceedings of the Midwest Association for Japanese Literary Studies* (West Lafayette: Purdue University Press, 1996), 230–52.
3. The reemergence of monstrosity in works of animation *(anime)* marks the end of this "lack" and indicates an openness about the artifice of motion pictures. As Susan Napier argues in her essay, metamorphosis of the body is particularly well suited to this genre. The monstrosity of *anime* counters the essential realism of the motion picture by making us aware of the movement from frame to frame.
4. This anesthetizing function is, of course, the purpose of modern narrative up until the time of writers such as Bertolt Brecht, who wished to disrupt the sympathy that could develop between an audience and an actor.
5. Abe Kôbô, *Sabaku no shisô* (Tokyo: Kôdansha, 1994), 287.
6. Masao Miyoshi, *Off Center* (Cambridge: Harvard University Press, 1991), 234–37.
7. Edwin McClellan notes this mixing of prose and more poetic passages a deeply rooted quality of even modern novels. See his reading of Shimazaki Tôson in "The Impressionistic Tendency in Some Modern Japanese Writers," *Chicago Review,* 17:4 (1965).
8. Of course, listing does not begin here. Jack Goody suggests that the forming of lists occurs as a consequence of writing at its earliest stages; see his *The Logic of Writing and the Organization of Society* (Cambridge: Cambridge University Press, 1986).
9. The importance of rhythm was brought to my attention by Keiko MacDonald.
10. Donald Keene, *The Four Major Plays of Chikamatsu* (New York: Columbia University Press, 1961), 39.
11. As pointed out by Svetlana Boym, the French *cliché* referred originally to "the typographic plate that allows multiple printings of pages, and also to the photographic negative. . . . The reproducibility of the cliché and the availability of mass reproduction form a necessary background for the Romantic

search for newness and for the cult of individual self-expression." Boym, *Common Places: Mythologies of Everyday Life in Russia* (Cambridge: Harvard University Press, 1994), 14.

12. This was my argument in an earlier study, "In the Scopic Regime of Discovery: Ishikawa Takuboku's *Diary in Roman Script* and the Gendered Premise of Self-Identity," *positions East Asian Cultures Critique* 2:3 Winter (1994), 542–69. Reprinted in *Formations of Colonial Modernity in East Asia,* ed. Tani Barlow (Durham: Duke University Press, 1997), 223–47.
13. We can hardly help wondering how long this privilege can last. Is it only becoming more private, as television and computer monitors become the principal means of delivery? Or does this intense privacy generate a new sense of community?
14. Irokawa Daikichi makes a similar observation: "Today the Japanese do not wear clothes to protect themselves from the elements; they do so to make themselves look beautiful, or because it gives them a sense of luxury, or because it gives them pleasure. The same is true of food: Japanese no longer eat to live. Today they all want to become gourmets. The emphasis in Japan today is on how to enjoy food and how to make food look beautiful so people can talk about it. The same can be said about sex and gender issues."

    Of course, there is nothing radically new about this dedication to style. We have only to consider Edo-period *sharebon, osetchi ryôri,* and *hyôbanki* to find well-established precedents. See Irokawa Daikichi, *Shôwa shi to tennô* (Tokyo: Iwanami Shoten, 1991). The quotation here is from Mikiso Hane and John Urda, trans., *The Age of Hirohito* (New York: Free Press, 1995), 60.
15. Here I am thinking of former Prime Minister Nakasone's famous comment that there were no "minorities" in Japan.
16. Ueno Chizuko, *Watashi sagashi gēmu,* (Tokyo: Chikuma shobô, 1987), 204.

PART TWO

REFLECTIONS OF IDENTITY

CHAPTER SEVEN

Where's Mama?

The Sobbing Yakuza of Hasegawa Shin

Alan Tansman

In the end, Chûtarô of Banba gets what we all want – Chûtarô of Banba gets his girl. For anyone from a psychoanalytically informed culture, Chûtarô's getting of his girl is a queasy scene to watch, for the girl Chûtarô gets is the girl we all don't know that we really want.

In the final shot of Inagaki Hiroshi's 1931 film *Mother Under the Eyelids (Mabuta no haha)*, mother and son embrace in a mist of tears and collapse to the ground, each folded into the other, a secure ball protected from the world. It has taken Chûtarô thirty years of destitution, wandering, and battles to reach the mother who abandoned him when he was five. In those years his losses have been great: he has forgone romance, conjugal love, and progeny, and has never settled down. In the course of the movie he travels to Edo looking for his mother, defending weak women and mistaking them for the real thing. To each he gives change from the purse he carries, as if purchasing their sympathy and paying down for the final product. The end of Chûtarô's longing demands the final sacrifice of his development as a man. In his end he returns to his beginning. Chûtarô has no choice but to return home to his mother, for he embodies his home and his name is inscribed on his identity. He is Chûtarô of Banba.

Mother Under the Eyelids, first written as a play and a novel by Hasegawa Shin in 1929, was staged hundreds of times and filmed repeatedly between 1931 and 1936. What accounts for the popularity of this hero who does not develop, and of this narrative that leads, through circles and repetitions, back to his beginning? Why have fifteen film versions been made of Hasegawa's play *Kutsukkake Tokijirô,* the tale of a poor gambler who lives his life to help a woman he has made a widow, a woman with tuberculosis who disappears from his sight only to appear at the end, deep in snow, plucking a samisen? Why, between 1929 and 1940, were seventy-six films made from Hasegawa Shin's plays and novels? Even given the rapid and voluminous production of films in these years, the numbers are striking. Hasegawa Shin wrote in a variety of genres, about violent samurai and suffering lovers. But the genre associated with him, and to which he gave name and fame (if not birth) in 1928, with the play *Traveling Shoes (Matatabi no zôri),* is the *matatabi mono,* the tale of the wandering yakuza in search, often, of a lost mother.

The tradition of popular literature criticism has seen in the *matatabi mono,* and in Hasegawa Shin, both deep connections to the concrete conditions of local life and universal meanings that transcend Japan. The popular novelist Osaragi Jirô, among others, argues that the *matatabi mono* are universal stories of the poor.[1] The heroes of Hasegawa's *matatabi mono* are gamblers – a convention that goes back to Hasegawa's own 1913 *The Gamblers (Bakuchi bachin),* featuring a yakuza as a hero; then to the gambler novels of the 1890s; and before that to the oral tale-telling *(kôdan)* tradition. Hasegawa's heroes' fighting spirit reveals their connections to the swashbuckling *chambara* genre, but they are weepy characters, and their loyalty is not to a lord, an emperor, or a state, but to the weak.[2] In Hasegawa's own words, the yakuza hero is "a man who is unproductive *(hiseisanteki),* usually illiterate, wearing a crown of thorns *(ibara).*"[3] His heroes serve women gallantly, and thus are anomalies in popular Japanese narratives. Satô Tadao, the hagiographic biographer of Hasegawa, praises his heroes for their emotional and ethical depth, their devotion not to abstract principles but to concrete situations of distress and to the discovery of their own selves in those situations.[4] This devotion to the concrete as opposed to the abstract is what marks Hasegawa, his heroes, and popular culture, as authentic in the worlds of popular literature and culture.

A genre that features the free movement of gamblers on the road who serve no master higher than themselves but only women in distress (and their own desires to regain an ideal), the *matatabi mono* seems to mark a resistance to a state calling increasingly for unified devotion to an emperor and a higher cause. Indeed, in *Mother Under the Eyelids,* Chûtarô finally gives up his sword for his frail old mother. Yet his giving up of the sword for the mother, I will argue, does not represent a rejection of militarist self-sacrifice. Rather, it denotes a redirecting of the passion for devotion to the state onto a body to which one feels as deeply connected as a citizen ideally should be to the Emperor. The movie repeatedly pauses for intense moments of emotional and bodily connection, so much so that what precedes these moments seems largely irrelevant. It can do this because it relies on generic conventions, understood by the audience, that allow for the foreshortening of the linear time of plot for the static space of scenes. Audiences who repeatedly saw films in this genre may have absorbed the emotional power of such scenes of physical bonding with a body one served. Here may be found the ideological import of the genre – the aesthetic dimension of politics that needs to be assessed in order to understand that politics.

Mother Under the Eyelids belongs to a film lineage that includes perhaps the greatest film about obsessive devotion, Alfred Hitchcock's *Vertigo.* While the *matatabi mono* were praised by critics for their concrete connections to everyday actuality, and while it can be argued that they take part in their political moment, the genre does seem to belong to a larger imaginative universe. But the *matatabi mono* were most certainly creations of a specific time in Japan, the late 1920s and the early 1930s, during which cultural products cutting across genres evoked images of loss and longing and of solutions to that longing; and the genre's particular popularity during that time (only one of these was made between 1941 and 1950, their content deemed first insufficiently prowar, and then, after the war, too feudalistic) can be linked to social and political contexts.

The narratives upon which the films were based drew from a well of a particular imagination. The figure of Hasegawa Shin has been seen by critics and audiences to lend an aura of authenticity to his narratives and to the films based on them. He has been evoked in writings on popular culture as belonging to the same local world of popular struggle as that of his characters. He himself was rumored in his lifetime to have been a yakuza, and his life story guaranteed to his audience that he was one of the people. Born in 1884 of working-class parents (he lived until 1963), he spent only a few years in school, worked as a laborer, and became a journalist at age seventeen at the *Yokohama Miyako Shinbun,* where he came into contact with other progenitors of popular literature, or *taishû bungaku.* He quit in 1926, and worked with Shirai Kyôji on the publication of *Popular Arts (Taishû Bungei).* By his forties Hasegawa was a successful playwright and novelist. His lack of education and his experience with manual laborers and their codes of loyalty have marked him, for critics of *taishû bungaku,* as authentically popular in his sensibilities.

Hasegawa learned his craft in a world of journalism that saw the beginnings of popular literature, and in a city, Yokohama, responsible for producing some of Japan's most important popular artists, including Yoshikawa Eiji, Shibozawa Kan, Osaragi Jirô, and the *enka* singer Misora Hibari. Critic Hiraoka Masaaki, himself a great lover of Yokohama and its popular culture, has called Hasegawa the Charlie Parker hipster of Yokohama, and the genre he created, the *matatabi mono,* his bebop.[5] This musical analogy may be apt, for Hasegawa's work has been thought to be "authentically" linked to an oral tradition of storytelling belonging to "the people."

Popular literature, or *taishû bungaku,* was born in the transformation from oral to written tales. One founding moment is thought to have occurred at Noma Kiyosada's magazine *Storytelling Club (Kôdan kurabu),* which published transcriptions of orally performed arts of tale-telling like *kôdan, naniwabushi,* and *rôkkyoku.* When the transcribers *(sokkisha)* responsible for recording *kôdan* went out on strike in 1913, only two years after the magazine began, Noma replaced them with writers from the *Miyako Shinbun* like Hasegawa Shin, who created what came to be called *shinkôdan,* or "new *kôdan.*" This, combined with the *ren'ai shôsetsu* (romance novel) and the *tsûzoku shôsetsu* (popular novel), became the *taishû shôsetsu* (literally, novel of the masses). The magazine went on to publish some of the gods of popular literature, including Yoshikawa Eiji and Edogawa Ranpo. The publication of the first chapters of Nakazato Kaizan's *Daibosatsu Pass (Daibosatsu tōge)* in 1913 (it was left incomplete with his death in 1941) marked the end point of the oral tradition and of popular literature's link to the oral performing arts of *jôruri, rôkkyoku, rakugo,* and *sekkyobushi.* It was in the mid-1920s, following the Great Kanto Earthquake and the explosion in readership of mass-circulation newspapers and magazines, that writers from the *Miyako Shinbun* and elsewhere, including Nakazato Kaizan and Hasegawa Shin, transformed popular literature into an industry.

Hasegawa began writing in this mixed milieu that included the remains of the verbal arts, or *wagei;* the *shinkôdan;* and the modern novel, already in full swing. Satô Tadao argues that in his early work, at least, Hasegawa owed more to the oral word than to the written word.

From the oral tradition he drew the melancholy heritage of Buddhist tale-telling in *sekkyobushi,* and the *kôdan*'s eschewal of philosophical musings about the meaning of the self and its concrete approach to spiritual questions. The more he wrote, however, the more Hasegawa lost that original orality, as an analysis of the stylistic changes not only in his plays, but in his novels as well, reveals.[6] By 1930 he had transformed himself finally into a written stylist like Osaragi Jirô; and it is perhaps no coincidence that he then devoted his energies not to imaginative literature, but to works of historical reportage, including studies of revenge tales and of Japanese prisoners of war.

Hasegawa's biography lends his work an air of authenticity that partially accounts for the popularity of his stories. How else might their popularity be explained? Nostalgia for a time when one sacrificed all for one's mother, empathy for a strong man wracked by the pain of loss, and admiration for the perseverance needed to get back home, may have fueled the emotional appeal of his plots. Between 1931 and 1936, when the *matatabi mono* peaked, the dramatic movement of poor, unemployed populations between country and city left many people wandering along roads, without homes, longing for a secure place left behind. (Japan's last great famine occurred in 1934.) The trope of loss, longing, and homelessness pervaded culture both high and low in these years, from the *enka* songs of Koga Masao to the iconic statements of Kobayashi Hideo.

Nostalgia for a time when roads led not into a new and unknown future, but along well-trodden paths, may also have helped lift the "wandering yakuza" genre to its status as cultural archetype. Repeated viewings of essentially the same plot may have comforted audiences longing for a lost ideal as they watched their hero's repeated attempts to find his mother. Repetition could lull one into sensing that what was happening on screen had always happened and always would; it could take the viewer outside the time of linear development – modern time – and place him in the circular time of myth, wandering the old roads with a yakuza hero. If modernity, according to Marx, meant the annihilation of space by time, these films, which foreshortened linear development and concentrated on intense moments of emotion, brought back space and interrupted time. In these films, time, even the circular time of Chûtarô's wandering, stops, at least for moments, leaving us in spaces where linear development has been extinguished by the love between mother and child. Glossing the image of mother and son as they become one,

Chûtarô says to his mother at the end of *Mother Under the Eyelids*, "Only the love between mother and son can overcome the passage of time."

The appeal of these narratives, then, might be explained by their proffering of a moment of escape from the forward movement of linear time. In this regard, the narratives of Hasegawa Shin drew from a rhetoric of crisis shared by numerous contemporaneous writers, some of whom flirted with an aesthetics of fascism that evoked moments in which the individual's own time – his life – would be, or should be, beautifully extinguished through sacrifice to a greater force. This does not mean, necessarily, that Hasegawa's narratives are fascistic. Indeed, though the content of other popular works, such as Yoshikawa Eiji's *Miyamoto Musashi*, has been linked convincingly by William Darrell Davis, among others, to the values of militarism and authoritarianism, the link between Hasegawa's narratives, which seem to have little connection to contemporaneous reality, and politics, appears, on the face of it, obscure. The connections of Hasegawa's narratives to politics are intriguing precisely because they were *not* created to galvanize support for the war through, for example, what Davis calls the "monumental style"; they were not intended to "lay out a space for a specific, essentially religious purpose of inspiring the faithful and fortifying the rectitude of their belief."[7] The political content of Hasegawa's *matatabi mono* is almost imperceptible and their ideology almost unrecoverable. For this very reason, their prominence in their time raises questions about the relationship between art and politics.

Between 1931 and 1936 a citizenry was being formed to accept state demands for self-sacrifice in the name of home and Emperor. What seems worth exploring, then, is how Hasegawa's narratives, in print and transformed into film, might have helped prepare an audience to see and feel in ways that would more easily allow them to become citizens amenable to the ways of feeling and seeing that were being prepared for them by the state. An exact accounting of the ideological effects of the "wandering yakuza" genre would be impossible; even worse, it would be uninteresting. One can only entertain the suggestive possibility that cultural experience connects to ideology in films like *Mother Under the Eyelids* to the extent that it provides little doses of ideology that, in concert with other such doses across culture, molds minds and hearts. In *Mother Under the Eyelids* an audience was being formed to accept, and admire, a son's sacrifice for a mother who had rejected him and yet retained his loyalty and devotion – a mother who does not deserve to be loved, or at least to be the object of unalloyed devotion. With Chûtarô one feels the pain of one-sided love, the *kataomoi* that characterizes the Japanese citizen's relationship to his emperor. This is a love one learns to believe in but that one can express only from afar, and that one can only hope will be reciprocated.

This relationship between Emperor and citizen had been in the process of formation for decades. From the time of the creation of a unified national polity in the 1880s, citizens were being trained to feel and think by the content of state propaganda disseminated through education and the media. They were also being trained to see, through an orchestration of visual images of the Emperor. The dissemination of state ideology and the orchestration of state spectacle were, of course, only part of the mental and visual landscape in which citizens lived, and their efficacy cannot be assumed to have been absolute. Japanese living through the first decades of the twentieth century were also immersed in a vast array of ideas and images unrelated or contrary to those that the state wished upon them. Willy-nilly, they were being trained in ways of listening and seeing through popular art and film and through new styles of architecture and urban design.

In drawing a connection between viewers of film and actors in society we need to keep in mind that the relationship between citizen and audience is not transparent; each is not necessarily at the same stage of formation as the other: an unformed citizenry may also be an audience with highly developed aesthetic sensibilities; or, to the contrary, narrative comprehension can lag behind citizen formation. In the late 1920s and the 1930s, however, both the audience and the citizen were still being formed.

The viewers of *Mother Under the Eyelids* were seeing a film that was itself in formation. To call a film "in formation" should not be taken to mean that it lacks completion and is on the way to becoming a greater, more fully formed film; it implies no aesthetic judgment. *Mother Under the Eyelids* was made in the last years of the silent era in Japan; by 1929, talkies were a force to be reckoned with, and the *benshi* – the raconteurs (often more the stars and the draw of the movie than the movie itself) who accompanied movies with narration and dialogue – were breathing their dying breaths. The increased use of intertitles was a step away from the aurality of the *benshi* toward the visuality of a more cinematic language. *Mother Under the Eyelids* continued use of the *benshi,* along with dramatically drawn intertitles and a complex visual language, creates a dual perceptual universe, both visual and aural, that forces the spectator to decode on two registers. The film creates a cinematic space straddled between the purely visual and the aural. Its cinematic operations are in formation, asking questions about itself. Should it veil or unveil the mechanisms of its production? Its theatricality – both in its connection to the stage-acting techniques of kabuki and to the oral arts of *jôruri* and *nagauta* – carries with it reminders of the past outside the world of the film, what Walter Benjamin called the aura of pre-mechanically produced forms, which lends the feeling of authenticity the narrative attempts to evoke.

The film is symptomatic of its stage of formation and, therefore, like its viewers, not fully baked, though it must be cautioned here again that the relative formation of a film and that of its audience do not necessarily map one onto the other. As a film in the process of formation, *Mother Under the Eyelids,* in its very technology *as* a film, requires us to think through the problem of time, of temporality and history. Is the film lacking for being less than consistently formed? This question, raised by the apparatus of the film, is asked as well by the narrative: Is Chûtarô lacking for being less than fully formed? What will he become when he is completed?

From this simple question asked about a fictional character, I would like to make suggestions that might elucidate the relationships among a film genre, its hero, the Japanese audience, and the press of political and social forces at the time. For its contemporaneous audience (as for us), *Mother Under the Eyelids* was set in the past; it presented a narrative of nostalgia. Through this nostalgic fictional filter, I would like to see not the past, but the contemporaneous present that evoked it. That present was, in a word, modern, in this context meaning structured by an ordered, unified, commodified space that was also alienating. Chûtarô, the searcher for his past, is modern only to the degree that his desires are nostalgic, though he also belongs to a premodern past. The degree to which *Mother Under the Eyelids* reveals its modernity at the same time that it exerts its oldness is suggested by the way in which the premodern figure of Chûtarô acts like a newly born modern *flaneur* – though his observant wanderings are not through city streets but through the countryside and the small town. As a *flaneur,* born as a consumer of things and of views, he carries a purse of change to distribute to the women he mistakes for his mother, as if in exchange for the hope and attention they give him.

Chûtarô's world was not the world of Chûtarô's audience, but as the product of their world it could not but belong to it as well. *Mother Under the Eyelids* is the product of new forms of sensual apprehension, at the same time that it offers an escape from a newly transformed sensual landscape. Japan in the 1920s saw the birth of a vibrant visual culture, in film, photography, advertising, and the electric lighting of streets. Mirrors came into vogue; slums were cleared for clean and neat-looking apartments. Aural culture changed too, with the birth of radio and the recording industry and with the replacement of the acoustic voice by the recorded. In the 1930s these changes were even more dramatic, as subways coursed underground, elevators rode to the tops of buildings to afford panoramic views, and the Yamanote train line circled Tokyo. This was a world where the copy replaced the original, a world one could escape from into the "authentic" space of a Hasegawa narrative.[8] That authentic space offered the possibility of human connection.

Changes in space and perception were fueled in part by the increased use of trains. In *Parallel Tracks,* Lynne Kirby shows how in the early years of American cinema the railroad functioned as a "proto-cinematic phenomenon" in which passenger perception conditioned cinematic perception, allowing a visualization of simultaneity and a new consciousness of time.[9] In Japan, too, the train was a force of sensual integration and of social linkage and cohesion, but it also fractured the senses, and dislocated and disrupted social cohesion. In *The Private Room and the Stare (Koshitsu to manazashi),* Takeda Nobuaki describes how, by 1914 in Japan, trains had unified the nation and linked it to the outside world through the tracks of empire. Space had become ordered as well through the "life improvement" *(seikatsu kaizen)* movement, which commodified and thus ordered and unified living space. Yet like trains, these new spaces left residents of newly designed houses and apartments alienated from one another in private rooms. Takeda notes the loss, during these years, of direct visual interaction between people, and though this seems somewhat speculative, his larger point, about the emergence of the possibility of isolation, should be seriously considered when thinking about *Mother Under the Eyelids.*[10]

In *Ranpo and Tokyo (Ranpo to Tokyo),* Matsuyama Iwao sees this weakening of human relationships in the fiction of Edogawa Ranpo as resulting from a new urban landscape and its sensual stimuli. The world of *Mother Under the Eyelids,* in which no trains move forward, but people only walk, offers an escape from the dramatically different sensual landscape of reality: no tracks lead out of the old circular Edo roads, and the only movement the camera shows is that of the travelers along those roads who are looking for the past. Yet framing this nostalgic content, the film's form, its use of flashback, montage, and quick cutting, reveals modern technological underpinnings and a new spatial consciousness of simultaneity. Furthermore, submerged beneath the nostalgic depiction of a wandering gambler, looking for his mother, is the tale of modern people with few chances to look each other in the eye and engage one another. The folklorist Yanagida Kunio noted in 1931 that stares between strangers on the streets of cities had become more intense in recent years, as men, fearing contact with strangers, became self-conscious and looked at each other even more intensely than before, as if insisting they did not fear one another. The intensity of visual contact coincided with a decrease in actual fighting; physical had given way to visual exchange.[11] It is perhaps no coincidence that therapist Morita Sôhô began his treatment of the "fear of others syndrome" *(taijin kyôfushô)* – a most modern of illnesses, born of alienation and sensual separateness – in 1920. Fighting, in the *matatabi mono,* might thus be seen as the social art of lonely men on the road that, through stares and swords, offered one way of interacting with another. The connection Chûtarô seeks, however, is of a more enveloping kind.

The diagnosis that urban Japanese in the 1920s and 1930s suffered from alienation took its most intimate form in the description of a dulled or fractured sensuality, made most pointedly by Kuki Shûzô in his 1928 *The Structure of Iki (Iki no kôzô).* Kuki described a modern world where senses had been fractured, and saw in the aesthetics of the demimonde of Edo Japan the possibility of a world where senses were integrated, the body was whole, and art matched to the body's senses. Paradoxically, that aesthetic universe of *iki* required not a static sensibility of things being properly in their place, but a sensibility alive to unresolved tension. Paradoxically, then, to see *iki* in *Woman Under the Eyelids* is to see nostalgia for a world in the past still whole, as well as grounded in a fractured present-day world. It is when the tension created by Chûtarô's longing for his mother is resolved, when he meets her at the end of the movie, that *iki* gives way to its aesthetic opposite, *yabo* (boorishness). And it is there, paradoxically, at the moment of resolution, that the movie reveals the mechanism of its nostalgia and shows its ideological underpinning in the contemporary world. That is, it reveals a desire for stasis in a world of crisis. When the project of nostalgia is still in process, and Chûtarô is still on his way home, the present is occluded; when the project is completed and Chûtarô reaches his mother, it can be seen for what it is. A crack opens, and the present glimmers through.

Of all the senses, once unified but now broken apart, vision occupied central stage for writers like Hasegawa and Kuki. The complexity of urban stimulation demanded the power of visual dissection. The cure for this condition of sensual fracture and visual mastery, for the mystery writer Edogawa Ranpo's characters in the 1920s and 1930s, was to seek the contrary experience, a feeling of wholeness made possible, in part, by the shutting of the eyes, as Ranpo discusses in his "On the Tactile Arts" *(shokkaku geijutsuron):*

> Other than the art one sees with one's eyes, and the art one hears with one's ears, and the art one analyzes with one's mind, there should also be an art one touches with one's hand. It is strange indeed that we have given much thought to our sense of vision and not considered our sense of touch. Why is this? Of course because we have eyes; because we are not blind. If, like dogs, people had an acute sense of smell, an art of smell would have developed. And if we had no eyes, a far more developed art of the sense of touch would certainly have developed.[12]

In *Mother Under the Eyelids* the cure for sensual and existential dislocation is found in the body of the mother. Before getting to that body, an elaborate dance of desire and forestalled satisfaction must occur until finally this tension is resolved. The *iki* dance in the movie is enacted through the social art of lonely men on the road in the literal swashbuckling scenes of *tachimawari,* and in the symbolic *tachimawari* between Chûtarô and the women he meets. For a movie about wandering, *Mother Under the Eyelids* involves mostly standing and talking, long lines of dialogue, and silence between people, alternating with rapid sword fights and quick travel along a road. The filmic time of scenes that do not move forward is considerably greater than the filmic time given to scenes of movement and travel. I will return to this point later.

The movie is not subtle: it opens with a shot of two chickens walking out of a gate, while a narrator places us in the nineteenth century. With a fade to a mother and child, and back again to a hen and her flock, we are made to understand the naturalness of the parent-child bond, that it lies beyond, or before, culture. We are introduced to the first of numerous mothers, crying for her son Hanjirô, wondering if his life has come to no good, waiting for his return.

Two ruffians arrive at a house looking for Hanjirô; his sister lies and says he's nowhere to be found. They give her a letter for him demanding that he meet them in battle. After stamping his feet and declaring he must do what he must do to be a man, he crumbles to the floor when his mother sees him with the letter. "Is it manly to leave your mother?" she demands. "Kill me instead!" she offers. The mother's withering look has slain her son, and the two cry in each other's arms.

A cut to a water wheel – time continues to circulate – then to a flock of chickens, one alone, another under a tree, leads us to another son: Chûtarô, who has been observing the scene. At the start of the film he glimpsed an image of what he himself seeks, the bond of mother and son, which is the image that will end the film. Calling on his friend Hanjirô, he is rebuffed, feared by both mother and daughter. Through *benshi* narration, intertitles, and facial expressions, we learn that he grows, and thinking of the image of a mother and son and of Hanjirô as a happy man, at last cries. Chûtarô's first dance, his first *iki* movement, his first *tachimawari,* begins: he leaves; Hanjirô calls him back; he leaves; Hanjirô cries. The tears in these scenes represent both the fullness of a bond and the loss of that bond, both wholeness and fracture.

The opening scenes have established Chûtarô's lost ideal and shown him to be a man trying to get back to that ideal. The back-and-forth movement between him and Hanjirô – the movement between separation and connection – shows him to be a hero with *iki,* whose attributes include the tension in the dance between longing and failed possession. For now, at least, Chûtarô is an *iki* hero, because he possesses an acute sense of circumstances that allows him to reveal his shame, examine his feelings, act coolly to exorcise his shame, and depart before he can witness the resolution or take credit for his part in it. It would be boorish, *yabo,* to stay for the credit; and *yabo* to have one's desires resolved. The end of the movie will be *yabo.*

The images of wholeness in the first scene – of mother and son, and of tears, which evoke an intensity of emotion that wipes out time and a blindness that is an escape from it – are images of stasis that now give way to the movement of travel. It is night, and following on the Chûtarô-Hanjirô dance the camera takes to the road, with shots of legs in movement, from front and behind. Preparations are being made for the next *tachimawari,* though here it will be a more literal one. The two ruffians from the earlier scene are chasing Hanjirô and his sister and mother; they are going to take revenge on Hanjirô for killing their friend, a scene shown to us in a flashback of furiously fast cuts. Ever the man, Hanjirô wants to fight: "I'm a man!" the intertitle, jagged with his emotions, tells us. As the mother is about to stop him, Chûtarô, who has been watching, calls out. The fight that ensues is another dance, with quick, jagged intertitles frequently appearing. Chûtarô kills one man, and the other runs off. This *tachimawari,* following Chûtarô's reflection on his aloneness in the previous scene, is not merely a *tachimawari* of swords; it has a less tangible, more human meaning, allowing Chûtarô close interaction with another body and an opportunity to fight for a mother. An *iki* hero, he will be off.

He explains that he is on his way to Edo in search of his own mother. This brings Hanjirô's mother and daughter to tears, signaling, through tears, at least the possibility, if not the attainment, of emotional wholeness. In the most moving scene of the movie – in which sentimentality is overcome by genuinely intense emotion – Chûtarô asks Hanjirô's mother to write a letter for him that he will leave with them, a letter meant to scare off any passersby with bad designs. Chûtarô's inability to write is a reversal of the common trope of the time, that of an unlettered woman offering solace to a male intellectual. The scene, perfectly evoking the intensity of Chûtarô's desires, was conceived by Hasegawa, but the director Inagaki has provided the perfect visual language for it. The mother guides Chûtarô's hand as he gazes upon her in longing, crying when he signs his name. The two faces merge on the screen. Chûtarô here approaches his first experience of nonlinguistic, physical bonding. At the same time, his silence, and the orality represented by the bond with the mother, are disturbed by the writing of the note, which interrupts the moment of bonding and sends Chûtarô on his way, with the image of his mother under his eyelids, as the intertitles tell us. He has experienced, only momentarily, the eyes-closed sense of physical wholeness felt by Edogawa Ranpo's heroes, and sought or evoked by many writers and intellectuals across Japanese culture in the 1930s. Chûtarô now struggles to re-create that experience: he closes his eyes and sees his mother – the

10. Chûtarô of Banba; Inagi Hiroshi, *Mother under the Eyelids* (1931).

mother under the eyelids (see Figure 10). He has continued to possess her as an ideal, and he can now take off, an *iki,* romantic, ironic hero who will not linger to take credit for his service and cannot remain in a condition of satisfied stasis.

On the way to Edo the film uses all its resources to collapse the images of travel, nature, and mother. We see moving feet, sky, the road from Chûtarô's view, his back, trees, feet, "Edo" written diagonally in intertitles, feet, trees, the road, flashes of the character for "mother" *(haha)* – like the popcorn and candy we're made to eat by subliminal messages – all cut with increasing rapidity. Writing continues to come between Chûtarô and his mother, disrupting their unspoken bond. She hovers above consciousness, and is not deeply implanted in him. The camera here neither shows Chûtarô nor shows the scene from his point of view. That is, Chûtarô is nowhere to be found and is unformed as a person as he travels on the road to his mother.

In Edo, Chûtarô continues his dance with desire, his movement toward and away from mothers, his brush with tears. The seasons pass, and still no mother. The long time of the seasons, like the time of travel, passes in the film in a few moments; they are nothing compared to the intensified, melodramatic time during which Chûtarô interacts with other people, in particular the false mothers he meets. Such a meeting will be his next *tachimawari.* He finds an old woman playing the samisen, and hopes she might be the one (her music can be read as an offering of some all-enveloping experience). He determines that though she had a son, he is dead; he gives her money and, moved, she cries, calling after him as he leaves her side. Next, he watches drunk samurai harassing and then beating two women; he watches one woman humiliated with kicks to her side in the dirt. Desperate for his mother, he asks this woman her age, if she has a son; she cries, because she too has lost her son. Chûtarô then wanders to the grave at which the samisen-playing woman has come to pray for her son; after seeing Chûtarô she missed him terribly, she says. He apologizes for making her remember and he prays; she gazes on him and feels her dead son come alive. Chûtarô, caught in his past, prods these mothers out of the present into their own pasts; he incites them to nostalgia. These women have been trying to mourn, and he will not let them. He keeps nostalgia alive. "Your mother must have been happy with a son like you," she says, and he wanders off. Hope, however, is not lost, because he explains his situation and she says she knows a proprietor of an inn named Banba. Before wandering away, Chûtarô, the consumer of tears, gives her money.

The final leg of his journey seems about to begin. At an inn people are happily celebrating the beginning of spring. We see a mother and daughter lovingly doting upon one another. Chûtarô seeks entrance to see this potential mother, but is blocked by her assistants. Hearing him from the hall, she allows him to enter – impatient, annoyed, anything but fearful of this stranger. His entry is shot like a travel scene, for this is the final leg of his journey, or, at least, so he hopes. The camera takes us quickly through corridors into the room, then dramatically closes up on the mother's face. He looks down; she, up. The climactic *tachimawari* has begun. Stiff and formal, with great pain in his face, he asks her if she remembers a son. She's suspicious. "Mother!" *(Okaasan)* he says, in jagged intertitles; she pulls back; he bows. She says she had a son named Chûtarô but he died; he says he is the son, and he cries. Rapid dialogue ensues, he arguing his case, she fending the argument off – thrust and parry – the camera cutting quickly between them. She demands he leave; hope gone, he takes out his money to give her and insists on calling her "Mother"; she denies him; he dissolves in tears.

Now the camera, stretching the time of the scene so slowly it becomes a space outside of time, moves across their faces that are wet with tears. Space is quickly interrupted by time as the emotional intensity is relieved with a cut to a teakettle, steam pouring out; then the camera moves back to Chûtarô as he wipes his face. Bitter, he resigns himself to his fate, and she seems to soften: "What if I am your mother?" In a moment of great stoic clarity she articulates the pain of loss. At the same time she declares the absolute loss of time: what's gone cannot be made real; the tragedy is too great. Her instinct, unlike his, is to accept the present and move on. She has mourned and is trying to heal; he has been trying to forestall that process. Finally, again the *iki* hero, he states that he is a *matatabi mono* – a wanderer – and walks out, slamming the door with great pluck. She collapses in tears.

Our own tastes might have been better satisfied if the movie had ended here, in the tension of separation and loss, in an *iki* moment; and indeed, the film's ending was not Hasegawa's original one. His sensibility seems to have been more ironic, because in his play he has Chûtarô walk away; in a second ending he walks away and the mother cries after him, to no avail; and only in a third ending are the two reconciled. In the movement from play to screen, resolution has replaced tension; *yabo* has defeated *iki*. Now, outside, the woman's daughter sees Chûtarô, and after demanding his identity from her mother, her mother finally admits, crying for forgiveness, that he is her son and her daughter's brother. The sister is furious; the mother claims this is for the best.[13]

The film will now bring together a literal *tachimawari* with a metaphorical one. The scene quickly shifts, with a jagged intertitle screaming, "Hanjirô!" We see that the mother and daughter have taken to the road to search for Chûtarô, who has become the object of their desire. Meanwhile, two ruffians are searching for Hanjirô to kill him. We see running feet and a road leading to a fight scene. The scene, with long, intimidating stares and quick cutting of shots of slashing swords, is the final *tachimawari* of the movie, and the longest (see Figure 11). It is the concrete visualization of the emotional *tachimawari* of mother and son that preceded it, and that will follow. Chûtarô kills one man, and the camera returns us to the adversary Chûtarô can't seem to vanquish: his mother (with his sister) by a carriage, in search of him. He overhears their cries for him, and ignores them, angry still, his heart hardened. Again he is attacked. The two men stare at one another, and Chûtarô asks: "Do you

11. Battling in the quest for Mother; Inagi Hiroshi, *Mother under the Eyelids* (1931).

have a parent? A child?" Hearing his "no," Chûtarô swiftly kills him and leaves the scene, his final filial act accomplished.

Perhaps now Chûtarô deserves his mother, but is any mother worth all this? His mother and sister arrive at his side in their carriage, but Chûtarô does not want to see them. He closes his eyes and cries, for he can no longer see the image of his mother under his eyelids; he has lost his *mabuta no haha,* his fantasy and dream. He is abandoning his romantic, ironic, *iki* sensibility of tension for a completion in stasis. If only he could hold on to that image, one cannot but feel, he might not have to return to her. What he has now is the real mother before him. She calls to him; he stares at her for a long time. Cut her down, one cannot help but think – "return to the mother in your mind." But the mother in his mind is gone. Now Chûtarô and his mother, like baby and parent, engage in a game of Freudian Fort-da, a hide-and-seek that will establish the reality of the mother for the baby. Chûtarô needs to be given an identity. "Call me again," he implores, asking to be renamed and reborn; and it is only after she does so that he relents and goes to her. After a lingering shot of a sword stuck in the ground the camera slowly pans to the parent and child merged into a black mound dissolving into tears (see Figure 12). The time

12. Chûtarô unites with Mother at last; Inagi Hiroshi, *Mother under the Eyelids* (1931).

of the film and the time of this man's development have ceased. We are back where we started.

Mother Under the Eyelids is certainly a film strictly guided by narrative conventions; by the obligatory swashbuckling scenes; the masterless, wandering protagonist; the melodramatic tears; the "happy" ending – which nevertheless lingers in the mind as a scene of surrender. The film must be seen in the company of its generic connections, alongside the hundreds of "mother tales" *(hahamono)* – where a mother, like Hanjirô's, sacrifices and suffers, unlike Chûtarô's mother – period dramas *(jidaigeki);* swashbucklers *(chambara);* Ito Daisuke's films of nihilistic, masterless samurai; Yamanaka Sadao's teary 1935 *Paper Balloons (Ninjô kami fûsen);* and the other *matatabi mono* filmed every year in the 1920s and 1930s.

I would like, however, to place the film as well in a larger context, alongside William S. Hart's 1925 classic silent American Western, *Tumbleweeds,* and in the company of perhaps the greatest film about the obsessive circular repetitions of a man in search of a lost woman, Alfred Hitchcock's *Vertigo.* The connection to the first film is a historical one, and should not seem strange. The even more forceful connection to the second film is a psychic and aesthetic one.

In the 1920s Japanese film drew not only from modern theater *(shinpa),* but also from the superior filmic art of directors like F. W. Murnau and von Sternberg, and from the more refined technology of American films. Hasegawa, indeed, was a fan of William S. Hart, of *Shane,* and of *Stagecoach. Tumbleweeds* is the American *matatabi mono,* but whereas Chûtarô lives in a society deeply structured and ordered, the cowboy in *Tumbleweeds* is on the prairie, where society barely has a foothold. The cowboy's dilemma is between preserving his life as a loner on the open range and settling in with a wife as one of the homesteaders who will soon claim and domesticate that wilderness. His struggle, for the land and the wife, is not easy, but in the end he marries. The final shots of the film show him standing with his bride looking over the new land, and then a single tumbleweed blows into a fence that, like his wife, stops forward movement. It is instructive to note that as the literal movement in this film is all in one direction, out West, the psychic movement also heads into the uncharted territory of marriage, which is an ending of one sort of a life, but a beginning of another. In his study of melodrama, philosopher Stanley Cavell describes marriage as a union leading to knowledge, requiring the imagination of another's inner being and an opening of one's self. The refusal of marriage, the choice of solitude, recognizes that one is not intelligible to another. Chûtarô – unlike Hart's hero – has chosen to be alone. He has forsworn the erotic exchange one wins through the daily repetition of marriage.[14]

His search is like that of characters in what Cavell calls the remarriage plot. He wants a second chance, and his desire requires the great imaginative capacity to wait. It also requires a great blindness that leads him to his mother. He is drawn to her like the protagonist in *Vertigo,* who falls in love with a phantom and watches her die, then transforms her into his *mabuta no haha* – his mother under the eyelids. When Scotty thinks he finds his lost love's replacement, he makes of her a repeat item, forcing her into the mold of his ideal. When he realizes his ideal is a masquerade, he repeats his earlier steps and frees himself of his fantasy and of his ideal: atop the tower whose heights he has feared, he has the real woman before him and has lost his vertigo; he no longer fears falling, or falling in love. But Scotty is doomed to repeat: a nun emerges before them, an image of conscience, or of the origin of all repetitions and desires – the mother. Scotty's phantom, now made real, jumps to her death; Scotty cannot shake his mother. Pathetically doomed as he is, Scotty wins our compassion. Chûtarô is more resistant to sympathy: it is not that he cannot shake his mother. All he wants is to have her, and to feel that she has yearned for him – to feel both his desire for her and hers for him, for it is only in this state of desire that he can be made into a person again. Without desire he is nothing.

His restoration to her at the end was certainly meant to be a happy ending. Yet the stasis it offers seems at odds with the tensions – the *tachimawari* – that filled the film. Until the last shot, the movie is *iki;* in the last scene it becomes *yabo.* While marked by *iki,* the movie maintains its ironic distance from a politics of stasis, even while it is nostalgic; when marked by *yabo* it reveals its collapse into an ideological connection to that politics. Until the last scene, *Mother Under the Eyelids* is a melodrama – but with a twist. Yomota Inuhiko describes the Japanese melodrama as requiring a situation in which a family is reconstituted after a male hero is expelled from a traditional family or social structure because of a woman, and begins a life of wandering; eventually, the woman dies, goes insane, or simply disappears, and the man is restored to the family.[15] In *Mother Under the Eyelids* a man – a boy, actually – is expelled by a mother, and does not rest until he gets her back. Until the end, the film shares with the melodrama an intensification of time in emotional moments where linguistic discourse gives way to tears; these moments of emotional intensity stretch on longer than moments of lived time, and are thereby given greater density in the film.[16] These moments are also always disrupted. The melodramatic dimension can be seen in the pathos of what Franco Moretti calls the "rhetoric of the too late," and the struggle of the protagonist against the passage of time, his attempt to break the connection between causality and linearity – that is, his attempt not to accept the narrative of his life as given.[17] At the end, *Mother Under the Eyelids* breaks with the melodrama, because Chûtarô accepts the narrative of his life as given, even though it seems that he has fought for this end. The end seems to show that it has not been too late for him – he has got what he wants. But it *is* too late for him, for it is now too late for him to be a man. This final moment will not, after all, be disrupted. It is when the generic convention collapses that the narrative becomes defamiliarized and reveals, to the informed viewer, its ideology. The film purports to show Chûtarô to be autonomous, to have been the master of his fate, to have chosen his destiny. We see here that this is an illusion.

Mother Under the Eyelids maintains a melodramatic tension until Chûtarô regains fullness and connects the circle with his mother. The gap between desire and the object that marks the melodrama is filled here, and the tears of the couple – tears which in melodrama, and which until now in this film, evoked the loss of fullness and the evocation of a lost ideal – now make the separate two one whole. It should be noted that all the crying in the film has occurred in still shots (tears are never shed on the road of frenetic travel), where people talk to one another, because still shots bring people in them close to that condition of stasis that they seek through one another. The generic conventions of *Mother Under the Eyelids* make it possible to create these moments of intensity, because, relying on the spectator's knowledge, meanings can be shorthanded and stereotypes called upon to condense the narrative into intensely emotive moments that might otherwise seem out of proportion to the narrative build-up of them. Indeed, scenes *must* be condensed in order to arrive at those moments. For moments, at least, generic convention releases the film and the viewer from time into space, from the modern present, in which time continues to move forward, to the eternal past. The structure of generic convention, approximating the working of memory, thus easily serves the interest of nostalgia.

The narrative structure of the film develops through an alternation of movement and stillness, but the amount of movement is not commensurate to the stillness it leads to. Too little prepares us for the too much of the still, but emotionally intensified scenes such as that at the conclusion of the movie. These scenes seem not so much caused by the preceding narrative as fated by motivations that precede the time of the film – like Scotty being fated by his unconscious. Even if they are disrupted along the way by an ironic sensibility, in the end there will be no disruption, no conditioning forces. They seem to have no cause, no linear development, no conditioning time behind them: they are the products of a nostalgic imagination (though still fractured by irony). Why does Chûtarô seek his mother? The conclusion of the movie raises the question of free will, which is a philosophical, but also a political question. Why is a man inexorably drawn, with no rancor, to a mother who abandoned him years before and went on to be happy? Why is such a man the hero of a genre? Why is such a woman forgiven?

And further: What can be said about the relationship of this narrative and of its popularity to the creation of a populace unified in a singular vision under the aegis of an Emperor in a time of increasing unity and in a state serving that Emperor? *Mother Under the Eyelids,* it might be clear by now, is pious and sanctimonious. It shows the fantasy of the formation of a subject whose sexual desire, by which I mean its longing for a connection to and contact with another body, has been suspended and channeled into the body of a mother and the metal of a sword. The linear narrative of the film, the trip to Edo, which cuts through the film's repetitions, displays the logic of the suspension of desire; it provides a dilatory middle delaying gratification before its closure in stasis. What is this stasis? Before the final shot of the movie, when mother and son embrace, we see Chûtarô's sword stuck in the ground. Does giving up the sword for the mother imply an antimilitarist analogy, or, rather, a move from feudal, decentered loyalties to a singular object of loyalty, the state? Or will fighting with the sword be replaced by fighting through other means? At the end of the movie, both, I suggest, remain. The sword is not buried, but is stuck in the ground for later use; and the energies behind the sword have been focused on the body of the mother. Chûtarô is even closer to his Emperor now – though he may not know it – and without his sword, he has perhaps lost his protection against him, and against his mother. That he does not know how close his Emperor is indicates how deeply he has internalized him as an unconscious, ideological force.

For the Emperor is nowhere to be found in the movie. Following Taki Kôji's argument in *The Emperor's Visage (Tenno no shôzô),* by the 1920s the Emperor had been turned, in forty years, from an irrelevancy into a figure viewed by the populace from roads through which passed imperial processions, a hidden and fetishized source of power whose image in schools and other public spaces helped give birth to a national space – "an anti-linguistic image to be sensed instinctually" *(chokkan dekiru higengoteki imeji).*[18] The Emperor might be found in such a nonlinguistic moment when language disappears into tears or into the embrace of two bodies. The final embrace in the movie can be understood in part as a visualization of the erotic connection between mother and son, left unrepressed. But the resolution of one-sided love, or *kataomoi,* in the *yabo* moment of embracing, seems so strikingly anomalous in the context of social norms that kept familial bodies apart, and so at odds with the even greater physical distance demanded between emperor and citizen, that it is difficult to explain without reference to its ideological import.

The Emperor is nowhere to be found in *Mother Under the Eyelids,* unless the Emperor *is* the mother under the eyelids, the idealized image of someone watching but never seen except in the mind's eye. One might consider this possibility in light, also, of Kato Mikiyo's argument that the Japanese emperor system represents a communal fantasy for the mother, and that the Emperor's relationship to his citizens is mediated through his mother's love *(boseiai)*. The Emperor, the argument goes, descends from the Sun Goddess Ameterasu, a nurturing god of crops.[19] I would add that the Emperor's love relationship with his people, like that of the mother with Chûtarô, is one-sided – *kataomoi* – and even if the reciprocation of his love was assumed, it was never expressed, and could not be guaranteed.

That the image of the mother might stand in for the image of the Emperor might seem more plausible if we consider the central place given women in these years. The years leading to and during the war have been characterized by Yoshiko Miyake as having created a "nationalistic maternal" *(kokkateki bosei)*. Women were assigned reproductive roles by the government, to serve the family and the nation. In 1937 laws that were enacted to protect single mothers recognized a shift to a mother-centered family, with so many men no longer on the mainland.[20] In the imaginations of male writers in the period, too, women bore a heavy burden: to many they offered emotional salvation from sensibilities fractured by abstract intellectualizations.

Devotion to women might thus be linked to devotion to the state, even while providing a temporary, sublimated refuge from the devotion demanded by the state. Satô Tadao suggests that the devotion of heroes like Chûtarô, to the weak, can easily be reversed, and become like that given to one's lord, country, or emperor. That is, though Hasegawa's understanding of loyalty in the *matatabi mono* derives from his work as a laborer, these local morals can easily become national.[21] Satô has suggested that Hasegawa's evocation of the willfulness of samurai, and his tales of revenge, might have been fueled by his increasing sense of Japan as having been made into a victim – like the *matatabi mono* hero – by the Western powers. Hasegawa sympathized with the loyalty the yakuza showed to the emperor and the ultranationalism of "the people" bonded with him. "It might be said that Hasegawa sympathized with the fascism in the emotions of the people," writes Satô.[22] Indeed, Hasegawa did come to endorse the ideology of national unified spirit, or *ichioku seishin*.[23] His later activities also indicate, at the very least, that he was not strongly antiwar or anticolonial. In 1938 he was sent as the PEN representative to China and Taiwan, where he wrote nationalist and promilitary pieces.[24]

These are biographical facts that merely make it more conscionable to link too literally an aesthetic creation to its political context; to make a political argument about what feels to be a nonpolitical film. The problem with an argument that attempts to link narrative and visual language experienced by viewers to ideology as it is acted out by citizens is that it seems to fail without evidence of how viewers' experiences of the film bore upon their sense of themselves as citizens in a state. Did any of this matter at all to an audience? Though there is no reason to assume that audiences were particularly sophisticated viewers of the film, and its genre, is there any reason to assume that a modern audience would be susceptible to the pious message of the story? Or if the message were not pious, but admonitory – saying that if you want a perfect home, this is what you get, this is the provincialism to which you will be condemned – is there any reason to assume that audiences would have been swayed by this admonition?

What might be said, however, is the following. We should recognize *Mother Under the Eyelids* to be a moving, imaginative creation born of a specific time and of particular literary and filmic imaginations and talents. The film also resonates, both emotionally and aesthetically, far beyond its time. To take the film as a sign of militarism or fascism is therefore to underestimate its aesthetic complexity and that of its relationship to its political, biographical, and aesthetic contexts. Nevertheless, its aesthetic context does reveal that during the years of its popularity, and that of its genre, there existed a confluence of images of loss and longing, and of solutions for that longing, in nonlinguistic union with a more powerful body. Its political context reveals that during these same years a similar ideal, through similar imagery, was being called for by the state in the form of self-sacrifice to the Emperor and nation through war. This suggests that such films as *Mother Under the Eyelids,* and such heroes as Chûtarô, were imaginative creations with oblique but discernible connections to less imaginative, but equally passionate – and more nefarious – acts in the real world.

NOTES

1. Ozaki Hotsuki, *Taishû bungeizu* (Tokyo: Sogensha, 1969), 89.
2. Satô Tadao, *Hasegawa Shin ron* (Tokyo: Chûôkôronsha, 1975), 20–29.
3. Hasegawa Nobuaki, ed., *Taishû jiten,* (Tokyo: Kôdansha, 1987), 796.

4. Satô, 33. This is a view shared as well by Ozaki. See his "Shomin kanjô no ketsusho – Araki Matazaemon, Mabuta no haha," in *Taishû bungaku no kanôsei*, ed. Ozaki Hokki and Tado Dôtarô (Tokyo: Kawade Shobô, 1969), 67–69.
5. Hiraoka Masaaki, *Menken kotoba no kutsukkake tokijirô* (Tokyo: Riburupôto, 1987), 23.
6. Satô, 199.
7. William Darrell Davis, *The Monumental Style in Japanese Cinema* (New York: Columbia University Press, 1997), 7.
8. Takeda Nobuaki, *Koshitsu to manazashi* (Tokyo: Kawade Shobô, 1989), 124, 179.
9. Lynne Kirby, *Parallel Tracks* (Durham: Duke University Press, 1997), 2, 50.
10. Takeda, 163–64, 211.
11. Matsuyama Iwao, *Tokyo to Ranpo: 1920 toshi no kao* (Tokyo: Parco shuppankyoku, 1984), 21.
12. Quoted in Matsuyama, 30–31.
13. The role of sisters in the film requires further analysis. They are buffers between angry mothers and their wandering sons, as Hanjirô's sister was in the opening scene of the movie. Here, Chûtarô's sister chides their mother, bringing her back to Chûtarô and to her role as a properly filial mother.
14. Stanley Cavell, *Contesting Tears: The Hollywood Melodrama of the Unknown Woman* (Chicago: University of Chicago Press, 1996), 23, 82.
15. Yomota Inuhiko, "Japanese Melodrama" in *East-West Film Journal* 2, University of Hawaii, (July 1993): 19.
16. See Joseph A. Murphey, "Melodrama, Temporality, Recognition: America and Russia," *East-West Film Journal 2,* (July 1993): 69.
17. Franco Moretti, *Signs Taken for Wonders* (London: Verso Books, 1983), 159.
18. Taki Kôji, *Tennô no shôzô* (Tokyo: Iwanami shoten, 1988), 26–30, 88, 196.
19. Kano Mikiyo, *Josei to tennôsei* (Tokyo: Shisô no kagakusha, 1979), 69. See also Takashi Fujitani, *The Splendid Monarchy: Power and Pageantry in Modern Japan* (Berkeley: University of California Press, 1996), 171–72.
20. For example, the *boshi hogo hô,* or Mother-Child Protection Law, established in response to a spate of mother-child suicides. See Yoshiko Miyake, "Doubling Expectations: Motherhood and Women's Factory Work Under State Management in the 1930s and 1940s," in *Re-creating Japanese Women 1600–1945,* edited, with an introduction, by Gail Lee Bernstein (Berkeley: University of California Press, 1991), 237, 272.
21. Satô, 23, 49.
22. Satô, 264.
23. Satô, 175, 183.
24. Ozaki Hotsuki, *Yokohama no sakkatachi – sono byakuteki fudo* (Tokyo: Yûrindô, 1980), 109.

CHAPTER EIGHT

Saving the Children

Films by the Most "Casual" of Directors, Shimizu Hiroshi

Keiko I. McDonald

Shimizu Hiroshi (1903–66) is something of a forgotten veteran among directors of Japanese cinema. He made over 160 films in a career spanning thirty-four years. Yet he is rarely studied in Japan or abroad.[1] Even the best of his films seem neglected, even by the Japanese.

Oddly enough, Shimizu's most significant contribution to the Japanese film history lies in a genre his country's cinema is famous for: films about children. It could be argued that posthumous neglect is the price he pays for having been a notably casual craftsman. His ruling passion, both in art and in life, had more to do with a kind of philanthropy. As we shall see, Shimizu aimed to do this weary old world some good by showing how children can be rescued, and maybe grown-ups, too.

How did he come to this? Why should he have become increasingly involved in the fate of children on screen – and in real life – beginning in the mid-1930s? What qualities made him a master of such films? In order to address these questions, we must first get him in perspective.

It could be that Shimizu's reputation suffers from a surfeit of good company in the Golden Age of Japanese cinema of the 1930s, including the versatile Ozu Yasujirō and Shimazu Yasujirō. These two we know as specialists in the *shomingeki* genre – the drama of middle-class family life. Shimizu was more of a generalist, a company man content to take up whatever projects came his way in that frenetic heyday of high-pressure production.

This is not to say that ambitious films of considerable artistic merit did not emerge with Shimizu in charge. Some did. But unlike the perfectionist Ozu, Shimizu was rather carefree in his approach. One critic's reminiscences preserve the experience of an acquaintance who would find Shimizu on the set, in the background, having excused himself for a friendly chat while the cameraman continued cranking away at the given scene.[2]

The working milieu of directors like Shimizu at the time is most vividly expressed in *A Heaven of Cinema* (*Kinema no tenchi,* 1986). This fascinating retrospective on its history was commissioned by the Shochiku Company to celebrate its Ofuna Studio's fiftieth anniversary.

This assignment was given to Yamada Yōji best known for his *Tora-san* series. Here, he begins by looking back at the turmoil of full-speed-ahead production at the Shochiku Kamata Studio. The coming of talkies in Japan shifts the scene to the newly built studio in Ofuna.

The director modeled on Shimizu in *A Heaven of Cinema* is given the name Ogura. He is shown launching a new face on the road to stardom, telling his heroine: "No projection of feelings." He is seen using long shots on location. In brief, he is seen developing cinematic traits that became hallmarks of Shimizu's mature work.

The film also explores Ogura/Shimizu's relation to the head of the studio, the legendary Kido Shirō. The careers of both men correspond to the cultural climate that helped to forward the burgeoning industry in the 1920s.

Kido was appointed head of the Kamata Studio in 1924, when he was just thirty. He quickly instituted radical changes in the company's production policy at Kamata, where Shochiku's staple *gendaigeki* films were made. His influence was such that "Kidoism" became a force to reckon with. He transformed the *shimpa* tragedy of stock figures like the cruel stepmother, the hateful mother-in-law, and the self-sacrificing wife into a more cheerful vein of comedy involving common people.

Early films in this line were *Father (Otôsan)* and *Sunday (Nichiyôbi),* both made in 1924 by Shimazu Yasujirō, working in close collaboration with Kido. (These films were made at the Kamata Studio while the main human resources of the Kamata were temporarily relocated at the company's Shimogamo Studio in Kyoto after the 1923 earthquake.)

Kido had this to say about his drive to create films capturing the flavor of everyday middle-class life:

> It's all right to go see a tragedy armed with plenty of hankies, but not every film has to be a tear-jerker. Entertainment should be healthy and cheerful too. If a film-

maker uses social irony and paradox, these cinematic means can offer a learning experience along with a good laugh. . . .

Tragedy is theatrical more than cinematic, better on stage than on screen.[3]

Interestingly enough, Shimizu's early films seem not to have developed along the lines of Kido's preferences. (All but two of his films from the 1920s have vanished, so we must work from secondary evidence here.) He made his first film in 1924, when he was twenty-one. Titled *Beyond the Mountain Pass (Tōge no kanata),* it was strong in local color. That same year Shimizu was transferred to Shochiku's *jidaigeki* studio in Kyoto. There he worked on several films in that genre, all apparently given a lyrical touch. (None survives today.)

For the next seven years (1925–32), Shimizu worked at Kamata, where he proved to be a prolific director – if making 80 films in such a span qualifies one as prolific. These works ranged from light comedy to melodrama, all done with a light and dexterous hand by a man who knew how to meet the production schedules demanded by Shochiku's competitive drive.

He excelled at melodrama, a genre not in favor with Kido. But it was melodrama different from rival Nikkatsu Studio's Shimpa-style tragic mainstay. *Shimpa* was a new form of drama that emerged as a reaction against the conventions of Kabuki. One radical departure was in its use of contemporary settings and situations. The *shimpa* repertoire ranged from comedy to suspense drama, but its mainstay was a subspecies of tragedy that staged "a grand display of the will of a woman who endures her fate in tears."[4]

Two surviving Shimizu films show how he wrung tears from such heroines. *Indestructible White Pearl* (*Fuwa no hakuju,* 1929) was based on Kikuchi Kan's novel of the same title. The story features a well-patterned causality as a suitor chooses between two sisters. His choice of the younger turns out to be a disappointment for him as well as for the older sister. The older is forced to marry an incompatible widower.

The Nikkatsu Studio would have treated this classical *shimpa* situation as an instance of the classical conflict between *giri* and *ninjô* (social obligation and personal inclination) with complications arising out of class differences. In such a treatment, any element of celebration must focus on abject self-sacrifice as the heroine endures her fate in submissive silence.

Shimizu's development of the drama, in contrast, follows the novel more faithfully. It studies the differences in egotism between men and women as a source of unrequited love and conflict. One critic sees this as a new element in the modernization of melodrama.[5]

Only a portion survives of *Blacksmith in the Village* (*Mori no kajiya,* 1929). It shows Shimizu blending melodrama with suspense. Here, the story concerns two brothers. The elder becomes a medical doctor because of his deeply felt compassion for his physically handicapped sibling. After many years away, the doctor returns home to his brother. He is then accused of taking money from the safe of the village headman. It happens that the girl he loves is being pursued by the headman's son. The plot becomes complicated as the lame younger brother sets out to defend his doctor brother's honor.

In later years Kido had this to say about Shimizu's stylistic strength as it grew out of the director's fresh and innovative approach to melodrama:

> In his melodrama, Shimizu composed his effects, not in terms of the facial expressions of actors, but in terms of the story itself. His compositions became themselves the expressive medium. This was his new method. Even in long shots, the over-all atmosphere says a lot about the given character. Even when the actor's back is shown, the scene itself expresses the mood of the piece. Instead of using facial expressions to draw the drama out, he dissolved the actor's movements into several fragments, each shot in a short take. This mounting tension of short shots becomes the propelling force of the story.[6]

A climactic scene from *A Blacksmith in the Village* shows this being done. The lame younger brother ventures outdoors in search of the doctor falsely accused of theft. A series of long shots focuses on his back, showing how pitifully he drags his feet. His helplessness is conveyed as his figure merges with the uninviting surroundings – a deserted yard with wind tossing in the trees.

Even this brief evidence points up the radically different approaches to silent-era melodrama taken by Shochiku and by Nikkatsu. At Nikkatsu, major directors like Uchida Tomu and Mizoguchi Kenji tended to stage *shimpa* dramas on the screen, relying heavily on the acting expertise of veterans trained on the stage. They even shot their dramas on stage sets most of the time.

At Shochiku, directors like Shimazu Yasujirō and Shimizu Hiroshi preferred to use the new faces of acting talent with no theatrical background. In their films, the actors took their places as part of natural settings shot on location. Shots tended to be on the short side, because these actors could not sustain the long takes that Mizoguchi's veterans were trained for.

Because most Shochiku actors lacked experience of *shimpa* and the Kabuki stage, their acting was free of the exaggerated, often highly formalized gesticulations of those theatrical traditions. Thus a kind of "weakness" became a kind of strength as these novice screen actors took on methods and manners being used to develop a "realism" expressive of everyday life.

In the 1930s, Shimizu's films achieved increasing consistency and sophistication using these methods. In 1936, the entire footage of *Mr. Thank-you (Arigato-san)* was shot on location. Here too, we see Shimizu's growing commitment to the spirit of realism understood as "fidelity to actual events."

The film is based on a short story by the Nobel prize winner Kawabata Yasunari. It offers a slice of life as it is lived by villagers and transient laborers – poor people who happen to live in a natural setting blessed with great scenic beauty. Various lives come into contact, sometimes contrasting, sometimes in parallel, as a bus driven by Mr. Thank-you picks up and discharges its passengers (see Figure 13).

Most of *Mr. Thank-you* is devoted to noncommittal views of daily events in the idyllic village as caught by the camera's nonchalant eye. Even so, some shots are strongly revealing. They speak for the plight of the masses who were suffering from the depression of the 1930s. A long

13. A slice of life on the village bus; Shimizu Hiroshi, *Mr. Thank-you* (1936).

shot studies a villager coming home from the city, still unemployed. Another telling long shot takes in a group of transient Korean laborers silently trudging along a mountain path.

Shimizu's dedication to "realism" called for the soft-touch screen idol, Uehara Ken, to learn how to drive his bus for real. The vehicle itself was a remodeled studio runabout. Even so long ago, the famous bottom line imposed its own realistic demands.

Scriptwriter and film critic Kishi Matsuo claims that Shimizu attempted to achieve "realism" as early as 1925 in his sixth film, *A Small Itinerant Performer (Chiisaki tabi-geinin).* Whether or not he is right, Shimizu's films of the 1930s and 1940s show clearly that his characteristic orientation developed most successfully in films concerning the fate of children.

This thematic orientation was rooted in a trend specific to the political and cultural milieu of the mid-1930s. In Japanese film history, the years 1935–37 are generally recognized as partaking of the upsurge of interest in the so-called *junbungaku* (pure literature) movement of the country's literary scene. Studio production schedules for those years indicate a vigorous marketing response to the public's interest in serious works of literature adapted for the screen.[7]

These adaptations *(bungei eiga)* drew on children's literature as well. In fact, filmmakers made such good use of it that the years 1937–41 are looked upon as a Golden Age of such pictures. Studios competed for the work of famous children's writers like Tsubota Jōji, Miyazawa Kenji, and Yamamoto Yūzō.

Ironically, this zeal owed something to twin grown-up horrors taking hold in Japan in these years: government censorship working in tandem with the rising tide of militarism. The outbreak of war with China in 1937 led the Home Ministry to institute regulations that, in effect, rationed film footage and restricted subject matter.[8] Scenes depicting frivolous behavior and individual freedom were taboo, and so was anything seen as encouraging Japanese women to adopt Western ways.

A Motion Picture Law that took effect in 1939 was even more draconian. Every script had to answer to its twenty-six articles of detailed prohibition. Studios had good reason to seek haven in the far less troubled waters of children's literature.

Shimizu had already made a good start with *Children in the Wind* (*Kaze no naka no kodomotachi,* 1937). The prestigious film journal *Kinema jumpo* ranked it the fourth best picture of the year. Shimizu himself adapted the script from the book by Tsubota.

The narrative pattern offers a clear progression of causality: stability yields to upset, struggle, and ultimately resolution.[9] Two boys, Zenta and Sanpei, are leading a careful, even idyllic life, when suddenly their father is charged with embezzlement and taken away by the police. Hard times follow quickly. Their mother is forced to get a job. Sanpei, the younger brother, is sent to live with an uncle. The rest of the story focuses on his boyish determination to return home. All does end well as the father is proven innocent.

Shimizu's cinematic rubric makes use of children as major actors in a natural setting. This contributes to a subtle yet forceful depiction of middle-class family life. Scenes showing the children in familiar outdoor surroundings are used to suggest a paradise soon to be lost.

One such scene shows an alleyway outside Sanpei's and Zenta's house. The alley runs down the center of the screen from the foreground to the back. This strong line becomes a basic compositional unit of the film. At the outset we see the house of Sanpei's rival Kintarō. It is a somewhat better house in the street where the alley ends. Sanpei comes out of his house and goes that way, leading a gang of boys. Kintarō is shown idling alone, then tagging along as the children set out on the day's adventures.

A series of dollying shots – all taken from a distance – shows the children at their innocent play, as if caught unawares by the camera's roving eye. They run across a field and swim in the river. Their restless motions are caught now here and now there by the camera's panning. We get a sense of children in perfect harmony with nature, their joie de vivre as yet unspoiled by knowledge of the grown-up world.

Though the scene is perfectly ordinary, its details prepare us for what is to come. Kintarō's exclusion from the happy group anticipates the crisis even then developing. His father is not just a stockholder in the factory managed by Sanpei's father; he is the one who accuses the manager of embezzlement.

Again, the alley is used to point up the contrast between innocence lost and experience gained. After Sanpei's father is taken away by the police, we see him standing alone in the lower front of the screen. He is the one left out now. In the distance, where the alley joins the street, Kintarō is shown taking his place as head of the gang.

A final scene uses the same real-world "set" to show a role reversal, now that the crisis is resolved. This time, it is Kintarō's father who is under arrest. The boy is seen alone once again outside his house. Sanpei leads the gang once more. As the camera follows the children at their play, we cannot help seeing their innocence contaminated now by knowledge of adult power and corruption.

Again, the alley localizes our sense of Sanpei's growth through experience, child though he is. The last several shots ironically reinforce a sense of clear division between the worlds of children and of adults. Sanpei invites Kintarō to join their gang. We see clearly that this reconciliation, so little likely in the grown-up world, is in fact a premonition of inevitable change as these small ones grow up to become knowledgeable and tragically fallible adults.

The modern-day audience may be surprised by the look of another scene used repeatedly to establish our sense of the children's world. Here, the road to the factory runs through the idyllic countryside, not the crowded tenements we expect. In place of the man-made horrors usually associated with industrialization, we have a road with tall trees leading away from the camera.

We first see this country road as Sanpei experience an important childhood "first." He is entrusted with his father's lunch box. He has long looked forward to this privilege and challenge. Now we see him in a long shot, running toward the camera. As his tiny figure moves against a background still untainted by modernization, the shot itself expresses the strongly felt reality of the little boy and all his childish joy.

The same road is used later on to convey the opposite emotion. At the factory, Sanpei sees the police take his father away. Sanpei and Zenta walk homeward, away from the camera. Shimizu uses a reverse-field setup to draw our attention to the sorrowful shuffling steps of the children. No closer view is necessary.

Some viewers will see a parallel with the memorable take in Ozu's *I Was Born, But* (*Umareta wa mita keredo,* 1932). There, two brothers have seen their father humiliated by his boss, the father of their playmate. As they leave the scene, they walk sadly down a road adorned only by two electric poles. Their felt reality is strongly transmitted to the viewer as they move away from the camera, their small figures taken in a long shot, merging with the night.

As it happens, Shimizu's take was inspired not by Ozu's cinematography, but by the novelist Shiga Naoya's *"Manazuru."* In his memoirs, Shimizu tells of finding himself in tears as he read in the short story about the little children shuffling along a road at night.

In *Children in the Wind,* the road serves the happy outcome. The brothers have found a letter establishing their father's innocence. A shot of the flag of the rising sun signals his release to us. Then we see the road, shot again at right angles to the screen. A long shot shows the brothers approaching. Their sprightly motions now speak of their expected happiness. This time, the idyllic scene is invaded by one of man's machines – the car bringing their father home. A cut to the inside shows him. Then a cut to the road shows the happy boys running toward the camera.

In 1939, Shimizu returned to the children's-novel writer Tsubota for a sequel, *Four Seasons of Childhood (Kodomo no shiki).* Here again, the plot involves the two young brothers Zenta and Sanpei, who are caught up in a familiar narrative scheme involving stability, upset, struggle, and resolution. This time, however, the action encompasses not just one summer, but a full year. Given this much more time, the children have that much more scope for suffering and growth. The chain of repetition works to resolve one issue, even as it helps establish another demanding resolution. As we shall see, each narrative element is also charged with more variety than is the case in *Children in the Wind.*

This is evident from the outset. Here, the causal chain is expanded by a sudden disclosure of withheld information. When the film begins, Zenta and Sanpei are living happily in their village. They make friends with Ono, a kindly old man in a neighboring village. His benevolent wisdom suggests an idyllic link between the worlds of children and of grown-ups.

Another stage of enrichment comes with the revelation that Ono is in fact their grandfather. By getting to know him, they have healed an old family rift. As so often occurs in Japanese tales of parent-child discord, it turns out that their father had married for love, without the consent of his parents, and was subsequently disowned by his family.

Even as finding a grandfather in their old friend makes the children's lives happier, this new situation leads to a threat from another quarter. Among their grandfather's friends is the rapacious villain, Rokai (literally, "a cunning old man"). He is determined to gain control of Ono's factory by making his own son the old man's heir. The sudden discovery that Ono has two grandchildren, and a son of his own, upsets this plan. Worse yet, Rokai is in a position to demand repayment of a loan from Ono's son. When he makes his demand, the father falls ill.

Suddenly life becomes very hard for the children. They must work to help their mother pay their father's hospital bills. They soon learn about the power of money in the adult world. Despite their efforts, the father dies. His legacy to them takes the form of final good advice: "A man should not be greedy."

Nevertheless, Part 2 of *Four Seasons of Childhood* begins with happiness regained to some degree. Ono manages to take them in. Under his protection, they begin to recover from the loss of their father. But the greedy villain Rokai must still be dealt with. He is legally entitled to seize Ono's factory in payment of the unpaid debt. Once more, the children become pawns in the struggle. They see their toys being confiscated, along with the rest of their grandfather's household goods.

It is important to note that the ultimate reconciliation in this film is made not by the warring adults, but by these innocent children. In *Children in the Wind,* the boys' playmate's relations act out a childish version of the adult power struggle going on around them. In *Four Seasons of Childhood,* the boys behave with a generosity in obvious contrast to the malice displayed by their elders. Despite the misery Rokai has caused them and their family, Zenta and Sanpei continue to play with the villain's son, Kintarō. Moreover, Kintarō shames his father by upbraiding him for taking possession of his two friends' toys. In the end, harmony is restored. Rokai, feeling guilty, does right by the family he has dispossessed.

As before, Shimizu's cinematic rubric unfolds unobtrusively as he follows the children around outdoors. Casual as he seems, he does evoke some telling, even powerful, responses in us.

For example, after the death of the boys' father, we see the children testing their courage with a classic childhood dare: Who can walk the tree trunk that has fallen across a stream? Zenta, Sanpei, and the others make it across. Kintarō loses his balance, nearly falls, and gives up. Long shot and deep focus together place the children for us, making them a part of nature's changing spectacle.

The tree spanning the stream is seen again after Rokai has broken off relations with the boys' grandfather. The dare is repeated with the same result. We get the director's point. The children haven't changed. Their bond has something in common with nature's continuity. It has survived the grown-up war going on around them at home.

Shimizu's *The Introspection Tower (Mikaeri no tô)* was given third place in the *Kinema jumpo* lineup of best pictures for 1941. This story is more grimly realistic, taking place in a 200-bed reformatory. Studying various case histories, the narrative moves from a pattern of enmity and alienation to one of understanding and cooperation.

Children from different social backgrounds are brought together for an especially contentious mix of young people's unhappinesses. Tamiko, for example, is the spoiled daughter of a wealthy businessman. Her unwillingness to abide by reformatory rules puts her in conflict, not just with the housemother, but with the other girls as well. A group of boys tries to escape, only to be caught. A small boy hides to avoid visits from a kindly stepmother. Clearly, the narrative problem has to do with staging a turnaround: how to bring these troubled youngsters in contact with convincing warmth and positive values.

Shimizu consults a means no doubt familiar to those who deal with juvenile delinquents: a common cause requiring close cooperation. An acute water shortage at the reformatory requires the construction of a water path. The film studies the progress of this hard work in great detail. Long shots of groups are mixed with medium and close-up shots of individuals at various locations along the way. This sequence, which critics consider reminiscent of King Vidor's *Our Daily Bread* (1934), ends with a shot of the water coursing along its hard-won path as the children follow.

The director's familiar cinematic rubric may be most tellingly illustrated in the final leave-taking scene. The theme of children being caught outdoors in traveling shots now shows several on their way home, successful graduates of the reformatory. The deep composition shows the introspection tower on its hilltop in the background. The camera follows a diagonal progress of children down the hillside. A long shot shows departing children in the foreground, with those waving good-bye in the background. The train (by now a Shimizu trademark) passes near the road. As the departing group continues to walk, the camera tags along. The final shot is an opposing dolly: as the party walking on the left moves out of sight, the camera veers right to show an idyllic country landscape with the soaring tower in the distance.

Shimizu's preoccupation with the lives of children continued after the war. A number of such films show him gaining mastery over a sustained power of realism, especially in outdoor scenes. Proof that this was his labor of love can be found in the fact that he used his personal fortune to care for a number of war orphans.

In 1948 he made *Children in the Beehive (Hachi no su no kodomo-tachi),* a film he financed himself. He cast it with his protégés and used amateurs for the supporting staff. The film was shot on location to save on production costs.

The first thing to say about *Children of the Beehive* is that it offers a vivid portrayal of the struggle for survival in postwar Japan (see Figure 14). This trauma shared by adults and children alike is studied through the sufferings of two representative types. One is the repatriate adult, Shimamura, who has no home or family to return to. The other is a group of war orphans lost in the shuffle in those difficult times.

Shimizu wastes no time establishing the harsh terms of survival meted out to his characters. Rather than presenting an objective case history, however, he studies the plight of the children through Shimamura's eyes. Point-of-view shots are used to show what this adult observer sees happening to these orphans.

In one scene a group of them is shown loitering around the station as a train arrives, packed with repatriates. Some of the children beg for food. Others try to steal. Still others are fixated on nabbing stray cigarette butts

14. The post-war struggle for survival; Shimizu Hiroshi, *Children of the Beehive* (1948).

– a fit image of the acute shortages then prevailing. These streetwise waifs are subject to adult exploitation too. It turns out that this group is led by a crippled man, himself a casualty of war, who forces them to steal, and steals from them in turn.

Shimamura comes to represent the antithesis of such a malevolent father figure. In the opening sequence, he shares his last bit of rations – bread – with them. Then, as their paths cross soon again, he shares their journey and struggle in which they find themselves in this world of dire want amid the ruins of defeat in war. The narrative pattern thus moves from extremes of alienation and discord to the achievement of unity and harmony.

Shimamura serves as the catalyst. Since he is himself a kind of orphan in this world, he is free to begin his quest for survival burdened with concern for those children he has seen at the station. He meets a gang of eight of them soon afterward, and their destinies are joined. He becomes a benevolent mentor and adoptive father, seeking to instill in them the values of honest hard work and camaraderie.

The children have already had to lend one another support in self-defense. From Shimamura, they learn true companionship. The older children begin to develop a more genuine concern for the younger ones. The strongest instance involves the sickly Yoshibo. Convinced that his mother is to be found in the sea, he begs the older Yutaka to carry him to see it. This involves a difficult piggyback journey up a steep mountainside.

Shimizu's camera studies this progress in exquisite detail, viewing the children from all angles, in a variety of shot sizes. At times it casts a long, fixed gaze on their tiny figures from afar; at other times it follows them at close range. At one point, Yutaka slips. A close-up studies his legs and the peril involved. Several shots more show him toiling ahead, not giving up. At last they reach the top of the mountain, in view of the ocean spread out below. But Yoshibo has died. The pace of filming picks up as Yutaka speeds down the mountain to tell the others of this tragic outcome.

Withheld information provides a surprise ending to the story. Throughout the film, the viewer expects the children's wanderings to be essentially directionless. Then, in the final sequence, the introspection tower looms up, offering reunion and settlement, after all. Significantly, the tower has come to represent an all-inclusive metaphor for an ideal family for orphans. Having escaped from the false family of their leader at the station, these children have found a truly benevolent father figure in Shimamura. Now, at the reformatory, complete with mother and father figures, they find a welcome "home." It even turns out that Shimamura was himself raised in that place.

Shimizu's favorite compositional ending returns here as the camera looks down a country road. A long shot shows a group of orphans, led by a teacher, running toward the camera. A series of long shots captures the moment of celebration as Shimamura and his children are made welcome.

Then, as in so many Ozu films, *Children of the Beehive* closes with a shot of uninhabited landscape: the country road with a mountain rising behind. Obviously, we are being invited to reflect on the difficult path these youngsters have had to take – and the struggle still rising steeply before them in war-torn Japan.

Children of the Beehive Part 2 (1951) takes up the story three years later. Here too, Shimizu's reputation for artistic nonchalance seems justified. Certainly he was willing to forgo remorseless perfectionism when his favorite subject was making its way on screen. This sequel, like the original, is cast with his own orphans. As a result, the film takes on the character of a documentary, set as it is on the farm he had bought for himself and his charges on the Izu Peninsula.

The source of peril required for a "plot" in this case was supplied by public relations. A newspaper reporter writes a piece about the peaceful, self-sufficient farming-cooperative community the children run and live in. Suddenly they find themselves besieged by well-wishers wanting to adopt them all away – and by other orphans clamoring to be taken in!

This state of affairs is rich in narrative potential, yet the film begins with a calm, commonsense gesture, locating the "beehive" community in its setting. The opening shot shows the Izu Peninsula on a map, then fades to an actual mountainside. A long shot then shows a woman walking along a path. The sound track blends music and birdsong.

The woman is soon identified as the first invader. She is the mother of one of the boys. Oddly enough, the boy is Yoshibo – the one who perished so touchingly in Part 1 of this film! What better example is there of Shimizu's casual goodwill toward his own productions?

Even so, we are quickly caught up in the sadly wry drama created by this episode's ironic twist. Because here, too, the child believes that his mother lives in the sea. Her sudden appearance would appear to confirm that fact. Yet the peculiar psychology of a child's long-cherished expectations takes charge as this mother fails to look like the one he has imagined for so long. She is just too ordinary looking. He rejects her and refuses to leave the farm.

Actually, the children's life on the farm is never under serious threat, so the film lacks that dramatic tension. Instead, Shimizu seems content to accumulate one episode after another, each being related to the invasion of well-wishers – would-be parents and orphans both.

The closest thing to a climax concerns the orphan Shinichi. A number of his former streetwise friends appear, eager to share his happy home. They prove more streetwise than farmwise and are soon discouraged by the very real hard work of this new life. They decamp – taking along various bits of property that don't belong to them.

Shinichi catches up with his friends at Atami. This is the only scene set outside the farm. Given the easygoing idealism displayed at every turn in this film, we are not too surprised by the upshot. After a tense confrontation, these young rascals see the light and return to the farm and all its benefits of rural life, among them, no doubt, reformation. A present-day corrections officer may well think that director Shimizu was born a good half century too soon.

The closing image of solidarity here, however, is not a school singalong of "Old MacDonald Had A Farm," but a session in a biology lab – for these orphans have solid academic achievement written large in their futures.

Shimizu's camera work throughout the film is as simple and economical as his faith in human nature is unburdened by doubt and cynicism. As might be expected, the standard unit is a long shot. As usual with him, the emphasis is on placing children in a wholesome natural environment – and on letting them act like children there. His camera imposes no artificial standard. The chosen shot is always appropriate to the matter at hand, as when it observes the shared values of these orphans as a group.

This is not to say that Shimizu's heartfelt concern for these youngsters fails to make itself known. As in the Part 1 film, a poignant instance of this concerns the plight of Yoshibo. Here we see him running away from the woman who claims him as her son. A high-angle, extreme long shot shows him near the beach, on a hill occupying the foreground. The sound-track music speaks for his yearning, for his childish dream of finding his mother – the one he imagines, not the one he is rejecting as being not the real one. The next shot records his plaintive cry as he looks out at a sea whose very calm strikes us as fit comment on the real world's indifference to this pitiful orphan's dream.

In *The Children and the Great Buddha (Daibutsu-sama to kodomotachi),* Shimizu returns to this theme, this time in a story involving just two wartime orphans. Again, his cast includes protégés who appeared in *The Children in the Beehive.* Here some do the work of stars. Even some adult roles are played by rank amateurs.

Shimizu is supposed to have been just amazingly casual about his casting. Apparently he thought nothing of giving roles to acquaintances who struck him as being right for them. In fact, a neighbor of my family in Nara was asked by Shimizu to play a fairly important role in *The Children and the Great Buddha.* So there she is, alive to this day on screen, cast as a visitor to Nara who decides to adopt one of the two starring orphans in this film of 1953.

This film was indeed set in Nara, the peaceful ancient capital that escaped bombing in the war. Two orphans, Toyota and Genji, lead a hand-to-mouth existence helping tourist guides. The operative motif here is the friend-and-mentor archetype. Ichiun, himself a war orphan and now a novice at the temple, teaches Toyota about historical buildings and statues. Ryohei, a painter from Tokyo, also instructs him. Toyota in turn helps Genji and various other children, teaching them the tour guide's singsong spiel, a vital survival skill in Nara in this difficult postwar period.

This film breathes a somewhat more gracious air, since these orphans lead a carefree life blessed with kindly adult contacts. Even the camera's gaze rests like a quiet blessing on the bonds being forged, especially between Toyota and Genji.

One scene in the famous Nara Park shows Toyota acting as elder brother and mentor. He is cutting little Genji's hair. He is in fact touchingly inept, leaving the little fellow badly cropped. But expertise is not the issue here. The shot is framed to emphasize the park's vast expanse of grass resplendent in warm spring sun. Tall trees uplift our gaze. The camera's distant gaze conveys a sense of a privileged view. True, these boys are orphans, but we see them in touching harmony with this beautiful natural setting – which clearly is what this scene is meant to do.

Even so, there are moments when the horrors of war revisit the children's lives. Toyota is in the habit of standing outside a different house each day, listening intently for radio broadcast news concerning repatriates. His father is still listed as missing in action.

Toward the beginning of the film Toyota is seen guiding a group of tourists. Suddenly he asks another orphan to take his place and he runs off, obviously in a hurry to get somewhere. Four shots explain what is going on. The first is a long shot of Toyota standing under the eaves of an old house set in a narrow alley near the Todaiji Temple. He is eavesdropping on a radio broadcast listing the names of soldiers just repatriated. Next, we see him in the background, moving away from the camera, away from the house. Obviously, he has not heard the name he was hoping to hear. He leaves the narrow alley, occupying the entire screen.

Mizoguchi is famous for the pains he took to let atmosphere express a character's emotions. Here we see Shimizu attempting the same thing, though more in the manner of shorthand. These two rather spontaneous shots do make their point. We sense the orphan boy's dejection and feel his pain, even though no word is spoken, and no close-up insists. The last two shots are similarly effective in an offhand way. They show a deserted alley lined with old houses with equally old earthen walls. The radio continues its litany of the names of soldiers who have returned.

Another variation on the theme of war and loss is offered in the following scene. A medium shot shows Genji standing near the entrance to an antique shop. It takes note of his look of concern – explained as the camera cuts to the interior of the shop, to a statue of the goddess of mercy. Genji and two other orphans gaze at it in obviously rapt sadness and hope.

Shimizu returns again and again to Genji's habit of standing outside the shop to gaze at the holy image. He offers no explanation and doesn't need to. The goddess obviously speaks for this little boy's yearning for his mother lost in the war.

The motif of separation that runs throughout the film takes on a more immediate poignancy toward the end when Genji is adopted by a woman tourist. Toyota, his friend and mentor, is desolate. Yet his loss is made good by an act of grown-up compassion. The painter Ryohei takes him back to Tokyo.

The final scene celebrates more than this new beginning. It reaffirms the bond shared by all these orphans – now orphans no more. On the eve of Toyota's departure he and Genji and a boy named Ichiun realize their dream of brotherly companionship. They contrive to sleep the night huddled together in the hand of the famous giant Buddha (a statue fifty-four feet high) (see Figure 15).

The entire film is done in long shots, a device that proves especially effective in this title sequence. A low-angle take reaffirms the benevolent parental archetype, showing as it does these three tiny figures peacefully asleep in the hand of the Universal Buddha. What better setting for a parting look at the camaraderie of waifs and strays used to the hole-and-corner existence of life in the streets?

This film represents an interesting departure from Shimizu's notoriously casual approach to cinematography. In fact, he is known to have

15. War orphans in Nara; Shimizu Hiroshi, *The Children and the Great Buddha* (1953).

taken charge of the camera himself – very much in contrast to his usual habit of letting a cameraman grind away while he himself chatted with visitors on the set.

Shimizu spent a year and a half studying Buddhist imagery, which seems a long time, considering that the film itself was shot in a matter of thirty days. In an interview with Kishi Matsuo, Shimizu had this to say about his cinematography:

> Kishi: "You used to say that the camera should be fixed at eye-level, seeing things as someone standing there would. . ."
>
> Shimizu: "Yes – in a drama whose focus is on human beings. It's different in a film whose stars are Buddhist images. They were originally made as objects of worship; they were made to be looked up to. . ."[10]

The use of holy icons as "stars" is in fact the significant difference that separates *The Children and the Great Buddha* from the rest of Shimizu's films about children.

The Buddhist images Shimizu chooses to work with are relics of the Tempyo period of art the Japanese are proud to see as distinctively their own. He makes powerful use of them too. The effect has the look of an exquisite art book well calculated to satisfy us aesthetically. But Shimizu does more. By making these holy icons an integral part of the everyday life of his orphans, he gives their transcendent, otherworldly character an immediate and entirely human interest that is everything to the success of this film.

One notable example of this is the scene set in a subsidiary temple of Nara's famous Tōdaiji Temple. This Sangatsudō temple houses an exquisite collection of Buddhist sculptures from the Tempyō era.

Shimizu is obviously anxious for the viewer to know and understand these images he has studied with such care, in preparation for making this film. So he offers a tour in great detail, deploying the camera's seeing eye in ways no visitor touring the gallery could manage. Nor is he content to let an uneducated view speak for these sublime expressions of spiritual thought and insight. Certainly his orphan guides, beloved as they are, are not up to the task. Instead, he lets the painter Ryohei guide our understanding of these powerful images the camera studies in part and in detail.

For example, we approach the Bodhisattva of the Moon by way of a long shot expressive of the atmosphere of peace and grace that radiates from this embodiment of the mudra of prayer. That done, the camera approaches to linger over details – her arm, her head in a close-up. Our attention shifts from this apparition of feminine grace and loveliness to the arresting menace of a diva, a guardian of Buddha. Here the camera begins with a low-angle shot, like a terrified, cowering first glimpse of the diva's angry face and gaping mouth.

Ryohei explains these things. His presence helps us connect these holy images with the orphans who revere them in their childish urchin way and who earn their streetwise living guiding gaping tourists in and out. Later we will see an extreme long shot of orphans and tourists together at the foot of a gigantic wooden statue of Nio, a guardian of heaven (sculpted by Unkei and Tankei).

Since Buddhism sees the purpose of existence as a process of compassion working to earn salvation, Shimizu is able to use these holy images as very real agents in the lives of these children.

When the statue of the goddess of mercy, which Genji considers his own, vanishes from the antique shop, the boy seeks out its purchaser, a lonely widow who has lost both husband and child in the war. It follows that she adopts this child now. Ryohei's decision to adopt Toyota is similar. He has long been engaged in portraying Buddhist icons, so he is, in effect, bringing precept and practice together.

The pictorially magnificent ending of the film celebrates the same kind of synthesis. In this case, a director whose love and compassion are centered on children has found a way to make the Buddhist case for union of sacred and profane. His final image says it all: that long shot of the children asleep in Buddha's hand, the hand so well known as it signifies a gift of serenity, of peace of heart and mind.

After such a closing, what next? It is almost surprising that Shimizu did in fact make two more films about children. In a sense, *The Shiinomi School* (*Shiinomi Gakuin,* 1955) does break new ground, since its children are handicapped, victims of the world's postwar polio epidemic. Some critics in fact see this film as the forerunner of a topic dealt with on television in the sixties. It may also be true that Shimizu was the first to treat the physical handicap as a topic of social relevance in life.

The narrative itself is a straightforward account of parents with two sons crippled by polio. The first half concerns their struggle at home in the city. The second half takes them to an idyllic country setting where they start a school for handicapped children.

All the temptations of the docudrama are here, and another director might well have stuck with a sober (if heartsick) clinical view of the situation. But these are children and Shimizu is Shimizu, so his account is well provided with sentimental, even melodramatic stress points.

It may help to remember that this film dates from 1955. That would account for the absence of larger social issues a director would expect (and be expected) to deal with today. Shimizu's focus is on these children in this situation: children cruelly handicapped and having to adjust to the life on offer at this school.

One focus of intensely charged emotion is the boy Tetsuo, whose parents have abandoned him. He is a child who has never learned to smile. Shimizu is unsparing in his history of the difficult adjustment such a child must make, not just to his crippled body, but to crippled emotions and expectations.

Shimizu uses deep space and the long take to emphasize the tiny bit of the world's vast space this suffering child occupies. At one point a long shot views him in the background weeping, his pitifully twisted body writhing. Two teachers arrive. This is not just a weeping child to be scooped up in a reassuring embrace. This child's body is itself an awkward, tormented obstacle to the everyday nourishment of human affection. Shimizu makes that point, training the camera's steady gaze at a well-meaning, but painfully maladroit struggle to calm Tetsuo and get him back into bed.

At other times, the camera suggests a more emotional involvement in this poor child's plight. Close-ups invite us to share his sense of dejection and loss, as he writes letters to parents who never reply, much less come to visit.

In the end, it looks as if the pathos of this situation got the better of Shimizu's critical faculty. Tetsuo dies in a scene that can only be compared to the classic tearjerker in which emotional content overwhelms intelligent control.

A long take shows Tetsuo in bed surrounded by classmates and their teacher. A girl begins to read the letter from his parents – a letter she has composed. A series of close-ups contrasts the boy's overjoyed expression with a rather troubled look on his teacher's face. Close-ups of their hands reinforce this difference of emotion. His lie open, receptive. Hers clench anxiously. The scene ends with a shot of the deserted garden, an obvious reference to earlier, happier days when Tetsuo was shown at long last a happy part of his group, playing with his classmates.

The Shiinomi School ends on the note of hopeful celebration of camaraderie one expects from Shimizu – complete with the countryside he obviously considered indispensable for growth and happiness. The camera pans left in a gesture conveying a sense of consoling admiration for the beauty of the scene. The film's theme song, "The Shiinomi School," is heard on the sound track, sung by the voices of children. The children enter while on their way to put letters of farewell in the mailbox. The seven-day memorial service for Tetsuo is over. A final shot pans over the mailbox with gently undulating mountains in the background.

Issues of children's welfare at the end of the twentieth century have vastly complicated every aspect of the subject, so Shimizu's views may seem exceedingly naive. Still, he was in effect an early advocate for children, and did some good at a difficult time in Japanese history. It seems appropriate to acknowledge one Japanese critic's assessment of his work on their behalf in film: "Shimizu's portrayals of children consistently focused on their beauty and innocence. He saw all children that way, the happy and the unhappy. Again and again he expressed his feeling that children are indeed angels."[11]

Shimizu's last children's film also appeared in 1955. It is something of a complex anticlimax to this aspect of his career. It shares the title of the novel it was adapted from, Shimomura Kōjin's unfinished five-part *Tales of Jirō (Jirô monogatari).*

The story, as it stands, takes the young hero from childhood through high school. It might as well be called *Jirō and His Mothers* since it studies the growth and development of a boy who experiences birth-mothering, foster-mothering, and step-mothering (see Figure 16).

Given such a maternal shuffle, one is not surprised to learn that the boy feels lost. His case may seem weighted, but the loss and learning are real, and show Jirō's growth in his understanding of the adult world and even of death itself.

Shimizu was not the first director to adapt this story to film. Shima Kōji did it in 1939. It may be helpful to see how he dealt with this material.

Shima confined his script to Jirō's childhood, which he viewed as a search for a satisfying bond. In a sense, the story views this need from an unexpected angle. Jirō, the second son, has been raised by a foster mother he must learn to let go of, since life has reunited him to his "real" mother. His emotions register the classic conflict between nature and nurture. Something in the boy leans to nurture, to the warm and loving woman who actually raised him.

16. Growing up with two mothers; Shimizu Hiroshi, *Tales of Jirô* (1955).

After an interval of separation, Jirō and his foster mother Ohama are reunited in a scene that resolves the drama in Shima's film. It is a local shrine festival, a nighttime celebration complete with festive music, firecrackers, and stalls of vendors selling all manner of treats and toys. It is one of those occasions of delirious childhood joy – and Jirō is enjoying it with the mother he loves best.

The camera pauses while Ohama buys Jirō a fox mask. Then it follows their progress through the crowd. It stops when Jirō drops his mask in a puddle and Ohama retrieves it for him. The camera pans to take in the lion dance that attracts their attention. It is performed on a makeshift stage. Ohama and Jirō take their place in the crowd scene captured by the camera's long take. No close-up of the woman and child is necessary. The scene itself speaks for Jirō's childlike joy in this unforgettable feast of delights.

His waking next morning also speaks for the keenness of his suffering, his sense of deception, of betrayal. Because Ohama is nowhere to be found. Here the camera cuts from room to room to follow his increasingly troubled search. A lateral pan speaks for his sense of a world so suddenly empty.

Overhearing his mother and grandmother talking, he learns the truth. Ohama has left for a new life far away. The camera follows the boy's desperate search outside. The scene ends on a country bridge. The camera shows the fox mask floating downstream, then over a waterfall. As the music on the sound track swells, we understand the boy's final gesture.

Shimizu's approach to the story is less subtle and considerably more energetic. The well-orchestrated, quick tempo of his narrative and the great care he gives to settings take the place of any real interest in the complexity of young Jirō's feelings.

Like Shima, Shimizu studies the boy's progress toward maturity. But like the novelist, Shimizu charts Jirō's progress in terms of three variations on the bond of motherhood. This Jirō is brought up by a birth mother, a foster mother, and a stepmother.

This screenplay also follows the novel in taking Jirō from childhood through junior high school. The story begins when Jirō is taken from his foster mother and returned to his family. He finds his birth mother cold and aloof and his siblings not that welcoming either. Shimizu follows the novel in pausing over the boy's sense of displacement. To make matters worse, Jirō is a second son, expected to occupy a subordinate position. That feeling is confirmed when he is farmed out to relatives again.

His sense of displacement eventually yields to overtures from his birth mother. But that reconciliation comes to grief, since she is ailing. Young Jirō gains a mother only to lose her to death – and then gain a stepmother after a decent interval.

As always, Shimizu's idea of a healthy environment is inseparable from rural charm. As the film opens, we see Jirō in Ohama's house. The camera surveys the entryway opening onto an earthen floor that leads into a rustic kitchen complete with a primitive hearth. The poverty of these peasants contrasts markedly with the wealthy home he was born into. But this simple country house is rich in affection and that makes all the difference to this child. Ohama (played by Mochizuki Yuko) is a chubby, down-to-earth, classic good country-woman kind of mother figure.

The moment he is returned to his own family's house, we see at a glance the world of difference that awaits this child. The camera's lateral pan makes a pointed survey of the imposing architecture of the house. We see how things stand. This child so happily nursed in the country was born into a land-owning family, prosperous, proud, and coldly respectable. We see room after room, all large, all filled with evidence of a distinguished family history.

Jirō, being a child and used to easygoing country ways, runs from room to room. He soon learns that noisy spontaneity won't do here. This "home" is all about mannerly behavior, proper and stiff. He can't seem to adjust. He starts wetting the bed. His confusion and shame are complete. Shimizu often uses deep space to suggest the distance that looms between Jirō and his mother and siblings.

For example, in one scene that shows the family's concern about the sick mother, her bedroom occupies the foreground. She is surrounded by the grown-up family members. Jirō watches from the courtyard in the middle ground. Beyond, in the background, his brothers and sisters gather in a room.

His mother being ill, Jirō is sent away again. Again, a lateral pan conveys a sense of his surroundings. The prosperity of this branch of the family derives from sake brewing, so the camera takes note of a large barrel and an imposing lattice door. We also see the assembled rural family seated in a large room.

Jirō's next visit to his own family home features Shimizu's version of the reunion/separation crisis involving Ohama. Shimizu's approach is predictably more direct, even artless. He lets the narrative sequence speak for the anguish that Shima dealt with symbolically. Shimizu uses just ten shots to tell this painful story. The effect is almost matter-of-fact, as if suggesting that Jirō is just passing through a phase, enduring pain that is only natural and therefore, well, endurable.

Ohama has come to visit in order to bid the family farewell. She is moving to a coal-mining town where her husband has found work. Jirō is overjoyed to see her. He is allowed to spend the night in her bed but doesn't disguise his desire to go with her the next day.

A long shot shows the nurse and child outdoors, aligned against a carriage. Ohama tells Jirō not to mention coming to see her off. He begs her to take him along but of course she must refuse. Ohama boards the carriage. A series of medium shots bears witness to Jirō's emotions as the carriage moves away from the camera. The absence of a close-up limits our involvement in his distress. The scene ends in a dissolve.

The next scene exposes us to the full brunt of emotions as his mother reproaches the disconsolate Jirō for having run after Ohama. A long shot shows the mother bedridden, the son forced by the size of the room to sit confined with her. The grandmother has positioned herself outside, near the room partition. Clearly she has reported the boy's behavior to his mother.

Jirō's mother reproaches him for behaving like such a big baby. She even asks which "mother" is more important, after all. Here the emotions involved are displayed directly. Close-ups register the mother's indignation, the son's mute rebellion. A medium shot shows both of them weeping.

Jirō's eventual adjustment is grudging. He is reconciled with his mother only as she dies. That done, the film picks up the pace as Jirō faces yet another stage in his development. A businesslike voice-over tells us that he is now in junior high school. His father has remarried.

The last part of the film seems perfunctory and anticlimactic. It may well be that his subject put Shimizu under obligation to the wave of postwar interest in the mother-genre film *(hahamono)*. That formula called for a suitable heroine to suffer a series of soap-operatic encounters with any or all possible mothers – birth, foster, or step.

Since young Jirō endures the encounters with all three, Shimizu was able to give three talented actresses equal time in the limelight. The screenplay itself takes a backseat to those performances.

Jirō's stepmother wins him over, not with patient insight into the boy's personal history, but with a gift of money. The dramatic high point of this part of the film is a school excursion. Jirō finds that his stepmother has tucked spending money into his kimono. His resistance to this new bond dissolves.

Back home, the camera follows him from room to room as he searches for her, calling out the word "mother" for the first time. The mother is clearly surprised, but this is sweet confusion, a scene well endowed with smiles and tears.

Interestingly enough, the camera maintains a discreet distance, as if observing some rule of detachment. The film ends with a long shot of mother and son embracing in the background. The camera's deep space orientation gives foreground magnitude to the earthen floor in view, an obviously hopeful likeness to the peasant house where Jirō was so happy. Soaring music on the sound track celebrates the love between mother and son as a voice-over narrative speaks of still more trials that are to come as Jirō grows into manhood.

It is of course a pity that Shimizu's last children's film is by no means his best. It does, however, contain some memorable outdoor scenes of the kind that contribute so much to his mastery of cinema.

One such scene concerns the bond between father and son. Here they are seen out taking a walk in sight of a mighty oak. Shimizu has used this setting before, in a short film made during the war: *Acorns of Oak and Pasania* (*Donguri to shii no mi,* 1942). Here the message is left unsaid and rightly so, being such a familiar old and enduring one. The camera does the talking, panning up to the tree admiringly as father and son linger nearby in a long shot. Given what we know, we see how things stand. How this father is saying to his neglected son, "Grow up strong like this oak!"

Shimizu has been described as a director whose idols were "children, monks, and athletes." Someone looking for a common denominator might come up with the idea that all three are expected to age gracefully and are apt to get noticed when they don't.

What then to say of a director whose work has aged into a kind of neglect? That he did the work the cinema industry wanted done before and after World War II? That at times he yielded too readily to studio production schedule pressures? That he stands too much in the shadow cast by giants like Ozu and Mizoguchi, monstrous perfectionists that they were?

I do think Hiroshi Shimizu warrants another look. True, he was easygoing to a fault. But in matters of the heart, in his concern for the fate of children on and off the screen, he stands paramount.

NOTES

1. For a brief study of a few representative films by Shimizu, see Noël Burch, *To the Distant Observer: Form and Meaning in the Japanese Cinema* (Berkeley and Los Angeles: University of California Press, 1979), 247–56.
2. Satô Tadao, *Nihon eiga no kyoshō-tachi* (Master filmmakers of Japan) (Tokyo: Gakuyo Shobō, 1979), 124.
3. Tanaka Jun'ichirô, *Nihon eiga hattatsu-shi* (A history of the development of Japanese cinema), vol. 2 (Tokyo: Chūō Kōron, 1976), 57. For a concise discussion of Kidoism in English, see David Bordwell, *Ozu and the Poetics of Cinema* (Princeton: Princeton University Press, 1988), 18–21.
4. Tadao Sato, *Mizoguchi Kenji no sekai* (The world of Mizoguchi Kenji) (Tokyo: Chikuma Shobō, 1982), 62.
5. Kishi Matsuo, Shimizu Akira, Sato Tadao, et al., *Kantoku kenkyû: Shimizu Hiroshi to Ishida Tamizô* (Study of directors: Shimizu Hiroshi and Ishida Tamizō) (Tokyo: Film Center, 1974), 19.
6. Kishi Matsuo, *Nihon eiga yoshiki-ko* (On Japanese cinema style) (Tokyo: Kawade Shobō, 1937), 19.

7. Donald Richie and Joseph Anderson, *The Japanese Film: Art and Industry,* expanded ed. (Princeton: Princeton University Press, 1983), 122–25.
8. Ibid., 124–25.
9. Concerning the canonic narrative pattern in the classical Hollywood film, David Bordwell points to this schematic pattern, which also fits these films about children by Shimizu. See Bordwell, *Narration in the Fiction Film* (Madison: University of Wisconsin Press, 1985), 157.
10. Quoted in *Nihon eiga kantoku zenshû* (Encyclopedia on Japanese film directors) (Tokyo: Kinena Jumpo, 1976), 207–8.
11. Kishi Matsuo, et al., *Kantoku kenkyû: Shimizu Hiroshi to Ishida Tamizô,* 28.

CHAPTER NINE

Ishihara Yûjirô

Youth, Celebrity, and the Male Body in Late-1950s Japan

Michael Raine

To borrow a line from Marlene Dietrich (*Touch of Evil,* 1957), Ishihara Yûjirô was "some kind of a man." Unlike Marlene, I think it *does* "matter what we say about people": the discourse on Yûjirô's celebrity speaks to us indirectly about the history of youth and masculinity in postwar Japan. In this essay I look at the early career of Ishihara Yûjirô as symptomatic of the social and aesthetic conditions of contemporary Japanese mass culture. I venture an explanatory critique of why and how Yûjirô's shifting impersonation of youth and masculinity was so successful, before going on to consider the consequences of that success for Japanese cinema and for Japanese visual culture in general. Japanese film study in the West has concentrated excessively on the art cinema and on the individual textual analyses. Yet the real interest of the Japanese program picture is distributed across a web of texts, filmic or otherwise, rather than being located in unitary moments. We need to trace that web if we are to understand cultural change in late-1950s Japan.

YÛJIRÔ'S "BIOGRAPHICAL LEGEND"

Ishihara Yûjirô emerged into public consciousness as the personification of the so-called *taiyôzoku* that scandalized Japan in 1956.[1] The word and the tribe were invented and popularized by the *shûkanshi,*[2] having been based on the stories of Yûjirô's older brother, Ishihara Shintarô.[3] Yûjirô appeared in the first Nikkatsu films based on Shintarō's work, impersonating the purportedly new subjectivity and the new body that the *taiyô-zoku* signified. However, the cynical, violent, sexually permissive, and suspiciously foreign image of the *taiyôzoku* was severely criticized, and Yûjirô did not become a star until he softened his original hard-edged and aggressive image.

By 1958, Ishihara Yûjirô was the biggest male star in Japan. He epitomized the sensitive tough guy in cinema and in popular music. In films such as *Sekai o kakeru koi* (1959) he became representatively Japanese, a "mixed-blood child of both Shitamachi ('downtown') and Yamanote ('uptown')," as he claimed in 1958. Later, Yûjirô's repertoire spread along with his waistline: in addition to the sailors, boxers, and jazzmen that made him famous, he played a teacher, an artist, a pilot, and a *sarariman* (businessman). He was still the principled hero when he played a traditionalist yakuza (in *Hana to ryû*) or even a right-wing assassin (in *Shôwa no inochi*). Although he died in 1986, he continues to be the subject of photographic collections, memoirs, and television specials: as the title of one biography has it, he was "the most beloved man in Japan."[4]

It is hard to anticipate that result from Yûjirô's early career. Instead of the legendary *bakuhatsu-teki na ninki* (explosive popularity – a phrase repeated so often that it has become a kind of epithet), we can see, in the first eighteen months of his career, an attempt to escape the delinquent image of his debut films and to become more acceptable to a wider audience. Far from explosive, his popularity underwent a deliberate inflation, with many agents of the Japanese mass communications industries manning the pumps.[5] The transformation was achieved through the distribution of public signs in newspapers, magazines, music albums, and other mass media. In the process Yûjirô became truly a multimedia star whose celebrity exceeded any particular medium. In addition to sparking the *teion* boom for deep-voiced singers, he also helped establish the fundamental *optique* of the Nikkatsu action metagenre of the 1960s,[6] and legitimated male fashion like no other actor before him.

Yûjirô's status was confirmed when he appeared on the first celebrity stamps issued by the Japanese post office. Actually, on two stamps: just as there were two Elvises there were at least two Yûjirôs, the old Yûjirô, star of TV police series such as *Taiyô ni hoero!*, and a younger incarnation associated with Nikkatsu youth films of the late 1950s and the early 1960s (see Figure 17). These two moments mark the beginning and the end of Yûjirô's "biographical legend," the version of his life that has gradually accreted around the repetition of exemplary stories – his hard drinking and surprising gentleness, his famous indifference to fame, his athletic body, his love

17. Ishihara Yûjirô, younger and older, on the first celebrity stamps in Japan.

of the sea. These stories consolidate Yûjirô's individuality; his "immediate" stardom is explained by his innate charisma. In fact, the younger image is itself the meliorated version of an even earlier, more dangerous Yûjirô. In the following section I excavate that earliest impersonation from underneath Yûjirô's "biographical legend," and follow the process by which it was transformed into the sporty young figure on the stamp.

YOUTH AND THE *TAIYÔZOKU* PHENOMENON

There is no space here to establish the social and economic grounds from which the *taiyôzoku* – or, rather, the scandal that created the *taiyôzoku* as its object – sprang in the spring and summer of 1956. This was the moment of *mohaya sengo de wa nai* (no longer the postwar) – the slogan that announced the beginnings of Japan's "economic miracle." The economy, thanks to hard work, procurements for the Korean police action, and the United States' support in international trade negotiations, had recovered from the war. Yet most Japanese were still impoverished, suffering the combined strains of scarcity and hard work in an export economy. While movies, LPs, and magazines proliferated, television sets – not to mention the cars and summer houses that fill the *taiyôzoku* films – were out of reach.[7]

Youth cultures were seen as a global problem in the mid 1950s, in literature, film, and popular discourse. From Francoise Sagan in France and J. D. Salinger in the United States to the Angry Young Men in Britain, literary old guards were in retreat. Films such as *Blackboard Jungle* and *Rock Around the Clock* marked the belated recognition by the film industry that its future lay with the youth market. Marking their international reach as well as the anxiety they generated, the former film scandalized Clare Boothe Luce and was withdrawn from the Venice Film Festival, while the latter occasioned dancing and riots in Europe. American popular cinema was soon named a chief suspect in the emergence of antisocial youth cultures: from the Teddy Boys in England to the *halbstarker* in West Germany and the *blousons noirs* in France.[8]

In Japan, Ishihara Shintarô's *Taiyô no kisetsu* won the prestigious Akutagawa Prize in January 1956 and sparked a debate on the relation between "popular" and "serious" literature, and on the influence of such works on contemporary youth. Treating Shintarō's novel as a social document, leading journalist Ooya Soichi endorsed the term *taiyôzoku* for the privileged but delinquent youth it described. Living it up at beach resorts such as Zushi and Hayama, or in mountain retreats such as Karuizawa, these youths made a mockery of Japan's postwar ideology of egalitarianism. The scandal marked a discursive shift in the meaning of *students,* a population which increased fourfold over the decade, from the hard-working *arubaito gakusei* (student working his way through college) to the irresponsible *Keiô boi* (rich kids at Keio University) or even the *kinbotan no yakuza* (college student "gangsters"). In this context, Shintarō's novel was a phenomenal best seller and Nikkatsu, which already owned the rights, rushed to make the movie in time for summer, while Shintarō wrote other *taiyôzoku* stories such as "Shokei no heya" and "Kurutta kajitsu."

Reviews of the *taiyôzoku* films all use the same vocabulary: *sengo* (postwar); *Nihon banare* (un-Japanese); *sekkusu* (already a translation), and *bōryoku* (violence). According to the *shûkanshi, sengo* in the *taiyôzoku* entailed a cynical, "dry" rejection of so-called traditional, wet human relations. Part of a larger discourse on the gradual desiccation or Americanization of Japanese culture, readers of the *shûkanshi* could check their own humidity by taking questionnaires that asked them to choose between whiskey and nihonshū, carpet and tatami – even between Nasser and Eden!

The very language of this new generation was different. In their breathless, present-tense reports, the *shûkanshi* would append explanations to now familiar *taiyôzoku* words such as *yabai* (dangerous) and *ikasu* (cool). Yûjirô was initially invited to the Nikkatsu studio to model the "Shintarō-gari" hairstyle that his brother's celebrity had popularized, and to work as dialogue coach for the actors in *Taiyô no kisetsu.* Publicity for the *taiyôzoku* films always stressed that this "dry boy" was the "*taiyôzoku no* champion," Shintarō's model for the *taiyôzoku* stories. We can hear these "un-Japanese" new speaking styles in an early scene from *Taiyô no kisetsu,* where the boxing club pals meet a group of bold young women in bathing suits from an English conversation school. High-velocity delivery and English-Japanese verbal confusion (the repartee includes several lines that can be understood in both languages; for example, *Shiga-ken* and "See you again") make ironic the boundary between native and non-native, while a low-level, low-angle shot fills the image with female bodies made foreign (they have English names and claim to be *Issei* – first-generation immigrants) (see Figure 18).

The connection between foreignness and specifically female bodies is not unique to this film – advertisements in *Heibon,* "a song and movie entertainment magazine," for example, touted special treatments to make girls grow taller and a device for inscribing eyelids with trendy double folds (see Figure 19). This last product was demonstrated by a Nikkatsu actress. Nikkatsu, in particular, was closely associated with the West through its recent history as a distributor of foreign films and of the successful series of youth films featuring nightclubs packed with gratuitous *gaijin* (Westerners), produced after the success of *Taiyô no kisetsu.*

Dressing up and style also figure prominently in *shûkanshi* reports on the *taiyôzoku:* the articles often begin *in medias res,* with a present-tense description of the spectacle of colorfully dressed new youths. *B-kyu taiyôzoku* (see note 1) men wear red and yellow, flowered shirts and tight, red swimming trunks, while *A-kyu taiyôzoku* wear white suits and inhabit *gaijin* spaces such as nightclubs and the resort town of Karuizawa. We can see the beginning of Yûjirô's reputation as the *ikasu otoko* (cool guy) in a scene from *Taiyô no kisetsu* where he visits a nightclub with four friends. The group patrols the dance floor, intimidating middle-aged businessmen types before moving in on three women sitting

18. Female and "foreign," *Taiyô no kisetsu* (1956).

alone. Yûjirô's white suit and slow, swaggering walk, with a slight hitch of his left leg, became a trademark, accentuated once fans started to imitate him after he became a superstar. Unlike previous tough-guy actors, Yûjirô was something of a dandy. As we will see later, this attention to body and image is crucial to our understanding of his role in late-1950s image culture.

Apart from being "postwar," "dry," and "foreign," the *taiyôzoku* films were also notorious for their tight imbrication of sex and violence. The *shûkanshi* accounts of the "real" *taiyôzoku* also stressed this relationship. Voyeuristic narratives follow policemen in search of fornicating teenagers in the woods, describe bodies draped on rocks by the sea in the moonlight, or speculate on illicit behavior in the yachts floating all night out at sea. Almost every magazine issue in the summer of 1956 has a cautionary tale about a young woman deceived by *kinbotan no yakuza,* or about young hoodlums terrorizing seaside resort towns.

In his second film and first starring role, Ishihara Yûjirô demonstrates the close link between sex and violence that made the *taiyôzoku* films so scandalous. Yûjirô confronts Kitahara Mie, who has begun an affair with

19. An advertisement in *Heibon* for an eyelid treatment.

his younger brother, when he discovers that she is already coupled with a middle-aged American serviceman. Kitahara admits this, and other affairs, but claims this time it's for real. As the jazz sound track, which was the aural condition of sexuality in late-1950s youth films, starts up, Yûjirô cynically suggests that Kitahara sleep with him too and forces a kiss on her. When she slaps him, the camera cuts to a low-angle extreme close-up of Yûjirô's heavily shadowed face as he wipes blood from his lips and fixes Kitahara with a sexual gaze (see Figure 20) light years from the look in *Aoi sanmyaku* (1949) that inaugurated the postwar sexual frankness of the youth film genre. Yûjirô then sexually assaults Kitahara – until, in a trope increasingly common after this period, she responds.

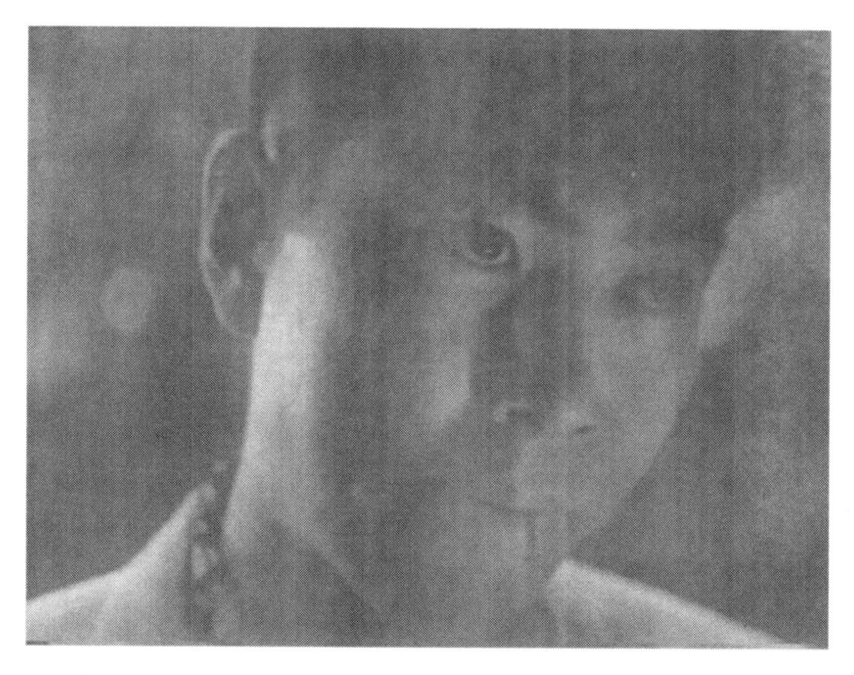

20. Yûjirô's sexual gaze.

Advertising and reviews for the film focused on the immoral but passionate relationship between these two characters. Given its source, this was hardly surprising. In *Kurutta kajitsu,* Nikkatsu aimed as close as possible at the forbidden *seifūzoku byōsha* (portrayal of sexual mores). Director Nakahira Ko even claimed that he had distributed the dialogue in the above mentioned sequence so that Eirin, the film industry's censorship body, could not cut a single shot without rendering the whole meaningless. Apart from the poster[9] (see Figure 21), a sultry still showing the two leads kissing was printed in the photographic front section of several film magazines, while contact sheets of the photo shoot itself were used in exposés of new film-star behavior. In the publicity for these films Yûjirô became a "carnal expert," whose knowledge was housed in a new, un-Japanese body.

CHANNELS OF CELEBRITY

Cinema reigned supreme as the most prestigious and highly capitalized branch of mass culture in the late 1950s. Attendance peaked in 1958 at

21. Portrayal of sexual mores in a poster for Nakahira Ko's *Kurutta kajitsu* (1956).

almost 1.2 billion. Film narratives were surrounded by parallel texts: posters and *chirashi* (film programs); reviews and star interviews in newspapers; photo spreads of the stars; and photo-novella-style versions of the texts in entertainment magazines such as *Heibon*. There were also more detailed accounts in the specialist film magazines – for example, *Eiga no tomo* for foreign films and *Eiga fan* for domestic films.

The early mentions of Yûjirô always describe him as "Ishihara Shintarō's younger brother." That is hardly surprising in 1956, the year of the "Shintarō boom," since one poll at least placed Shintarō with the pro-wrestler Rikidozan, and above top film star Nakamura Kinnosuke, as the biggest celebrity in Japan. Overshadowed though he was, in *taidan* with his brother, the early Yûjirô embraced the role as model for Shintarō's stories. He introduced readers to the new visual pleasures of the Ginza "golden time," that hour after work when, according to Yûjirô and the *shûkanshi,* male and female groups would prowl the Ginza, striking up promiscuous conversations. Yûjirô was also the subject of a two-month-long serial column in *Sports Nippon,* in which he would criticize existing actors, explain new words, and generally personify the new generation.

However, the early discourse on Ishihara Yûjirô was far more concerned with his body than with his mind. They talked about his "un-Japanese" strong physique, his long legs, his *taiyôzoku* clothes, and his *Shintarō-gari* hairstyle. At this early point in his career, Yûjirô also insisted on his own foreignness, claiming that all Japanese actors before him "stank of acting" and comparing himself to Marlon Brando and even John Wayne. In sum, he eagerly contended with Kawaguchi Hiroshi to epitomize the *taiyôzoku.*[10]

Taiyô no kisetsu and *Kurutta kajitsu* were hugely profitable for Nikkatsu, which had restarted production only two years earlier. Along with *Gyakkōsen* (written by Iwahashi Kunie, the "female Ishihara Shintarō" and starring Kitahara Mie) and Daiei's *Shokei no heya,* the films sparked a debate about the malign influence of cinema on Japan's youth. Regional housewives' groups, PTAs, and other guardians of social order picketed the cinemas and demanded that the films be censored or banned. As the Minister of Education declared: "Youth today has *taiyôzoku* tendencies – these must be removed!" Shintarō fanned the flames by attacking the "boredom" *(taikutsusa)* of a Japan controlled by old men, and by declaring, "Mishima Yukio told me that Japanese literature is full of mental cruelty: I wanted to show active physical *(nikutaiteki)* cruelty instead." While the *shûkanshi* reports on the phenomenon are characterized as much by titillation as by disapproval, the attacks on the *taiyôzoku* by newspapers and magazines such as *Fujin kōron* produced results. Eirin, the film censorship body, was reformed and film studios announced that they would make no more *taiyôzoku* films and would cooperate with the Ministry of Education in making films that encouraged moral behavior.[11]

In the short term at least, film studios tried to dissociate themselves from the *taiyôzoku* films. Nakahira Ko, director of *Kurutta kajitsu,* parodied the genre in *Gyūnyūya Frankie,* while Yûjirô experimented with different genres throughout the rest of 1956 and most of 1957.[12] He appeared as a polite youth (*Ubaguruma,* 1956), a dandified yakuza (*Chitei no uta,* 1956), and a human torpedo (*Ningen gyorai shutsugekisu,* 1956), as well as costarring in a number of jazzy musicals (for example, *Jazz musume tanjō,* 1957). He finally found a successful balance of tuneful romanticism and tough-guy bravado in three films made at the end of 1957: *Ore wa matteru ze, Washi to taka,* and *Arashi o yobu otoko,* the film that inaugurated the "Yûjirô boom" of 1958. Yet this formulaic film-historical account is still incomplete. Although it at least avoids the "explosive popularity" label that ascribes Yûjirô's position in postwar mass culture to his natural charisma, it still regards him as a fixed quality (of individuality, freshness, energy, sexuality) in search of a vehicle to communicate that quality to his waiting public. If we think of film as an unbounded text among texts, written, drawn, or photographed, we can build a denser explanation of his developing celebrity.

Most accounts of the "Yûjirô boom" begin with the release of *Arashi o yobu otoko.* In yet another conflation of his role and Yûjirô's metamedia celebrity, this narration of drummer Kokubu Shoichi's success in the jazz world is punctuated by montages that show his rise to the top of the *ninki tōhyō* (popularity polls) that both measured and advertised celebrity in the late 1950s, just as Yûjirô's own approach to stardom was mirrored and instigated by film and entertainment magazines. By 1958 there was a Yûjirô photo spread at the beginning of each entertainment magazine almost every month, while at least once a year he appeared on the cover or on a pullout calendar. In the yearly readers' polls for magazines such as *Heibon* and *Eiga fan,* he barely features for 1956, is just behind period stars Nakamura Kinnosuke and Okawa Hashizō in 1957, and is the clear winner by the end of 1958 (see Figure 22). The combination of *haha-mono* melodrama, jazz musical, and slugfest – and the moody affect of Nikkatsu's heavily shadowed wide-screen color style – made *Arashi o yobu otoko* the biggest New Year film of 1958. In an often-repeated story, cinemas were so crowded for the film that fans were standing within fifty centimeters of the screen. The first special edition on Yûjirô was printed in March 1958 in *Eiga Fan,* along with various songbooks and other paraphernalia, while *Sea and Trumpet,* an early example of the *shashinshū* (photographic collection), was published later in the year. That spring Yûjirô sang with Japan's most popular singer, Misora Hibari at the Kokugikan.[13] It seemed that all the trappings of stardom were in place by

22. Yûjirô's prominence in entertainment magazines soared by 1958.

the late summer, when Yûjirô published his first autobiography at the age of twenty-three and started to complain about fans waiting all night outside his house for an autograph.

How did Ishihara Yûjirô achieve this stardom? He arrived with a nice body and a bad attitude: both together made up his impersonation of a new kind of modern young masculinity associated with the *taiyôzoku.* But with the attacks on the *taiyôzoku,* he lost the attitude and kept the body. Yûjirô's interviews and Nikkatsu studio publicity during the remainder of 1956 and throughout 1957 worked to dissociate him from the excesses of the *taiyôzoku.* Even though he still often plays "dry" types, those hard exteriors concealingly reveal depths of inner liquidity. Yûjirô's language is still hypermodern – the *taidan* (verbatim interviews) in which he appears are dense with katakana representing his unconventional pronunciation or neologisms – but the aggressiveness is gone, replaced by a rough and ready friendliness. No longer a rapist, he's a favorite older brother. In response to the critiques of the *taiyôzoku* as "Americanized," Yûjirô stresses his fundamental old-fashionedness. In girls' magazines such as *Shin joen* he insists that the modern but dutiful student in the literary adaptation *Ubaguruma* (1956) is closest to his own character, and he claims that underneath he is a traditionalist who loves his mother and enjoys folk singing. We can see this in the shift from the Zushi cosmopolitanism of the *taiyôzoku* films to the nationally coded spaces of Shitamachi (downtown) in films such as *Ashita wa ashita no kaze ga fuku* (1958), in which Yûjirô first appears carrying the *mikoshi* (shrine) in a local festival (see Figure 23). Even the action films have a "wet" sensibility: for example, Yûjirô's tearful reconciliation with his mother at the end of *Arashi o yobu otoko* (see Figure 24).

However, as the musical genre reminds us, the main channel by which Yûjirô avoided the *taiyôzoku* ghetto was not film, or film publicity, at all. The song "Ore wa matteru ze" was played extensively on the radio in early 1957. It sold thousands of copies and became a *jazz kissa* (jazz coffee shop) staple, as well as the pretext for a film that established the trademark "mood action" so influential over the following decade. According to music critics, Yûjirô was one of the first deep-voiced (*teion*) stars, along with Frank Nagai and Mifune Hiroshi. During that year he developed the *nanpa* (lover) aspect of his star persona in albums directly addressed to his female fans. Between the songs, Yûjirô chats seductively

23. Yûjirô carries a shrine in *Ashita wa ashita no kaze ga fuku* (1958).

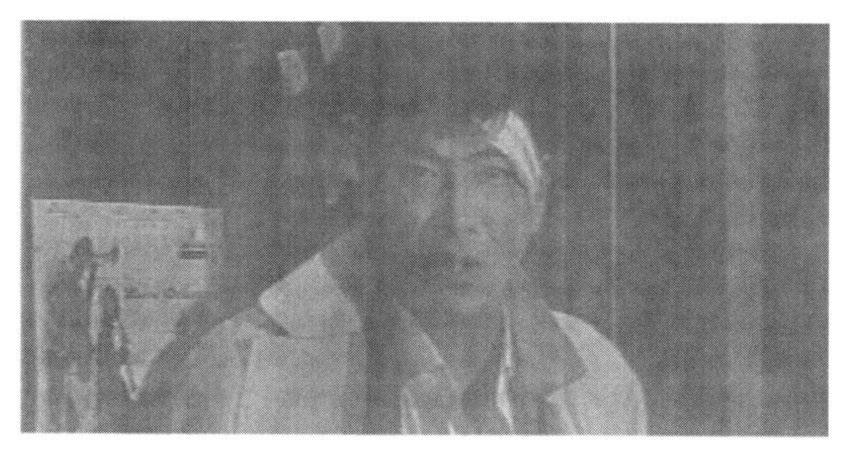

24. Yûjirô "wet" in *Arashi o yobu otoko.*

with a virtual interlocutor, apologizing for keeping "you" waiting, pouring "you" a drink and telling "you" how happy he is to be alone with "you" together on this imaginary date. No wonder, then, that his label, Teichiku, dubbed him *Nihon no koibito* (Japan's lover). *Arashi o yobu otoko* was released simultaneously as film and record – from this film on, the title song is so important to Yûjirô's films that the opening sequence is extended to accommodate the entire tune.

Yûjirô insisted in interviews that singing was just part-time work, yet by one count he still managed to release or re-release four albums, eighteen EPs, and forty-three singles in the first two years of his career.[14] He was just as diffident about acting as about singing: in the Platonic sense that undergirds the culture of celebrity, Yûjirô was neither an actor nor a singer. He was a personality first and the medium through which his celebrity circulated was of only secondary concern. Instead of the formulaic answers of typical star interviews – "I want to continue as long as I can," "I just want to portray ordinary people" – he declared, "If it gets boring I'll quit" or, "I never learn the lines, I'm just myself on the screen." Yûjirô's semiotic body was always a text-above-the-text, separated from the diegesis by the title song, which was sung under his own name at the beginning of the film and then repeated by his character, often in quasi-direct address to the camera (for example, in *Washi to taka*), during the film. His appeal was based on his individuality, separate from the characters he portrayed, even in period films such as *Bakumatsu taiyôden*

(1957). The musical *Subarashiki dansei* (1958) demonstrates this personalized celebrity. Hardly a dancer, and with a rough (though distinctive) singing voice, Yūjirō stands outside the diegesis as an example of the "wonderful guy" of the film's title. In the grand finale, the play on "Yū" (his nickname) and "you" again confuses Yûjirô as celebrity and the character he plays.[15]

Fashion, too, is an important part of this metatextual representation of self (*jiga*) and individuality (*kosei*). As he became famous, Yûjirô's style was adopted by many of his fans. For example, he was the first Japanese male star to wear jewelry. He also popularized styles such as high-waisted pants and the boat-neck collar, *yakuza* accessories, and even inspired young fans to imitate his way of speaking and his swaggering walk. Fashion works metatextually, like a trademark, across his early films. For example, the variety of tiny hats he wears tipped back on his head, or even the formulaic way he was introduced by his famously long legs (see, in particular, *Kurutta kajitsu, Shimizu no abarenbō,* and the extended opening sequence of *Washi to taka*). This was even parodied by Nakahira Ko: when he cross-dresses in *Aitsu to watashi,* we are introduced to this gender-impersonation through a shot, under the changing-room door, of Yûjirô's hairy legs in a skirt. Yûjirô's style was described as "treating expensive things casually": it was part of his impersonation of *ikasu otoko,* the cool guy who ignored convention and did things his own way.

NEW BODIES

How was Ishihara Yûjirô able to overcome the long tradition of the *binan* (beautiful male) in Japanese film and theater in order to become a romantic star? Critics in 1956 thought that Yûjirô was too big and too ugly to be a star. No star had been that large: cinematographers complained that he changed the shot scale, making two-shots hard to achieve. No star had had such uneven teeth – and done nothing about them. Yet if we look at other aspects of masculinity in this period, perhaps we can see why visual culture was ready for a new kind of male impersonation. One such aspect is the popularity of sports, especially Sumo, aided by the spread of television. Although television ownership was still low, in their "plaza TV" tactic, TV companies advertised the medium itself, and the sports it predominantly conveyed, by displaying

TVs in public places such as train station plazas and electric-goods stores. Sumo wrestlers became *ninkimono* (celebrities). They would pose for photographs outside the ring, in playgrounds, or dressed up as cowboys. In one photograph, the *sumotori* Kotogahamaseki is described as "otoko ippiki" – something like "man-animal," one of the epithets that was assigned to Yûjirô in the press sheets sent to each cinema along with a film (see Figure 25). In general, these magazines aimed at young people conflate opposing signs of hypermasculinity and cuteness. Yûjirô, too, was even called "kawaii," recalling the root sense of "lovableness," rather than its current saccharine emphasis. Perhaps this broken terrain makes Yûjirô's own combination of violence and sensitivity less surprising.

Violence and *struggle* were also key terms in the discourse of economic development in Japan, especially after the "Japanese Economy and Economic Growth" white paper that introduced the phrase *mohaya sengo de wa nai.* As Ichikawa Kon's *Man'in Densha* (1957) and Masumura Yasuzō's *Kyojin to gangu* (1958) seek to dramatize, contemporary Japanese were underpaid and overworked in the speedup economy. One solution was injectable testosterone, as advertised in *Shūkan yomiuri* alongside a discussion of the *taiyôzoku* in 1956. Like the new popularity of bodybuilding in 1955 (Mishima Yukio was an early enthusiast, as his appearance in *Karakkaze yarō* testifies [see Figure 26]), hormones promised to make men strong and women young – the still-current "dimorphic ideal." In this context

25. No longer the beautiful male, Yûjirô as man-animal.

26. Mishima Yukio buff in *Karakkaze yarô.*

Yū-chan's body, like the sumo wrestler's, became a kind of joke. No longer threateningly antisocial, his violence now was just exciting, part of his latest male impersonation. As one Nikkatsu publicist put it: "32-inch inseam (see Figure 27), second longest of any actor in the world: monster Yûjirô!" Perhaps this last reference to *kaibutsu Yûjirô* gives us a clue to what happened to his semiotic body in the interests of mass cultural popularity – Yûjirô, like Godzilla, began as a terrifying and alien force but was soon domesticated and became ineffably, albeit somewhat violently, Japanese.[16]

27. Yûjirô's 32-inch inseam.

CONSEQUENCES OF THE *TAIYÔZOKU*: "CULTURAL WRITING" IN LATE-1950S JAPAN

This essay has argued that celebrity in the late 1950s extended across a range of "cultural writing," from the image-signs (visual and aural) of cinema to the publicity discourses that preceded them and the magazines and other media that exceeded them. Cinema was not a self-contained cultural object, but part of a system of "wording the image." In that cultural writing, Yûjirô's initially threatening *taiyôzoku* persona was normalized and nationalized as a condition of his becoming a major star. However, this brief period of scandal and retrenchment was not without consequences. I speculate that the shifting imbrication of word and image marks a shift in the semiotic regime of Japanese cinema, and perhaps even of Japanese literature and mass culture as well.

In cinema, those consequences include changes to poster design and shot scales caused by the emphasis on body over face. Yûjirô's later films also created the stereotypically male roles of Nikkatsu action: boxer, sailor, jazzman. The slightly later *mukokuseki eiga* (films without nationality) added a parody of the U.S. cowboy series so popular on Japanese TV, featuring performers such as Kobayashi Akira and, most memorably, Shishido Jo[17] (see Figure 28). Taken together, we might call this the Nikkatsu Action *optique* (see note 4).

Beyond Nikkatsu, we could also make the case for a new temporality in Japanese cinema: at the beginning of this period Satō Tadao could write that Japanese film was fundamentally "slower" than Western cinema.[18] There are of course many counterexamples to this claim – for example, prewar *chanbara,* or Ichikawa Kon's early films – but it does represent a developing ideal of 1950s Japanese cinema, especially after that "oriental" temporality was rewarded with prizes at European film festivals. Against this orthodoxy, in 1958, Masumura Yasuzō propagandized the importance of "speed" in shaking off mainstream cinema's "premodern" trappings. Masumura meant something more Eisensteinian than simply fast cutting: a cinema of shocks that sent spectators careening out of their comfortable orbit around *ningensei* (humanness) and *jinsei no aji* (flavor of life). The privileged trope, turning up in almost all the new youth films, of this new temporal distortion is the montage sequence that usually telescopes time but introduces a new dynamism even when it expands time, as in the final scene of *Kurutta kajitsu,* Nakahira Ko's first

28. Domesticated cowboy.

released film. This is the scene that so excited Oshima Nagisa, who wrote, "In 1956, when Nakahira Ko burst onto the scene with *Kurutta kajitsu,* . . . sensitive people heard in the sound of the woman's skirt tearing and the roar of the motorboat that cut through the older brother a petrel's cry announcing a new age of the Japanese cinema."[19] Oshima himself was promoted by Shochiku at the tail end of industrial and semiotic changes that began in films directed by Nakahira Ko, Kurehara Koreyoshi, Masuda Toshio, Inoue Umetsugu at Nikkatsu; Ichikawa Kon and Masumura Yasuzō at Daiei; Sawashima Tadashi at Toei; Okamoto

Kihachi at Toho; and several others. As cinema attendance declined in the 1960s, overwhelmed by the same tide of television and individuated consumption that washed over other parts of the world, this accelerated mode of filmmaking continued in subgenres such as Nikkatsu's *mukokuseki eiga* and Toho's city comedies. Aaron Gerow has written, of 1920s Japanese cinema, that the image was taken over by the "regime of the word" in sound cinema after the *Jun'eigageki undō* (pure cinema movement). In counterpoint, the 1950s action *optique* resists the tight hold of the word – as *gensaku* (original story) and as *naiyō-shugi* (content-based) criticism – in the pleasures of the optical, reclaiming its link to the visual experimentation of the 1920s.

Turning from visual images to writing, Ishihara Shintarō claimed an affiliation to Camus and Hemingway, saying that his stories were not social-problem texts, but *kannen shōsetu* (novels of ideas) in which writing was a kind of cinema – not like a film scenario but built of images, immediate perceptions. Perhaps this is why older writers such as Satō Haruo claimed he wasn't writing "literature" at all. Ishihara's stories simply narrate a play of gazes and moments of self-conscious perception, linked by cinematic devices such as abrupt flashbacks and even superimpositions. Perhaps we can see an echo of Shintarō's emphasis on self-consciousness, surface, and vision, if not of his (sexual) politics, in the Yoshimoto Banana phenomenon, as analyzed by John Whittier Treat.[20]

We might also claim a new kind of temporality for *shûkanshi* "cultural writing." Accounts of the *taiyôzoku* start in the middle of things and use few time markers; the narrative point of view frequently adopts the role of a camera, passively registering the passing scene or actively seeking out delinquent couples. Magazine culture in general enabled an accelerating cycle of scripted "booms" that is as old as Japanese mass culture itself, including the "Shintarō boom" of 1956 and the "Yûjirô boom" of 1958. They cheered on the development of Japan's economy with articles about new *danchi* (apartment blocks) and the electric goods that they contained. They also assisted in the development of Japan's domestic consumer economy, as it at last began to take off after the "income doubling" pledge, made in response to the social protests of the 1950s that culminated in the Anpo demonstrations of 1960. In general, mass cultural writing seems, in this period, to aspire to the condition of cinema – at least, to the immediacy of the visual image. As the threads that bind these speculations to the substantive claims made in this essay about

Ishihara Yûjirô's "semiotic body" begin to fray, perhaps we could grasp for a formulation of "post-postwar" Japanese consumer culture as increasingly image-oriented, even before it was technically and economically able to communicate through photograph rather than copy, image rather than word. Since I began this essay by stealing a line from Orson Welles, perhaps I should end it by stealing a line from one of Welles's biggest fans. Like Bazin's "myth of total cinema" that blazed the way for cinematic technology, it is the 1950s *shûkanshi*'s "myth of total imagery" that has reached its apotheosis today.

NOTES

1. *Taiyôzoku* is usually translated in English as "sun tribe." It was coined in response to the rich, bored, and vicious youth of Ishihara Shintarō's *Taiyô no kisetsu,* to refer to the privileged youth who would gather in their family villas at beach and mountain resorts for supposedly decadent purposes. By extension, it referred to the Japanese students and young workers who aped the lifestyle of the privileged bourgeoisie, camping out at the same resorts during the summer months, away from the supervision of their parents. Rather than villas or *ryokan* (Japanese inns), these kids slept in tents and "bungalows" (tents or plywood erected over a wooden base). The two groups were often divided into "A-class *taiyôzoku*" and "B-class *taiyôzoku,*" but this stable classification was undermined by a proliferation of terms that blended into other "zoku" that the mass media had invented since the war: for example, *shayōzoku, manbozoku, bungarozoku, gekkōzoku, eiseizoku, kaminarizoku, danchizoku,* and so on. Whatever the sociological merits of these categories, the public reputation of this "arbitrary young generation" is probably best described by an English caption in the graphic magazine *Asahi gurafu:* "These young people in their teens or early 20s seek action before reason and are keen about the pleasure of the flesh."
2. Populist weekly magazines that were initially published by newspaper companies before World War II but were augmented by publishing companies and other enterprises (e.g., *Shûkan shinchô*), creating the "*shûkanshi* boom" of 1956.
3. Ishihara Shintarô won the Akutagawa Prize in 1956 for the novella *Taiyô no kisetsu.* The ensuing debate over whether this work constituted literature or pornography, and the surprising support for Shintarō's outspoken critiques of gerontocratic Japanese society, made him one of the most famous people in Japan. A student of Minami Hiroshi, he claimed to have Communist leanings at the time, but is now best known as a right-wing politician, author of *The Japan That Can Say "No"* and the current mayor of Tokyo.
4. The flow of memorabilia never ends: in the past year Nikkatsu has released 12 of his films on video for the first time and a double CD-ROM collection

containing a multimedia presentation of various Yûjirô fetish-objects, such as his "beloved Benz convertible."

5. Komatsu Shun'ichi's memoir *Ore no Yûjirô* gives many details of this process. Komatsu was in charge of Yûjirô's publicity at Nikkatsu for the first three years of his career.
6. See Dudley Andrew's *Mists of Regret: Culture and Sensibility in Classic French Film* (Princeton: Princeton University Press, 1995) for a sophisticated discussion of a film *optique.*
7. Japanese wages averaged one-tenth of American wages in the mid-1950s, a time when the Americanization of Japan was a constant topic in opinion magazines. This cultural "pollution" was realized as fantasy long before Japanese could afford to emulate the American consumption of things. There is no end to salient detail in the analysis of this mode of cultural fantasy. In addition to establishing the comparative intertext between Yûjirô and American stars such as James Dean and Elvis Presley (whose celebrity swept Japan in 1956 and 1957, respectively), a longer version of this project links the vicissitudes of Yûjirô's persona to larger social processes such as economic recovery and the (re)development of Japanese commodity culture, as well as to discourse on masculinity and the *minzoku* (National Folk). It would also seek to demonstrate that these films were active in those processes, assisting in the work of producing fit subjects for both accelerated production and individualized consumption.
8. See James Gilbert, *A Cycle of Outrage: America's Reaction to the Juvenile Delinquent of the 1950s* (New York: Oxford University Press, 1986) and T.R. Fyvel, *Troublemakers: Rebellious Youth in an Affluent Society* (New York: Shocken Books, 1962) on juvenile deliquency in Europe. See also Stanley Cohen's *Folk Devils and Moral Panics: The Creation of the Mods and Rockers* (Oxford: Martin Robertson, 1980) for an early analysis of the function of mass media in generating a social consensus through publicizing outlaw groups.
9. Posters were a hugely important part of film culture in this period. Almost always in a dramatized, painterly style, they were posted in several formats outside cinemas and were copied for the enormous *kanban* (billboards) over the entrance to the cinema. Yûjirô's films, in particular, changed the representational mode for these posters. Until then they had operated according to a simple code: the bigger the head, the bigger the star. Posters were usually composed around a big close-up of the main star's head, with portraits of minor characters arranged along the side. But Yûjirô's impersonation of a new masculinity in his posters emphasizes his body, especially his legs. As Ozu Yasujirô recognized in a fascinating article in *Eiga hyōron,* he could never use Yûjirô in his films, because he acted with his whole body, not just with his face.
10. Kawaguchi's extraordinarily confrontational performances in films such as Ichikawa Kon's *taiyôzoku* film *Shokei no heya* (1956) and *Man'in densha* (1957), and Masumura Yasuzo's *Kuchizuke* (1957) and *Kyojin to gangu* (1958), kept him outside the mainstream. He is now remembered chiefly as

one of the first film actors to appear in a TV commercial in the early 1960s, a measure of the comparative failure of his career. Yûjirô, on the other hand, modified his persona in response to the inevitable backlash against the *taiyôzoku* and the films that represented it.

11. Although Nikkatsu cancelled production of *Hai-iro kyōshitsu,* the taiyôzoku films produced permanent changes in Japanese cinema. While the overt immoralities of the *taiyôzoku* – drugging and raping women, torturing men to death – were avoided, the more important shifts in editing rhythms, ranges of shot scales, and antimelodramatic irony soon returned at other studios in the work of Masumura Yasuzo, Okamoto Kihachi, and (somewhat belatedly) Oshima Nagisa. Mishima Yukio even attempted Yûjirô's dangerous bodily presence in *Karakkaze Yarô,* while nothing in the *taiyôzoku* films surpassed the breathtaking brutality of Katsu Shintaro's *Heitai Yakuza.*
12. The agency of this search is of course open to question. An answer would focus on Nikkatsu's advertising and production divisions – in particular, publicist Komatsu Shun'ichi and producer Mizunoe Takiko, who acted as Yûjirô's mentor, even bringing him to live with her near the Nikkatsu studio.
13. See Alan Tansman's "Mournful Tears and Sake: the Postwar Myth of Misora Hibari," in John Whittier Treat, ed, *Contemporary Japan and Popular Culture* (Honolulu: University of Hawaii Press, 1996), for an account of Hibari's extraordinary fame. If Yûjirô was the king of postwar mass culture, Hibari was most surely its queen, having been commemorated on a stamp from the same series that included the Yûjirō stamp. Tansman concentrates on Hibari's later career, where she came to embody the enka tradition. Yet in the 1950s she was one of the three stars of trendy comedies such as *Romansu musume* and *Janken musume,* riots of product placement and *Heibon*-style pastel fashion. Perhaps *Romansu musume* recognizes *Heibon's* role in constructing ideal forms of masculinity in the scene where Hibari and pal Eri Chiemi construct a "photofit" picture of the boy Yukimura Izumi is looking for by cutting and pasting parts from an issue of the magazine. A more disturbing indication of the increasing importance of body image was the acid attack on Hibari in 1957, by a young fan who wanted her to be as "ugly and worthless" as she felt herself to be.
14. *Ishihara Yūjirō eiga Korekushon* (Ishihara Yūjirō film collection), (Tokyo: Kinema Junposha, 1994).
15. These quasi-direct address performances also point to a mode of reception that differed significantly from the supposedly self-enclosed and "illusionist" mode of representation claimed for the "classical cinema." Yûjirô's appearance on the screen was met with wild applause and cries of "Yū-chan" from the audience. A dedicated cultural purist could claim this behavior for the kabuki tradition of calling out to favorite performers, but it seems in this context to have more in common with the organized frenzy of 1950s live music. For example, Watanabe Productions organized several "Western carnivals" in Tokyo that started the rockabilly craze. Watanabe Misa (the model for the Kitahara Mie role in *Arashi o yobu otoko*) staged a direct relation between performer and fan by passing out the paper stream-

ers seen in the "drum contest" at the heart of that film (and satirized in Masumura's *Kyojin to gangu*).

16. This transformation was complete by 1959. From representing a threat to the Japanese social order, he came to represent Japan itself – explicitly so in *Yûjirô no Ōshū kakearu ki,* a documentary about his trip to Europe to make *Sekai o kakeru koi,* the first Japanese feature shot mainly in Europe.
17. These films also solidified the Action *optique's* heterosexual, homosocial masculinity, perhaps most overt in the finale to *Shimizu no abarenbō,* when "older brother" Yûjirô is shot by a distraught Akagi Keiichiro and has to slap him to his senses, smearing his own blood across the younger man's face in the process. The final exchange of loving gazes in extreme close-up couples the two men and leaves Akagi's sister, played by Ashikawa Izumi, as a spectator. Going beyond the cinema that was one of its main stages, the invention of new forms of masculinity in the late 1950s is coincident, perhaps reciprocal, with the representation of male effeminacy. Although there are earlier examples of gender confusion (*Jiyū gakkō* [1951], *Bakushū* [1951], *Ashi ni sawatta onna* [1952]), these hints become more common in films such as *Arashi o yobu otoko* (1957), *Hi no ataru sakamichi* (1958), *Yami o yokogire* (1959), and many others, as well as in the "fashion boy" craze of 1955 when words like "gay boy" and "sister boy" also came into currency.
18. Satô Tadao. "Nihon eiga no tempo," in *Eiga hyōron* 12.5 (1955), 27–33.
19. Oshima Nagisa. "Sore wa toppaguchi ka? Nihon eiga no kindaishugisha tachi" (Is it a breakthrough? The modernists of Japanese film), *Eiga hihyō,* July 1958. This essay appears in Oshima Nagisa, *Cinema, Censorship, and the State: the Writings of Nagisa Oshima* (Cambridge: MIT Press, 1992), 26.
20. John Whittier Treat, "Yoshimoto Banana Writes Home: The Shojo in Japanese Popular Culture," in John Whittier Treat, ed., *Contemporary Japan and Popular Culture* (Honolulu: University of Hawaii Press, 1996).

CHAPTER TEN

Otoko wa tsurai yo

Nostalgia or Parodic Realism?

Richard Torrance

How to account for the extraordinary popularity of *Otoko wa tsurai yo?* It is the most prolific film series in the history of world cinema – forty-eight films since the first movie was created in 1969, preceded by a twenty-six-episode TV series. For much of the life of the series, individual films were attracting two million viewers per film, and it is thought that half the population of Japan has seen at least one of the films at some point. As Mark Schilling has observed, the star of the series, Atsumi Kiyoshi – who played the hero, Kuruma Torajirô, nicknamed Tora-san, a short, square-faced loser who cannot hold a steady job, did not graduate from junior high, and never once got the girl – could, on any given day, beat out the likes of Harrison Ford, Mel Gibson, or Michael Keaton in the Japanese market. Atsumi Kiyoshi died on August 4, 1996, from lung cancer. He was posthumously awarded the People's Honor Award *(Kokumin Eiyôshô),* the twelfth person to receive the honor. Despite the fact that Atsumi Kiyoshi did not wish a public funeral and the public was not informed of his death until after his cremation, well over 100,000 people have paid their final respects at Shôchiku's Ôfuna Studio near Kamakura. Those who have made this pilgrimage appear to have been representative of Japan's population as a whole – men and women, children, the elderly, young couples, and the middle-aged.[1]

Critics writing in a journalistic style tend to ascribe the popularity of the series to some single source: the formulaic quality of the plots, nostalgia, or

I would like to thank David Desser, Linda Ehrlich, Norma Field, Dennis Washburn, and the anonymous reader for this volume for their comments and suggestions.

the fact that the series came to perform a ceremonial function of celebration at New Year's, when one of the movies in the series was often released. These sources of appeal are commonly identified with a specific sociological characteristic of the Japanese, for example, the audience for these films as "cogs in the great Japanese export machine," or as the proverbial nails that have gotten hammered down. Nostalgia, or something like it, is one of the most frequently cited sources of the films' appeal for a mass audience by writers for an English-speaking readership.[2]

This mode of argument seems reductive, for it depends on assumptions that disparage the audience it attempts to explain. The term *nostalgia* is historically a designation in English of a pathological condition of longing for the geographical location of home. The connotations of illness are reinforced in current usages of the term in the rhetoric of postmodernism by which nostalgia presupposes "the idea of history as decline; the sense of a loss of wholeness; the feeling of the loss of expressivity and spontaneity; and the sense of loss of individual autonomy." Thus the Japanese audience's responses of familiarity, affection, intimacy, and laughter are reduced, according to the nostalgic paradigm, to symptoms of transglobal capitalism's alienating effects.[3]

On the other hand, such critics as Satô Tadao and Yoshimura Hideo have written substantial studies that illustrate the extraordinary complexity of the series, both formalistically and in terms of sociohistorical content. Satô argues in great detail that *Otoko wa tsurai yo* constitutes a parody of almost every major genre of Japanese film. Yoshimura provides an account of the film series as a mirror of the history of the manners and customs of the postwar period.[4] An adequate account of the reasons for the popularity of the series, then, would probably require a book-length study reconceptualizing the sophistication of Japanese popular culture and the idea of "the masses." Moreover, a consideration of the representation of class in the context of popular culture in contemporary Japan should take into account the *Otoko wa tsurai yo* movie series – first, because in the context of popular culture (*minshû bunka, taishû bunka*), an idea that has clear class connotations in Japanese, the series is the most popular in the sense of "mass appeal"; and second, as will be argued below, because this popularity is attributable in large part to its comedic play on class signification. As a preliminary inquiry into the issues the series raises, *Otoko wa tsurai yo*'s contemporaneity and realism will be the aspects of its popularity considered here.[5]

PARODIES OF POPULAR ENTERTAINMENTS

Otoko wa tsurai yo parodies something for just about everybody. The formula that had evolved by about the fifth film would remain, with variations, the one used throughout the series: dream sequence/parody of mass media; Tora-san awakens in the countryside/parody of the pastoral; Tora-san returns home to Katsushika Shibamata/slapstick along Edogawa behind opening credits and title; Tora quarrels with his family/parody of home drama; he travels to the countryside to peddle his goods, and meets a romantic interest/parody of pastoral romance; he returns home and the Katsushika family meets the love interest/parody of home drama; Tora doesn't get the girl and leaves for the provinces/parody of romance-melodrama.

Tora-san himself is a walking parody of movie *yakuza* (Japanese gangsters). The television series appeared as the boom in idealized treatments of yakuza, with Takakura Ken often in the lead, was becoming predictable and mannered. In the television series that preceded the movies, Kuruma Torajirô appears in sunglasses and a flowered shirt, the image of a young gangster, *chinpira,* as the TV series' director, Kobayashi Shunsuke, conceived of the character (see Figure 29). Almost every film in the series opens with the self-introduction of Kuruma Torajirô and the song in which Atsumi, in the role of Tora-san, sings to his saintly half-sister, Sakura, about his status as a ne'er do well yakuza: "Dôse orera wa yakuza na aniki, wakatcha iru-n-da imôto yo/Itsuka omae no yorokobu yo na erai aniki ni naritakute" ("You know, young sister, your brother's a yakuza. One day I'll become a brother you can be proud of"). Tora-san's formulaic self-introduction (*jingi,* verbal decorum) is a sort of stylized play on words that harks back to the prewar traveling gangster introducing himself and his status to the boss of the gang he has encountered in his travels: "Watakushi, umare mo sodachi mo Katsushika Shibamata desu. Taishakuten de ubuyu o tsukai, sei wa Kuruma, na wa Torajirô, hito yonde fûten Tora to hasshimasu" ("Born and raised in Tokyo's Katsushika Shibamata, baptized in the waters of the temple of Taishakuten [*Sakra devânâm Indra*]; last name, Kuruma [revolving wheel] given name, Torajirô, people call me 'The tiger who wanders on the wind' [Fûten Tora]").

Throughout the life of the series, though less in later years, the conventions of yakuza films are parodied. The fights Tora-san gets involved in degenerate into posturing and shoving in which no one is really hurt.

29. Atsumi Kiyoshi, as Tora-san, parodies a gangster in the *Otoko wa tsurai yo* series.

When he is arrested on some minor charge, he sheepishly calls his family, who immediately bails him out of jail. But most important, in contrast to the strong silent movie yakuza such as Takakura Ken, Tsuruta Kôji, or Ando Noboru, whose stoic expressions testify to a willingness to die at a moment's notice, Kuruma Torajirô is constantly talking, creating narratives. He is a *tekiya,* a street vendor living by his verbal wits, who often peddles goods at festivals. Tora-san is adept at a sort of street performance called *tankabai,* which is designed to attract a crowd on the street or at a festival in order to sell useless or shabby or misrepresented goods (see Figure 30). An example of this kind of street performance by Tora-san is as follows:

> Saa, mono no hajimari ga ichi naraba, kuni no hajimari wa . . . Yamato no kuni, shima no hajimari wa Awajishima . . . Nee . . . bakuchiuchi no hajimari wa Kumasaka no Chōhan, akai akai wa nani mite wakaru, akaiiro mite ugokanu mono wa, kibutsu, kanabutsu, ishibutsu da, senri hashiru kisha de sae, akai hata furya chito tomaru to yû yatsu. . . Dô desu, tsuzuita sûji ga futatsu. . . Nee, dô . . . Nî-san yotterasshai wa, Yoshiwara no kabu, Nikichi ga tôru Tôkaidô,

30. Tora-san as *tekiya,* street vendor and performer.

nikumare kozô, yo ni habakaru . . Saa, Nikki Danjô shibai no ue de no nikumare yaku, to yû no . . . Tsuzuita sûji ga mitsu, hora, san san rokupo de hikeme ga nai. San de shinda ka Mishima no Osen, Osen bakari ga onnago jyanai yo, kano yûmei na Ono no Komachi ga Kyôto wa Gokurakuzaka no monzen mikka miban nomazu, kuwazu notareshinda no ga, sanjusan . . . Tsuzuita sûji ga yotsu, Yotsuya/Akasaka/Kôjimachi, charachara nagareru Ochanomizu, ikina nêchan tachishonben (*Torajirô komoriuta* [Torajirô's lullaby], 1974).[6]

(If one is the origin, then the start of the nation was the country of Yamato, and the first island was Awaji. . . The start of gambling was Kumasaka no Chôhan, and the first color is red. Red, red, nothing's unmoved by red, not wood, not metal, not stone. Even the locomotive that runs for a thousand miles will stop at the waving of a red flag. Let's move on to two. Brothers, you're now the second sex, so gather around. The second son, Nikichi, is a highwayman along the Tôkaidô and is despised by the world. The second generation actor Nikki of the famed kabuki family Danjô, he always plays the villain. Which brings us to three, for when Nikki does the hopping three-step up to the stage, there are no fans cheering him in the audience. Osen from the Third Island died in the third night of labor, and she's not the only one. Ono no Komachi spent three days and three nights without food or drink in front of the palace at Kyoto's Gokurakuzaka and died there when she was thirty-three. Let's go on to four. Four districts around Edo Castle, first is the fourth, Yotsuya [Four Valleys], next is Akasaka, next is Kôjimachi, and then we come to Ochanomizu, where the waters flow and chatter and beautiful young ladies piss standing in the street.)

There are a number of variations on this sort of "street rap" – every film in the series seems to have a different one. Atsumi Kiyoshi was trained in comedy on the stages of strip theaters in Asakusa in the days of the Occupation. He was thus able to handle the cadenced delivery of a verbal comedic art that was essentially taken from the street of *shitamachi* Tokyo in a way that most present-day actors cannot, and it seems that he took part in creating some of the dialogue for the series. The screenplays were all written or cowritten by Yamada Yôji, who directed forty-six of the forty-eight films and conceived of the Kuruma Torajirô character after meeting Atsumi Kiyoshi. Yamada has been deeply influenced by the traditional comedic performance arts, especially *rakugo,* and his entire career is evidence of a profound respect for common (*shomin*) society and the Japanese vernacular.[7]

The source of Tora-san's power over women and others is his comic eloquence. Of course, yakuza are known for their insults and low, obscene speech, but in *Otoko wa tsurai yo,* vulgar ridicule is taken to an eccentric extreme that is comic. One of Tora-san's most famous insults, one that appears in almost every film, is, "Kekkô kedarake, neko haidarake, oshiri no mawari wa kuso darake" (Fine, that's fine, a cat's fine fur is covered with ash, and your ass is covered with shit). Or again, "Taishita mon da yo, kaeru no shonben. Miageta mon da yo, yaneya no fundoshi" (Real impressive, like frog's piss. Something to look up to, like a roofer's underwear).

Given the complexity of the 5/7 syllabic meter and the literary and extraliterary allusions in the passages cited, one can understand the cleavage between a body of criticism for a domestic audience – numerous volumes of serious studies of the *Otoko wa tsurai yo* series – and journalistic criticism intended to "explain" Japan to the West. Every genre has languages specific to it – dialects, registers, traditional literary languages – and when multiple genres are parodied in a single film, usually by extraliterary language, with one film building on the next, the resulting complexity is virtually untranslatable in the context of a subtitle. Something of the literary quality of the screenplays can be judged from the fact that they have been published as collected works and are continually reproduced in such forms as *The Wisdom of Tora-san,* or as best lines from *Otoko wa tsurai yo.* However, when one subtracts the language and the comedic experience of the ensemble cast that articulates it so brilliantly, one is left with a formulaic plot of little interest, once seen, and what can only be termed visually derivative images. Humor that owes so much to language, literary allusion, and specific class/cultural associations cannot be "internationalized," and it is unlikely that the series will ever win much of an English-speaking audience.[8]

As Satô Tadao argues, the audience's enchantment with linguistic rhythm, complexity, and sophistication is integral to *Otoko wa tsurai yo's* popularity, and this quality of the language is in turn inseparable from the class milieu it represents – class, in Pierre Bourdieu's formulation, is "defined as much by its *being perceived* as by its *being,* by its consumption . . . as much as by its position in the relations of production. . ." For our purposes, food preferences, fashion, living spaces, and, most important, dialects and social registers, create a "linguistic sense of place," which in the *Otoko wa tsurai yo* series is immediately identifiable with patterns of commoner (*shomin*) life.[9] Those who regard the masses as a positive social force tend to ascribe this source of the series' popularity to a sympathetic portrayal of working-class and *shomin* life, an objective and function of the arts consistent with naturalism and social realism.[10]

Yet another genre parodied in every movie of the series is the home drama. *Otoko wa tsurai yo* began as a television home drama, which has antecedents in the prewar *shomingeki* (theater of commoners), a genre that was the special pride of Kido Shirô, president of Shôchiku. Yamada Yôji was trained at Shôchiku and while he did not work directly under Ozu Yasujirô, Shimizu Hiroshi, or Saitô Torajirô, who were at the Ôfuna Studio while he was there, he had to be influenced by what he termed "Kidoism," a set of guiding principles promulgated by Kido, principles that promoted humanistic stories of everyday urban life, as in the *shomingeki,* and emphasized family values appealing to an audience of the petite bourgeoisie, especially women.[11] On the frequently pointed-out Ozu influence on his work, Yamada has said:

> I had never intended for there to be influence from Ozu, but people have told me repeatedly that my work has come to resemble his. If I belong to his school, or if I have somehow received his legacy, one should probably think of it in terms of something I absorbed through the skin while growing up at Ôfuna while Ozu and the rest were there. I think the influence, that transcends consciousness, is probably the tradition of realism they created at Ôfuna.[12]

In scene after scene in the series, Yamada Yôji created an atmosphere of an idyllic family conducting their business – a *dangoya,* or rice dumpling shop – from their house in a neighborhood of small shopkeepers that is harmonious, at least until Torajirô returns home, when all hell breaks loose. But the social origin of this "happy family" forms a comic/tragic genealogy. Kuruma Heizô and Kuruma Ryûzô are brothers of the same father. An illegitimate child, Kuruma Torajirô, is born to Heizô's lover, Okiku, who abandons the infant at Heizô's house. Tora is raised by Heizô's legal wife with two half siblings, an older brother and a younger sister, Sakura. Tora, who does not get along with his father, runs away from home at about the age of fifteen to join a gang of itinerant peddlers/yakuza. Several years later, in about 1950 or so, Heizô dies from alcohol-related causes. Shortly thereafter, his legal wife and oldest son die as well. Ryûzô, Oichan, and his wife, Tsune, who are childless, take over the operation of the Katsushika Shibamata shop and raise Tora's half-sister as their own daughter. In 1969 (1968 according to the TV series), when Tora-san is thirty-six and Sakura is twenty-four or twenty-five, Tora returns to the shop in Shibamata for the first time in twenty years.

When critics refer to *Otoko wa tsurai yo* as preserving that "furuki, yoki, natsukashiki Nippon" (old, good, nostalgic Japan), they are referring to this family and their neighborhood. However, the family situation, as noted here, is hardly "Ozzie and Harriet," and Katsushika Shibamata is not a traditional *shitamachi* neighborhood, but an industrial suburb of Tokyo that owes its economic existence to expansions of the economy in the 1930s and to the chaotic growth in small-scale manufacturing in the 1950s and 1960s. Furthermore, the family's web of ties in this neighborhood constitutes a very eccentric community indeed.

In back of the *dangoya,* first called Toraya, and later changed to the Kuruma Kashiten, is a printing shop owned by Shachô, also known as Tako (the Octopus), Torajirô's perennial straight man. The Toraya forms a sort of shortcut between the main street and Shachô's small factory, and Shachô is in and out of the shop frequently every day. Shachô's live-in factory workers, addressed by Tora-san as "rôdôsha shokun" (comrade workers!) form the permanent proletariat in the series, and from the ranks of these workmen, Sakura takes a husband, Hiroshi, in the first movie of the series, after she has been rejected by a young man from an elite family. It is through negotiations over marriage that issues of class conflict and solidarity often come to the fore. Hiroshi, a shy young man who adores Sakura, becomes the voice of common civic responsibility, goodness, and wisdom throughout the series. With the birth of their child, Mitsuo, they move to a nearby apartment, then buy a house in the neighborhood. Sakura continues to work at the Toraya, and the couple and child take meals there, so they are always around. In later movies in the 1980s, plots concerning Mitsuo and Shachô's daughter, Akemi, become central. In addition, there is the head priest, Gozensama, of the local temple, Shibamata Daikyôji, also known as Taishakuten.[13]

This neighborhood, probably typical enough, in its class mix, of many urban neighborhoods in Japan, is receptive toward newcomers, supportive of the weak within its midst, and much concerned with keeping up the standards of morality and common respectability within the community. In the series, the mood of the *shomingeki,* or home drama, is composed, usually around the dinner table in the evening, and then the peace and harmony of the Kuruma family and neighborhood degenerate and finally are completely destroyed through the antics of Tora-san. For example, in the twenty-first movie in the series, *Otoko wa tsurai yo Torajirô waga michi o yuku* (Torajirô does it his way, 1978), the Japanese economy is in recession, and the Kuruma family is united in its desire that Tora-san return and take over the family shop. When asked how he would improve the dumpling business, Tora-san responds as follows:

Tora: Every month we should have a special sale. Cut the price of dumplings in half for that one day. We won't make a bit of profit. But the word of how delicious Toraya's dumplings are will spread far and wide.
Shachô: Hmmm.
Tsune: Old people like us just can't come up with such enterprising ideas.
Ryûzô: I guess so.
Hiroshi: You *have* been thinking about this, haven't you.
Tora: There's more. We keep getting more and more customers. This small shop isn't able to handle the business, so we take decisive action and tear the old place down!
Tsune: Oh my!
Tora: We construct a brand new building made of steel and concrete. First floor is the shop, second floor is living space, third floor is the retirement apartment for our old couple here. By that time, Shachô's business will have gone bankrupt, so we buy up his property, take over his workers,

turn the whole thing into a dumpling factory. No more handmade dumplings with snot all over them. Automation is the key. A dumpling rolls out of the machine every second. Poton, Poton, Poton. Of course we can't have slightly dirty old people in the shop. We hire fresh, pretty young girls, dress them in matching outfits. "Welcome to the Toraya, please come again." The business expands. We open one new chain store after another. The Toraya dumpling empire extends from Hokkaido in the north to Okinawa in the south. We buy television advertising. "Tonight's programming, *The Toraya Ballad Drama Hour,* is brought to you by the Toraya, makers of your favorite dumplings. Sleep little child, don't you cry, where has your mother gone. . ."

(Tora looks around. His audience looks very depressed.)

Ryûzô: I'm going back to bed. My head's started to hurt again.

Tsune leaves too: There's no point to growing old. No hope for happiness in the future.

Almost all of the films have similar scenes. These parodies of a happy, working-class home and neighborhood life result in Tora's departure, for he realizes again he does not fit in with contented domesticity. It would be facile to dismiss such scenes with the observation that they follow a formula. Each is different, each is constructed with extraordinary care, and most can be seen again and again with interest. Much of the everyday urban life of the masses *(shomin)* is formulaic, variations on the same situations: birth, death, marriage, love, departing and returning saying good morning and saying goodnight. The popular realistic depiction of everyday life has to be carried out in a way that rearticulates, in an entertaining manner, innumerably recurring speech genres. Not only have the filmmakers and cast managed this with undiminished inventiveness, but they have also incorporated the representation of changing circumstances. The Kuruma family is not a collection of stagnant stock figures or archetypes. A similar scene of happy domesticity around the dinner table works toward a politically significant parody that addresses the difficult issue of class identity in the postwar period. The following is taken from *Torajirô wasurenagusa* (Torajirô's forget-me-nots, number 11, 1973), in which Torajirô explains to his assembled family the difficult life led by Lily, a woman entertainer whom he has recently met:

Tora: Traveling alone is hard for a grown man like me. Imagine what it's like for Lily. Aunt, you're a woman. You know how difficult it is for a woman on a journey all by herself.

Tsune: I certainly do! First of all, there's the problem of going to the bathroom. Men can go anywhere, but. . .

Tora: Impossible! I shouldn't be talking to people like you who've never suffered. Lily has such a sad life. How can a middle-class housewife possibly understand!

Tsune: Are we a middle-class family?

Tora: Of course you are.

Ryûzô: I don't think so.

Tora: Then what are you?

Shachô (enters): Good evening, everyone.

Tora: One of the upper classes has arrived.

Shachô: Me?

Tora: Yes, you.

Shachô: Upper class? Me?

Tora: Yup. You're the boss, and bosses are upper class.

Shachô: Really?

Tora: Yes.

Shachô: But I've never thought of myself that way.

Tora: You're upper class and you just don't know it.

Ryûzô: Then what class are you Tora?

Tora: Huh? Me? Well, I guess I'm about middle class, right Hiroshi?

Hiroshi: Probably not middle class, I don't think.

Shachô: That's right! To be middle class, you have to own a color TV and a stereo, and stuff like that.

Tora: I see. I don't have any of those things.

Ryûzô (laughing): All you've got is that square suitcase you carry around. I don't know what's in it, though.

Tora: Get off my back.

Hiroshi: Wait a second. Just because people have possessions doesn't mean they're superior.

Tora: Absolutely right!

Hiroshi: There are plenty of awful people who have lots of land and big houses. And there are plenty of fine people who have nothing. In fact, it's people without property who tend to be the better people.

Tora: I like the way this man talks.

Sakura: You don't have a color TV or a stereo, but you have something priceless that others don't have.

Tora: Have you been snooping in my suitcase, Sakura?

Sakura: I'm not talking about material things.

Tora: What then, something like a fart?

Sakura: Of course not. How shall I express it. . . ? It's love. The capacity to love people.

Shachô: Tora has more than enough of that!

Tora: What do you know about it, idiot!

Hiroshi: Sakura's right. You can't buy what you have, no matter how much money you spend.
Tora: (obviously pleased): You're joking!
Ryûzô: Tora has something that valuable? We'll have to assign him to the upper class.

This exchange is a parody of the intellectual discourse, starting in the 1970s, concerning Japan's status as a postindustrial society, with most of its citizens, even Tora-san, identifying themselves as middle class. In 1973, there was probably no one, among the 2,390,000 people seeing this movie, who considered the extended Kuruma family to be middle class. Most of the audience was probably reminded of the similarity of the Kuruma family's economic situation to that of their own. However, the Kuruma family does not look backward with nostalgia in the course of the series. In 1980, Hiroshi and Sakura buy a small house. In 1983, Hiroshi is able, by means of an inheritance from his father, to become part owner of Shachô's printing company. By 1988, when Sakura and Hiroshi finally get Mitsuo into college, there was probably not one person in the audience who did not consider the extended Kuruma family to be middle class. But what can be the meaning of class categories that change so radically during the period of a little over a decade? As several sociologists have concluded, the statistics of social stratification "cast doubt on the emergence of 'the new middle mass' in Japan." Indeed, the most stable class formation in Japan since World War II appears to be exactly the urban petite bourgeoisie, which is represented by the Kuruma family.[14] Certainly, the consumer society's old televisions and stereos seem dirt poor when compared to the enduring value of class cultural capital that the Kuruma family has built up generationally in the Katsushika Shibamata neighborhood.

A constant source of humor throughout the series arises from the disjunction between "reality," as the films' naturalistic techniques portray it, and images of postindustrial life projected by the mass media. Take, for example, the recurring dream sequences that open most of the films. In these, Tora-san is in the countryside dreaming of himself as the hero of popular entertainments who inspires the admiration of the people back at the Toraya. *Torajirô waga michi o yuku* (Torajirô does it his way, number 21, 1978) opens with a parody of *Star Wars, Close Encounters, Planet of the Apes,* and the Pink Lady's "UFO" in which Tora-san emerges to announce he is really an alien who has assumed the identity of Sakura's brother. A hat-shaped spaceship arrives to take him home to Planet X. In an obvious parody of "West Side Story," the opening of *Hana mo arashi mo Torajirô* (Flower and storm and Torajirô, number 30, 1982) has Tora-san restoring peace to Brooklyn after facing down a Mafia chief. In *Torajirô Shibamata yori ai o komete* (Torajirô with love from Shibamata, number 36, 1985), Tora-san dreams he is Japan's first astronaut, chosen because he is the most typically Japanese male (see Figure 31). These are amusing parodies of mass entertainments. Yet on another level, at the moment of Torajirô's awakening, one becomes aware of the ephemerality of the pervasive images of the mass media when compared to the rural workaday realities around him in his waking world. Looking past the mass media, one discovers that the basic structures of everyday life remain unchanged over the intervening decades, and perhaps the "new middle class" or the "revolution in public consciousness" is illusory. In any case, the *Otoko wa tsurai yo* series forces its audience to address the disjunction between a rapidly changing economic order and long-enduring class cultural patterns of life.

31. Tora-san dreams he is an astronaut; *Torajirô with love from Shibamata* (1985).

A CHRONICLE OF CONTEMPORARY MANNERS, FASHIONS, AND CUSTOMS

Tora-san is an unabashed anachronism. As early as 1971, in *Otoko wa tsurai yo: junjôhen* (The innocence chapter, number 6), he is shown doing his "sales rap" for a group of college students who are recording it as if it were a piece of folklore. However, the world this comic anachronism observes changing around him is resolutely contemporary. With its continuity of a repertory of actors, characters, story lines, and direction, the series provides the most detailed, unified narrative history of film of Japanese manners, fashions, and customs from the Occupation until the recent Kobe earthquake. The accurate representation of changing manners, customs, and fashions extends to every aspect of the films, from the goods that Tora-san hawks to the prices of the dumplings sold at the Katsushika Shibamata shop.[15] Sakura wears a sixties mod style at the start of the series but becomes more conservative as she grows older; women, except for geisha, stop wearing kimonos as time goes on and favor jeans and T-shirts. Sakura's bicycle gives way to a shiny new motorbike; Ryûzô and Tsune's radio is replaced by television and then color television; and by the end of the series, Shachô's factory is air-conditioned and has converted to offset printing.

In terms of human relations, the most significant aspect of this postwar history is found in the stories of the lives of fifty or so typical Japanese women. In the contexts presented in the films of the social dislocations caused by Japan's high growth in the 1960s, the oil shocks of the 1970s, the widespread distrust of elites and the political process of the 1980s, and the almost complete social alienation of the 1990s, this history of popular manners and customs in the postwar period becomes a matter of the "attitudes" of the individual women Tora-san comes in contact with. The main story line of any given movie revolves around Torajirô's chivalrous befriending of a woman and then his gradual falling in love, always ending in rejection or in the realization of inadequacy and his subsequent lone departure. These movies, then, are romances, often pastoral, in which Tora-san never gets the girl. In Satô Tadao's formulation, they are a parody of melodrama: "Handsome men and beautiful women are always the central focus of romantic tragedy in modern Japanese drama *(shinpa-geki),* but Tora-san is the exact opposite of the handsome leading man, and so the more serious and intense the romantic situations in these movies, the more comical they become."[16]

Romantic chivalry and Platonic love are the motives for Tora-san, the comic anachronism, to gain access to women's stories in the contemporary world. The stories proliferate, feeding off each other, until by the end of the series, any given film has been taken over by women. The women include Tora-san's aunt, Tsune, wise in the ways of the neighborhood; Sakura, the younger half-sister, keeper and protector of Tora-san and ordinary domestic *shomin* life in the face of the threats of modernization; Akemi, daughter of Shachô, countercultural admirer of Tora, and Mitsuo's love interest; Izumi, a girl from the provinces; Izumi's mother, Reiko; and Tora's current love interest, the so-called Madonna, who changes from one movie to the next.

Though the role of Madonna is played by a well-known actress, usually one popular at the time the movie is cast, her character is as a rule integrated into realistic stories about ordinary life. The actress almost never plays herself and never becomes a sexual object in an obvious way.[17] The performances are often quite subtle and beautifully handled, and these talented women keep the individual films varied, contemporary, and popular and allow viewers in the present to construct a taxonomy of characters in the context of the age and generation that finds them attractive.

The basic types are pretty much established in the first 12 movies, and the rest of the films do contemporary variations. The types are: (1) the conscientious, usually cultured, daughter devoted to her parents, who is engaged to a prospective groom or becomes engaged in the course of the film – 6 movies, numbers 1, 2, 5, 9, 23, and 30; (2) the independent small-business owner/entrepreneur – 7 movies, numbers 3, 8, 10, 38, 39, 44, and 45; (3) the respectable wife who has been recently separated from, or divorced from, her husband or has been widowed – 8 movies, numbers 6, 19, 13, 22, 28, 32, 34 and 38; (4) the woman in a caring profession, the nurse, teacher, and so on – 6 movies, numbers 4, 14, 16, 18, 36, and 40; (5) the young woman up from the provinces who is trying to make a life, find a decent job, get an education, in Tokyo – 9 movies, numbers 7, 20, 26, 35, 37, and 42 through 45; (6) the woman who, like Tora, is a drifter, often involved in the demimonde, entertainment, or peripherally with the yakuza worlds – 9 movies, numbers 11, 15, 17, 21, 25, 27, 33, 43, and 48;

(7) other types, the majority of which have something to do with the West – 6 movies, numbers 12, 18, 24, 29, 31, and 41.

Arranged marriages *(omiai),* a situation driving innumerable plots of popular romances in the prewar period, die out in the course of the series. After the second film, featuring an extraordinarily appealing performance by Satô Orie as the devoted daughter of Tora-san's former teacher, the Ozu-like purity and self-sacrifice for parents fades away. Love in the postwar era is carried on by lonely individuals. It is haphazard, awkward, and comic. Arranged marriages are for the elites, and usually involve a violation of privacy no "ordinary" woman would submit to. Utako (Yoshinaga Sayuri) in number 9 (1972), inspired by Tora-san, defies her father to marry an impoverished potter. In number 23 (1979), Hitomi (Momoi Kaori), rebels against her parents twice, first by fleeing from her wedding to a spouse chosen for her by her parents, and then by allowing the same young man to win her over and marry her in opposition to her parents' wishes. By 1982, in number 30, starring Tanaka Yûko as Keiko, the young woman lead has come to regard *omiai,* with its attendant detective reports that maintain that Tora-san is her lover, as a foolish disgrace, and she brushes off her parents' offers as an insult. By the early eighties, then, the *omiai* situation, such a rich vein mined continuously in popular dramas since the Meiji period, was exhausted in the series, and this undoubtedly reflects the custom's growing irrelevance to contemporary audiences.

The independent woman business owner is a durable and widespread presence in modern Japanese society, and so it is no surprise that this category winds its way through the series from 1970 to 1995. Number 8 (1971) features Takako (Ikeuchi Junko), the owner of a local coffee shop, who expresses the desire to accompany Tora-san on his travels. Ochiyo (Yachigusa Kaoru) in number 10 (1972) proposes marriage to Tora-san. Setsuko (Yoshida Hideko) in number 44 (1991), the owner of a restaurant and an inn in Tottori, wishes she had married Tora-san instead of the former husband who left her the business. And in number 45 (1992), Choko (Fubuki Jun), who has her own barbershop, declares to Tora-san that she will depart with the first man who walks in and asks her to leave with him. As is usually the case, Tora-san evades these offers by reference to his outlaw status – his life is no life for a woman. These portraits of intelligent women with independent means, eager to marry the penniless

Tora-san, probably speak of the drudgery involved in running an independent business, for Tora-san is nothing if not a diversion.

The films featuring the role of the respectable wife separated from her husband reveal two transformations in male and female roles. First, there is the appearance of the weak, neurotic salary man (white-collar worker) who suffers a kind of breakdown due to intense pressures at work and then disappears, embarking on a roaming journey in search of himself. Such men are the victims of Japan's economic miracle. Tora-san helps the desperate wife locate her missing husband, and the family is reunited. Number 34 (1984), starring Ôhara Keiko as the wife and Yonekura Sakatoshi as the husband, is a good example of this subgenre. Second, when comparing the first film in this category, number 6 (1971), and the last, number 38 (1987), we see the destigmatizing of women who leave abusive husbands. In number 6, the sickly, kimono-clad wife is, after much weeping, reconciled with her husband. In contrast, in number 38, the athletic, independent Takeshita Keiko returns home to her father for a time, but then realizes the meaninglessness of nostalgia for home, and departs again for the city to make a life for herself.

The rise in living standards apparent throughout the series results in a greater independence for the women portrayed. This is evident in the films that feature women in caring professions. In number 4 (1970), Kurihara Komaki plays a kindergarten teacher; number 14 (1974) features Toake Yukiyo as a nurse; number 16 (1975) has Kashiyama Fumie as a graduate student in archeology and an instructor at the university; number 18 (1976) features Dan Fumi as an elementary school teacher; in number 36 (1985), Kurihara Komaki appears again as a profoundly inspirational teacher at the middle school level; and number 40 (1988) has Mita Yoshiko as a doctor. It is clear that there is an upward trajectory of women's careers in terms of education, responsibility, pay, and competence.

The frequency of the appearance of young women up from the countryside in the series reflects a central problem Japanese society continues to face in the modern period. Here, too, however, the filmmakers are not content to present a stereotyped situation but work hard to keep the issue contemporary. The seventh film in the series (1971) opens with trainloads of young people, some just out of middle school, departing, amid the winter snows of the north, to work in the factories and shops in Tokyo. The presentation of this social problem (*shûdan shûshoku,* of mass emigration for employment) is pure social realism. Sakakibara Rumi plays a slightly retarded girl, lost in Tokyo, who is being intimidated by a policeman, and whom Tora-san befriends and finds work for in Tokyo. In the early films in this category, numerous male and female laborers from the provinces appear in Shibamata and the circumstances of these immigrants are desperate. They are fortunate to have work of any sort, and losing a job means returning in disgrace to families in the provinces. Women have the added burden of maintaining their chastity and reputation, for a decent marriage is the only way out of menial, ill-paying work. The incorporation of regional dialects (see, for example, number 20 [1977], with a wonderful performance by Ôtake Shinobu in the Aomori dialect) into the series adds yet another layer of linguistic complexity. However, conditions change over the life of the series. By the twenty-sixth film (1980), the girl from the provinces, Sumire (Itō Ran), has been emboldened enough to physically attack a policeman who suspects Tora-san of trafficking in provincial girls. By 1985, in number 35, the young woman up from the country has become a great deal more independent. Wakana (Higuchi Kanako) is a typesetter whose family in the countryside is Christian. Living alone in Tokyo, she has changed jobs several times due to poor working conditions, but, she assures Tora, she is not going to starve to death: something will turn up. Virginity at marriage is no longer of critical importance. There are, however, still ceilings to the social advancement of those provincially born, as is clear in the case of Izumi (Gotô Kumiko), Mitsuo's love interest in numbers 42 through 48. Izumi is largely provincially educated and has transferred to other schools several times. Even during boom times in the Japanese economy, long-established shops only recruit permanent employees from nearby high schools, and of course provincial public schools leave non-college-bound students ill-prepared for entrance examinations. Discrimination against young people of unorthodox, provincial backgrounds remains a prominent feature of Japanese society and is dealt with by the series up until the end.

Perhaps the most memorable women in these films are the ones who can compete with Tora's verbal dexterity. Equality of fluency in certain social registers and dialects implies equality of class. Lily, played by Asaoka Ruriko, appears the most often as Tora-san's love interest (see Figure 32). She is a singer, divorced, who wanders around the country appearing at one cheap engagement after another. She is the most like

Tora and the most independent of all the women characters in the series. In *Torajirô aiaigasa* (Torajirô and the shared umbrella, 1975, number 15), there is the following exchange:

> Lily: A man's going to make a woman happy? Thanks so much. Do you really believe a woman needs to borrow a man's strength to be happy? Don't make me laugh!
> Tora: But they say a woman's happiness depends on her man.
> Lily: First I've ever heard of it. I've never once felt that way. If men say such things, it's just male arrogance!

Lily appears in four of the movies, from number 11 in 1973 until the last, *Torajirô kurenai no hana* (Torajirô red flower), in 1995. Women in the entertainment trades and the demimonde understand Tora-san best. Perhaps this is because they comprehend his willful perversity in a love of women that requires nonpossession, for possession would spell the end of his engagement with multiple stories from his contemporary society.

Most of the women characters in the last category are fluent in foreign languages and serve as translators for Tora-san. These are among the least

32. Lily, played by Asaoka Ruriko, matches Tora-san's verbal dexterity.

successful in the series, for Tora-san is deprived of his linguistic fluency and lacks standing to parody conventions he is not familiar with. The humor tends to be rather broad because it arises from Tora-san's ignorance rather than his insights.

The categories discussed earlier all portray women in the process of individual transformation in changing social circumstances. In broader class terms, women are the pillars of working-class life, a "feminine realm" that is the repository of decency, progressive ideas, and humanity in Japanese society, especially when contrasted to the "masculine realms" of Japan's economic and intellectual elites.

FOOLS AND VILLAINS

As has frequently been observed, recognizable working-class life in the contemporary world is either ridiculed or ignored by the mass media. Elites, "the new woman," or the "new white collar worker" are identified as typical of the nation in the sense of being the wave of the future, and depictions of long-standing patterns of everyday life are dismissed as appeals to nostalgia. The *Otoko wa tsurai yo* series is exceptional in that a sympathetic portrayal of an urban petite bourgeoisie family is presented comically in a way that has attracted a mass audience for almost three decades. The audience feels affection and respect for a cultural rather than economic pattern of life that is largely of their own making and has its roots in the commoner's life of the prewar period. It is in part defined by the satirical treatment of elites.

The Japanese intelligentsia are repeatedly satirized, for intellectuals have most vocally advocated the end of "feudal common society" since the end of World War II. In *Torajirô yumemakura* (Torajirô's dream pillow, number 10 [1972]), the professor at Tokyo University is described by Ryûzô as "a type Tora dislikes most," and the professor calls Tora a remnant of feudalism. In number 16, *Katsushika risshihen* (Torajirô's determination to succeed, 1975), which is an extended parody of the intelligentsia, Tora confronts a professor, "You start right off preaching. It's the worst thing about college professors, that's why women reject you." In general, intellectuals are portrayed as blind to the realities of common life around them and are most often the objects of laughter and derision.[18]

Another frequent target throughout the series is big business. Shachô frequently complains in a number of the films that what's good for large enterprises is bad for small and medium-size businesses. Applicants for employment at large corporations are treated shamefully, with executives brutally attacking those with even slightly unorthodox backgrounds (see, for example, Wakana's interview in number 35, mentioned previously). First-rate companies drive their white-collar employees to the point of nervous exhaustion and attempted suicide, as in number 15 (1975) and number 34 (1984).

Similarly, the cultural zone of the upper classes, Den'en Chôfu, is frequently satirized. An aristocrat's son living in Den'en Chôfu acts just like an aristocratic villain from a Meiji-era melodrama (number 19 [1977]). The "asobase" of the cultured ladies from Den'en Chôfu is parodied in Shibamata as "asobabeba" (number 23 [1979]). Finally, state welfare institutions are not trusted by the people (number 39 [1987]), and high schools and colleges are seen primarily as tools of social stratification (see, for example, number 26 [1980]).

CONCLUSION

Those aspects of Japanese society that are projected internationally as the personification of Japan are shown in the series to be atypical, repugnant, and cruel from the perspective of the Japanese masses, which are defined in the series as the rural population, the self-employed, employees of small and middle-size businesses, working women, and students. Is this definition of ordinary life realistic or nostalgic? Of course, the class demographics of contemporary Japan are precisely in accord with the image of the masses projected by the *Otoko wa tsurai yo* series.[19] In the end, the filmmakers' adherence to their formula revealed more about contemporary Japanese society than it obfuscated. The diversity of what constitutes the masses and the transformation of the concept during the postwar period are approached in the series through a parodic realism; that is to say, a realism which parodies from a common perspective (necessarily a class perspective) the representations of reality by other genres of the mass media and exposes as comical the stereotypes of popular entertainment, which are first created and then undercut. The wonder is not just that the series lasted for as long as it did, but that it lasted so long with content consistent with naturalism. Directors, screenwriters, crew, and cast have to be credited with integrity, commitment to their contemporary society, and originality in continuing to engage, through comedy, social problems in changing aspects for over twenty-eight years, while many other filmmakers have retreated to the exoticism of the past, the future, or to a Japan that by and large resembles foreign movies. The continued support for the series speaks of the sophistication of Japan's mass audience.

The appeal of the series, then, lies not so much in nostalgia as in the realistic portrayal of long-standing continuities in patterns of everyday life revealed through changing economic circumstances. The series is a means of taking stock, of asking how prevalent is the past in the present. Demographics aside, how one answers this question depends on one's experience.

NOTES

1. Atsumi Kiyoshi o okuru kai, ed., *Tora-san, arigato!! Sore o itchaa, oshimai yo* (Hyôgo Pref., Nishi-Miya-shi: Rokusaisha, 1996), 5–6 and 310–33; Masako Nakagawa, "Tora-san, A Japanese Hero," *Education About Asia* 2:2 (fall 1997): 56–57. Mark Schilling, "Into the Heartland with Tora-san," *Japan Quarterly* 40:2 (April 1993): 199–200.
2. Ayako Doi, "Rite of Passing: Kiyoshi Atsumi, and 'Tora-San' Are No More," *Japan Digest Forum,* 12 September 1996, p. 5; Masako Nakagawa, "Tora-san, A Japanese Hero," 56. As Yamada Yôji has stated, "I've come to be criticized for 'Forever depicting the old Japan in a nostalgic way.'" He goes on to state that such was never his intention, but that perhaps the world changed around him while he was making the series. "Shiroyama Saburô no 'Tairon Nihonjin wa kawatta ka': Yamada Yôji 'Tora-san ga oshiete kureta jinsei-ron,'" *Gendai* 31, 6 (June 1997): 44. See also, for example, Aaron Gerow, "Tora's Lost World," *The Daily Yomiuri,* 28 December 1995, 9; Kevin Sullivan, "The Death of Japan's Immortal Everyman," *Washington Post,* 10 August 1996, sec. C, p. 1, col. 1; or Andrew Pollack, "Japan Mourns an Actor, and a Lost Way of Life," *New York Times,* 14 August 1996, sec. A, p. 4, col. 3.
3. I am indebted here to a talk at Ohio State University by Philip A. Kafalas on "nostalgia" in Western and Chinese contexts. See Philip A. Kafalas, "Nostalgia and Reading of the Late Ming Essay: Zhang Dai's 'Tao'an mengyi'" (Ph.D. diss., Stanford University, 1995). For quote, see Roland Robertson, "After Nostalgia?," in Byran S. Turner, ed., *Theories of Modernity and Postmodernity* (London: Sage Publications, 1990), 53. The psychoanalytic counterpart of the nostalgia reading is that Tora-san represents a "mother

yearning syndrome," in which longing for a fictitious place and time in the past is displaced by a longing for mother, but the characterization of the Japanese mass audience as pathological remains the same. As noted and critiqued in Linda Ehrlich, "Wandering Fool: Tora-san and the Comic Traveler Tradition," *Asian Cinema* 8:1 (spring 1996): 19.

4. Satô Tadao, *Minna no Tora-san* (Tokyo: Asahi Shinbunsha, 1988); Yoshimura Hideo, *"Otoko wa tsurai yo" no sekai* (Tokyo: Shine Furontosha, 1981).
5. For an excellent interpretation of Tora-san as an archetypal figure with religious associations, see Linda Ehrlich, "Wandering Fool: Tora-san and the Comic Traveler Tradition," 3–27.
6. Yamada Yôji and Asama Yoshitaka, *Otoko wa tsurai yo Tora-san no jinsei goroku* (Tokyo and Kyoto: PHP Kenkyûjo, 1993), 12.
7. Yoshimura Hideo, *Yamada Yôji no sekai* (Tokyo: Shine Furontosha, 1984).
8. Titles dealing substantially with passages and quotes from the series' screenplays include: Kagurazaka Tora-san Fuan Kurabu, ed., *Otoko wa tsurai yo Tora-san to nazo* (Tokyo: Jitsugyô Nihonsha, 1993); Yamada Yôji and Asama Yoshitaka, *Otoko wa tsurai yo Tora-san no jinsei goroku;* Inoue Hisashi, ed., *Tora-san taizen* (Tokyo: Chikuma Shobô, 1994); Atsumi Kiyoshi o Okuru Kai, ed., *Tora-san, arigatô!! Sore o itchaa, oshimai yo.* To my knowledge, only one of the *Otoko wa tsurai yo* films with English-language subtitles is presently available for distribution in the United States. *Tora-san Goes to Vienna* (no. 41, 1989), concerns Tora-san's adventures in Europe and is available from New Yorker Films. Though many of the films in the series were released in the United States with English titles and subtitles, these are apparently no longer available. I have chosen to provide my own translations for the titles and dialogue I cite here.
9. Satô Tadao, interview in "ETV Tokushu: 'Otoko wa tsurai yo' mei serifu o yomitoku," NHK, broadcast 9 September 1996; Satô Tadao, *Minna no Tora-san* (Tokyo: Asahi Shinbunsha, 1988), 18 ff. Quote is from Pierre Bourdieu, *Distinction,* trans. Richard Nice, (Cambridge: Harvard University Press, 1984), p. 483. The notion of a "linguistic sense of place" in relation to class identification is taken from Pierre Bourdieu, *Language and Symbolic Power,* trans. Gino Raymond and Matthew Adamson (Cambridge: Harvard University Press, 1991), 82.
10. Yamada Kazuo, "'Otoko wa tsurai yo' no nijû-shichi nen," *Zen'ei* 680, no. 12 (December 1996): 140–49; Yoshimura Hideo, *"Otoko wa tsurai yo" miryoku taizen* (Tokyo: Kôdansha, 1992), 16–22 and 109–11.
11. Kido was Yamada's great supporter at Shôchiku, and Yamada edited and explicated a posthumous collection of Kido's writings. See Kido Shirô, *Waga eigaron,* ed. Yamada Yôji (Tokyo: Shôchiku Kubashiki Kaisha, 1978), for Yamada's explication of "Kidoism" and for his deep sense of gratitude toward him. On *shomin-geki,* the genre's tendency to realism, comedy, and development into "home drama," see Joseph L. Anderson and Donald Richie, *The Japanese Film: Art and Industry (expanded edition)* (Princeton: Princeton University Press, 1982), 96–126, and Satô Tadao, *Currents in Japanese Cinema,* trans. Gregory Barret (Tokyo: Kodansha International Ltd., 1982), 139–44.

12. As quoted in Yoshimura Hideo, *Yamada Yôji no sekai,* 202. It might also be noted that Yamada employed a number of actors also used by Ozu, including the regular Ryû Chishû, Kagawa Kyôko, and Kyô Machiko.
13. The cast: Sakura/Baishô Chieko; Kuruma Ryûzô (Oichan), Sakura's uncle and stepfather/Morikawa Shin, Matsumura Tatsuo, and Shimojô Masami; Ryûzô's wife, Tsune/Misaki Chieko; Sakura's husband, Hiroshi/Maeda Gin; Sakura and Hiroshi's son, Mitsuo/Yoshioka Hidetaka; Shachô/Dazai Hisao; Gozensama, head priest of the local temple/Ryû Chishû.
14. Hiroshi Ishida, *Social Mobility in Contemporary Japan: Educational Credentials, Class and the Labour Market in a Cross-National Perspective* (Stanford: Stanford University Press, 1993), 238, and 172.
15. In the early 1970s, a box of dumplings is 300 yen. It rises to 500 yen during the dollar and oil shocks of the mid-seventies, and, with growing prosperity, goes to 1,000 yen in the 1980s. During the literature craze inspired by Kawabata Yasunari's winning the Nobel Prize for literature, Tora-san begins selling remaindered fiction on the street. With the oil shock he peddles the electric animator bracelets that stimulate the central nervous system with solar energy. In the early eighties, he begins selling panty hose. Trade surpluses in the late eighties inspire the purchase of impressionistic paintings by Japanese capitalists, and Tora-san hawks reproductions of Van Gogh. In 1990, it is CDs, and the success of *Jurassic Park* in 1993 results in Tora-san's selling cheap models of dinosaurs. The series is a sort of museum of popular culture's junk.
16. Satô Tadao, *Minna no Tora-san,* 18.
17. The one exception is Miyako Harumi in *Tabi to onna to Torajirô* (Journies and women and Torajirô, 1982). The fact that Japan's most capable actresses desired these roles is evidence of how well the parts were written and of Yamada Yôji's extraordinary ability as a woman's director.
18. Yoshimura Hideo, *"Otoko wa tsurai yo" no sekai,* 125–33.
19. Yamada Kazuo, "'Otoko wa tsurai yo' no nijû-shichi nen," *Zen'ei* 680:12 (December 1996): 146.

CHAPTER ELEVEN

A Working Ideology for Hiroshima

Imamura Shôhei's *Black Rain*

Carole Cavanaugh

Japanese cinema returned to the atomic bombing of Hiroshima, after an interval of three decades, with Imamura Shôhei's *Black Rain (Kuroi ame).* The documentary stylistics of the 1989 film are consonant not only with the *vérité* approach of many of Imamura's film and television works on other subjects but also with the treatment of nuclear warfare in film internationally. The global nature of atomic weaponry brings *Black Rain* into a worldwide subgenre of fictional nuclear films that share in the gravity of the historical event they recall, or forewarn, and that, more significant, strive for the look of nonfiction.[1] Examples range from films that quote from evidential or factual footage, such as Resnais's *Hiroshima, Mon Amour,* or Kubrick's *Dr. Strangelove,* to those that follow the visual or structural regulations of the documentary, such as the provocative simulations of Peter Watkins's television drama *The War Game* (1966). The tendency of nuclear films and television dramas to strive for the transparency of nonfiction urges observation of the veristic procedures at work in *Black Rain* and an inquiry into their ideological implications for Japanese film a half century after the end of the Pacific war.

Perhaps nuclear film simulates or incorporates documentation as a way of returning to its own censored origins, for no images were kept so scrupulously from public view for so long as the films that recorded the actual aftermath of the bombings of Hiroshima and Nagasaki.[2] In the days and months immediately following the destruction of those cities, both the United States and Japan endeavored, in different ways and for different purposes, to forestall the dissemination of pictures, particularly moving pictures, of the effects of nuclear bombs.[3]

The stories of Japanese military suppression of newsreel footage of Hiroshima in the days before surrender, and of the American classification, for years afterward, of film shot in Nagasaki, are by now familiar. The career of these films in the decades following the war illustrates not only the potency of the moving image, but also the process of commodification of certain images as their status shifts from documentation to representation, or as their function changes from historical evidence to political tool to cultural artifact. Moreover, their censorship gestures toward the complicated relationship, at once collaborative and competitive, between Japan and the United States in fixing the visual symbols of defeat, victory, and victimization. The mushroom clouds blossoming on American television and auditorium screens throughout the cold war proclaimed superpower ownership over the ultimate symbol of mass destruction, an icon that demonstrated the dominance of science as it denied the historical reality from which the political power of modern physics derived. Images of the dead and deformed undermined the nuclear message that survival unscathed was not only possible but also guaranteed to individuals who accepted responsibility for their own welfare in an age under constant threat of atomic war. Nuclear aesthetics expressed a mysteriously survivable end to history but never history itself.[4]

The disavowal of the recent past symptomatic of cold-war Hollywood film worked to sublimate the facts of nuclear annihilation into science fiction and film noir, where disintegration, invasion, violence, and secrecy are frequently associated with nuclear fear.[5] In Japan, symbolism of atomic destruction became localized, contained as it were, in the museum – in Hiroshima and Nagasaki exhibitions that reinforced the specificity of the bombings as limited, almost causeless events.[6] In the Japanese national media, representations of the devastation of those cities were confined in the cold-war period to a handful of minor films.[7] Noteworthy is the mid-fifties shift in emphasis from the bombings themselves to the psychological effects of a future nuclear threat, a change marked in Kurosawa's *Record of a Living Being (Ikimono no kiroku, 1955).* With this film Japan's most "international" director redirected nuclear cinema along the psychological lines of the American B movie, and it was his apprentice, Honda Ishiro, who would turn that threat into the cartoonish *Godzilla* (*Gojira,* 1954), the first in a globally successful series of monster films for export.

Because cinema in Japan, as in Hollywood, situates itself at the political center to subdue and absorb, rather than to critique or dissect, it is not surprising that film reduced Hiroshima to the nuclear subtext of creature movies produced for the world market. During the cold war, atomic iconology and the limitations it imposed on the real, the political, and the historic encouraged Japanese film to engage in a fantasy of futuristic monsters, at the cost of confronting the monstrous reality of the past. Cinematic suppression of the bombings encouraged Western critics, if not Japanese, to look for symbolic representations of survivalism in a postnuclear world in, for example, Kurosawa's *Rashomon* (1951) and Teshigahara's *Woman in the Dunes* (*Suna no onna,* 1964). An honest reconnection with history beyond allegory was not to occur, perhaps partly due to a sense among survivors *(hibakusha)* that silence was their only authentic response to the bombings.[8]

The reluctance of victims to speak out was ironically consonant with the aura of political secrecy surrounding all matters nuclear in the United States, from the inception of the Manhattan Project to the development, testing, and build-up of genocidal hydrogen-weaponry. During the increasingly tense decades of nuclear escalation, the United States, China, and the Soviet Union were in continual confrontation through their proxies in Korea and Southeast Asia, a program dependent on the cooperation of client states like Japan. But by the late 1980s, the nuclear powers were working more steadily toward disarmament, a movement that contributed to Japan's reassessment of its international relationships. Imamura's film on Hiroshima was released in the same year that the collapse of the Soviet Union brought the cold war to an end.

The belated appearance of *Black Rain* among those few films in Japan dealing with nuclear reality gives pause. The global import of the subject of the film and its international distribution confess a desire for attention outside Japan – recognition justly received in prizes at Cannes and Ghent – but a desire that should make us wonder if this commemorative anticipation of the fiftieth anniversary of the destruction of Hiroshima has some work in mind for itself beyond cinematic memorialization. But what work? The routine job of cold-war films about nuclear weapons was to warn against their use, but in 1989, Imamura's film labored in vain if it set itself the task of omen or cautionary tale. *Black Rain* arrived in a nuclear world far less threatening than the one in which its source text, Ibuse Masuji's novel *Kuroi ame* (Black rain), was published in 1966. The

Nonproliferation Treaty, SALT I, and SALT II were in place, and the Strategic Arms Reduction Talks (START) between the United States and Russia were moving forward with optimism. The atmosphere of these negotiations, and the end of the cold war they augured, added to *Black Rain* not the aura of oracle but the veneer of history.

The time of its release gave the film a sense of something over and done with, rather than the urgent political currency Ibuse's breakthrough novel enjoyed. Black-and-white film with very low contrast,[9] Ozu-esque camera placement and narrational effects, and the judicious use of documentary-style voice-over give *Black Rain* the feel of archival material seamlessly blended into a movie made in the forties. This semblance leads to questions about the psychological impact of historical film and, more important, to concerns about the ideological potential of a fictional film that achieves the look of cinema produced at the time of its temporal reference. Realism is, of course, an aesthetic choice, but, as I will argue, the atmosphere of authenticity borrowed from verism and its styles gives additional authority to a revisionist view active subliminally in the film, a view that fantasizes Japanese nonresponsibility for the war. The task that *Black Rain* sets for itself is not only to retell Ibuse's novel, but to adjust his 1960s reading of the Hiroshima bombing to accommodate a 1980s Japan.

The intimacy of the richly drawn domestic environment that provides its setting allows the film to pull the enormity of Hiroshima into the more modest dimensions of a single, simple story. Modesty is further secured by direct references to Ozu's 1949 film *Late Spring (Banshun),* to which this discussion will briefly return. *Black Rain* modifies its more immediate source by replacing Ibuse's mode of multiple narration with a linearly constructed plot involved increasingly with Yasuko, a character whose presence noticeably fades in Ibuse's novel. The film opens moments before the bombing, but most of its narrative takes place in 1950, when the protagonist, Shimamura Shigematsu, tries to arrange a marriage for his niece. Yasuko is by then twenty-five and has lived with her aunt and uncle in a village just outside Hiroshima since sometime during the war. Her rumored radiation sickness has been the cause of three failed engagements. Shigematsu, who himself suffers from the disease, turns to family diaries of the bombing as proof his niece was outside the city at the time. These recollections appear as a series of flashbacks that ironically work against Shigematsu's purposes, for they prove that he deludes himself about Yasuko's exposure to radiation, in degree no different from his own. At the close of the film, Yasuko, who has formed a mutually redemptive relationship with Yuichi, a shell-shocked soldier, is near death, and it is clear that Shigematsu's end is also imminent. In the penultimate scene the very ill Yasuko reaches a hallucinatory epiphany when she sees a giant carp leaping from a pond. Shigematsu is with her and, throughout the scene, speaks as though his niece will marry and survive him. Only in the final scene, which closely replicates the ending of Ibuse's novel, does Shigematsu seem resigned to her certain death.

The film takes a single story out of the interweave of testimonial narratives that constitutes the novel, and by so doing proposes the possibility of coherence and univocality for a historical event that Ibuse's novel (like many other works of atom-bomb literature) is able to express only through multiple voices and points of view.[10] The relationship between *Black Rain* and a previous text brings up the issue of adaptation, but the connection the film has to Ibuse's novel unveils not only the ordinary mechanisms of transference from one medium to another but also, more significant, the ideological structure of the film. There are any number of dissimilarities to be noted between book and movie – differences in content, pace, and style – but the overriding variance is external to both. Ibuse wrote *Black Rain* when the Japanese government was most deferential to its client relationship with the United States, just a few years after the two countries had signed the 1960 Japan-U.S. Security Treaty, an agreement that provided for U.S. military bases and troops in Japan. The Kishi government endured enormous domestic protests against this treaty, rather than opposing the intensifying presence of the United States in Asia. Two decades later, the eye of the United States was on commerce rather than conquest in Southeast Asia, and Japan's own global vision had dramatically emerged. When Imamura's film was released, Japan had become a superpower economically and "the Japan that can say, 'No!'" to the United States politically. By 1989 the nation's international confidence had reached an unprecedented peak.

That historical difference accounts for the remarkable discrepancy in ideological structure between the film and its source text. Nöel Carroll argues that a film is ideological not simply because it is a social construction, but only if it "promotes ideological ideas – either false beliefs or categorical schemes that function to support some system of social domination."[11] Whether a film is ideological or not is a function of its rhetorical organization – internal structures that "lead the audience to fill in certain ideas about human conduct in the process of rendering the story intelligible to themselves."[12] The film *Black Rain* makes a strategic move beyond the novel when it adds the mentally tormented veteran Yuichi to Yasuko's story – in my view, an ideological supplementation that encourages the audience to assign, or "fill in," the victim status of Hiroshima to those who victimized others during the war. The film accomplishes this task through the union of Yuichi and Yasuko, an unlikely interclass alliance possible only because both are handicapped by their wartime experiences. Because the rhetorical structure of heterosexual romance assumes that a man and a woman who love each other are equally good and worthy of our sympathy, the romantic story added to the film version of *Black Rain* "leads the audience" to transfer Yasuko's indisputable innocence to Yuichi. The structure of the film persuades us that her genuine victimization is shared equally by him. Soldier and civilian have both suffered and their suffering is the same. The "naturalness" of this construction is further ensured by the film's division of victimization between mind and body according to gender: the diseased body is female, the diseased mind is male. They unite to form a single victim, the body politic of home and country. The romantic unification of these characters organizes the film rhetorically to promote the ideological conception of Japan as a nation undivided in its victimization and violation by the war.

The Yasuko-Yuichi romance and its division of labor are points to which we will return, but for the moment, while in no way begrudging the power of this film to move us by the tragedy of its subject matter, we can recognize that in working to enlarge the victimization of Hiroshima, *Black Rain* must not only remember and memorialize the *hibakusha* survival experience, but must also repress the war that preceded that experience. The only images in the film of life before the bomb include three minutes of Yasuko loading a truck with her grandmother's kimonos; her participation in a tea ceremony; her uncle and other wartime commuters boarding a train; a dog, and a clock. The film opens with shots of Yasuko in the truck, and the atmosphere of evacuation gives the sense of a city under siege. Her voice-over explains that on that morning she took her grandmother's kimonos and other belongings for safe storage to the home of an acquaintance. The bleached cinematography, the voice-over narration, and the fact that the person whose image we see is retelling in present-tense events as they occur, are *vérité* effects that not only underwrite the authenticity of the story about to unfold but also instantly situate the viewer within the limitations of the historical framework the film has chosen. In other words, the urgency and unmediated quality of the opening montage allow reflection only on those few hours and moments before the bombing. This rapid but narratively dense interlude preempts questions about the war itself that a film beginning immediately with the bombing would have provoked or one that alluded to wartime Japan might have answered. The disavowal of the historicity of the war and its displacement with the idealization of Japanese culture are formalized in references to the preservation of kimonos and in shots of a tea ceremony that takes place, by most Japanese standards, at an unusually early time of day. The bomb interrupts not an ordinary breakfast but a sacred and timeless ritual with strong domestic and religious connotations.

The 1949 film *Late Spring* also begins with a tea ceremony, one more social than spiritual, and the first of several parallels Imamura's film draws with Ozu's.[13] In some ways *Black Rain* answers the question of what Ozu might have done had the postwar ethos or his own sensibilities allowed him to complicate the domestic relations so dear to him with the politics of the times. Imagine Noriko in the 1949 film suffering from radiation sickness, a thought not so far-fetched when we recall the mention her father makes of his concerns about her blood count and the bodily fatigue she continues to endure due to wartime work. Obviously her condition is not related to the atomic bomb for she and her father live in Kamakura, but here no less authority than Ryū Chishū casually inaugurates the female body, in the person of the iconic Hara Setsuko, as a vessel that harbors lingering effects of the war. Her desire not to marry and her dedication to her father anticipate Yasuko's bravely stated recommitment to her aunt and uncle after it becomes clear that she will never marry. Shigematsu and Yasuko share the same relationship of affection and responsibility complicated by daughterly sacrifice and fatherly guilt as Professor Somiya and Noriko. Just as Noriko seems to fantasize the creation of a new sexless "marriage" of devotion with her father, Yasuko more pragmatically looks toward the creation of a new kind of post-nuclear family tied not by patriarchal blood but by a cancer of the blood. The *Late Spring* intertext persuasively authorizes these relations and embeds them in the cultural timelessness Ozu claimed for the cinema of domesticity. In the end Imamura does not so much add history to *Late*

Spring as find, in the Ozu style he so detested and in its reconciliation of Japanese tradition with Occupation liberalism,[14] a precedent for history denied.

Black Rain continues to persuade us by establishing a range of characters whose conduct and views are unimpeachable. The most convincing of these characters is Shigematsu, the patriarch to whom the film continually returns for its sense of balance, normalcy, and forbearance. Appropriately, it is in Shigematsu where both remembering and forgetting (demonstrated in his paradoxical combination of both pragmatism and denial) exist side by side, never the one overruling but, rather, one continually recycling and replenishing the other. When he enlists his wife, Shigeko, and Yasuko to recopy their stories of the events of August 6, 1945, and the days following, this solution to the marriage problem implies that collaborative remembering will eventually work to undo the past. He stipulates that this process is not one of revision (as he must do under the ethical regulations of the film) and thereby secures our faith in his integrity, despite his attachment to an irreconcilable interpretation of transpired events.

"Sono mama seisho shite dasunjya" (Make a fair copy just as it is), he tells his wife, who wonders if the record of Yasuko's transit through the bombed Hiroshima will confirm the truth of the rumor they hope to dispel. The statement authenticates Shigematsu as the film's moral center. His virtue is unquestioned and it is always this character whom the film consults for its sense of decency and for a practical faith in the logic of the everyday – an earthbound intelligence that gives primacy to the normal routines and expectations of the family, to relearning the sacred rhythms and repetitions of rural life, and to the power of those routines and rhythms to restore what has been lost. But his statement, "sono mama seisho shite," ironically demonstrates a slippage at the center, a denial not of the experience of the past but of its consequences for the present. He seems to grasp events in isolation, not as they connect casually to other events, past or future. The incongruity of Shigematsu is that he is able to cast his lot with the written word as he disavows the source of its power. He relies on the documentation of health certificates, the authenticity of journals, the authority of deeds and contracts, but fails to endorse the historical continuity that both underlies and supersedes them. "Black rain is black rain, it wasn't the bomb that hit her," he protests to the reluctant Shigeko, a statement that pleads a misguided faith in the exonerating force of documentation the recopied diary seems to represent (see Figure 33).

Shigeko counters with the ominous reality of their present situation, "Ima jya dokuso wa atta koto minna shitte orimasu kei" (But *now* everyone knows that the black rain was poisonous). Unlike her husband's, Shigeko's realm is legislated, for better or for worse, by gossip, rumors, and superstition – a language that binds people together, or traps them, in unbreakable communal relationships. Hers is a world where word-of-mouth and hearsay carry a more powerful truth than do the written texts on which her husband relies. Shigeko reminds us that the film allies itself with local, communal, and familial concerns, and remains suspicious of the urban and global (if not the national) forces that have intruded on village life. Under these conditions, Shigematsu's withdrawal from history, despite the film's references to contemporary historical events (peace demonstrations and the escalating war in Korea), becomes ethically persuasive. The removal of its protagonist from history (a removal similar to, and corroborated by, the tragic marginalization fundamental to actual

33. Pelted by nuclear debris; Imamura Shôhei, *Black Rain* (1989).

hibakusha experience) allows *Black Rain* to exploit *hibakusha* alienation while releasing itself from responsibility for the past.

The emphasis the *Black Rain* narrative gives to the value of textual transcription and verification (of diaries, sutras, and documents) is symptomatic of the film's desire to call upon the authority of the past to do the bidding of the present; that is, the film offers itself as a historical documentation of the current consensus in Japan on national victimization. *Black Rain* takes a position similar to Shigematsu's with regard to the task of recopying the diary; the film makes "a fair copy just as it is" of Hiroshima victimization but deludes itself about the deeper implications of the historical context it fails to represent or acknowledge.

Shigematsu's urge to remain outside history is inscribed early in the film when he guides his wife and niece through the horrors of the bombed city with the protective admonition "Miru na" (Don't look!). A similar marginalization will be imposed on him after the war, as he, a *hibakusha* survivor, is abandoned by the historical movement his experience has initiated. In the first scene that takes place in the film's present, the year 1950, a sound truck, announcing a rally against nuclear power, blares: "We are all victims of the bomb." The politics of the future drives by, leaving Shigematsu, an actual victim of the bomb, on the sidelines. The cultural incongruities of the film are fully in place in this scene: *hibakusha* are absorbed into the larger community when they serve a political purpose but are in practice barred from the normal relations of society, such as marriage and employment. The slogan "we are all victims of the bomb" takes on a more subtle and pervasive meaning as the film works to achieve its own political aim, that is, to make literal the shared victimization Hiroshima seems to allow.

The film plots Shigematsu's marginal location so carefully that in a flashback to the emperor's radio surrender, we are not surprised when he retreats to gaze at a stream outside where baby eels swim against the current. The emperor's trickle of speech interrupts a series of water scenes: Yasuko and her aunt bathe in the poisoned river shrouded with the stench of cremation, while on the bank Shigematsu dutifully officiates in Buddhist ceremonies for the dead. A few days later, his absorption in the movements of the little rivulet, just when the tide of history has carried Japan to defeat, is abruptly cut by present-day rice-planting, an obvious sign of postwar prosperity. Nature, in these images of water, eels, and agriculture, seems to have won; the constant ebb and flow of the natural world apparently triumphs over the explosive discontinuities of politics and history. But this interpretation must be weighed against a tendency to view the war as part of the sweep of events over which, like a natural disaster, Japan had no control and thus no responsibility.[15]

As an alternative we can reimagine the film's references to nature in terms of their affirmation of the fundamentality of human labor: the daily labor of agricultural life; the labor of mourning the dead and the duty of returning their souls to nature's cycles of rebirth; the labor of survivors who struggle for meaningful work despite their disabilities. In other words, in the worldview of *Black Rain,* it is only through work that human beings can relate to each other and to the natural world. The labor of raising carp unites Shigematsu and his friends who are suffering from radiation sickness and, though they remain separated from the community, the visibility of their work resituates them within its structures of productivity. While labor is especially relevant to the rural setting of *Black Rain,* its treatment is consonant with the role of labor in most Imamura films, where work is often the only way an individual can integrate with society. For Imamura, as for the bomb survivors he portrays, work is identity, selfhood, and reconnection with others.

The importance of labor in Imamura's cinema and its thematic significance in *Black Rain* return us to the film's ideological proposal: that is, its division of the tasks and burdens of victimization between the female body and the male psyche. I have noted that this task is accomplished by the addition of the traumatized veteran Yuichi, but before we turn our attention to him, Imamura's insertion of this significant character urges us to scrutinize other characters the director adds to Ibuse's novel.[16] The most striking are two working-class women far removed, both socially and in terms of their place in the film, from the family of Shigematsu, Shigeko, and Yasuko, who occupy the narrative center. It is easy to understand how the introduction of Yuichi and the romantic element he allows strengthen the plot structure of *Black Rain* and provide greater depth for the characterization of Yasuko, who interacts with him in a way unavailable to her counterpart in the novel. But the addition of the two women is more difficult to justify from the viewpoint of structural coherence. One is the "cigarette woman," a kind of local prostitute who voices the village suspicion that the men with radiation sickness are just lazy; and the other is her daughter, a cabaret waitress returned from the city to escape a gangster boyfriend. These characters reflect the social complexity of the postwar village, providing the narrative with realistic texture. The daughter suggests potential subplots (why has she returned home? will her boyfriend cause trouble in the village? is one of the men with radiation sickness her father?) but these stories never develop. In the end we realize that the two women have no plot function, no narrative of their own, and do not touch the main story even peripherally. While the roles of all the other minor characters are resolved, the mother and daughter simply drop out of the film.

But before they do, we cannot help but notice that these women are similar to the exploited female characters who command so much attention in several of Imamura's other works – for example, the victimized bar hostesses and prostitutes in his documentaries *History of Postwar Japan as Told by a Bar Hostess* (*Nippon Sengo shi: Madamu Onboro no seikatsu,* 1970) and *Karayuki-san* (1975); or the haunted widow in his earlier work, *The Pornographers (Jinruigaku nyūmon).* It is almost as if the sardonic cigarette woman and her permed and painted daughter have stumbled into *Black Rain* from another Imamura film, one more challenging than this conventional picture. Imamura readily acknowledges his fascination with the generation of working-class women who lost everything during the war and who "contributed to the destruction of the old family system in Japan."[17] If this film tells a story about tenacious survival, the lives we can imagine for these characters speak eloquently to Imamura's purpose. But why does any deeper acknowledgment of these women go unspoken in *Black Rain?* Why add these characters only to abandon them?

The cigarette woman and her daughter remind us that the patriarchal system that *Black Rain* upholds has its own victims, "comfort women" sold into prostitution and women in the sex trade who catered to soldiers during the American Occupation. I have already pointed out that Shigematsu is a character of political ambivalence – immersed in history, he continues to deny its force. I want to suggest that Imamura's addition of these marginal women points to the director's own ambivalence about Japanese restrictions on victimization (who is included and who is not) in this unusually cautious film. That ambivalence testifies to the deep uncertainty Hiroshima generates in its twin calls for remembrance and repression.

With no narrative of their own, the mother and daughter are displaced and unabsorbed by the family melodrama that occupies the film's center.

Their displacement is inscribed in the film when the villagers stage a mock skirmish to subdue Yuichi by participating in his obsessive reenactment of battlefield trauma. The apparent superfluity of the added women stands in sharp contrast to the focal position the young man begins to occupy. Men from the local bus he tries to "bomb" belly along the road in feigned combat. It is a poignantly comic scene that points in all seriousness to Yuichi's special, unspoken standing in the community – the veteran soldier. The two women, stunned, watch from the sidelines. Are they surprised at the lengths to which the villagers will go to care for a disabled veteran, or are they shocked to see how deftly the film moves Yuichi to the heart of the narrative at the very moment it abandons them? In another scene, when the cigarette woman cynically asks an old lover why he wants to help Yasuko find a husband but doesn't do anything for the girl who could well be his own daughter, she voices an unanswered protest against the fathering structures of society that legislate not only her own life but Shigematsu's and Yasuko's as well. It is the very "storylessness" of the two women, the fact that they *do* wander into the narrative only to disappear, that gives them ironic significance in Imamura's otherwise conventionally plotted film.

But more important is the fact that the two women represent a clear contrast to Yasuko, a negative alternative defined in terms of sexuality. It is essential to the ideological purpose of *Black Rain* that Yasuko be sexually innocent. The promiscuity of the other women certifies her blamelessness, a bodily innocence that in turn substantiates the spiritual innocence the film hopes to secure for the soldier Yuichi through his alliance with her. Neither the cigarette woman nor her daughter can be the heroine of this story, because ideological victims (even *hibakusha* apparently) must be pure. In this light, the seemingly nonchalant addition of these characters becomes crucial in defining victimization for the *Black Rain* viewer, and for reinforcing the fundamental goal of the film's division of labor.

On one side of the equation the female victim is sexually pure and her body is violated by radiation; on the other side, the male victim can be presumed to be spiritually pure and it is his mind that is violated by war. The female-body/male-psyche division and the unification of victimization it strives toward are at work across the entire film. Any psychological effects Yasuko may suffer from her failed engagements and her worsening health are left undramatized. Emphasis on the physical nature of her illness is presented again and again, first when the black rain falls directly on her upturned face and hands; later in three sequences where we see her unclothed (bathing in the river and at home); and in scenes where she secretly eats medicinal aloe, applies a plaster to a lesion, or finds her hair falling out in clumps in her hands (see Figure 34). All of the women in the film live in the realm of the physical or are engaged in physical labor. The cigarette woman is almost always seen with a heavy pack on her back; her daughter works in a cabaret for the benefit of a ne'er-do-well boyfriend; and the workers in the rice fields, in accordance with tradition, are all female.

The suffering of the men or their labors are, in contrast, mental: Yuichi, a tank bomber, has apparently suffered no physical injuries during the war, though his psychological wounds are severe. Shigematsu, whose cheek was burned by the flash of the atomic blast, suffers emotional rather than physical distress; we never see him in a bout with the radiation sickness that physically debilitates, one by one, those around him. The film has little to do with his physical activities and can be understood

34. Yasuko's body violated by radiation; Imamura Shôhei, *Black Rain* (1989).

to take place entirely in his head – the narrative is a series of his memories, problems he must figure out, and decisions he must reach.

When we do catch a glimpse of the female mind it is a dark and haunted place. The charming delusions of Yasuko's senile grandmother turn ominous when, mistaking her granddaughter for Yasuko's own dead mother, she warns her not to marry or else she will die. Shigeko brings the feminine occult to the surface of the film most dramatically. Convinced the family troubles lie in the realm of her dead sister-in-law, she consults a shamaness, an obvious charlatan, whom Shigematsu upbraids in perhaps his most heroic moment. But Shigeko's own demons are not as easily exorcised; before her death, she is tormented by visions of Shigematsu's deceased friends. Shigematsu's dealings with the dead, on the other hand, are enacted sacramentally and cerebrally in terms of institutional Buddhism. To dispose of the countless corpses after the bomb with decency and respect, he is enlisted to recite the ritual prayers before cremation. The beautiful language and the enduring wisdom of the sutras contrast sharply with the incomprehensible babble uttered by the shamaness. While neither Shigeko's superstition nor Shigematsu's pragmatic faith achieve workable solutions for Yasuko's problem or their own illnesses, the disparity between their beliefs and actions favors Shigematsu, and, more significant, limits female psychology to the irrational, delusional, mystical, and obscure. Implied in this consistent limitation on the female psyche is the film's sense that it is only within the body that female "memory" and knowledge can reside, unexpressed and unfulfilled beyond the physical sphere.

Memory returns us to Yuichi, for everything about him is an expression of his repressed past; he literally "presses out" from the unconscious into obsessive reenactment. He restages the private torment of his wartime experience as a tank saboteur according to the local bus schedule for daily public viewing. The contrast with Yasuko could not be more stark. Where Yuichi's psychosis emerges full-blown in the light of day, Yasuko's illness creeps furtively in the night. She keeps her plight secret at all costs, and not only must she hide any hint of radiation sickness, but also all physical signs of the disease are a source of shame. The significance of the difference in the conceptualization of their conditions intensifies when Yuichi and Yasuko emerge as an idealized romantic pair parallel to the mundane older couple represented in Shigematsu and Shigeko. Yuichi's relationship to her forces us to interpret Yasuko's disease, characterized as shameful, as the oppositional counterpart to his. Their pairing implies that his disability is by contrast not a stigma in the community but a badge of honor, a sign of distinction. The conventionality of the rhetorical construction of *Black Rain* – demonstrated in the classic use of parallel couples and romantic idealism – naturalizes the heroic status of Yuichi's affliction.

In all but his final scene Yuichi is "acting out" his past, replaying himself as an absurd hero in the theater of memory. As already noted, others follow his lead in supportive roles or inscribe themselves as spectators in the bus scene that moves this minor character to center stage. Later, his cathartic retelling of the battle experiences that have produced the compulsion to reenact them is the film's most histrionic moment, complete with footlights, spotlights on the carved faces of his statue "actors," and Yasuko as audience.

But the drama of reenactment here implies not so much artifice as art. Yuichi's expressiveness, its nonrationality, and his obsessive creativity in isolation mark him as a creative force. He passes his days compulsively chiseling stone statues of Jizo, the Buddhist patron of children, whose benign countenance is endlessly replicated in temple carvings of the familiar little deity throughout Japan. But the faces on Yuichi's Jizo are contorted in anguish, terror, pain, thereby becoming outward reflections of inner turmoil. The religious aspect of his work links it with spirituality and transcendence; again it is Yuichi's soul, in contrast to Yasuko's body, that is expressed by the symptoms of trauma. His obsessive stonework is not a decorative feature of *Black Rain* but is fundamental both to plot and to the ideological implications of the film. The statues not only solidify the romantic connection between Yasuko and Yuichi, but they also iconically cement together the victims of Hiroshima with Japanese soldiers in battle.

The use of idiosyncratic artwork in a film about the nuclear bomb has deep historical and psychological significance. Art is an expression of the personal but is also a repository of public memory, because it allows us collectively to process the past by what we choose to aestheticize, demonstrate, exemplify, or censor. Within *hibakusha* experience, art in its public mode has had a unique function as "a special distillation of group psychic response"[18] and, for many survivors, has had rehabilitative power within their own lives. Moreover, beyond the shared psychological and individual therapeutic capacity of artistic expression, censorship of nuclear-war photographs and films gave political urgency to the preservation of images of Hiroshima and Nagasaki in the plastic and literary arts. *Hibakusha* used pen and brush not only to respond creatively to the event but also to record impressions and images they feared would otherwise be lost.[19] Only art could rescue what cold-war politics hoped to suppress.

Within this context, Yuichi's portrayal as a romantic and an isolated artist is the film's most brilliant stroke. His passion for expressing and preserving the inexpressible in stone accrues innumerable layers of meaning. On a narrative level, the Jizo sculptures that Yuichi struggles to bring to Yasuko's garden stand as sentinels of affection, guardians of love disfigured by the hatred and cruelty of war. We are uplifted by this aspect of the story, rehabilitated by the hope it gives us that even the insanity of war can be cured, that even a fatal illness ravaging the body can be postponed. And while we must embrace this interpretation and the trust in human goodness it allows, we must also be aware of its ideological implications.

When Yuichi restages the horror of combat for Yasuko, his memories illuminate and emphasize the distortions of the stone faces of the Jizo he has carved. Are these the anguished expressions of Yuichi's comrades? Or the disfigured victims of the atomic bomb? Is this Hiroshima? Or a battlefield in the Philippines? The film persuades us that there really is no difference between battle and bomb. In the iconographic use of Jizo, *Black Rain* successfully reconstructs innocent suffering as equally shared in Japan by men and women, soldiers and civilians, children and adults, and so fulfills the national desire to visualize the war in terms of Hiroshima and Nagasaki alone. The Jizo sculptures not only unite Yasuko and Yuichi in their love for one another, the statues literally "carve in stone" an identification of the soldiers who waged the war with the victims of the atomic bomb.

Black Rain styles itself as history to give validity to a consensus in Japan on national victimization unencumbered by wartime responsibility, a consensus defended by the bombing of Hiroshima. In the words of John Dower, "Hiroshima and Nagasaki [have become] icons of Japanese suffering – perverse national treasures capable of fixating Japanese memory of the war on what had happened to Japan and simultaneously blotting out recollection of the Japanese victimization of others."[20] The higher purpose of *Black Rain* is to honor those who were killed or injured or sickened by the unforgivable and immoral use of atomic weapons by the United States on Hiroshima, and the film succeeds in this objective through its honest portrayal of the painful lives of those who survived. The more questionable task of this internationally promoted and acclaimed film is to fixate world memory on the "icons of Japanese suffering" while simultaneously blotting out recollection of Japan at war.

One of the last scenes in the film is Yuichi's embrace of Yasuko – a romantic picture rare in Japanese cinema and one that persuades us of their devotion and the purity of their love for one another (see Figure 35). Yasuko, who suffers the physical debilitation of radiation sickness, and Yuichi, a man psychologically traumatized by combat, redeem each other spiritually and provide a sense of narrative closure to an episode in history that will never be morally resolved. In their embrace the characters satisfy our need for a romantic story. The problem is that their union also works to fulfill the film's more subtle political purpose. The single character to be rehabilitated in *Black Rain* is not Yasuko or Shigematsu, but Yuichi, who by the end of the film rides with the dying Yasuko in an

35. Yûichi bears the burden of his love for Yasuko; Imamura Shôhei, *Black Rain* (1989).

ambulance, clearly no longer plagued by a compulsion to obliterate the sound of an engine that once triggered memories of the machines of war. *Black Rain* here expresses the hope that a shared embrace of Hiroshima victimization can work as a kind of national therapy, but at what cost, we must ask, to those others not included in the cure?

NOTES

1. Robert Jay Lifton, in *Death in Life: Survivors of Hiroshima* (Chapel Hill: University of North Carolina Press, 1991), suggests that film holds special creative potential for A-bomb re-creation but notes that "most attempts have stuck to the other side of the film equation, the apparent literality of the photographic image, without realizing that this is a 'dreamed reality.'" He writes that "filmmakers have often tried to reproduce the atomic bomb experience exactly as it happened" (453), with little success in convincing those who actually experienced the event.
2. All prints and negatives of the films were thought to have been confiscated for the Strategic Bombing Survey, but in 1952 an incomplete copy kept hidden during the American Occupation resurfaced in Japan. It was not until 1967 that the United States returned a complete print of the film to the Japanese government, which refused to show it. In 1982 a private Japanese group was able to purchase the nearly million feet of remaining film on the bombings from the U.S. National Archives. See Kyoko Hirano, *Mr. Smith Goes to Tokyo: Japanese Cinema under the American Occupation, 1945–1952* (Washington, D.C.: Smithsonian Institution, 1992), 59.
3. For a detailed description of the "complex history of suppressions" in the making of one such film, *The Effects of the Atomic Bomb on Hiroshima and Nagasaki,* see Abe Mark Nornes, "The Body at the Center – The Effects of the Atomic Bomb on Hiroshima and Nagasaki," in Mick Broderick, ed., *Hibakusha Cinema: Hiroshima, Nagasaki and the Nuclear Image in Japanese Film* (London and New York: Kegan Paul International, 1996), 121.
4. The discourse on atomic weapons derived its authority from Civil Defense educational programs. The Federal Civil Defense Administration pamphlet *Atomic Attack: What to Do* (1951) mentions Hiroshima and Nagasaki only in terms of survivability: "In the city of Hiroshima, slightly over half the people who were a mile from the atomic explosion are still alive. At Nagasaki, almost 70 percent of the people a mile from the bomb lived to tell their tale. Today thousands of survivors of these two atomic attacks live in new houses built right where their old ones stood. The war may have changed their way of life, but they are not riddled with cancer" (4).
5. Mark Osteen, "The Big Secret: Film Noir and Nuclear Fear," *Journal of Popular Film and Television* 22 (summer 1994): 79–91. For a compilation of American films correlated to historic nuclear events, see Brian Fruth, Alicia Germer, Keiko Kikuchi, Anamaria Mihalega, Melanie Olmstead, Hikaru

Sasaki, and Jack Nachbar, et al., "The Atomic Age: Facts and Films from 1945–1965," *Journal of Popular Film and Television* 23 (winter 1996): 154–61.

6. For discussions of the psychological, literary, and historical dimensions of atomic symbolism in media other than film, see Robert Jay Lifton, *Death in Life: Survivors of Hiroshima* (Chapel Hill: University of North Carolina Press), 397–478; John Whittier Treat, *Writing Ground Zero: Japanese Literature and the Atomic Bomb* (Chicago: University of Chicago Press); John W. Dower, "The Bombed: Hiroshimas and Nagasakis in Japanese Memory," in Michael J. Hogan, ed., *Hiroshima in History and Memory* (Cambridge: Cambridge University Press, 1996), 116–42.
7. The first Japanese motion picture to address the atomic bombings was *Bell of Nagasaki (Nagasaki no kane),* directed by Oba Hideo in 1950; this was followed in 1953 by Shindo Kaneto's *Children of the Atom Bomb (Genbaku no ko),* based on the novel by Osada Arata. In the next year, Sekigawa Hideo produced another version of the same story, titled *Hiroshima.* David Desser outlines the sketchy history of Japanese nuclear film in "Japan: An Ambivalent Nation, an Ambivalent Cinema," but goes on to say that "even [Kurosawa's] jidai-geki (period films) *Rashōmon* (1950) and *Kumonosu-jo* (*Throne of Blood,* 1957) may be profitably seen as thinly veiled responses to the destructiveness of the bombs." (*Swords and Ploughshares, The Bulletin of the Program in Arms Control, Disarmament, and International Security,* University of Illinois at Urbana-Champaign, vol. 9, [spring-summer 1995]. Online: http://acdisweb.acdis.uiuc.edu/homepage_docs/pubs_docs/S&P_docs/S&P_Sp-Su_1995.html. August 15, 1995.) If Desser's interpretation of these films is valid, then his reading reinforces the fact that, in the fifties, mainstream Japanese cinema collaborated with Hollywood in its refusal to face the reality of nuclear history. If Kurosawa was then the "only filmmaker in Japan" preoccupied with the atomic age, his singular absorption in allegorizing nuclear issues intensified the perception of Japan as a postwar victim of a holocaust with no historical cause or context.
8. Robert J. Lifton, *Death in Life: Survivors of Hiroshima* (Chapel Hill: University of North Carolina Press, 1991), 304.
9. "I have no color reference for that period," claimed Spielberg about *Schindler's List.* In this sense Imamura's film anticipates Spielberg's, though Kawamata Takashi's cinematography is less ripe than Janusz Kaminski's. Armond White, "Toward a theory of Spielberg history" *Film Comment,* March-April 1994, n. 2, 51.
10. Japanese and Western works that try to encompass the bombing of Hiroshima, both textual and visual, often resort to multiple levels of narration or combinations of individual stories. John Hersey's *Hiroshima,* the first widely read work to confront the bombing, is four separate narratives; Resnais's film *Hiroshima, Mon Amour* plays upon its own inability to offer a coherent statement about the nuclear destruction of the city. The writing of individual *hibakusha* often presents itself as adding another voice to an event that can never be grasped in its entirety. John Treat writes, "The literature . . .

struggles in vain to succeed – to overcome the contradictions implicit in a form of writing that would give a beginning, middle, and conclusion to events defying such narrative domestication" (3).

11. Noël Carrol, *Theorizing the Moving Image* (Cambridge: Cambridge University Press, 1996), 279.
12. Ibid., 281.
13. Imamura's aversion to the style and direction of Ozu Yasujiro, whom he assisted at Shochiku, hardly bears repeating, except to say that his famous antagonism implies more in Imamura's quotations from *Late Spring* than homage. Audie Bock points out that in *Stolen Desire* (1958) "Imamura set out to put in everything Ozu leaves out of [*Story of Floating Weeds* (1934)]" (*Japanese Film Directors* [Tokyo: Kodansha, 1990], 290–91). Something similar happens in *Black Rain,* a film that deals more honestly with the anguish inherent in the institution of arranged marriage. The difference is that *Black Rain* does not critique *Late Spring* but, on the contrary, returns to the Ozu film as a source of cultural authenticity.
14. David Bordwell, *Ozu and the Poetics of Cinema* (Princeton: Princeton University Press, 1994), 307.
15. This view is paralleled in the United States, where atomic iconology has focused on the bombs as apocalyptic storms rather than as acts of war. While in the novel *Black Rain,* we can agree with John Treat that, "the power of the natural world rushes in to fill the void vacated by the political collapse of power" (293), the same cannot be said for the film, which offers no location, past or present, where the workings of human society are not in force.
16. Yuichi is probably based on the lieutenant in Ibuse's "Yohai Taicho."
17. Ed Murray, "Witness to Hell," *Living Marxism* 73 (1994): Online. Internet. Available http://www.junius.co.uk/lm/lm73_Living.html. 3 December 1996.
18. Robert J. Lifton, 397.
19. John W. Dower, 128.
20. Ibid., 123.

PART THREE

OUTSIDE THE FRAME OF CULTURE

CHAPTER TWELVE

Piss and Run

Or How Ozu Does a Number on SCAP

Edward Fowler

From everything I have seen, the Japanese people have great respect for our power and will be highly sensitive to our wishes as long as that power is not seriously weakened.

– 25 October 1945 letter from "Ted" de Bary in Tokyo to "Don" Keene in Tsingtao[1]

We, the Japanese people, acting through our duly elected representatives in the National Diet, . . . do proclaim that sovereign power resides with the people.

– The Constitution of Japan (1946)

Who are the agents of cultural transformation in one nation when it is ruled by another? With the word *culture,* in its sense of both generator and custodian of social norms, we typically associate such notions as *indigenous, organic, traditional:* What happens to it when a value system – however well-intentioned – is imposed from without, as was the case during the Allied (and principally American) Occupation of Japan from 1945 to 1952, following World War II? Are the tenets of democracy and individualism, so central to American life, universally desirable, regardless of the social context into which they are introduced? Are they superior or preferable to the "feudal" values of communal loyalty and selflessness they are called on to replace? Finally, does the very process of cultural transformation, when it assumes a blatantly alien mantle, inherently undermine its product? What is left, in other words, after the rebound from foreign rule?

These questions are raised, subtly yet unmistakably, in Ozu Yasujirô's (1903–63) brilliant but little noted *A Who's Who of the Tenement* (*Nagaya shinshiroku,* 1947), set in a working-class neighborhood of postwar Tokyo.[2] *A Who's Who of the Tenement* is an anomaly in many ways, not the least of which is its very title in translation. Distributed in English as *Record of a Tenement Gentleman,* the film does not provide a chronicle *(roku)* of the life of some "gentleman" *(shinshi)* who happens to live in an old, wooden row house, but rather portrays the lives of several tenement dwellers – a veritable "Who's Who" *(shinshiroku)* of lower-class citizens, as David Bordwell rightly point out.[3] The translation is a "howler" a denotative and connotative mismatch that is at least as misleading as, say, rendering *hamburger* into another language as a cold sandwich containing ham.

I dwell on this mistranslation because it is emblematic of the film itself, which appears, even upon repeated viewings, to be a series of misleading signifiers – whether in the form of title or scene or situation – that resists easy connection with readily identifiable signifieds. Nowhere is this more strikingly apparent than in the opening scene. Tashiro, a fortune-teller from Kyushu who rooms with Tamekichi, a tinker who deals in used goods, returns home with an (apparently) abandoned child he has picked up while working in the city, and finds his roommate engaged in conversation with a nonexistent audience. Tamekichi is asking for a divorce. "Yes, but even the moon is shadowed by clouds once in a while," he begins, "so what do you expect of us small/frail human beings, who pale like faint stars by comparison? . . . Your sweet words and concern make me feel as though I'm stabbing you in the back . . . but I ask that you please agree to separate." Tamekichi makes this odd request with no little feeling – indeed, with a certain theatricality that contrasts notably with the dry personality we come to know later in the film. (Unbeknownst to Tashiro, he is actually reciting a passage from a well-known stage play, *Onna keizu,* by Izumi Kyôka.) Overhearing Tamekichi's soliloquy from the entranceway, Tashiro quite naturally asks if someone is visiting. "Forget it," (*Iya, kotchi no kotta* – literally, "No, it's my own business"),[4] is the ambiguous reply. The subject is never taken up again, except in a very abstruse way that is in itself notable and that will be examined later.

And so we are presented, right at the beginning, with a fragment, unglossed and apparently without connection to what follows, which threatens to undermine the film's unity and perhaps its very coherency. Yet this is a film, we remind ourselves, by a director with, by every other measure, a consummate interest in design. Indeed, it is hard not to assume that this fragment is presented to us at the outset *precisely* by design – a design, it should be noted, that most certainly toys with notions of spectatorship, problematizing the viewing, as well as the filmed, subject. For we are obliged to ask ourselves, as we witness this dramatic performance reminiscent of an actor's delivering his lines on a stage, what is *our* relationship to this nonexistent audience? How do *we* constitute ourselves as viewers here and throughout the film, and what are we to be looking for when viewing it? If these questions are posed only obliquely in the film's prologue, in accordance with the oblique angle from which the soliloquy is shot, they are posed directly at the film's end, where Otane – the woman, living opposite Tamekichi, who takes in the lost boy he rejects – delivers a monologue of her own on the state of postwar morality, facing the camera head-on in the usual Ozu style. Such a "direct" confrontation with the audience, followed as it is by a series of closing shots of a well-known Tokyo locale (the Saigô statue in Ueno Park), which propels the fictional story line into the "real world" of postwar deprivation, compels us to reconsider our own subject position as spectators of the film we have just viewed.

I use the word *we* advisedly, for I refer not simply to the fiction by which we Americans vicariously appropriate the role of a Japanese national watching a first-run Ozu film of the postwar period more than half a century after its release. I refer as well to our seemingly improbable, yet in fact crucial, role of intended audience; for it turns out that we Americans, *as Americans,* have been implicated in its viewing – have indeed been constructed as viewing subjects – from the very beginning.

In her informative book on Allied censorship of Japanese cinema during the Occupation, Kyoko Hirano briefly notes the concerns that censors had about *Nagaya shinshiroku* – ones that seemingly pale before more serious concerns about other films, many of which Hirano chronicles in detail.[5] She recounts the finding of one censor who characterizes the treatment of the boy as "too cruel," and surmises that at least two scenes – first, of the choosing, by lottery, which of the tenement dwellers would accompany the boy back to his alleged home outside Tokyo; and second, of the boy shouldering a heavy bag of potatoes back to the tenement afterward – survived in the final version only through the intervention of another censor, and might have been facilitated by a bribe from the studio.[6]

Hirano's instructive account of Occupation film censorship in Japan leaves no doubt about the significance of the *American* viewing of *any* Japanese film made during the postwar period. It is clear that the Supreme Commander of the Allied Powers (SCAP) placed great importance on cinema as a potentially democratizing element in postwar life, and went to extraordinary lengths in an effort to ensure production of what it considered to be not simply wholesome, but also ideologically correct, entertainment. Not surprisingly, SCAP was concerned with correcting previous excesses of Japanese cinematic production, and banned, on the grounds of being "ultra-nationalistic," "militaristic," or "propagating feudalism," more than two hundred films (roughly half the total) made during the fifteen-year period (1931–45) of war on the Asian continent and with the United States. But it did not stop there. It acted, through the Civil Information and Education (CIE) section and the Civil Censorship Detachment (CCD), to censor films made during the Occupation years as well – not once, but twice over, in both the preproduction and postproduction phases. Screenplays had to be translated for review by the CIE, and completed films had to pass inspection by both the CIE and CCE.[7]

What is astonishing is how quickly, after Japan's surrender, the Occupation acted to institutionalize the censorship of film. From very early on – well before the end of the war, in fact – a number of U.S. governmental agencies saw cinema, along with the press, the publishing world, and other media, as a way of transforming Japan into a democratic nation more amenable to American values. Scarcely a month after the Emperor had announced Japan's surrender and barely a fortnight after General MacArthur had himself set foot on Japanese soil, SCAP commenced its policy of "guidance" of film and of other entertainment industries. By 22 September 1945, the CIE had been formed and had summoned a group of prominent Japanese film executives, producers, and directors to a meeting at which it presented a list of suggested desirable subjects and directions for future films.[8] The institution of double censorship (preproduction and postproduction) was formalized by January 1946 and continued until June 1949. Postproduction censorship through the CIE continued until the very end of the Occupation in April 1952.[9]

In addition to its list of "desirable subjects and directions" for films, the CIE listed subjects considered taboo under the Occupation. They included themes of a violent, militaristic, nationalistic, antidemocratic, "feudal," chauvinistic, xenophobic, suicidal, or discriminatory nature, as well as those exploitative of women and children and, finally, those "at variance with the spirit or letter of the Potsdam Declaration or any SCAP directive."[10] This last restriction proved an anomaly that was never to be fully resolved. The Allies "had come to Japan," as Hirano puts it, "to bring democracy; however, in order to disseminate and inculcate democratic ideas, they had to suppress some of the ideas that might have inhibited the growth of the new ideology."[11] This left the Occupation censors in the uncomfortable position of concealing their work in the name of creating a more open society – a contradiction that would not only lead to extreme actions on the part of SCAP (including the actual burning of banned films, a practice not instituted even during wartime),[12] but also baffle Japanese advocates of Westernization in the process.

The obvious contradiction of their own position notwithstanding, the fact remained that Occupation censors were an integral part of *any* Japanese filmmaker's audience throughout the postwar years. To script and direct a film in this period without considering the American response to it was, quite literally, unthinkable. No film made in Japan could escape the watchful eyes of CIE, which, as noted above, observed stringent (and at times arbitrary) prescriptive and proscriptive guidelines at several stages of the filmmaking process.[13] It is in this context that we must review Ozu's film, which eloquently speaks to, even as it is shaped by, these conditions.

A Who's Who of the Tenement, Ozu's first postwar production and first film in five years (he had previously directed the well-known *There Was a Father [Chichi ariki],* in 1942), was released in May 1947, the same month that the so-called MacArthur Constitution officially went into effect. The postwar constitution, drawn up as early as February 1946 by MacArthur's staff at SCAP and promulgated in November of the same year, blatantly betrayed its foreign origins, drafted as it was "in secrecy within General MacArthur's headquarters, sprung upon a distraught Japanese Cabinet, and forced through a reluctant Japanese Diet after a few minor changes had been permitted to the Japanese."[14] It was praised or denounced (depending on the critic's political persuasion) because of those origins, and for its radical departure from previous (late 1945) attempts by Japanese officials at token revisions to the 1889 Meiji Constitution.

The very secrecy of the new constitution's production, resembling a kind of bureaucratic sleight of hand that masked its origins, recalls the process of censorship in general during the Occupation.[15] Democracy was "served" by an intricate monitoring system to which no reference was allowed. Not only did the censors take great pains to conceal their existence in an attempt to avoid criticism, but they also took equal pains to avoid commendation, which in their eyes was just as damning to their project.[16]

What is the link between Ozu's screenplay of a boy apparently abandoned by his father and taken in unwillingly by a middle-aged widow living in a row house, and the Allied program of postwar censorship directed at violent, militaristic, nationalistic, and other antidemocratic elements in Japanese cinema? As I will argue here, it is the play of spectatorship, which operates at wildly varying levels of concealment. If, as I believe he did, Ozu succeeded in communicating an extraordinarily blunt and indeed xenophobic message to his Japanese audience without getting caught by his American one, it is because the director managed to disguise that message in a way that made his respective audiences focus on essentially two different stories. When making a film that is guaranteed as critical a viewing as it would receive during the Occupation years, the stakes are high in betting correctly on just what will be seen, and missed, by a particular audience.

A Who's Who of the Tenement is in some ways a postwar film in name only, for it is an extension of Ozu's interest and accomplishment in the *shomingeki* (drama of the lower classes) genre, in the development of which Ozu himself played a crucial role from the early 1930s; it has a very different feel to it than his later explorations of middle- and upper-middle-class life that began in earnest with *Late Spring* (1949). The film is set in the *shitamachi* or "Low City" side of Tokyo – not in Sunachô (the setting of several other *shitamachi* films) but near Tsukiji. The Honganji Temple, which survived the U.S. air raids, dominates the landscape in several exterior shots.[17]

The signature of Ozu's mature directorial style informs the film throughout: the low camera angle, made particularly effective in this film due to the presence of the small boy; the cluttered depth of the interior shots contrasted (both visually and musically) with the vacant spaces of the exterior shots, the latter made even emptier due to the backdrop of wartime devastation (rubble and charred remains dot the urban landscape); the predominance of the still frame (broken only by two dolly shots of the boy running after Otane on the beach at Chigasaki and by a vertical wipe, imitating a shutting camera lens, of a photography studio where Otane and the boy have their picture taken); the numerous parallel scenes and actions (the boy and later his father are seen shouldering sacks of potatoes); homeless boys fish in a canal near Tsukiji in the middle of the film and loiter about the Saigô statue in Ueno at the end; Tamekichi and Otane give "speeches" in the film's beginning and penultimate scenes, respectively); and the ceaseless attention to design, from the footpaths delineated by Otane as she hurries over the dunes on the beach, to the studied placement of household objects as props in the tenement alleyways. Indeed, the film's formal qualities tempt us to incorporate it unthinkingly into what critics, particularly with reference to the late films, have come to regard as the "transcendent,"[18] and consequently timeless and apolitical, Ozu aesthetic.

The stamp of the film's gritty postwar setting, however, with its evocations of the aftermath of total war in nearly every exterior shot, is too pronounced for the viewer – especially the American viewer – to ignore. It is all the more remarkable, therefore, that the only scenes that Occupation censors appeared to have challenged during their review of the film were ones depicting "cruelty," of a personally motivated sort, to the boy, as already noted. Did they not observe the physical backdrop – and by extension the political and social context – against which the alleged "cruelty" took place and to which we would expect the censors to be particularly sensitive? This question begs an even more urgent one: What exactly did the censors "see" when they viewed the film? Or to put it another way, what in the film was visible, and invisible, to them?

One way of approaching the question is to reconstruct the scenario in a manner that reconciles the story of an apparently orphaned and cruelly treated boy and the backdrop of a postwar Tokyo tenement neighborhood. Given the times in which Ozu's film was made – one thinks of course of the suggested and proscribed themes issued by the CIE – the matter of deciding what a film was about was surely no mere exercise in plot summary but in fact central to its ultimate status as a viable cinematic entity. Occupation censors had the authority to delete scenes, or even take a film out of circulation, in accordance with what they saw.

The question, once again, is what they did in fact see. Any cinematic narrative, just as any text, is a plenitude – indeed, an overload – of signs that, reorganized in our reading/viewing, we are conditioned to edit into some coherent pattern through which we can naturalize a host of recalcitrant details. This process inevitably creates a hierarchy of images out of which we construct a plot. Plot, then, is *not* some predetermined story line, equally obvious to any reader/viewer, but a narrative that each of us invents from all the details, most of which end up going unaccounted for. It is the details we must direct our attention to here, however, for as David Bordwell reminds us, "The film does not tell the story; it prompts the spectator to *construct* the story."[19]

Just how differently viewers construct a narrative is revealed in a survey of the English-language synopses of Ozu's film. Donald Richie and Joseph Anderson, for example, summarize it as follows:

> [A] cycle of [postwar] films about children began in 1947, when Yasujiro Ozu made his first film in five years, *The Record of a Tenement Gentleman* (Nagaya Shinshi Roku), which was about one of many homeless boys who roamed the streets directly after the war. The boy meets his father, but eventually rejects him to go off on his own and make his own life.[20]

Here is Richie's own summary in his later study of Ozu: "A war orphan is found on the streets of Tokyo and sent to live with a middle-aged woman. At first she finds him a bother, but eventually she comes to love him. The boy's father is found and she must give up the child."[21] Here is Audie Bock: "A war orphan found on the streets of Tokyo is sent to live with a middle-aged woman. She finds him a nuisance at first, but grows to love him. His father is eventually found and she has to give him up, but she opens an orphanage, in a very un-Japanese ending."[22]

Certain contradictions in these descriptions are immediately apparent: for example, what these critics call "orphanhood" is actually a temporary condition in this film. (The boy's father turns up in all three citations.) Bock's erroneous assertion, moreover, that the woman who takes care of the boy later opens an orphanage curiously mirrors Richie's assertion following his summary cited above: "At the end of the picture the middle-aged woman decides to open a center for war orphans like the one she had come to love. This unlikely, one may almost say un-Japanese, resolve almost ruins the film."[23] And perhaps it would, were this in fact what really happens.

The most recent and detailed summary is to be found in David Bordwell's study of Ozu, which presents synopses and analyses of every film that Ozu directed. Bordwell notes:

> Otane, a widow who runs a kitchenware shop, is forced to take care of Kohei, a homeless boy. At first she hates him and does all she can to evade responsibility, but he will not be put off. After he wets his bed one night, he runs off and she anxiously searches for him. He turns up, and she realizes that she has grown to love him. She takes him to the zoo and to a photography studio. That night his father appears, relieved to have found his son. Moved both by her concern for the boy and the evident love of father and son, she resolves to adopt a child.[24]

Bordwell's summary is in fact the most accurate in the sense of containing no gross errors – which is not, however, to say that it is a true or adequate account of the film. The very elaborateness of Bordwell's formalist analysis, which follows the summary and extends over five pages, suggests otherwise: that a viewing cannot be contained by a mere "plot" outline, however rigorously the latter sets out to encapsulate the film's temporal, spatial, and causal relationships. To characterize the film, then, as being about the growing, if grudging, affection that an older woman shows a boy she has been forced to take in, is at once to identify the film (i.e., differentiate it from other films) and to skew it beyond recognition, Bordwell seems to be saying – rendering, if you will, the proverbial hamburger into a cold ham sandwich.

Given the eyebrow-raising examples (all by critics who presumably saw the film) gleaned from the previously mentioned survey, it would seem that this very preoccupation with plot – a desire to figure out what the cinematic narrative is about – is what blinded the Occupation censors to a number of visual cues that transcend the story of boy-taken-in-by-unwilling-woman: cues so visible that they were entirely overlooked by officials more interested in *reading* a story than in *seeing* a film. (Perhaps the censors' vision had become blurred, after the manner of Otane when she contracted trachoma as a child, upon viewing too many peep shows, as she recalls during the film's marvelous ballad recitation scene!) This film's dynamism, however, lies precisely in the way that Ozu puts the film image at war with the story line.

I do not use the word *war* lightly. The film makes no verbal reference whatsoever to the hostilities between Japan and the United States; yet traces of the war and its aftermath infuse the film: we hear talk of rations (of flour, matches, and candles) and of general scarcity of goods (there are inquiries for such things as a bicycle tire and a rubber hose); of inflation (the winning lottery ticket is paid off in "new currency"); and, most tellingly, of how people lived and behaved at a time – identified nostalgically but cautiously as "before" *(Mae wa. . .)* the present – when they were not so selfish and more willing to let children grow up as children.

These muted references suffice to place the postwar present in a distinctly uncomplimentary light, but they pale before Ozu's visual representation of late-1946 Tokyo.[25] We are actually presented with two cities, and the contrast between the pleasantly cluttered, lived-in space of the interior sets and the empty spaces of the war-damaged urban setting is striking.[26] The plenitude of daily life in the confined but richly occupied space of the row houses stands out all the more starkly against the sheer paucity of living things in the external shots, characterized, as the latter are, by rubble-filled lots behind the tenement, by the imposing but vacant concrete office buildings nearby, and by streets virtually devoid of pedestrians (and these only in extreme long shots).[27] Indeed, the most prominent feature in one exterior shot (in which Otane searches for the boy she had taken in) is a fire-charred tree trunk, no doubt consumed by a wartime air raid and the only bit of urban foliage to be seen in the film.

Two visitors to the tenement reinforce the contrast between a morally preferable (even if not idyllic) world of the past and a contemporary world in decline. The first is Kikuko, Otane's friend from school days, who reminisces with Otane about the nobler ways of an earlier time (in a way that anticipates the appearance, at the film's very end, of the Saigô statue at Ueno Park around which homeless youths congregate). The second is Yukiko, Tamekichi's daughter, who lives away (we are not told where) and arrives empty-handed and with an appetite. Kikuko, dressed in a kimono, offers gifts of food to Otane and to the boy. Yukiko, dressed in slacks, blouse, scarf, and sun shades, has gained weight at other people's expense, we are led to believe; today she has arrived with designs on lunch. The link of the one character's dress and attitude to a communal prewar ethos and of the other's to a self-centered postwar ethos is hardly subtle, and here again we wonder why the Occupation censors did not "see" this damning juxtaposition (amounting to nothing less than a character assassination of the thoroughly "modern" and Westernized *après-guerre* figure of Yukiko) as a stinging critique of democracy and individualism, so vigorously championed by SCAP and shortly to be institutionalized by the new constitution.

All of which brings us back to the "divorce" scene at the film's beginning. Tamekichi, who asked a fictional spouse to agree to a separation, has a real offspring, it turns out, the product of an upbringing that has, according to our visual and verbal cues, gone awry. The daughter's presence lends credence to an actual divorce having taken place; but in the absence of the spouse, this rupture is expressed through a father-daughter separation: it is as though the father has sworn off association with her, even though he may have lingering feelings of guilt about "stabbing her in the back." Given the daughter's appearance, however, one might go one step further: Does not Tamekichi in effect swear off association with the American-made values that have made his daughter what she is?

Such speculation might seem a bit far-fetched were it not for one more telling visual detail, deftly "concealed" yet prominently placed in Ozu's tale of postwar Japan. I refer to the central object of Ozu's criticism: the very symbol of America itself. The boy that Otane has unwillingly taken in enrages her by wetting his bed overnight. For this act the boy must pay by fanning her futon dry on the line behind the row house. Ozu's camera lingers on the bedding: we see it in a series of long shots and close-ups, and from both directions (see Figure 36). An old piece of bedding, the futon is patched on two corners, front and back. But no ordinary patches, these! White starry shapes on a dark rectangular background: a replica, excepting the plaid pattern that camouflages the stripes, of the U.S. flag that is hung, in the final insult, upside down.[28]

Lest the viewer miss it the first time around, Ozu shows us the futon again, this time from behind and in painstaking detail, after the boy wets his bed a second time (see Figure 37). The boy is not there to fan it, for he has run away in anticipation of Otane's wrath. It is a clear case of *neshonben no tarenige* (piss and run), Tamekichi declares wryly when he hears the story. Yet it is precisely this infraction and subsequent flight that endears the boy to Otane, who sets out in search of him and later realizes, during a chat with Kikuko in which they inveigh against the selfishness of contemporary society and talk wistfully of a bygone era, that she indeed has feelings for him. The boy's irreverent trashing of the United States, then, awakens Otane to her own selfishness and opens her eyes to a set of values that she had known and cherished all along.[29] In the manner of Poe's "Purloined Letter," Ozu succeeded in concealing from cen-

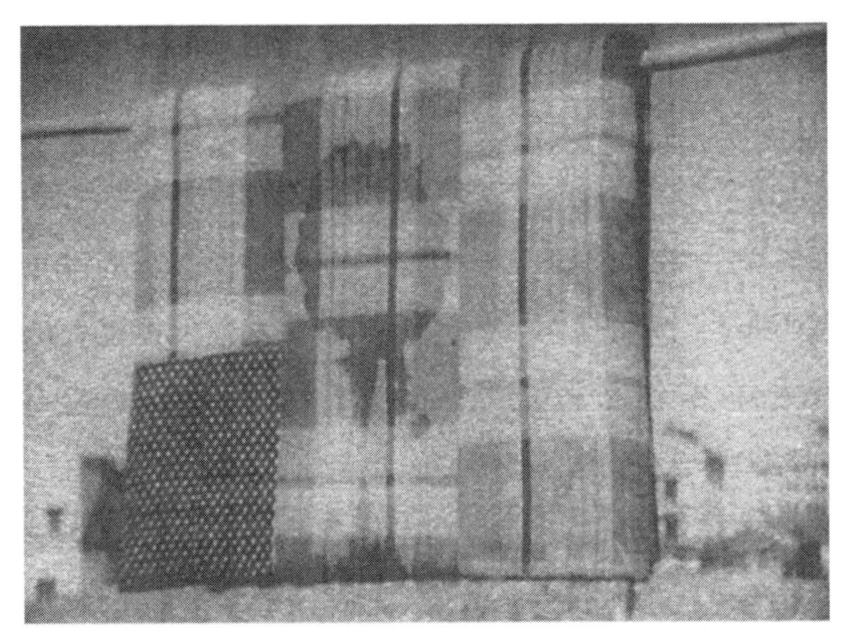

36. Futon or flag?; Ozu Yasujirô, *Record of a Tenement Gentleman* (1947).

37. A prominent symbol invisibly defies Occupation censors; Ozu Yasujirô, *Record of a Tenement Gentleman* (1947).

sors that very thing they were charged with looking for, by making it all too visible.[30]

This act of concealment is no small feat, given that it is executed the first time around in a series of exterior shots that, as noted earlier, are so dominated by vacant space. Where we expect presence – in the form of building structures or human habitation or activity – we find little or none. The "presence" of the United States, therefore, in the form of bombing rubble and the "flag" in the futon-drying scene, as if it were filling a vacuum that a Japanese presence alone could not fill, looms very large indeed. "All of Ozu's 'intermediate spaces' exemplify a dialectic of presence and absence," David Bordwell writes, "but in *Record of a Tenement Gentleman* this becomes prominent throughout the film's stylistic organization."[31] Bordwell has in mind the speech Tamekichi makes to a nonexistent wife, but he refers (without, however, actually identifying it as such) to the "flag" scene as well: "The quilt scenes . . . tend to present empty space when we expect to see characters."[32] Yet as we have seen, empty space has in fact been "occupied" – without invoking a single image of a GI – by an unmistakable, if unexpected, symbolic presence.[33]

What, then, motivated the director to defy the Occupation censors in this way? Despite certain excesses and a wrenching change of course in 1947–48, brought on by the Cold War, from a program of New/Fair Deal-style liberalism to reactionary anticommunism, the American presence has been almost universally characterized as a benign one in which rapport between the occupiers and the occupied was exceptionally good.[34] Such a "rapport," however, would seem to have everything to do with what Edwin Reischauer describes as the ability of the Americans to be good winners and of the Japanese to be good losers.[35] Thus, the rapport was "good" in this complex scenario of military occupation only because both victor and vanquished adjusted quickly to the required roles. Reischauer attributes this success to the serendipities of national character. The assessment of "Ted" de Bary (cited at the outset), however, with its observation, at once naïve yet prescient, about the importance of brute power, may well be closer to the truth.

It would seem to be precisely at that sort of brute power that Ozu, on one level at least, was thumbing his nose, in a recalcitrant, *ama-no-jaku*-like gesture that anticipates writings on the Occupation period by the likes of Kojima Nobuo and Nosaka Akiyuki in the 1950s and 1960s.[36] Having no contribution to make to the frenzied postwar quest for a new social order, he presents a profoundly conservative worldview, seemingly unconcerned about the issue of war guilt and appealing to a prewar ethos. Yet on another level, he can be seen as mobilizing values and institutions (such as the neighborhood association, vilified by postwar reformers) that had been tarnished and discredited, but that he saw as still useful in binding (quite literally, one feels, when viewing the film) a broken and empty society.

This is not to say that Ozu favored a wholesale return to prewar or wartime life and ideology. Although he paid lip service, in several interviews he gave to correspondents while serving on the front, to "making films that would be of use to the state,"[37] there is no evidence that he was enthusiastic about the military regime or about Japan's imperialist mission.[38] At least one script he wrote (*The Flavor of Green Tea over Rice* [*Ochazuke no aji,* 1939]) was rejected by Japanese censors as "unserious,"[39] and he went on to make two important contemporary films, *The Brothers and Sisters of the Toda Family* (*Toda ke no kyôdai,* 1941) and *There Was a Father* (*Chichi ariki,* 1942), which treat daily life in a way that transcends and challenges the militarist agenda. Like many other directors, he was recruited to make propaganda films (much as were Frank Capra and others in the United States), and was dispatched twice to the Asian continent, first to Nanjing (1937–39) and later to Singapore (1943–46), where he became a prisoner-of-war under the British for half a year and spent a good many hours, we are told, watching American films. Aesthetics (Ozu's appreciation of American cinema is well known), in this instance, took precedence over politics.[40]

As the generator of both a cinematic aesthetic and a political zeitgeist, then, the United States was doubtless foremost in Ozu's mind during the immediate postwar period when he reestablished his career in Tokyo. And yet it is wrong to characterize (and implicitly dismiss) *Nagaya shinshiroku* as being "the first and last time Ozu can be caught making a nod in the direction of civic endeavor, an idea imported from abroad that enjoyed a brief popularity during the Occupation."[41] For as we have seen, Ozu distanced himself as much or more from SCAP's agenda as he did from the militarists', at a time when distancing of any sort was not that much easier than during the wartime years.

In an era of "democratization" and of a nearly universal rejection of the prewar ethos, then, Ozu's subversive act stands out as nothing less than revolutionary in its way. And this is why, more than half a century after its release, the film still rings true. It is not just out of the feeling of rooting for the underdog, for the party out of power, whichever it might happen to be (a feeling that would make perhaps any viewer of this film, in an unthinking moment, want to piss on the American flag). It also comes from the recognition that Ozu's sense of national identity seems just as valid for a great many Japanese today – more than four decades after the end of the Occupation and in this era of ostensible internationalization – as it did before. And it is because of this startling recognition, even more than because of the technical expertise so much in evidence, that I agree with Bordwell's assessment of *Nagaya shinshiroku:* "If Ozu had made only this seventy-two minute film, he would have to be considered one of the world's great directors.[42]

NOTES

Japanese-language books cited here are published in Tokyo, unless otherwise noted. The author wishes to acknowledge the very useful comments of James Fujii, Thomas Kierstead, Lucy North, and Linda Williams on earlier drafts of this essay.

1. *War-Wasted Asia: Letters, 1945–46,* ed. Otis Cary (Tokyo: Kodansha International, 1975), 112.
2. Like so many critics, Hasumi Shigehiko dismisses Ozu's work of the immediate postwar period in an attempt to valorize the more famous later films (beginning with *Late Spring* [*Banshun,* 1949]), which typically feature the bourgeoisie (often with a focus on a daughter's prospective marriage and its impact on her family): "*Late Spring* is unquestionably a richer film than either *Nagaya shinshiroku* or *A Hen in the Wind* (*Kaze no naka no mendori,* 1948)." (*Kantoku Ozu Yasujirô* [Ozu Yasujirô, director], Chikuma shobō, 1983, 88.) Noël Burch's study, *To the Distant Observer* (Berkeley: University of California Press, 1979), provides a useful corrective to the standard appraisal of Ozu, but it, too, makes only the briefest reference to *Nagaya shinshiroku.*
3. See Bordwell's *Ozu and the Poetics of Cinema* (Princeton: Princeton University Press, 1988), 296–301. Bordwell's is the only substantial discussion of this film in English.
4. Here and above, I have revised the film's English-language subtitles.
5. Kyoko Hirano, *Mr. Smith Goes to Tokyo: Japanese Cinema under the American Occupation, 1945–1952.* Washington: Smithsonian Institution Press, 1992.
6. Hirano, 74; see esp. note 82.
7. The information in this paragraph and the quoted words are taken from Hirano, 6. The hands-on policy of preproduction/postproduction censorship has more in common with the somewhat more lenient (although still quite

effective) policy of self-censorship within the United States through the Motion Picture Producers and Distributors Association (MPPDA) during the 1930s than with the scurrilous blacklisting and purging tactics of the House Committee on Un-American Activities in the late 1940s and early 1950s. For Occupation censors, the latter stance would have clashed with their policy of ensuring their own invisibility (see note 15). For a comprehensive review of film censorship in the 1930s, see Lea Jacobs, *The Wages of Sin: Censorship and the Fallen Woman Film, 1928–1942* (Madison: University of Wisconsin Press, 1991), esp. the section entitled "The Model of Self-Regulation," 18–26. Thanks to Linda Williams for introducing me to this book.

8. Hirano, 27, 37–38. As early as April 1945, the first "Basic Plan for Civil Censorship in Japan" was in place, with practical guidelines for all areas of communication. See Etô Jun, "The Sealed Linguistic Space: The Occupation Censorship and Post-war Japan," trans. Jay Rubin, in *Hikaku bungaku zasshi (The Annual of Comparative Culture),* vol. 2 (1984), 29.
9. Hirano, 6, 40.
10. Ibid., 44–45. The list of thirteen prohibited themes, itemized by Hirano, was announced in November 1945.
11. Ibid., 45. Criticism of SCAP censorship is by no means limited to Hirano. Richard B. Finn, in his otherwise highly favorable narrative of the MacArthur years, calls "excessive censorship" a "black mark on the occupation record." *Winners in Peace: MacArthur, Yoshida, and Postwar Japan* (Berkeley: University of California Press, 1992), 162. Also to be noted is Etô Jun's sweeping critique, of which the article in English cited in note 8 is only a part. See *Tozasareta gengo kûkan: senryôgun no ken'etsu to sengo Nihon* (The enclosed linguistic space: the Occupation censorship and postwar Japan [Bungeishunjû, 1989]). Although it can be faulted for inferring – erroneously and dangerously, I believe – that the Occupation years were worse than the war that brought it on, the book nevertheless contains important investigative work on this period.
12. Hirano, 45. For summaries of prewar film censorship in Japan, see David A Cook, *A History of Narrative Film,* 2d ed. (New York: Norton, 1990), 781–83; and Donald Richie and Joseph L. Anderson, *The Japanese Film: Art and Industry,* expanded ed. (Princeton: Princeton University Press, 1982), 69–70, 128–32.
13. The differences between the German and Japanese experience with Allied censorship policy are instructive. In contrast to Japanese cinema, Americans saw German cinema as an economic as much as ideological threat after the war. (In the 1920s, it was Hollywood's only serious competitor on the world market.) The Allied censors were not the only regulators in the German case, moreover. The churches also intervened in the battle for the nation's moral conscience, which was seen as being in a vacuum following the Nazi demise. See Heide Fehrenbach, "The Fight for the Christian West: German Film Control, the Churches, and the Reconstruction of Civil Society in the Early Bonn Republic," in *German Studies Review* 14 (February 1991): 39–64; and Ralph Willett, *The Americanization of Germany: Postwar Culture*

1945–1949 (London: Routledge, 1989). Thanks to Eric Rentschler for alerting me to these sources.

14. Kazuo Kawai, *Japan's American Interlude* (Chicago: University of Chicago Press, 1960), 51–52. Information in this paragraph is gleaned from this source (see the chapter on the new constitution, 51–70) as well as from Hugh Borton, *Japan's Modern Century* (New York: Ronald Press, 1955), 400–11; and W. G. Beasley, *The Modern History of Japan* (New York: Frederick A. Praeger, 1963), 280–85.
15. See the CCD document (25 November 1946) on media censorship, which, among other things, proscribes "any reference to the part played by SCAP in writing the new Japanese Constitution" and any "indirect or direct references to censorship of press, movies, newspapers, or magazines." Cited in Etô Jun, "The Civil Censorship in Occupied Japan," in *Hikaku bunka zasshi (Annual of Comparative Culture),* vol. 1 (1982), 5. (Etô's article also appears, minus the footnotes, under the title "The Censorship Operation in Occupied Japan," in *Press Control around the World,* ed. Jane Leftwich Curry and Joan R. Dassin [New York: Praeger, 1982], pp. 235–53.)
16. Hirano notes that a Japanese magazine editor's comment "praising the 'democratic' attitude, thoughtfulness, and efficiency of American censors, compared with the wartime Japanese censors, was also suppressed by the American censors" (46). Hirano adds: "Occupation censors required Japanese film producers to rework and smooth over deletions to keep the flow of the narrative consistent, whereas the prewar Japanese censors did not care how inconsistent the film looked after being cut and patched, despite the protests of the filmmakers" (ibid.). This description, reminiscent of the Hollywood ideal of continuity editing, aptly characterizes the method that the censors used to disguise their operations.
17. In an essay on Ozu, Yomota Inuhiko notes that the following films are set in Tokyo's poorer industrial district, which spreads east from Tsukishima to Sunachô: *Passing Fancy* (*Dekigokoro,* 1933), *An Inn in Tokyo* (*Tôkyô no yado,* 1935), *The Only Son* (*Hitori musuko,* 1936), and *A Hen in the Wind* (*Kaze no naka no mendori,* 1948), in addition to *Nagaya shinshiroku.* See *Tsukishima monogatari* ([Tales of Tsukishimá; Shûeisha, 1992), chap. 11 (142–58), esp. 144.
18. I borrow this term from Paul Schrader's well-known study of three directors (*Transcendental Style in Film: Ozu, Bresson, Dreyer* [New York: Da Capo Press, 1972]). An important book, it is limited by its privileging of Ozu's later films in the author's analysis of his chosen directors' spare, "transcendental" style. In the introduction to his study of Ozu, David Bordwell rightly advocates a "historical poetics" that allows the critic to conjoin poetics (i.e., "the study of how films are put together and how, in determinate contexts, they elicit particular effects") with specific historical context (*Ozu and the Poetics of Cinema,* 1–2). I do not think that he goes far enough, however, at least in the case of the film under discussion. Indeed, the very format of his book, with its emphasis on formalist analysis ("With Ozu, we must adopt new viewing strategies, recognizing that film style can claim our attention in its

own right"; ibid., p. 178), blinds him to his own shrewd insight about the importance of historicizing a film, to wit: "Placed in a social context, the films are less indebted to Japanese aesthetics and Zen Buddhism than to a vibrant popular culture and, more indirectly, to ideological tensions" (2). It is of course to the "ideological tensions" that this essay directs its attention.

19. *Ozu and the Poetics of Cinema,* 73.
20. *The Japanese Film: Art and Industry,* 191.
21. Donald Richie, *Ozu: His Life and Films* (Berkeley: University of California Press, 1974), 232.
22. Audie Bock, *Japanese Film Directors* (new paperback ed.) (Tokyo: Kodansha International, 1985), 95.
23. Richie, *Ozu,* p. 233.
24. *Ozu and the Poetics of Cinema,* p. 296. Ozu himself provides the following plot summary, as dictated by Tanaka Masumi: "A homeless child is taken to a tenement in a burnt-out section of Tokyo. Otane cares for the boy, but he leaves when his father comes to retrieve him." Tanaka Masumi, ed., *Ozu Yasujirô: sengo goroku shûsei* (Ozu Yasujirô: a collection of postwar conversations), Firumu Aato Sha, 1989, 131. For a detailed description of the film in Japanese, see Ooba Masatoshi et al., *Ozu Yasujirô o yomu* (Reading Ozu Yasujirô). Firumu Aato Sha, 1982, 186–89.
25. Although *Nagaya* was not released until May 1947, an Occupation censor's work diary shows that Ozu's film had been sufficiently completed for review by the CIE by December 1946. (See Hirano, 74, n. 82.)
26. Satô Tadao notes this contrast and refers to the tenement dwellings, miraculously left standing after the devastating air raids on Tokyo, as a "Lost Paradise" – a nostalgic, if illusory, image of domesticity for refugees in the audience who had returned to the city and which, however much a contradiction in dramatic terms (juxtaposed as the serene dwellings are with the burnt-out ruins), represents Ozu's deep yearning for a better time. See Satô, *Ozu Yasujirô no geijutsu* (Asahi Shimbun Sha, 1978), 52–53.
27. Adults are never shown close-up, with the exception of the woman interviewed by Otane (shot only from behind), who had let a room to the boy and his father. This interview takes place in Chigasaki, however, not in Tokyo. Youngsters fishing near Tsukiji and gathering around the Saigô statue in Ueno Park figure far larger in the frame.
28. Admittedly, the actual number of "stars" over a dark field is not identical to that on the American flag: on the one side of the futon it is greater; on the other side, less. I would argue, however, that the Japanese viewer was far more sensitive to the *pattern* of the starred field/striped background, which the futon replicates quite closely, than to the number of states (forty-eight) that the United States comprised. The futon's geopolitical significance is not lost on Shinoda Masahiro, the renowned director who worked early in his career as one of Ozu's assistants, and who recalls being reminded of a world map upon viewing the film. See his *Nihongo no gohô de kataritai* (Nihon Hôsô Shuppan Kyôkai, 1995), 220–21. Thanks to Mitsuhiro Yoshimoto for steering me to this passage. My observations on the futon-as-flag have been

immensely aided by class discussions in my winter 1993 course on Japanese cinema at UC Irvine. I am particularly grateful to James Nagaya for initiating the discussions.

29. That Ozu's mode of critique is not wholly idiosyncratic is confirmed in an important new study by Mitushiro Yoshimoto, who notes the ambivalence that Japanese moviegoers felt toward the U. S. during the Occupation period, taking as an example their negative reaction to the "Americanized refashioning" of Tanaka Kinuyo after the star actress's return from a goodwill mission to Hawaii, San Francisco, Chicago, New York, and, of course, Hollywood in 1949–50. Widespread criticism of her Western clothes and newly expansive demeanor was embodied in the sobriquet *ameshon joyû* (*ameshon* actress). The neologism's first term, a combination of *ame*rika (America) and *shon*ben (piss), plays on the slang expression *tachishon[ben]* (pissing on the street); thus, "Pissing in America." According to Yoshimoto, the term "was used to refer to a person who has stayed in the U. S. for a brief period of time (i. e. just enough time to 'piss') yet pretends to know everything about America after coming back to Japan." See Mitushiro Yoshimoto, *Kurosawa: Film Studies and Japanese Cinema,* (Durham: Duke University Press, 2000), p. 408, n.23.
30. Occupation censors were certainly vigilant in (and perhaps distracted by) their search for images of *other* flags in films – red flags, in particular. With the Cold War on in earnest by the late 1940s, officials took a dim view of any representations of communism. For example, a scene displaying a red flag and "Communist marchers" in a 1948 film about postwar corruption, and "a close-up, full view, of a waving 'red flag'" in a 1949 film on the national railway workers union, were cut. Also cut, in other films, were a poster with the slogan "Workers of the World Unite!" and a tryst scene in front of the Nikolai Cathedral (simply because it is a Russian Orthodox Church!). See Hirano, 242.
31. Bordwell, *Ozu and the Poetics of Cinema,* p. 300.
32. Ibid.
33. Yomota Inuhiko notes that GIs were never shown in *any* Japanese film made during the Occupation, and only finally made an appearance (and then with a vengeance) in 1961, with Imamura Shôhei's *Pigs and Battleships (Buta to gunkan).* (See *Tsukishima monogatari,* 158.) Censors encouraged filmmakers to remove any trace of American presence whenever possible, including, for example, English-language signs, Occupation facilities, and even the sound of airplanes flying overhead! (See Hirano, 56–57.) In a censor's memorandum to SCAP in June 1947, recommended cuts in *War and Peace (Sensô to heiwa)* include: "Scenes of man negotiating for date with streetwalker, both using . . . sign language. Reason for deletion: Criticism of Allies. Man has face well hidden, and both using . . . sign language . . . infers that allied personnel is involved." Etô Jun, "The Civil Censorship in Occupied Japan," 13–14.
34. The following assessment, by Edwin O. Reischauer, is representative: "The military occupation of one advanced, modernized nation by another, instead

of proving the unmitigated disaster that most people might have expected, turned out on the whole to be a resounding success." *The Japanese Today: Change and Continuity* (Cambridge: Harvard University Press, 1988), 105. John Whitney Hall makes an even stronger assessment: "Certainly no occupation, other than one of outright conquest, has been so dedicated to political and social reform. And certainly few other societies have been as thoroughly "made over" in so short a time as was Japan between 1945 and 1952." *Japan: From Prehistory to Modern Times* (New York: Dell, 1970), 349.

35. "The truly surprising success of the American occupation of Japan might in fact be partially explained in terms of the particular qualifications of the American and Japanese in their respective roles. The concept is at best vague and hardly susceptible of proof, but an imaginary substitution of roles will help to indicate its validity. The Japanese, who showed some extraordinary virtues in defeat, demonstrated all too clearly in China and the Philippines how overbearing, unsympathetic, and cruel they would have been in victory. On the other hand, we Americans, who played our part as victors with surprising altruism and good will, would scarcely have made tractable or coöperative losers." *The United States and Japan,* 3d ed. (New York: Viking, 1965), 234.
36. See, for example, Kojima's "American School" ("Amerikan sukûru," 1954), and Nosaka's "American *hijiki*" ("Amerika hijiki," 1967), both in Howard Hibbett, ed., *Contemporary Japanese Literature* (New York: Knopf, 1977).
37. Peter B. High, *Teikoku no ginmaku* (The empire's silver screen), Nagoya Daigaku Shuppankai, 1995, 155.
38. Here, I am in agreement with the views of David Bordwell over those of Joan Mellen. See *Ozu and the Poetics of Cinema,* 282–83 and passim; and *The Waves at Genji's Door: Japan Through Its Cinema* (New York: Pantheon Books, 1976), pp. 151–59, respectively. Mellen is probably correct in her evaluation of the director's politics: "Ozu had never valued a democratic philosophy and always found it a threat to the preservation of the old ways" (153). The question is just what those "old ways" were, and if by rejecting democracy Ozu was embracing militarism. All indications are that he did not.
39. Richie, *Ozu,* 226. The script was eventually made into a film in 1952. Its original title was *Kareshi Nankin e yuku [He heads for Nanjing],* but was not at all a narrative about the front. See High, *Teikoku no ginmaku,* 156.
40. High argues persuasively that whatever enthusiasm Ozu may have had for making a war movie was cooled by his run-in with censors over *The Flavor of Green Tea over Rice.* Rather than bouncing back with a film that lauded the war effort, Ozu, falling back on a policy of "safety first," reverted to the *hahamono* (films about mothers/families), the result being *The Brothers and Sisters of the Toda Family.* See *Teikoku no ginmaku,* 155–56.
41. Richie, *Ozu,* p. 233.
42. *Ozu and the Poetics of Cinema,* p. 301.

CHAPTER THIRTEEN

In the Realm of the Censors

Cultural Boundaries and the Poetics of the Forbidden

Leger Grindon

Over twenty years have passed since *In the Realm of the Senses (Ai no korida)* provoked a sensation at the 1976 Cannes Film Festival, where the film earned Nagisa Oshima the Best Director Prize. An unprecedented thirteen screenings were mounted to meet the public demand. Subsequent screenings at the New York Film Festival and in other countries spread the furor incited by the film's portrayal of explicit, continuous, and shocking sexual activity. Though shot in Japan with a Japanese cast and crew and based upon a tale that arose from the Japanese legal record, the film was never screened in Japan. Japanese censorship prohibited anything but a highly edited and otherwise circumscribed public showing. Nevertheless, the furor surrounding its production and reception arguably had its greatest impact in Japan. Even today this notorious exile haunts the film culture that produced it.

The impact of *In the Realm of the Senses* invites a paradoxical comparison with the screening of *Rashōmon* at the 1951 Venice Film Festival. *Rashomon* gained international recognition for the sterling achievement of Japanese cinema and led the way for other Japanese films, produced before and after, to cross cultural boundaries and assume a more influential and celebrated role in world cinema. In spite of its intentions, *In the Realm of the Senses* bore witness to the barriers blocking international exchange; its controversial reception in Japan illustrated the difficulty that arises in crossing boundaries and the power of culture to retract as well as to expand. More pointedly, it expressed the conflict within Japan between the drive to become a cosmopolitan leader and an opposing need to identify itself as distinct, homogeneous, and apart.

In the Realm of the Senses was conceived and produced as an international film in the tradition of the European art cinema. Testing the bounds of sexual representation had long provided a commercial edge for the art cinema, which depended not on a national audience, but rather on the sophisticated metropolitan moviegoer in cultural centers throughout the free world. What could be more international than sex? For years the challenging aesthetic practices of filmmakers such as Alain Resnais, Federico Fellini, and Ingmar Bergman had been made more attractive to audiences by the promise of a more explicit treatment of sexuality than portrayed in Hollywood productions. By the late 1960s, Hollywood had released itself from the old Hays Code constraints and in 1969 an X-rated film, *Midnight Cowboy* had even won the Academy Award for Best Picture. But in 1972 the commercial success of *Last Tango in Paris* once again proved that the international art cinema could distinguish itself and earn big profits, if it could exploit its traditional association with erotic daring.

In the summer of 1972 Oshima stopped in Paris after the Venice Film Festival and met Anatole Dauman, French producer of films by Jean-Luc Godard and Claude Chabrol. Meeting in the lobby of a private screening room, Dauman proposed to Oshima, "Let's collaborate on a film, a coproduction. A porno. I'll leave the content and the actual production all to you. I'll pay for it, that's all." The offer took Oshima aback, but after his return to Japan he sent Dauman two sets of plans, including the story of Abe Sada. "I want to go with Sada," the producer replied. But Oshima backed off and for three years let the prospect linger. Dauman, however, continued to press the director and his offers of financial support increased.[1] Why did Oshima hesitate?

Reservations that arose within Oshima after the completion of *Pleasure of the Flesh* in 1965 offer a clue. Though the film was a commercial success, the director felt compromised. While Oshima was drafting the screenplay, the Motion Picture Code of Ethics Committee warned the filmmaker, and finally compelled Oshima, to omit important episodes. He also regretted not engaging actresses from soft-core pornography, which he felt would have encouraged a more explicit treatment of sex. After *Pleasure of the Flesh,* Oshima explains, "I carefully avoided the kind of filmmaking that makes the sexual act its central concern . . . I had resolved not to make that kind of film if there were no possibility of complete sexual expression."[2] Then in the spring of 1975 conditions changed. In April the French government instituted a complete legalization of pornography. On June 17 friends returned to Japan from the Cannes Film Festival and reported to Oshima on the explicit sexual films swamping the screening rooms. On that night the director resolved to go ahead with the Abe Sada story.

Unusual production practices were adopted to ensure Oshima's freedom. Film stock was imported from France, shooting took place in Japan from late in 1975 until mid-February 1976. The exposed film was then shipped back to France for processing and editing. International procedures themselves were central to the conception, financing, and execution of the film. As Oshima explained, "If the method of making films doesn't change, the films won't change. A new film will not emerge without a new production method."[3]

The various titles for the production further emphasize its international status. The Japanese title, *Ai no korida,* whose literal translation is *Bullfight of Love,* invokes the famous ritual sport of Spain to characterize the relationship of the protagonists. For its French release, Dauman proposed, and Oshima warmly accepted, the title *L'Empire des Sens,* a pointed allusion to the Roland Barthes book, *L'Empire des Signes,* a semiological study of Japan. Unlike the English title, these names underline a cross-cultural exchange already at work in the production. Maureen Turim has noted that the film marks "a change in Oshima's career from an initial status as a participant in a national cinema hoping to get foreign distribution to a director working within a multinationally financed, intentionally international art cinema. Oshima's films since 1976 have been aimed as much or more at non-Japanese 'markets' as they have at his compatriots, and this condition is not just an economic necessity. Oshima is a filmmaker who has become a spiritual exile."[4]

Nonetheless, while in New York for the opening of *In the Realm of the Senses* Oshima was accused of making his film too Japanese and not sufficiently international. The filmmaker conceded to his audience that "I'm a Japanese director and make movies for Japanese people."[5] Indeed, as I will argue here, Oshima fashioned his film around a poetics of the Japanese forbidden. The filmmaker took advantage of his French production circumstances to address conditions and an audience in his home country. Such an expression and its subsequent impact would have been impossible if he had attempted to produce it solely in Japan.

Around the exhibition and the reception in Japan of *In the Realm of the Senses,* a struggle arose between authority and resisters that resembles guerrilla warfare. The resisters engage in forays and retreats at the margins of acceptability, realizing that a straightforward assault would never succeed. On the contrary, the authorities institute their own attacks and skirmishes even though they realize that totally vanquishing the enemy is unlikely. For example, the film was screened in Japan, but with forty-nine major cuts, one-third of the total film, and other images masked to block objectionable material. Blocked at home, many Japanese saw the film abroad, and travel agencies obliged by arranging "Realm of the Senses" tours to Paris. Capitalizing on the notoriety surrounding the film, a book including the screenplay and production stills was published, but in August 1977, Tokyo bookstores were raided by the police and the publication seized. As Oshima explains, "*In the Realm of the Senses* became the perfect pornographic film in Japan because it cannot be seen there."[6] The book prompted an indictment of Oshima Nagisa for violating obscenity statutes, and legal proceedings continued for over four years before Oshima was cleared by the Supreme Court in 1982. In spite of this verdict the expense and delays of the legal proceedings deterred film producers from challenging the obscenity statutes.

In his text challenging the indictment, Oshima emphasizes the conflict between the cosmopolitan and the parochial that underlies his case. *In the Realm of the Senses* was screened throughout the free world, Oshima noted, and among "advanced countries," only Belgium and Japan banned the picture. Of course, such practices limited, but did not prevent, Japanese from seeing the film. For example, by the beginning of 1978 Oshima estimated that over 70,000 of his compatriots had watched *In the Realm of the Senses* in Paris alone. "Why is something that is not considered 'obscene' in a foreign country considered 'obscene' here? Isn't Japan one of the advanced countries? Isn't Japan part of the free world?" Oshima asked.[7] Furthermore, the defendant claimed that the charges against the book were only a pretext. Rather, the government attack was based, argues Oshima, not on a violation of the law, but was a personal vendetta of the authorities motivated by his long history of opposition to official censorship, and by his attempt to circumvent Japanese restrictions by collaborating on a film with foreign producers. "The police and the public prosecutors hated the person who made a film that went beyond the confines of sexual expression in Japan by means of an international collaboration," accuses Oshima. "Out of hatred, the police and public prosecutors fabricated a crime."[8] In conclusion, Oshima explains, "I am struggling in this trial to expand freedom of sexual expression, however minimally."[9]

Though Oshima was judged innocent on appeal, his case did not change the censorship codes governing Japan. Those codes themselves are based upon an anatomical prohibition against the representation of pubic hair and genitalia that gives little regard to the sexual experience portrayed. As Ian Buruma notes, "Rape, sadism, torture, all this is permissible in popular entertainment, but the official line is drawn at the showing of pubic hair. This is more reminiscent of schoolmasters measuring the length of their pupils' unruly mops than an indication of any deep moral conviction."[10] But these conflicts reveal that authority is at issue as much as, if not more than, sexuality in these battles over censorship. The official bureaucracy guards their power to patrol cultural boundaries and to protect their prerogatives against incursions, foreign and domestic.

Viewed from this perspective, the controversy generated by *In the Realm of the Senses* is a manifestation of what Edwin O. Reischauer describes as the struggle between "Uniqueness and Internationalism" in Japanese culture. In the closing chapter of *The Japanese Today,* Reischauer describes the nation as "simultaneously world leaders and world loners" caught up in the debate over what it means to be Japanese and their proper relationship with other cultures.[11] In the case of *In the Realm of the Senses,* Oshima used sexuality as a provocation, on the one hand, to promote Japanese film culture around the world and, on the other, to invoke international standards as a means of relaxing censorship in Japan. The pointed defiance and the aggressive posture of both the filmmaker as legal defendant and the film as a violator of taboos prevented the Japanese from maintaining a harmonious disregard. Oshima succeeded in breaking down their *tatemae* (public posture) while forcing their *honne* (private feeling) into the public arena and thereby affronting the harmonious national consensus prized by his countrymen. Oshima's insistence on the conflict between the cosmopolitan standard of free expression and the peculiar Japanese censorship codes was the first instance of the Japanese forbidden raised and violated by *In the Realm of the Senses.*

But, you may ask, how can you overlook the salacious content of this film by subsuming it into a discussion of cross-cultural relations? Even if one places legal prohibitions aside, shouldn't the moral reservations of decent people, or the demand for complexity in art among the sophisticated, raise objections to the obsessive and perverse focus on sex portrayed by *In the Realm of the Senses?* To answer this, one must turn to the film.

In the Realm of the Senses is exemplary in addressing the experience of sexuality. That is, the sexual relations of the protagonists are not portrayed as a window onto other topics, emblematic of contending social forces, or otherwise at the service of ulterior human concerns. I will argue that *In the Realm of the Senses* designs its drama around the transformation of the sexual into either eros or thanatos. This issue is posed within the specific context of Japanese culture and, as I have noted previously, draws upon what I call the poetics of the Japanese forbidden.[12] For the purposes of my discussion, eros is understood to be a life force expressing the capacity of the sexual instinct to project its power beyond the immediately sexual and invest its energy into people, such as the beloved; objects, such as one's bicycle or tennis racket; or activities, such as art making, child rearing, or general career goals. I assume that marriage, or any long-term relationship with a sexual partner, depends upon the generation of sexual energy and its transformation into an erotic force that charges the field of the relationship with the sexual energy that was particularly intense at its initiation. Thanatos, of course, poses an opposition to eros in being a death drive. It is manifest in the compulsion to repeat, the inability to project sexual energy outside the self, or to transform the force of sexuality into extrasexual life activities and relationships. Thanatos is vividly expressed in the notion of a return to the womb, the transformation into a still inner self, as opposed to a social self, that retreats from the activity of life. The compulsive repetition of the sexual act itself carries with it an undercurrent of thanatos.

The relationship between sex and death, or thanatos, in *In the Realm of the Senses* has been widely discussed by commentators on the film.[13] My essay intends to add to our understanding of the film by specifically locating the sexual transformation unfolding in the film through a close examination of the narrative design, and through an exploration of its expression in a series of conflicting figures and motifs. These expressive properties, I will argue, while portraying an essential dynamic of the sexual, are located within the particular tradition of the Japanese forbidden. The three principal aspects of the Japanese forbidden I will explore are, first, the prohibition against pollution and its manifestation in the wife/maid figures and the cleaning motif; second, the prohibition against passionate attachment to a sexual partner and its manifestation in the geisha/teacher figures; third, the prohibition against an idealized carnal sexuality that refuses erotic projection and its manifestation in the turn from double suicide and in Sada as a revision of the demon woman.

However, before proceeding with the analysis, it is necessary to acknowledge a tension arising in the discussion of the film. In his public statements, Oshima, complementing his crusade for open sexual expression, idealizes the experience of his protagonists, Sada and Keichi. For example, talking with Ruth McCormick, the filmmaker explains, "It's really wonderful that, at that time [1936], when everyone was thinking of nothing but the country, of war, these two were able to pursue their own pleasure."[14] A few years later Oshima tells Peter Lehman, "For all Japanese men, what we would want is to be able to meet a woman who would be that intense about us in love."[15] Though some commentators, such as McCormick, appear to share the director's positive understanding, most analysts [see, for example, Peter High, Dana Polan, Ian Buruma, David Desser] describe the experience of the lovers as at least misguided; indeed, High and Buruma emphatically place Sada in the Japanese tradition of the demon woman preying upon her male partner.[16] I share the belief that *In the Realm of the Senses* offers a cautionary tale rather than a model for behavior. But, as with any successful artwork, one's experience of the work excites a complex response grounded in the play of formal elements and resistant to a simple summary. Maybe Maureen Turim's claim that the Oshima film provokes "fascination and terror" provides the best invitation to a closer examination.

The sensation created by *In the Realm of the Senses* bears witness to the violation of widespread, if not universal, taboos against sexual representation – taboos upon which the pornography industry and censorship have flourished across cultures and throughout history. Pornography's relationship to this film has been discussed by numerous commentators, such as McCormick, Oshima himself, and, most notably, Peter Lehman.[17] A task in this essay is to address neglected aspects of the forbidden, and their expression in figures particular to Japanese culture as portrayed by

In the Realm of the Senses. Explicit sexual expression itself, rather than being forbidden, arises as essential to achievement of Oshima's work.

The narrative of *In the Realm of the Senses* divides into three acts, which I identify as "the liaison initiated," "rivals contested," and "the specter of death" (see Appendix 1 for a precise division of scenes). The narrative design is typical of a romance, with the central couple meeting and overcoming various obstacles in the pursuit of union. Act 1 brings Sada and Keichi together and ends with their departure from the brothel, owned by Keichi and his wife, to the inn of their rendezvous after the wife openly acknowledges Sada as a rival. Act 2 extends through three phases of its own: in the opening scenes the wife is contested and overcome by the lovers; in the second phase, a male rival, the teacher, is overcome; and, in the closing scenes, sex is given absolute priority over other activities, such as eating, childbirth, or business. The final act plays out a quest for a physical unification through sexual ecstasy. This quest supersedes bodily needs, with life itself being held in the balance.

The wife is characterized by cleanliness, home, and work in the first act. On the three principal occasions when she appears, at the beginning and the end of act 1 and at the beginning of act 3, the wife is presented dressing, bathing, or shaving Keichi. Each of these gestures of almost ritual purification results in the husband and the wife having intercourse. Cleanliness arises as a counterpoint and complement to conjugal sex, serving to purify the physical element of marital union. Otherwise, the wife is presented as the manager of the brothel, which serves as a combination home and business. The brothel is populated by a covey of female servants including Sada, but we never meet any customers. The husband, in the tradition of the *nimaime,* idles about, apparently the only one being served. As a result, the wife appears to manage a staff, in the service of her husband, among whom she is the leading, but not the exclusive, woman. This multiplicity of women will later contrast with Sada's determination to possess Keichi solely.

The cleaning motif addresses the prohibition against pollution, an aspect of the Japanese forbidden. Cleaning serves as a check marking the containment of the carnal. The wife's cleanliness is associated with the various maids who appear to wait on the lovers throughout the film. Sada, in her second encounter with Keichi, works as a maid cleaning the courtyard porch. But in response to Keichi's advances she abandons purification for pollution. Soon Sada insists on disorderly quarters ripe with the smells of lovemaking, and this pollution marks her rivalry with the wife. The association develops into a sharp conflict, between Sada and the cleaning maids, that culminates in Sada's attack on a servant, who only manages to flee when Keichi restrains his lover (see Figure 38). The link between Sada and pollution embraces a long-standing element in the Japanese forbidden that Ian Buruma traces to the earliest Shinto myths. He writes, "Though absolute Evil seems to be absent from Japanese thought, every form of pollution, including wounds, sores, blood, death and even simple uncleanliness is to be feared. The traditional antidote to the polluting forces of nature is purification. . . . Naturally, purification in one form or another exists in religious ceremonies everywhere, but in few cultures is it taken as seriously and is it as much a part of daily life as in Japan."[18]

The first five scenes of the second act portray the vanquishing of Keichi's wife. The act begins with the lovers traveling in a carriage. Here the pollution motif carries an undercurrent of foreboding, as Keichi responds to Sada's menstruating by reaching under her clothes and then

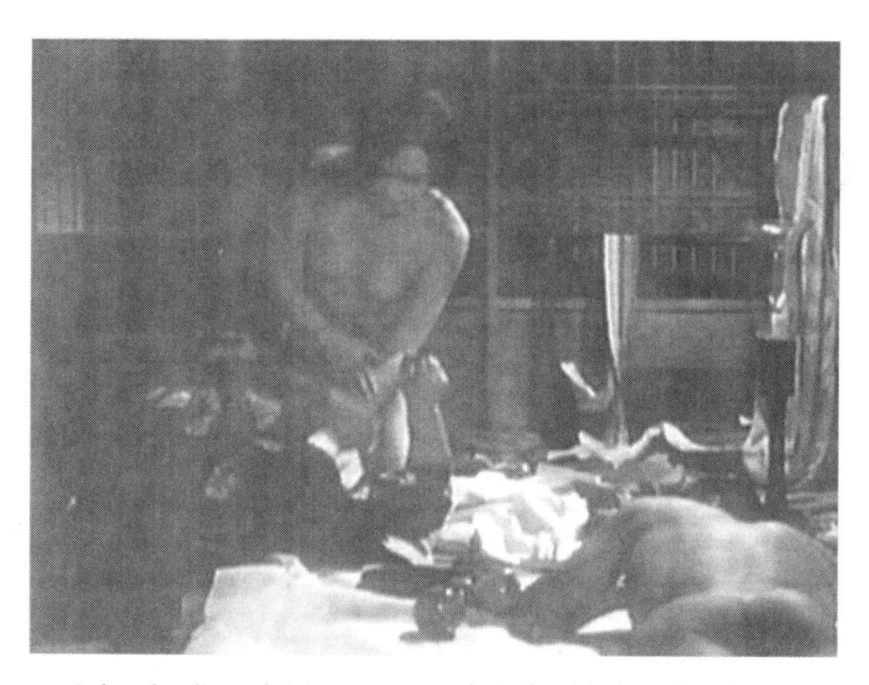

38. Sada strikes the maid; Oshima Nagisa, *In the Realm of the Senses* (1976).

licking his bloody fingers. In retrospect, the blood anticipates his own postmortem mutilation and the fearsome consequences of his attachment. At the inn of their rendezvous a mock wedding ceremony presents a ritual celebration of the new union. The following morning Sada claims Keichi's soul and immediate sexual attention. Scene 13 refers back to scene 5 from the first act. In the earlier scenes Keichi flirted with, but withdrew from, Sada after they were observed by an unidentified woman on the interior courtyard of the inn. Scene 13 returns to a similar courtyard location, only now the lovers indulge in intercourse outdoors and under the observation of an elderly woman. The inhibitions of the initial encounter are overcome and the female observer serves as a wife surrogate who can no longer restrain Keichi and Sada. Walking in the rain, another unidentified woman is chased away by the couple with their umbrella, continuing and concluding the motif of the vanquished female rival.

The next four scenes present Sada's preparation for, travel to, and meeting with, the couple's male rival, the teacher. All the while, she ensures that Keichi will remain prisoner at the inn of their rendezvous by taking his clothes. Faced with separation, Sada and Keichi engage in sex with partners who serve as substitutes for their absent love. Keichi, forlorn and melancholy, abruptly rapes a maid. Sada demands that the teacher slap her, pinch her, and pull her hair as an implicit punishment for abandoning Keichi. The attack serves to arouse her into having sex with the teacher, but Sada later confesses to Keichi that she thought only of him.

The teacher, a slight, older, bespectacled man, represents tradition, learning, and emotional detachment. He serves as a counterpart to the wife, for he is another figure of orthodox values that the reckless couple overthrows in their pursuit of the Japanese forbidden. Though he desires Sada, when she suggests that they travel on a holiday together, the respectable teacher refuses, explaining that he would kill himself if their liaison was discovered. He honors the social discretion that limits his sexuality and guards against reckless emotion.

The teacher is associated with a related figure who reappears throughout the film, the geisha. Together they address another aspect of the Japanese forbidden, the prohibition against a passionate attachment to a sexual partner that can produce an obsessive disregard for sexuality's harmonious integration into the social order. Like the maid, numerous geishas assume a growing significance as the film unfolds. While the maids are allied to the wife, the geishas are linked to the teacher. Within Japanese culture the geisha is associated with artifice, learning, and eroticism, but also with emotional detachment. The geisha is an actress in the theater of desire. She is trained to arouse and flatter, but only a fool takes the geisha's amorous play as sincere. The geisha defines eroticism as a pose that rewards detachment and destroys those who surrender knowledge to feeling. Throughout *In the Realm of the Senses* the appearance of the geishas warns of the dangers of unbridled passion.

In the opening act Sada is characterized first as a cleaning maid and then as a geisha. When Keichi and Sada initially have sex a geisha knocks, interrupting them. A figure of erotic knowledge, the geisha enters with the understanding glance of a mistress in the matching of pleasure with constraint. Later, Keichi insists that Sada continue to act the geisha, sing and play the samisen, while they make love, as a ruse to deceive his wife. The pose of the geisha cautions the couple against abandon. In *In the Realm of the Senses* the geisha functions as a sign of the Japanese forbidden, the surrender of one's emotions to sexual passion and the danger of carnal obsession. Sex, discreet, detached, playful, is acceptable, but to fall under the sway of feeling, to lose oneself in a devotion to the beloved, only brings destruction. At the mock marriage, when the three geishas rape their virgin companion with a dildo and engage in group sex, their activity is treated as play independent of any tenderness or attachment. They act as a counterpoint to the wedding ceremony that underscores the exclusive devotion of Keichi to Sada; the orgy serves as an antidote to the desire for union with the beloved.

With the male and female rivals overcome, the balance of act 2 demonstrates the lovers' overriding devotion to sex and anticipates the violent culmination of the film. After the reunification of the lovers, Sada reports on her encounter with the teacher. In response to the blows Sada endured, Keichi asks her to strike him, thereby demonstrating his willingness to endure pain for the sake of their union. In the next scene, the couple takes a respite from lovemaking, to eat. Sada puts food to her genitals before feeding it to Keichi. Keichi places a boiled egg into Sada's vagina, telling her to push it out. After she does, Sada forces Keichi to eat the egg. These acts affirm the priority of sex over eating and childbirth, which is first mocked, and then the product of Sada's womb is devoured. In the next scene, Sada threatens to cut off Keichi's penis if he has sex with another, and a pact of loyalty is sealed (see Figure 39). The act ends with

39. Sada threatens Keichi with a knife; Oshima Nagisa, *In the Realm of the Senses* (1976).

another walk through the rain. The couple stops at a cafe, and when the proprietor asks them to leave at closing, Sada raises her skirt and offers herself if the owner will serve them. The proprietor declines, claiming impotence. The businessman's attention to commerce is central, for his condition sets business and sex at odds. The second act ends with the couple making love in the rain, underscoring the absolute value sex has assumed in relation to common activities, such as eating, childbearing, or business, which may subsume sexuality. The episodes also prepare for the final act, in which sex is set into opposition with life itself.

The distinctive excess of *In the Realm of the Senses* arises because obstacles to the romance are not merely rivals, parental figures, or social mores, but even physical needs or other satisfying activities that may divert the lovers from sexual gratification. Central to the forbidden activity of the film is not the explicit representation of sex, but the quest for an idealized carnal sexuality that engulfs all other experience until the obsession extinguishes life itself. In this regard sexuality abandons its special ability to project its energies onto other people, pursuits, or ideals, a fundamental quality of the erotic, and becomes an agent of thanatos, the drive to death. In its movement toward death, the film invites comparison with the Japanese tradition of double suicide in dramas of passion, an association widely acknowledged by commentators on the film. Oshima has staged implicit variations on the double suicide motif in his earlier films. For example, in *A Cruel Story of Youth* (1960) the filmmaker concludes by crosscutting his hero, beaten to death by thugs, with the heroine, who ends her life by jumping from a speeding car. Both young lovers are mentally and spiritually united in their apparently simultaneous and willful acts of self-destruction.[19] Of course, *In the Realm of the Senses* rejects double suicide, for only Keichi is slain. Hence, the tradition of the demon woman, like Lady Wakasa in *Ugetsu* (1953), becomes linked as a counterpoint of reference. But the double suicide option is suggested, even by Keichi himself. How is the turn from double suicide to be understood?

In the final act of the film, as Keichi becomes increasingly melancholy and passive, Sada grows bolder and more determined to satisfy her carnal longings. The practice of strangling Keichi during coitus, to inflame Sada's pleasure, is initiated. In order to continue, the inhibiting specter of death must be exorcised. In scene 25, act 3, the maid and the geisha offer their final warnings to the couple and the lovers meditate upon death.

The scene begins with a maid bringing sake to the lover's chamber, and in the process she reports that others gossip about the "disgusting" behavior of Keichi and Sada. Keichi dismisses her news with a chuckle, but Sada flies into a rage, attacks the young woman with a flurry of slaps, and, after being restrained by Keichi, she asks him to rape the maid. As the servant hurries from the room, an old geisha appears at the door and plays the samisen as the couple moves into another sexual embrace. During intercourse, the geisha compliments Keichi on his virility and Sada offers to command her lover to give his attentions to the sixty-eight-year-old woman. At first the geisha acknowledges the offer as a polite gesture, but then Sada dispatches her companion. As Keichi has sex with the geisha, Sada watches enraptured, but Keichi, toiling away, looks to Sada. At orgasm the old woman urinates and then lies lifeless on the floor. Sada approaches, declaring to Keichi, "You look as if you've seen a ghost." "I had the impression I was holding my mother's dead body," he replies. Then the lovers briefly discuss the deaths of their parents. "Everything must have an end," Sada concludes, apparently unmoved.

By contrast, Keichi grabs his lover's hand in distress and ends the scene with his forlorn reply, "Let's be happy together."

This context, established by death and the geisha as a traditional participant in double suicide, turns the lover's cliché, "Let's be happy together," into an understated invitation from Keichi; that is, in the traditional Japanese tale of passion, when the lovers cannot overcome obstacles to their union, double suicide becomes a means of perpetuating the spirit of their love, of being happy together (see Figure 40). Double suicide serves to transcend the carnal romance and realize a spiritual union. Keichi has turned pale at this harbinger, this ghost embodied in the geisha. Death is prescribed by the sexual passion that has engulfed him. The union of Keichi and Sada is inevitably doomed by its grounding in the physical. Seeing his destiny, Keichi resigns himself to death and asks his lover to travel with him across the boundary of life. But Sada fails to respond. She attacks and puts to flight reprimands inhibiting her desires; even death fails to intimidate her. She is not interested in an extra physical love, the transcendent union val-

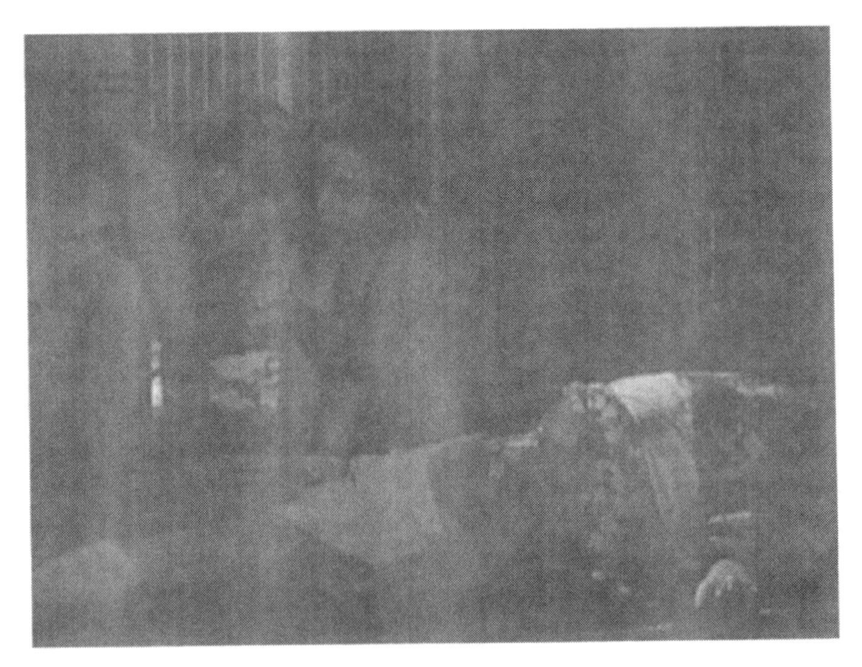

40. Keichi and Sada before aged geisha; Oshima Nagisa, *In the Realm of the Senses* (1976).

orized by double suicide, but in a heroic, or foolhardy, quest for physical union grounded in an ever-intensified carnal ecstasy. The explicit representation of sex in the film is necessary to express the corporal basis of her adventure. In Sada, Oshima portrays the demon woman as a folk heroine who bestows on her lover the death he seeks and who pursues her carnal quest to its quixotic end. Her values are so focused on the flesh that its concluding gesture underscores a grotesque, disquieting irony when she later writes with Keichi's blood on his dead, castrated body, "Sada/Keichi: two of us, together."[20] Sada embodies the third prohibition against an obsessive carnal sexuality.

The quest for physical union is inflected by the privileging of Sada's point of view. Though the film generally assumes an objective, detached third-person stance, significant variations on this mode bring Sada's sensibility to the fore. In this regard, it is useful to remember that the tale is based on an incident in the legal record from 1936, a homicide trial in which Sada was the accused and the principal witness. So from the initial source, one may assume the woman's perspective. In addition, the film begins and ends with its heroine, and, in the course of the film, Sada is the only character whose interior mental experience is dramatized. In the concluding scene of the opening act, the film presents Sada's wishful vision of Keichi's wife slashed, presumably by Sada, with a straight razor. In the second act, as Sada travels to the teacher, her longing for Keichi is expressed in her vision of him running after the train. These instances of simple wish fulfillment are a prelude to Sada's complex concluding vision, which occurs at the moment when she simultaneously ascends toward her aspiration and dispatches her lover. In discussing *In the Realm of the Senses,* Stephen Heath contrasts the film's explicit presentation of sex to *Letter From an Unknown Woman* (1948), in which the pivotal sexual encounter is elided.[21] The elision of Keichi's moment of death for Sada's vision seems an equally central absence in which a culminating experience is confined and deflected. Most important, however, is that rather than achieving any heroic union with her lover in ecstasy, Sada is psychically alone, absorbed internally, and finally stricken by solitude and anxiety. So, what is the content and meaning of her vision?

Sada's vision is presented in a five-shot sequence during which Sada is encircled by a young girl and Keichi chanting multiple times, "Where are you now? I'm not there yet" (see Figure 41) (see Appendix 2 for a detailed

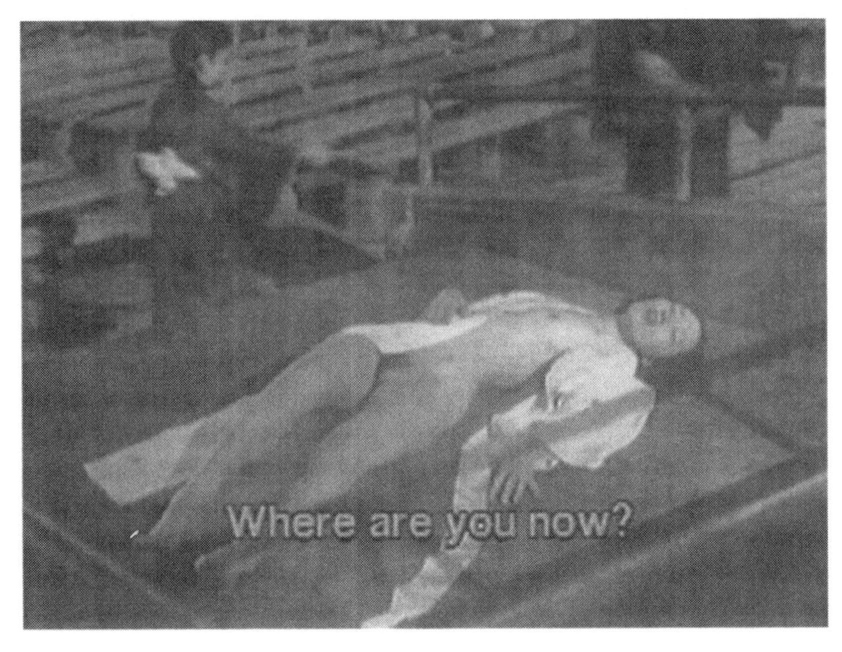

41. Sada on platform with a girl and Keichi in background; Oshima Nagisa, *In the Realm of the Senses* (1976).

shot description). The chant evokes a child's game of hide-and-seek in which the call and response mean, "Is it okay now for me to come and look for you," answered by, "No, not yet, I'm still looking for my hiding place." In the context of the deadly sex play in progress, the exchange implies Sada asking, "Is it enough now, or do I keep choking you," answered by Keichi's, "No, I'm not dead yet."[22] The daydream appears to take place in an empty stadium, possibly a reference to the titular bull-fighting, a deadly arena of lovemaking. The young girl serves as an alter ego for Sada whereby her sexual experience is portrayed as active, play-ful, and unfettered by social prohibitions. The dream condenses two chil-dren's games; hide-and-seek is evoked verbally while the movement of the players is more like a chase. The girl runs after the man; though he moves almost within reach, she is uncertain about his presence. His age, even more than distance, separates them. Keichi's passivity, resignation, and withdrawal become embodied in the adult-child contrast. The cir-cling chase around the platform presents an intensifying repetition approaching resolution. The chase presents the couple's quest for union, but Keichi's hiding place is death and promises separation. The dream-like condensation presents sexual ecstasy, physical union, and death as contending, intersecting prospects. In the first three shots the scale builds intensity, moving from long shot to extreme close-up, while the length expands slightly, matching the repetition of the chant. Movement within the image shifts from the childish chase to the rolling of Sada's head. In shot three the dream comes to a climax as Sada's head stops and eyes open with the realization that Keichi's voice and his image have left the scene. Solitude, rather than union, is acknowledged as the outcome. "Where are you now?" repeats the girl, staring down at the still woman. The answer comes in shot five. Alone and in extreme long shot, Sada anxiously looks about, isolated in the empty stadium. Finally, she wails for her beloved, but the echoing cry only underlines her separation. The psychological episode runs contrary to the unrelenting physicality of the film. The vision questions Sada's carnal quest even as it arises from her own consciousness.

The anxiety and isolation the vision expresses appear to be subtly acknowledged when the film returns to an objective view of Sada for the closing scene. The woman, deliberate and composed, looks down upon the dead man and proceeds with the postmortem castration. Finally, she lies next to the body upon which she has written her testament with his blood, "Sada/Keichi: two of us, together." Sada seizes the penis as a keepsake and writes her epitaph on Keichi's remains, taking her final leave.[23] The vision informs these acts with melancholy. The carnal quest reaches a disquieting conclusion, but the film invests the demon woman with an uncanny, heroic dignity. The camera looks down from above, maintaining a distance elaborated by the voice-over, which relates the arrest in the coming days and confirms the nonfiction basis of the tale. The final image stares deadpan, refusing to condemn Sada as demonic, but rather seeming to bear witness to, without evaluating, her insistence on the physical basis of her idealized, but impossible, union.

The ambivalence of the conclusion is elaborated and intensified by offering the events from the perspective of the demon woman. This figure from Japanese culture, a variation on Circe, the femme fatale and the vamp, is remarkable because she is presented with sympathy. In this regard, the turn from double suicide is crucial. For if the woman in a

42. Sada and Keichi in sexual embrace; Oshima Nagisa, *In the Realm of the Senses* (1976).

destructive passion is willing to join her lover in death, the mutual sacrifice attains a spiritual valor. However, Sada's survival, compounded by the dismemberment of her lover, confirms her demonic association and underlines its basis in the physical. For Oshima the intangible abstractions of nationalist war cries or Buddhist spirituality are swept aside by Sada's insistence on the body, her grounding in the realm of the senses. Even though the lovers' sexuality confronts a dead end, a zero point of erotic projection and social force, its quest for value seeks a ground in the corporal (see Figure 42). The excess of its failure strikes a lonely note against nihilism. In her insistence on the carnal, Sada, the demon woman, gains an enduring dignity as a folk heroine. I suspect that Oshima Nagisa would insist upon it. Because he has turned to the most feared woman in the tradition of the Japanese forbidden and embraced her. "Now I don't want to get my ideas from anywhere except the pain experienced by the women who live in the lowest depths of society," writes Oshima, "I made *In the Realm of the Senses* with that in mind."[24]

APPENDIX 1

In the Realm of the Senses: Plot Segmentation

ACT 1: LIAISON INITIATED

1. Credits
2. Morning – Sada [S] wakened by woman making sexual advances. S resists. Together they spy on Keichi [K] having sex with wife [W] as W dresses K.

3a. Day – S walking with female companions comes across children tormenting old derelict man, who claims to know S as prostitute.

3b. Night, snowfall – old derelict comes by inn [Wife's Inn = WI] where S works & in courtyard pleads for sexual favors. S willingly exposes her genitals, but man cannot get an erection.

4. Same night – S reenters kitchen & fellow woman worker accuses her of being a "whore." S goes after her with knife. W, innkeeper, breaks up quarrel. K enters after commotion, meets S & flirts.
5. Day – S washes floor of courtyard porch. K approaches, flirts, reaches under S's clothing. S reluctant. Woman sees them from across courtyard & they separate to social distance.
6. K in room at WI drinking sake. S enters to wait on K. K kisses S, gropes under her clothing. S climbs on top of sitting K; intercourse. Geisha [G for various geishas] knocks. K asks G to wait. S disengages & leaves. G enters.
7. Late same night – K comes upon S in hall, brings her to his room where they have sex through the night.
8. Another night [?] – S & K copulating w/S fully clothed as geisha & playing samisen, as she sits atop prone K. K tells S that she must continue to play & sing, so W will assume she is geisha entertaining.
9. Morning – S comes upon W shaving K. W asks S to fetch water & when S returns, K & W are having sex. S has fantasy of cutting W with razor. W speaks to S while having intercourse, asserting her claim to K.

ACT 2: RIVALS FOR LOVE CONTESTED

A. Obstacle of Wife Contested

10. K & S depart from WI in carriage. K reaches under menstruating S's clothes & licks bloody fingers. At another inn [Inn of

Rendezvous = RI] K undresses S as hotel maid [M for various maids] overhears & watches couple embrace.

11. Mock wedding at RI. K & S robed at ceremony attended by 4 geishas. K & S have sex. 3 Gs make young G watch & then forcibly penetrate her with bird dildo. Old man in dance; camera retreats to reveal K & 5 women indulging in group sex.
12. Next day, noon. S in RI chamber, fondles K's penis as he sleeps. S sends away M, who wishes to clean. K wakes, wants to pee, but S insists that K penetrate her immediately.
13. S & K in RI courtyard. They have sex in open, fully clothed, w/S sitting atop K while elderly woman watches from across yard.
14. Night – S & K walking in rain with umbrella, cross footbridge, S holding K's penis under clothing. They chase away woman who walks nearby. K says they must part. S wants him to have sex with her there in street.

B. Obstacle of Teacher Contested

15. RI chamber, another day – M comes w/sake for K & S. S dresses elegantly preparing to meet Teacher [T]. K sprawled on disorderly floor. While M serves, K hops upon S & has intercourse from behind while she talks of T. M rushes from room in shock, but stays in hall listening to couple. After sex, S takes K's clothes so K will not leave room.
16. S on train looking out window. Fantasy of K running after train. S goes to compartment & wraps K's clothes around her in longing.
17. RI – K sits forlorn. M urges him to eat, but K only wants drink. Suddenly K hops upon M & rapes her.
18. S lies quietly in bed w/T, a slight elderly man with glasses. S demands that T slap, pinch her, pull her hair painfully. Excited by attack, S mounts T for sex.

C. Sexual Gratification Dominates

19. K & S reunite at railroad station. In rickshaw, S displays money to support them. Back in RI chamber, S speaks of T to K. S explains that she thought of K; received blows, lost control. K asks S to strike him . . . harder.
20. RI – K & S in robes, eat while G plays. S puts food to her vagina & give it to K. K puts boiled egg in S's vagina & tells her to force it out. She does & then makes K eat egg.

21. RI – S threatens to cut off K's penis if he sleeps with another. K pledges loyalty; says she will be sorry if she kills him. S clips off some of K's pubic hair.
22. Night – K & S walking in rain with umbrella. At cafe S raises her skirt & offers herself to proprietor if he will serve them a drink after closing. Proprietor declines, claiming impotence. S & K have sex in rain.

ACT 3: THE SPECTER OF DEATH: UNITY VS. SEPARATION

23. Early morning, WI: K & W in bed together wakened by noise. Later in morning, K draws blood shaving. W pours water over K & climbs onto his lap for sex. Noise, K pushes W aside & pursues sound. Encounters S in another part of inn. S attacks K with knife. Threatens him for leaving her for 3 days. "Punish me," K. "Don't ever leave me again," S. Reconciled.
24. RI, morning. M enters to clean & is chased. S proposes strangulation to increase pleasure. K tries strangling S, but reluctant to hurt S. S strangles K w/pleasure, but K pulls away her hands because he is choking.
25. RI. M enters. Claims others gossip about S & K, "disgusting." S attacks M, K intervenes to allow M to flee. G appears at door & plays samisen while K & S have sex. S offers K's services to old G. S watches while K has sex w/G in hallway. G lies as if dead. K & S discuss death. "Let's be happy forever," says K.
26. Day, outdoors. Fish kites mark "Boy's Day" festival. S with T, T says S looks troubled. S suggest that they go away for holiday together. T refuses, saying he would have to shoot himself if their liaison were discovered.
27. Day. K leaving barbershop. Passes marching troops in street with women & children waving flags at soldiers.
28. RI. In chamber, S with knife in mouth wearing open red & white robe, begins strangling sex, now with scarf. K asks S to tie his hands, so he won't stop her. "I'm going to kill you," S. Ecstasy.
29. RI. S watches K as he sleeps. K wakes, wan & dazed. S ready to resume strangling sex. K passively says, "This time don't stop. Too painful afterward." S begins again, cut to
30. [Fantasy] Day – among empty stadium benches red-robed girl chases black-robed K. On platform amid benches, S, wearing red & white robe, lies almost naked & exposed while girl & K chase

around the platform. S writhes in pleasure & turns head in CU. Girl standing at edge of platform looks down at her. Back to S head shot. Return to mid-shot, K & girl have disappeared. S sits up & looks about. She is alone.

31. RI chamber – S stands looking down at dead K. S takes knife & cuts off penis & testicles. She writes in blood across K's chest, "Sada/Keichi: two of us, together," & lies next to K's body. Voice-over reports that S was found wandering thru Tokyo 4 days later holding K's bloody genitals; the year was 1936.

End credits.

APPENDIX 2

Sada's Fantasy/Keichi's Death

Transition Shot: Extreme close-up of Sada's face surrounded by her black hair. Camera looks down from above forehead. Hair darkens image. Sound bridge offers voice from next shot. Noise of running feet, "Where are you now?," in a girl's voice. Keichi's reply begins with the cut, "I'm not there yet."

Shot 1 [14 seconds]: Long shot of empty stadium benches, a little girl chases Keichi among the benches in a childlike game. As she runs, she shouts three times, "Where are you now?," and Keichi replies each time, "I'm not there yet." The girl is dressed in a red robe with a white sash; Keichi, in a black robe with a grey sash. Running from left to right among the benches, they reach a railed, empty, concrete platform and continue to chase around it. The camera moves slowly from right to left. There is no sound aside from the call and response and the sound of running feet.

Shot 2 [18 seconds]: Still camera looks down from a slightly high angle at a full body shot of Sada lying centered and at a slight diagonal on the concrete platform. She lies, almost naked, on her open red robe with white trim. Her eyes are closed; her head rolls slightly; one hand clutches the robe, the other moves slightly near her stomach; she breathes deeply. Apparently she is experiencing sexual pleasure. Around the platform at the edge of the image, the little girl and Keichi continue the chase and the call and reply of their chant, three more times. Neither Sada nor the 2 runners acknowledge the other's presence. The runners go in and out of the frame as they chase. Their shadows fall across Sada's body.

Shot 3 [20 seconds]: Still camera, extreme close-up of Sada's face, horizontal across the image. As before, her eyes are closed, her mouth moves in heavy breathing. Her head rolls to the top of the image and down to the bottom. From offscreen comes the questions from the little girl, "Where are you now?," repeated three times, but no longer is there a reply. As Sada's head rolls down for the third descent, her head stops and she opens her eyes wide looking stunned.
Shot 4 [6 seconds]: Still camera, medium shot of little girl in extreme upper left corner of the image. She is standing with her hands on the railing of the concrete platform and looking down toward the camera and Sada. Sada's prone body lies horizontal across the bottom of the image, head left just beneath the little girl. Her body is covered by a white robe. Sada's head is turned away from the camera and seems to look up at the girl. Neither figure moves. The girl repeats her question, "Where are you now?," twice more without a reply.
Shot 5 [24 seconds]: Still camera in extreme long shot, even further from the platform than shot 1. The camera looks down slightly from above, across empty stadium benches to the concrete platform in the center at the top of the image. Sada lies flat on the platform. She rises slowly to a sitting position looking left, her upper body naked, sitting on her robe. Suddenly she turns to look behind her, first over her right shoulder, away from the camera, and then over her left shoulder. Slowly she turns, looking directly toward the camera, and cries out in a mournful wail, "Keichi-san."
Cut to Sada standing over Keichi's dead body covered by bed-clothes on the floor.

NOTES

1. Oshima Nagisa, "Theory of Experimental Pornographic Film," in *Cinema, Censorship and the State: the Writings of Nagisa Oshima, 1956–1978,* edited, with an introduction, by Annette Michelson. Translated by Dawn Lawson (Cambridge: MIT Press, 1992), 258–59.
2. Ibid., 256–57.
3. Ibid., 260.
4. Maureen Turim, "Signs of Sexuality in Oshima's Tales of Passion," *Wide Angle* 9:2 (1987): 33.
5. Ruth McCormick, "An Interview with Nagisa Oshima," *Cineaste* (winter 1976–77): 35.
6. Oshima, "Theory of Experimental Pornographic Film," 253.
7. Oshima Nagisa, "Text of Plea," in *Cinema, Censorship and the State,* 266.

8. Ibid., 282.
9. Ibid., 286.
10. Ian Buruma, *Behind the Mask* (New York: New American Library, 1984), 58.
11. Edwin O. Reischauer, *The Japanese Today* (Cambridge: Harvard University Press, 1988), 395.
12. A word about my use of *eros* and *thanatos:* these terms are, perhaps, most readily associated with Freudian concepts, though they have a currency that precedes Freud and certainly extends beyond him. Nonetheless, I think my use of these terms is consonant with psychoanalytic usage, though it may not carry the full implications invested in them by Freud and his followers.
13. In addition to the work, cited in this essay, see two useful reviews, Michael Silverman, "L'Empire des Sens," *Film Quarterly* (winter 1976–77), 58–61; Tony Rayns, "Film Festival Preview: Tony Rayns on *In the Realm of the Senses," Film Comment* (September-October 1976), 37–38.
14. McCormick, "An Interview with Nagisa Oshima," 34.
15. Peter Lehman, "The Act of Making Films: an Interview With Oshima Nagisa," *Wide Angle* 4:1 (1980): 58.
16. see Peter B. High, "Oshima: a Vita Sexualis on Film," *Wide Angle* 2:4 (1978): 62–71; Dana Polan, "Politics as Process in Three Films by Nagisa Oshima," *Film Criticism* 8:1 (1983): 33–41; Ian Buruma, *Behind the Mask,* 50; David Desser, *Eros Plus Massacre* (Bloomington: University of Indiana Press, 1988): 97–99, 185–87.
17. In addition to *Cinema, Censorship and the State,* see Ruth McCormick," *In the Realm of the Senses," Cineaste* (winter 1976–77): 32–34; Peter Lehman, "Oshima: the Avant-Garde Artist Without an Avant-Garde Style," *Wide Angle* 9:2 (1987): 56–61; Peter Lehman, "The 'Gift' and the 'Keepsake': *In the Realm of the Senses:* Castration Fantasies," in Peter Lehman, *Running Scared,* (Philadelphia: Temple University Press, 1993): 169–95. Lehman offers a particularly detailed and balanced account comparing the similarities and differences between Oshima's film and the conventions of hard-core films, among other forms of pornography. Lehman concludes that *In the Realm of the Senses* "displaces the usual pornographic emphasis on male sexuality" but poses a contradictory structure that retains phallocentric values.
18. Buruma, *Behind the Mask,* 9.
19. For a more detailed discussion of double suicide in *A Cruel Story of Youth,* see Catherine Russell, "Oshima Nagisa: the Limits of Nationhood," chap. 3, in *Narrative Mortality: Death, Closure and New Wave Cinemas* (Minneapolis: University of Minnesota Press, 1995), 111–23. In the same chapter Russell offers illuminating insights into *In the Realm of the Senses,* to which I am indebted.
20. Linda Williams has noted that "together" produces a pun on "alone" and "cut" in Japanese, intensifying the film's irony in the inscription. See her *Hardcore: Power, Pleasure and the "Frenzy of the Visible"* (Berkeley: University of California Press, 1989): 221.
21. Stephen Heath, "The Question Oshima," in *Ophuls,* ed. Paul Willemen (London: British Film Institute, 1978), 75–76.

22. I am indebted to my colleague at Middlebury College, David Stahl, professor of Japanese, for his translation of the call and response as well as an elaboration of its implications. David generously contributed these ideas, among others, to my essay.
23. For the idea of the severed penis as a keepsake, I am indebted to Peter Lehman's "The 'Gift' and the 'Keepsake': *In the Realm of the Senses:* Castration Fantasies."
24. Oshima, "Text of a Plea," *Cinema, Censorship and the State,* 285.

CHAPTER FOURTEEN

The Arrest of Time

The Mythic Transgressions of *Vengeance Is Mine*

Dennis Washburn

Imamura Shôhei has been a sharp, sardonic critic of postwar Japanese culture, and his efforts to expose through art the effects of social inequality and political corruption display a sympathetic interest in individuals who live on the peripheries of mainstream culture. Donald Richie has noted this interest, and, citing such works as *The Pornographers,* observed that Imamura's films frequently celebrate "a completely amoral, vital, and overflowing rejection of Japanese collective beliefs."[1] Imamura's opposition to the repression of freedom and individual desire is grounded in a discontent with the ambiguities and hypocrisies of postwar culture, and this attitude of resistance has been crucial in framing his aesthetic vision. The most striking, even paradoxical, aspect of this attitude is that while it champions the individual over and against a false, degraded society, it is expressed in terms of an economy of values so absolute, so "overflowing," that it appears mythopoeic.

My intent in noting the coexistence of the mythic impulses of Imamura's aesthetics with his individualist rejection of the coercive force of a collectivist state is to suggest that he has embraced apparently contradictory attitudes, and, thereby, to foreground a dynamic tension in his work. This tension, moreover, is bound up with his self-consciousness as an artist; that is, Imamura has consistently demonstrated an awareness of the intrusive, artificial presence of the camera – an awareness that sparked his rejection of the methods of his early mentor, Ozu – and an eager willingness to expose that artifice in his films. This self-consciousness with regard to the narrative machinations inherent in Imamura's art renders unstable any simplistic categorization of his oeuvre and at the same time exemplifies a particular turn in modernist aesthetics that is the subject of this essay: the rejection of the authority of rationality and of the historicized temporality of language in favor of intuition and the timeless spatiality of image.

A number of scholars, notably David Desser and Satô Tadao, have provided a good overview of the common threads that run through Imamura's films as well as a comparative view of Imamura vis-à-vis other directors.[2] Since it has proven useful to view Imamura's films within the context of his development as a director, it may also prove instructive to situate his work more broadly within the ideological contexts of contemporary Japanese aesthetics and politics. Specifically, I shall look at the way his discontent with the culture of modernity shapes the treatment of violence in *Vengeance Is Mine* (Fukushû suru wa, ware ni ari, 1979) and the presentation of the motives of the film's murderous protagonist, Enokizu Iwao. The violence depicted in *Vengeance Is Mine* is an extreme challenge to the norms of social behavior: an attempt to arrest the progression of social time in order to secure values that are genuine and timeless. The film transforms individual acts of violence into sacred transgressions by giving them both an ideological and a mythical significance born out of a concern with achieving authentic culture. This aesthetic representation of violence as an expression of desire at once rejects the modern and inscribes its aims and desires; it serves as a critique of modern culture and yet is deeply implicated in it. Such deep ambivalence, inherent to the process of turning violence to aesthetic ends, underlies a large number of literary, historical, and cinematic narratives produced by artists in Japan who came to maturity during the two decades immediately following the end of the Pacific war.

AESTHETIC VIOLENCE AND THE DESIRE FOR FREEDOM

> The requirement for transgression, preliminary to immolation, appears aberrant and unintelligible to us when we observe it in the context of human sacrifice "in the strictest sense," yet it figures in the literary rites which moderns play out themselves every time they canonize a "damned" poet or a demented philosopher. The process remains rooted in the collective murder which it reproduces ritually in a form that is simultaneously caricatural and attenuated. . .
>
> René Girard[3]

Near the end of *Vengeance Is Mine* the convicted serial murderer, Enokizu Iwao, is visited in Kokura Prison by his father. The meeting, as one would expect in such a situation, is exceptionally tense. The narrative momentum of the film, with its explicit depiction of Enokizu's crimes, has created an expectation of violence; and with that expectation comes a feeling of dread and suspense that is further heightened by the primal psychological confrontation between father and son.

As the scene opens, subtitles, which are used throughout the film, inform us that we are in the special visitor's room. Enokizu is led in and immediately complains that his wife and father have been talking to the press and putting all the blame on him. He then sits down opposite his father, who has brought two pieces of news. The first is that Enokizu has been excommunicated by the Catholic Church. Enokizu laughs at that – laughter that conveys not only his genuine disinterest and contempt, but also his sense of the absurdity of the act. The father, however, has ulterior motives for informing Enokizu of his excommunication, since it means that his ashes cannot be placed in the family grave. This leads him to the second bit of news, which is that Enokizu's mother died the previous day. Enokizu's reaction to this is muted. His father points out that now Enokizu cannot be buried with his mother, and he continues by saying that since they both share the blood of the devil he has asked to be excommunicated along with his son. He tells his son that he must live in fear of god, but in what is perhaps an echo of Camus's *The Stranger,* Enokizu claims that he has no need of God – that he killed innocent people and that he must now die for it.

Enokizu's father cannot accept the seemingly nihilistic atheism of his son and tries to goad him on the point. He asks Enokizu why he kept running, implying that he must have felt there was something of value in life. Enokizu answers pointedly that he just wanted to be free. Deflected by this response, the father wonders, almost rhetorically, if this is all their relationship as father and son means. Enokizu, who is now standing and moving toward the door, says that they will always be apart, and that though his father cannot forgive him, neither can he forgive his father. Then, in a menacing afterthought, Enokizu looks down at his father and says that he should have killed him instead. The father stands to face the challenge and confidently asserts that his son could not kill him – he didn't have the courage to kill his father because the only people he could kill were those for whom he felt no resentment. Then, in an act of extreme psychic violence, the father spits full into his son's face. Enokizu, struggling to keep his rage in check, calls his father a son-of-a-bitch, and utters his final line in the film: "I want to kill you" (see Figure 43).

This chilling confrontation, brilliantly acted out by Ogata Ken and Mikuni Rentarô, provides an emotional and intellectual climax to a highly charged film; and this single scene crystallizes some of the most important recurring themes in the corpus of Imamura's work. The story of Enokizu is based on Saki Ryûzô's journalistic novel of the same title.[4] The book, which calls to mind Truman Capote's *In Cold Blood,* depicts the career of the real-life serial killer, Nishiguchi Akira. Given his critical view of the collectivism of modern Japanese culture, it is perhaps not surprising that Imamura was drawn to the story of such an apparently amoral and utterly antisocial individual. One of Enokizu's primary motives for his murder spree was, as he told his father, the desire to live freely; and the film narrative is carefully structured to depict Enokizu as, above all, a creature of desire, a man who lives in the present, unconstrained by the norms of social behavior. Enokizu is a man of prodigious sexual appetite capable of living by his wits, according to the circum-

43. Confrontation between father and son; Imamura Shôhei, *Vengeance Is Mine* (1979).

stances of the moment, and able to change identities quickly and convincingly. Indeed, in our first view of him, in the opening shot in the police car that is taking him to his arraignment, Enokizu complains to his police captors that it is not fair that he is going to his death and that after he dies they will all still be alive and having sex. Enokizu's desire, his longing for perfect autonomy, is expressed as a resentment against the desires of others and the inexorable passing of human time, both of which he resents not being able to control.

Enokizu's antisocial rebellion, his desire for total freedom, is a particular manifestation of a mythic notion of the subject that serves as the basis for Imamura's critique of postwar society. Allan Casebier has argued that for Imamura the ontological ground of the subject in Japan is irrationality, a term he uses to indicate an intuitive, nonverbal understanding of the world that stands in contrast to the worldview of scientific rationalism. Casebier claims further that "Imamura seeks, through his films, to recover what is essential to being originally Japanese."[5] I would qualify Casebier's analysis somewhat by pointing out that Imamura does not necessarily valorize images of irrationality, but tries to establish a critical distance that allows him to play those images of irrationality off against the degraded false values of contemporary society in order to find something culturally authentic – a point I will return to later. However, I want to stress here that the story of Enokizu's crimes, which are by his own admission unreasonably directed against the innocent, provides a striking example of the kind of irrationality Casebier traces out for us in Imamura's other films.

Enokizu's irrationality is manifested in his crime spree, but it is rooted in his rebellion against the authority of his father. Beyond the obvious psychological implications, this conflict is made to bear enormous cultural significance. The structure of the narrative determines our understanding of the complex personality of Enokizu's father, who represents the communal, political, and religious norms Enokizu hates. From the son's perspective the sins of the father are legion: the father is a weak collaborationist during the war; his Catholic beliefs, though deeply rooted in the marginal culture of the Hidden Christians on Japan's western islands, retain their stigma of foreignness; and the father harbors sexual desires for his son's wife. The personal experience and values of Enokizu's father are situated clearly for us in their particular historical contexts; and yet the narrative time line of the film is lifted into the timeless realm of mythic narrative by casting the story as a primal conflict of generations, and, more important, by giving to the father characteristics that resonate with modern notions of genuine Japanese identity – that is, the father's Catholicism is pre-Tokugawa, his birthplace is a fishing village, his business is a hot-springs spa, and his desires are incestuous. The father is thus invested with both the oppressive authority of collectivist norms and certain features of cultural authenticity.

That is a tough act to follow, and the contradictions of the father give rise to the conflicted identity of the son. Enokizu's resentment against his inherited condition, more than his sense of outraged justice, is the origin of his vengeful rage.[6] His irrational violence, which evokes a comparison to figures of Japanese myth and legend, such as Susano-o or Yamato Takeru, suggests that somehow his desire for freedom is an expression of something genuine, of "original Japanese identity," as Casebier puts it. And yet his transgression is not just against order, but against the primal desires and irrationality of his father as well. As noted previously, the confrontation between father and son is complicated by the association of certain cultural traits with the father that also carry mythic significance. When Enokizu's father tells his son that he can only kill those he does not resent, he is in effect spitting the dialectic of their relationship in his son's face. Enokizu's transgressions depend upon his opposition to his father; and he cannot destroy the father who engendered him any more than he can break through the culture that establishes his identity. The struggle of the individual against the prisonhouse of modern culture is elevated to mythical status as an act of resistance to what Girard terms "the collective murder."[7] In the case of *Vengeance Is Mine,* Enokizu is effectively scapegoated insofar as his own impulses to violence, which on one level are reactions to the hypocrisy and violence of his society, are turned back on him by that very same society, which condemns him to death. In the end, unable to act on his most profound desire to avenge himself on the ontological ground of his identity, he is left with nothing more than the empty language of violence. This desire is conveyed by the meaning of the Japanese title of the film, *Fukushû suru wa, ware ni ari,* which is a translation of a statement attributed to God (*Rom.* 12:19 – rendered in the King James version as "Vengeance is mine"). Significantly, this phrase could also be read as "the act of vengeance is I," an interpretation that equates Enokizu's very being with violence.

IRRATIONAL VIOLENCE AS SACRED TRANSGRESSION

> None of the properties of creativity is adequately expressed in metaphors drawn from the life process. To beget and to give birth is no more creative than to die is annihilating; they are but different phases of the same, ever-recurring cycle in which all living things are held as though they were spellbound. Neither violence nor power is a natural phenomenon, that is, a manifestation of the life process; they belong to the political realm of human affairs whose essentially human quality is guaranteed by man's faculty of action, the ability to begin something new.
>
> Hannah Arendt[8]

There is an element of the culture of modernity that is distinguished by the ritualistic impulse to transgress against established order, even when that transgression is self-consciously recognized to be nothing more than a prelude to immolation. The effort to make everything new, to make everything begin now by the process of creative dissolution, is an effort to transgress against time itself – to free the individual by exploding the temporal progression of the established order. In the logic of this form of transgression, transcendence depends upon an annihilating revelation.

The act, or process, of creative dissolution, however, can never be transcendent by itself. As Arendt points out, violence and power belong securely in the human, political realm. An act of violence, whether physical or aesthetic in nature, is essentially political because it is both instrumental and expressive. It is instrumental in that it is a means to achieve power, impose control, or universalize a set of individual beliefs or desires. It is expressive in that violence, especially on the personal, domestic level, allows an imaginary reconfiguration, or confirmation, of social order. Violent transgressions against the innocent or powerless may seem irrational, but violence of an intentional nature always suggests that the perpetrator believes there is some underlying justification for it; and that intentionality is what defines the political nature of violence for Arendt.

Arendt's analysis explicitly sets aside an extended examination of violence that lacks intentionality (that is, what I would term, in the context of this essay, irrational violence) on the grounds that violence and power derive from the ability to begin something new – an argument that in its very wording is caught up in the impulse for creative dissolution that has had an important influence on the culture of modernity. At first reading

Arendt's argument seems skewed by its assumption that violence is invariably intended or motivated, since the notion, for example, of insanity as an unintended or unmotivated cause of violence is well established as a legal/moral principle. Nevertheless, the violence of a sociopath is still viewed, within the terms of Arendt's analysis, as intended, or political, because such violence remains motivated, even if by irrational fears or by antisocial desires that justify its containment, or suppression, within the economy of social norms.[9] This view, while it assumes that violence operates according to an order of motives, acknowledges that that order may be utterly capricious or even outside the bounds of accepted social norms. But once irrational violence is defined by its place outside the bounds of social norms, can it then continue to be described in political terms? Can it be understood as an act of human volition, as something intended? Violence that we are forced to explain as motivated by a will, or a desire, that lies beyond conventional values and rational comprehension, is somehow felt to belong to a separate realm of mythic transgressions.

The dual nature of violence, seemingly both political and apolitical in nature, finds its analogue in the destructive/creative impulse that has haunted the culture of modernity. Violence motivated by values or desires that are thought to be genuine and permanent can only realize that motivation by an act that is inherently finite and temporal. This paradox is best illustrated in the fascist imaginary, where violence is depicted as a kind of cleansing or purging of the body politic in response to the malaise of modern civilization.[10] In this imaginary, temporal and spatial orders of bourgeois culture are represented both as the supreme achievement in the teleology of progress and as an alienating site where the expression of genuine feeling and identity are suppressed. As a result, there is an ongoing struggle between submitting to the modern order and longing to transgress it. Saul Friedlander locates one instance of that struggle within fascist ideology: "Submission nourishes fury, fury clears its conscience in the submission. To these opposing needs, Nazism – in the constant duality of its representations – offers an outlet: in fact, Nazism found itself to be the expression of these opposing needs."[11]

Fascist violence aimed for a resolution of the contradictions of modern culture by obliterating the present and reconfiguring it as an authentic (mythic) past. The fascist aesthetics of violent purification and suppression of the body is, however, only one manifestation of the modern ideology of violence, which invariably purports to be an expression of freedom, even in its leftist variants. The aesthetic potential of violent transgression may be expressed in very different ways: as a desire to liberate from social rules and customs – imagined as a return to an original, ordered state of nature; or as a desire to liberate by imposing social constraints and a sense of order – best captured in the chilling slogan "Work will make you free." In both cases violence is justified as an effort to assert control in order to alleviate the anxiety created by the spare time that modern urban, technological communities have made possible and by the perceived crumbling of affective ties that governed so-called traditional notions of human relationships. At the core of the modern experience of individuality is an emphasis on self-realization through activity, rather than through inherited status or qualities, that has weakened both socially determined boundaries of self-definition and any stable center of the personality.[12] Thus, violence, in both the narrow political sense that Arendt uses and the apolitical sense of it as mythic transgression, is bivalent, and may be justified by the need to suppress the heightened awareness of the contingency and createdness of the modern sense of self, and by the desire for natural, authentic culture.

The recourse to violence and its justifications as political act or aesthetic expression can never be more than a temporary escape from the awareness of time, from the self-consciousness of language and thought that mark the culture of modernity, into an imagined past or future. The spatial and temporal orders of the present give way to a cyclical, mythic time that, in its constant return, runs counter to the longing for the transcendent experience that elevates the present to an eternal moment. For that reason fascism, in particular, among modern political ideologies, made violence routine, systematic, and institutional.

Because of the actual violence inscribed upon the body in certain modernist ideologies, best exemplified by fascism, care must be taken when discussing the expressive function of violence. There is the danger of abstraction that can aestheticize the effects of physical violence on individuals, transforming violence into a cultural fetish.[13] Such a transformation is readily apparent in the work of an artist like Mishima Yukio, and the phenomenon became widespread in the 1960s and 1970s when, for example, the works of Sade were treated as liberating texts, or aspects of the Nazi regime were eroticized in films such as *Seven Beauties* or *The Night Porter.* At the same time it would also be ethically questionable, and historically misleading, to divorce violence from its expression in language and thereby fail to address the (admittedly uncomfortable) nature of its aesthetic appeal.

The aesthetics of violent transgression figures over and over in the rites of twentieth-century literary and cinematic narratives, and has resulted in the modernist canonization of mad poets, outcast ideologues, or charismatic criminals.[14] Pound, Lewis, and Genet come most immediately to mind as representatives of this particular turn in modernism. The mythopoeic impulse that dominates their art, with its breaking and recasting of worlds, is undoubtedly the defining attitude of what is now sometimes referred to as high modernism; and it is an impulse that has clear political ramifications. The archetypes of myth destroy both the sense of present time and space, conflating the past and present and sweeping away the historical imagination, which always strives to account for the contingent in human affairs. The collapsing of historical depth that results from myth-making permits the individual to escape into the unconditioned realm of organic, or natural, culture, or to submerge the self in a collective culture that rejects the claims of individualism.

In Japan the desire to get beyond language and thought and return to an authentic culture has played an important role in the formation of cultural identity. The rapid and jarring transformations of Japanese society have given rise to an almost obsessive concern with defining the essential features of being Japanese. Modern Japanese identity is profoundly alienated because it is so heavily tied to modes of production and representation that are often perceived as failing to embody the true values or spirit of Japan. As a result the nation has been wracked by spasms of individual violence and by the violence of coercive social control. This alienation has been chronicled in numerous literary works: the brooding novels of Natsume Sôseki; the despairing irony of Akutagawa and the antirational solipsism of Shiga Naoya; the kitschy individualism of Mishima and the myth-making of Ôe Kenzaburô or Nakagami Kenji. The concern with the authentic and the retreat to an imagined Japanese past are also reflected consistently in the rhetoric of Japanese cinema. Nöel Burch's claims notwithstanding, there is in fact considerable continuity in the language of cultural archetype from prewar to postwar films. The modernist preoccupation with a pure Japanese space and time, where the essential values of the one true culture can be discovered, are embodied in images of the country village, the working-class neighborhood, or the feudal hero that have dominated all mass cultural artifacts in Japan.

This is not to say that we can simply collapse the historical distinctions between prewar and postwar films, and I want to stress again that I am not suggesting that there is a some equivalent of a unified field theory for modern Japanese culture. For example, both Mizoguchi's *Furusato* (Hometown) and Yanagimachi's *Himatsuri* (Fire Festival – a film, it should be noted, written by Nakagami) make important use of the image of the rural village and of nature to suggest a pure Japanese space and time that is the object of the respective protagonists' desire. The key difference in these films is that although the conflict in *Furusato* arises when the temptations of false modern (i.e., Western) culture threaten to lead the hero astray, the possibility of living in the imagined space of an authentic Japan remains. In *Himatsuri,* produced more than a half century later, the longing for a pure cultural space is just as strongly expressed, but the film makes it clear that the possibility of realizing that desire is zero. The protagonist's realization of that impossibility, his awareness of his own belatedness, leads to a violent conflagration, which is presented as the only way for him to escape the warp of modernity. Having noted the difference in attitude in these two films toward an imaginary Japan, I want to reiterate that the use of violence as aesthetic expression, especially where that expression seeks to justify the obliteration of the rationality of modern culture, has shaped both the discourse of resistance and the understanding of authenticity in Japan.

THE AUTHENTIC IMAGE

> It seems to me that before the photograph can exist as art it must, by its very nature, choose whether it is to be a record or a testimony. Whatever special lenses are used, and however the subject is thereby distorted, the camera only knows how to relate things directly. However abstract the composition, therefore, the individual meaning of the objects related inevitably remains as a kind of indispersible precipitate. The photographer's whole job is to filter this off by one of two methods. It is a choice between record and testimony.
>
> Mishima Yukio[15]

Mishima's reduction of the essence of photographic art to what he calls a choice between record and testimony touches upon a problem of special significance to all the photographic arts, including the cinema. His reduction derives from a distinction between what he calls the "absolute authority" of an object recorded on film and the distortion of an object that expresses the subjective judgment of an artist whose testimony is, in Mishima's words, "everything." In his account a struggle arises between the overt willfulness of the camera – expressed by the choice and contextualization of subject – and the sheer physicality (or "foundness") of the subject, which survives even in the most radically antirealist, or presentational modes.

Mishima's view of photographic art reflects his own peculiar preoccupation with the nature and meaning of authenticity. This preoccupation is at the heart of his film *The Rites of Love and Death,* based on the short story "Yûkoku" (Patriotism), where scenes of love-making and ritual suicide are carried out beneath a large scroll painting of two Chinese characters meaning "the attainment of sincerity." This word-image, which dominates the camera frame, creates both a textual and photographic space onto which Mishima can transfer his obsession with authenticity, with finding the genuine and sincere expression of cultural meaning and self-identity, and, through that transference, experience a state that normally lies beyond the individual in a timeless realm – the realm of ideology, art, and myth.

The aesthetic tension embodied in the calligraphic slogan that is the visual ground of *The Rites of Love and Death* is a clear, perhaps heavy-handed, expression of the tortured dialectic that is characteristic of that strain of modern aesthetics marked by the impulse toward creative dissolution. Mishima's observations on the nature of photographic art raise a valid point, though one that is hardly original with him, about the distorting process of an art form that depends upon the mass-production technology of the camera: a distortion that casts serious doubts about whether a photographic image, which can be widely copied and distributed, can ever be considered an authentic art form. Photography, in order to be art, depends on something apparently extraneous, that is, the willfulness or self-consciousness of the artist who confers aesthetic meaning and form on a subject. If the aesthetics of photography is determined by the attitude of the artist, then it may be rejected as false or fake art due to its subjectively grounded, created nature. The predicament that envelopes the modern artist, which Mishima locates in the dialectic of the art of photography (the choice between record and testimony), is that the self-consciousness necessary to make art possible is aesthetically and epistemologically unstable.

Mishima's awareness of the artifice of the camera, and his own willingness to make use of that artifice to express his concern over the problem of cultural authenticity, is a quality he shared with a number of postwar artists, including Imamura – though I do not want to take this connection any further here since their political outlooks were very different. The self-consciousness of the artist toward the production of art and the danger of "bad faith" establishes a critical distance that forces us to question if Imamura is in fact valorizing the equation of violence with novelty, oblivion, and transcendence. To answer that question, and to consider the meaning of, and the aesthetic motives for, depicting violence, we must examine the formal arrangement of *Vengeance Is Mine,* its narrative structure, and the attitude toward violence that the structure conveys.

Vengeance Is Mine is perhaps most famous for its graphic, at points almost matter-of-fact depiction of murder, which has the unsettling effect of making this film both compelling and difficult to watch. The crimes of Enokizu Iwao are especially disturbing since they are presented in a manner that strips them of the kind of overt stylization found, for example, in the work of Sam Peckinpah. By not overtly containing the depiction of violence within the space of aesthetic play, Imamura intentionally blurs the distinction between film as art form and film as documentary medium, and forces us to confront at least the visual, affective reality of violence. The unmediated view of murder, like the graphic depiction of sex in Oshima's *In the Realm of the Senses,* is designed to foreshorten representational distance and thus deprive the viewer of the reflective space where violence can be put into some controlling context and comprehended. The order of events in *Vengeance Is Mine* throws the first two murders at us early on with little explanation, before we have the time to understand Enokizu's motives, and forces us to confront normally invisible assumptions about the nature and aesthetics of violence.

The shock of seeing "realistic" violence disrupts expectations of both representational and ethical norms. By presenting violence that initially seems to have no meaning or motive, Imamura brings us squarely, if momentarily, into the worldview of a serial killer. This disruption of expectations is certainly unpleasant, but in a strange way it is also key to the aesthetic appeal of *Vengeance Is Mine,* which, together with *The*

Ballad of Narayama, is among the most formally satisfying of all Imamura's films. The compelling nature of the film is partly an effect produced by the work of a brilliant ensemble of actors. However, the primary source of the film's achievement is the narrative structure – a complex, nonlinear series of testimonial and confessional flashbacks that initially disrupts our sense of the temporal flow of the narrative in much the same way as the depiction of seemingly unmotivated violence disrupts our spatial and ethical bearings. The most distinctive aspect of *Vengeance Is Mine* is that the unsettling quality of its narrative structure so completely conveys the unpredictable nature of Enokizu's violent transgressions.

The formal structure of *Vengeance Is Mine* is noteworthy, but it is not especially ground-breaking since the narrative techniques and themes of this film have clear antecedents in Imamura's earlier works. For example, the examination of antisocial behavior and of individuals on the margins of mainstream society is a central element of *The Insect Woman, Intention of Murder,* and *The Pornographers.* Similarly, the disruptive erasure of the boundary between the techniques of documentary and fiction is something that Imamura has explored in *A Man Vanishes, The History of Postwar Japan As Told by a Bar Hostess,* and *Karayuki-san. Vengeance Is Mine* also shares a tendency toward myth-making, most obviously with *The Profound Desire of the Gods.*

Vengeance Is Mine is thus the mature product of a daring director who brought many of his earlier experiments to bear on its production. Even so, in pulling together the recurring elements of his earlier films Imamura finds a way to vary those techniques, especially the film's primary narrative device, the use of flashback. A brief comparison of the narrative structure of *Vengeance Is Mine* with some well-known films, *Citizen Kane* or *Rashômon,* that employ flashback as a major narrative element will illustrate Imamura's use of this technique.

The complexity of *Citizen Kane* or *Rashômon* is created by the apparent division of the flashback sequences among a number of narrators (I say "apparent" only because the frame of the camera provides a constant narrative reference point), whose competing perspectives give the audience the illusion of a more objective viewpoint (i.e., the constant point of reference provided by the camera frame that denies any privileged perspective), while at the same time rendering indeterminate any final judgment of the truth of the story. In the case of *Kane,* this indeterminacy is resolved, and the narrative given complete aesthetic closure, with the final shot of the sled burning, giving us the ultimate God's-eye view of the reason for the life story of Charles Foster Kane.

Rashômon, on the other hand, makes no attempt to resolve the indeterminacy that arises from competing versions of the truth, but rather makes the epistemological indeterminacy of narrative itself a metaphor for the true condition of humanity. Yet even in *Rashômon* the open-endedness of the flashbacks is provided with a formal resolution through its final shot of the life-affirming act of the woodcutter taking responsibility for an abandoned baby – an act that defers the problem of epistemological uncertainty. In a sense the film cops out by suggesting that although we can never be sure of anything in this world, life goes on.

The key difference from these films in the use of flashback narrative is that *Vengeance Is Mine* does not clearly set out the context of the narration at the beginning. *Kane* of course sets up its Gothic mystery with the cryptic phrase "Rosebud," but the flashback sequences are set up for us from the start as an attempt to answer that mystery through the investigation of a newsreel reporter. Similarly, the scene of narration is clearly laid out for us at the beginning of *Rashômon,* which takes its title not from the Akutagawa story on which it is based, but from the Kyoto gate that is the scene of narration. Imamura, in contrast, does not initially make the scene of narration unambiguous. We certainly understand that the context of the story is the police interrogation of Enokizu – a fact established first by the opening scene of Enokizu's arrival at the police station, and second by the use of subtitles in the scenes immediately following the opening credits. Nevertheless, the temporal jumps that confront the viewer at the outset create a sense of disorientation wholly appropriate to a tale of murder.[16] After the opening credits we move back in time without explanation to a scene of a woman tending her vegetable patch and complaining to her daughter-in-law in undisguised racist terms about the "drunk Korean" who has collapsed in her field. The daughter-in-law, who is also the target of the woman's ill-temper, finds that the Korean is in fact a "real" Japanese who has been murdered. This scene then cuts to the arrival of the police, and subtitles provide the essential police blotter facts about the case: the name of the victim and the cause of death. There follows another cut to the arrival of the police at the scene of a second murder, with the same use of subtitles.

As soon as we find out that both murders took place on October 18, 1963, the narrative jumps forward to January 9, 1964, to the police headquarters where the interrogation is taking place. Enokizu refuses to talk, so the police tell him the story of the murders, which are then acted out in brutal detail. By this point the spatial and temporal bearings of the narrative are gradually fixed, and the flashbacks take on a more sequential form. Even after the film establishes its bearings, however, the narrative point of view remains unstable. Once Enokizu begins to confess, the film is dominated by his version of the story, but his perspective is constantly qualified and fleshed out by facts gained through the police investigation and reported to us by Enokizu's lovers, by the media, by witnesses, and, most important, by his family. In arranging his story in this manner Imamura takes considerable license with the more straightforward narration of Saki Ryûzô's novel; and while the structure of his film is never radically disorienting (compared to, say, *Last Year at Marienbad*), it nonetheless succeeds in making a complex variation on the technique of flashback.

In pointing out the initial temporal confusion created by the uncertain context of the early flashback sequences and by the shifting narrative perspective in subsequent scenes, I do not want to suggest that the film structure is chaotic, or even necessarily difficult to follow. While the film tries to recapture the shock of murder and the disorientation at its discovery, the narrative is gradually given temporal and spatial order by the documentary-style use of subtitles that either announce the specific times and places of events or fill in important information. Moreover, certain words and images give the film a tight symmetry. For example, the Hidden-Christian song that Enokizu sings in the patrol car at the beginning is repeated at several points in the film: when his family is on the ferryboat taking them to their new home in the hot-springs resort of Beppu, and again at the very end of the film when Enokizu's father is disposing of the bones of his executed son. Similarly, certain images recur at important moments. Right after the first murders, when Enokizu returns to his room, the light cord is tied in the shape of a hangman's noose. This image is even more prominent later in the film in a scene at an eel hatchery where a rope and a pair of rubber boots explicitly foreshadow the fate that awaits Enokizu.

The narrative of *Vengeance Is Mine* oscillates between fact and interpretation, between the straightforward documentation of the police blotter and the aesthetic reordering of time through flashback. The disorientation created by the nonlinear narrative of the opening scenes and by the direct, unstylized depiction of violence reconfigures the real past into unreal narrative time that disrupts the movement of the story. At the same time, the random acts of murder committed by Enokizu are framed by a highly structured arrangement of imagistic and aural elements that points to the presence of a controlling aesthetic vision. It is as if the film is trying to achieve at once both options, that of record and of testimony, that Mishima asserted were available to the photographic artist.

The tension that results from the blending of fact and interpretation (of trying to be both documentary and fiction) contributes to a marked ambivalence toward the nature of Enokizu's violence. As disturbing as his actions are, the film makes him sympathetic at points – even appealing (here again it may be the sheer élan Ogata Ken brings to the role that makes this character wickedly appealing). At certain moments his violence seems incomprehensible; he embodies unbridled desire and hatred, and there seems to be no individuated self at the core of his being. For that reason Enokizu is chameleonlike and capable of assuming a wide variety of roles: interpreter, lawyer, laborer, college professor. At other moments the film takes its cue from Saki's novel and seems to go out of its way to provide some rationale, however inadequate, for Enokizu's vengeful rampage. The primary motive is his enmity for his father, and that enmity has political origins. Enokizu's rebellious nature – and it is crucial to recall that this description of him is his father's – begins with the compliance of the father with the orders of the militarist regime of the 1930s, and is thus tied directly to the momentous political decision by Japan to go to war and fulfill its imperialist destiny.

The connection of Enokizu's rebellion to the political situation in Japan continues on into the Occupation. Here his rebellious instincts work against both native authority and foreign control. The father's voice-over narration informs us that after the war his son spent a couple of years in jail for having stolen a U.S. Army vehicle, but that he also worked as an interpreter for the American forces. This volatile mix of complicity and resistance is brought out clearly in the scene where Enokizu rescues a young woman, Ômura Kazuko – who is first shown to us in farm dress working in a rice field – from being raped by drunken GIs. He later becomes Kazuko's lover, and when she gets pregnant he marries her over his father's objections. The father's narration throughout these scenes of Enokizu's youth and young manhood is meant to explain the son's crimes by pointing out his history of antisocial behavior. However, in political terms Enokizu emerges as likable, if not quite heroic, by virtue first of his resistance to the militarists in Japan and then to the raping of Japan, embodied in the agrarian figure of Kazuko, by American imperialists. A measure of sympathy for Enokizu is also created when he marries Kazuko out of physical attraction; and when that attraction is betrayed by her and his father it suggests a reason for his crime spree that is, all other moral considerations aside, at least emotionally comprehensible.

The romantic and political aspects of Enokizu's appeal come together in the story of his relationship with Asano Haruko, who runs a small inn used primarily as an out-of-the-way love hotel. Their relationship constitutes the longest sustained subplot in the film, since it takes place over much of the seventy-two days Enokizu is a fugitive. In many respects Asano's story recalls the type of women whose lives were ruined by the war or by social circumstances. Such stories figured prominently in the films of Ozu, Mizoguchi, and Naruse in the 1950s, but in *Vengeance Is Mine,* Asano's life-story serves as a counterpoint to Enokizu's, for what has ruined her life is that her mother, who perhaps lost her husband to the war, was forced to work and ended up murdering her employer, an old woman who mistreated her. Having a convicted murderer for a mother drove Asano to the demimonde as a kept woman running a cheap house of assignation. It is through her life at the margins that she encounters Enokizu, who, in his role as a college professor, represents to her a romanticized ideal of normalcy that she cherishes as a buffer against her own sordid life.

Because she idealizes him, the moment when Enokizu's true identity is revealed to her is significant in that it brings together those political and romantic aspects of his life-story that make him sympathetic. The revelation comes at a movie theater when a police bulletin about Enokizu is shown on the screen. This bulletin is sandwiched between a maudlin newsreel on the assassination and funeral of the young idealist John F. Kennedy and a ponderous-looking Soviet film titled "The Liberation of Europe: Part 3." Certainly the use of this sort of material allows Imamura to establish the historical context of his story. However, projecting on a film screen, between two polar images of the Cold War superpowers, the face of a murderer who is violently nihilistic and an embodiment of

Japanese resistance provides a knowing, self-referential image that foregrounds the aesthetic frame Imamura has constructed around the subject of his film. It also imbues the figure of Enokizu with a political significance that suggests some vague ideological motive for his crimes, which is not spelled out, and sets the stage for his transformation into a mythic figure.

The political associations of the unmasking of Enokizu dissolve immediately into Asano's romantic impulses as she resolves to play out her life according to the kind of story she is conditioned by circumstances to accept as appropriate to a woman in her situation – that is, she decides that when the time comes she will die with Enokizu. Soon after, however, she abruptly changes her mind and decides, in a version of yet another old story, that she will not die, but will have his child. This decision, and the pragmatic, nurturing values it depends upon, is eventually undercut by Enokizu's overwhelming desire for control. He strangles her while she is making pickles, a homely image of traditional agrarian culture. Asano explains that she enjoys making pickles because she comes from a farming family. Enokizu then remarks, in words similar to those he used to the police in the opening scene, that she will continue to make them long after he is gone. Not sure how to respond to this disturbing thought, she tries to pamper him by playing the coquette. Her hands are smeared with the pepper paste she has been applying to the vegetables, so she asks for a drink of his beer. He all but pours the beer down her throat, which he stares at menacingly, then starts to strangle her (see Figure 44). For a moment he relaxes his grip, as if he has had second thoughts; but instead of fighting she tells him that she wants to go far away. His pained look of recognition implies that he has understood her wish to die; and after he kills her he merely says, "Thank you." The build-up to Asano's murder makes it clear that Enokizu's gratitude stems from the fact that she has shared his desire to escape an oppressive culture; and the violent fulfillment of her desire, the moment of climax and death in which he recognizes and rejects Asano's love, is the moment when Enokizu also recognizes that his crimes are nothing more than a prelude to immolation.

Shortly after he kills Asano, he kills her mother as well and tries to pawn the furnishings in the inn. He is recognized by a prostitute he slept with, and is finally captured. In completing his confession to the police Enokizu insists that he killed a total of six people, including the baby he was sure was already growing inside Asano. Here we swing back away from political and romantic ideologies as an explanation for his desire for

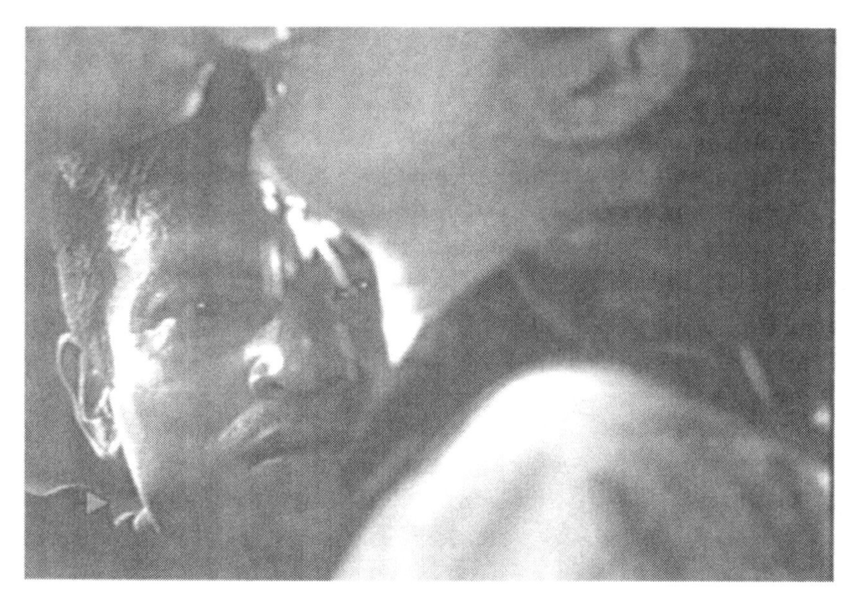

44. Violence and aesthetic vision; Imamura Shôhei, *Vengeance Is Mine* (1979).

vengeance and are left with a kind of incomprehensible rage. His rage is directed at overcoming his father, and yet that rage is deflected because he cannot kill the man whose existence defines him. Instead, by killing Asano he has destroyed himself as a father; and by that violent act he realizes that the only way he can resist the culturally determined identity imposed on him is the self-erasure of his very existence.

THE ARREST OF TIME

> In Japan . . . the appreciation of beauty, the sexual climax and the attainment of selflessness when face to face with death, are all moments when language is driven from man's mind and time is conquered. . . . And, at the same time, the conquering of time becomes the conquering of space between self and other. In short, violence is a kind of 'communitas.'
>
> Brian Moeran[17]

Vengeance Is Mine ends with a formal coda. Following Enokizu's climactic confrontation with his father, the narrative jumps forward five years to a time immediately after his execution. His wife, Kazuko, and his father are on a cable car carrying his ashes and bones to the top of a mountain. The place is not specified in the subtitles, though the time is, but it is clear that we are moving into a sacred realm. For as the father and Kazuko ascend, a group of religious pilgrims descends in another car.

Kazuko tells her father-in-law that she received a letter from Enokizu ordering her not to have another man. They laugh and the father says that it is just like his son to write such a thing. Certainly it is in keeping with the portrait of Enokizu that he would try to control the desires of others even after his death. The letter also warns Kazuko that her father-in-law is a crafty man, suggesting one last time that Enokizu's rebellion was partly motivated by his hatred of hypocrisy. The father agrees with his son's assessment, but that does not faze Kazuko, who, it turns out, is attracted to the father because of his hypocrisy.

When they reach the top of the mountain they begin to throw Enokizu's bones from an observation platform while the father sings the song of his Hidden Christian heritage. As they throw the bones into the sky, however, Imamura uses a stop-action shot that leaves the bones suspended in both time and narrative space. The father and Kazuko register surprise and then apparent consternation. Each time they hurl Enokizu's remains the bones halt in midair. The meaning of this strange, small miracle is difficult to gauge, especially in light of the eclectic mix of religious imagery involved in this final ritual. The miracle could be interpreted as either the apotheosis of Enokizu's spirit to the mythic status of a willful *kami,* or the assertion of egoistic desires so powerful that they continue to act, even after death, to try to arrest the progression of time.

The most interesting aspect of this scene is the sudden change of narrative mode employed by Imamura. Just as he sharply divides the mundane and sacred worlds to bring a sense of narrative closure to *The Ballad of Narayama,* Imamura makes a modal break to provide a formal closure for *Vengeance Is Mine.* Although the linear progression of time is disrupted early in the film, the mode of representation has been for the most part realistic. The sudden intrusion of the supernatural, conveyed by the use of the stop-action shots at the very end, is as jarring as the murders that take place at the beginning. Moreover, the mode of the very last shot, which shows the father and Kazuko throwing the bones right at the camera, is abruptly presentational (see Figure 45).

45. Arrest of time; Imamura Shôhei, *Vengeance Is Mine* (1979).

The presentational shot that ends *Vengeance Is Mine* lays bare the artifice of the narrative, leaving an ironic, distanced effect that fully exposes the film's ambivalence toward violence. The self-consciousness of the final shot suggests a critical skepticism toward myth-making, and yet the ending of the film tries to leave the viewer frozen in time and space, in the realm of myth – at least until the credits roll. Enokizu's violence becomes transfigured as a spirit of pure, irrational desire that seeks the arrest of time. His transgressions are at once deplorable and sacred, morally reprehensible yet culturally essential; and their moral and political ambiguities derive from the aesthetic propensities of Imamura, whose self-consciousness about the artifice of film is a manifestation of his interest in the possibilities of myth, of an ideal authentic world he is compelled to construct and then fling, like a handful of bones, into the viewer's face.

NOTES

1. Donald Richie, *The Japanese Movie* (Tokyo: Kodansha International, 1982), 188.

2. David Desser, *Eros Plus Massacre* (Bloomington: Indiana University Press, 1988), 81–87 and 122–27; and Satô Tadao, *Imamura Shôhei no sekai* (The world of Imamura Shôhei) (Tokyo: Gakuyô shobô, 1980).
3. René Girard, "The Founding Murder," in *Violence and Truth: On the Work of René Girard,* ed. Paul Dumouchel (Stanford: Stanford University Press, 1988), 240.
4. Saki Ryûzô, *Fukushû suru wa ware ni ari,* (Tokyo: Kôdansha, 1978).
5. Allan Casebier, "Images of Irrationality in Modern Japan: The Films of Shohei Imamura," *Film Criticism* 8:1 (fall 1983): 42. Taken out of context, as it is here, Casebier's comment may appear to be a sweeping generalization that verges on the acceptance of an essentialist view of Japanese culture. However, his statement is descriptive of an essentialist view of Japanese identity that he is correct, I believe, in ascribing to Imamura.
6. Hannah Arendt, *On Violence,* (New York: Harcourt, Brace & World, 1969), 65–66. Arendt argues that, historically, the reaction to hypocrisy, more than to injustice, is often the cause of political violence and unrest.
7. Girard, 241.
8. Arendt, 82.
9. Michel Foucault, in his famous study *Madness and Civilization,* argues that the asylum that emerged in the eighteenth century was not a space of nature, but a uniform domain of legislation, a site of moral syntheses that would eliminate insanities born on the outer limits of society: "Formerly, unreason was set outside of judgment, to be delivered, arbitrarily, to the powers of reason. Now it is judged, and not only upon entering the asylum, in order to be recognized, classified and made innocent forever; it is caught, on the contrary, in a perpetual judgment, which never ceases to pursue it and to apply sanctions, to proclaim its transgressions, to require honorable amends, to exclude, finally, those whose transgressions risk compromising the social order." Cited from *The Foucault Reader,* ed. Paul Rabinow (New York: Pantheon Books, 1984), 157–58.
10. David Forgacs, "Fascism, violence and modernity," in *The Violent Muse: Violence and the Artistic Imagination in Europe, 1910–1939,* ed. Jana Howlett and Rod Mengham (Manchester: Manchester University Press, 1994), 20–21. It is worth noting in passing that the fullest visual expression of the fascist aesthetic of the purified body is provided by Leni Riefenstahl's *Olympiad.*
11. Saul Friedlander, *Reflections of Nazism: An Essay on Kitsch and Death,* (Bloomington: Indiana University Press, 1993), p. 135.
12. William Bouwsma, *A Usable Past: Essays in European Cultural History,* (Berkeley: University of California Press, 1990), 182.
13. The aesthetics of violence is a primary concern in the 1930s in the work of members of the Japanese Romanticists (the *Roman-ha*), especially in the writings of Yasuda Yojûrô. I mention this in passing since the influence of these writers on the generation coming of age during that time – that is, the generation of people like Imamura and Mishima – was enormous.
14. René Girard, "The Founding Murder," p. 240.

15. Yukio Mishima, "Preface," in *Ordeal by roses: photographs of Yukio Mishima by Eikoh Hosoe* (New York: Aperture, 1985).
16. Satô Tadao emphasizes the elements of the detective story in his reading of the film, and criticizes Imamura for disrupting the viewers' expectations for the conventions of the genre – a move he finds morally puzzling. See Satô, 183–201.
17. Brian Moeran, "The Beauty of Violence: Jidaigeki, Yakuza and 'eroduction' Films in Japanese Cinema," *The Anthropology of Violence,* ed. David Riches (Oxford: Basil Blackwell, 1986), 116.

CHAPTER FIFTEEN

The Frenzy of Metamorphosis

The Body in Japanese Pornographic Animation

Susan J. Napier

The body and animation were made for each other. As *Sight and Sound* defines animation, "Appropriately enough, the word comes from the Latin *anima* meaning breath or spirit. Thus, an animator gives life to inert materials" (June 1996: 12). Or, as the *manga* (comic book) artist Yukito Kishiro puts it, on seeing his drawings transformed into animated video, "(When) I saw the finished video (I) thought to myself, 'Whoa, it's *moving!*' and 'Whoa, it's in *color*'" (*Animerica* 1, no. 8 (1993): 8.

Animation of course can animate any sort of "inert material." Indeed, Japanese animators can do marvelous things with nature (Miyazaki Hayao's *Nausicaa,* for example); with urban architecture (Otomo Katsuhiro's *Akira,* for instance); and with technology in general, (practically any science fiction animation out there). The greatest challenge in animation, however, as in art in general, is clearly the human body.

More than any other genre (with the possible exception of horror, with which it is often linked[1]), pornography brings the body to the fore, not only in terms of sexuality, but also in relation to aesthetics, gender, and, perhaps surprisingly, social identity. The related themes of power and domination are played out in pornography in the interaction of male and female bodies. Often these themes are played out in surprising ways, especially in Japanese animation.

There is no question that much of Japanese pornographic animation portrays disturbingly violent relationships between men and women. I would like to stress, however, that, as with the slasher films so popular in the West, it is impossible to reduce all Japanese pornography to a simple vision of brutal male dominance. Even the most appallingly violent films, such as *La Blue Girl* or *Twin Dolls,* show a more complex vision of male-female interaction than simply dominance and submission.

As Kellner says of Hollywood films, "[E]ven conservative ones . . . put on display hopes and fears that contest dominant hegemonic and hierarchical relations of power; . . . [they] put on display both the significant dreams and nightmares of a culture and the ways that the culture is attempting to channel them to maintain its present relations of power and domination."[2]

Kellner's point is a vital one for appreciating all forms of popular culture and it is important to remember just how popular animation is in contemporary Japan, including the highly sexualized films this essay discusses. I would like to argue, however, that what is most interesting about the films under discussion is that they often show the *failure* or at least the confusion of the attempts to "maintain [the] present relations of power and domination." Far more than live-action pornography in either Japan or the West (and even live-action pornography has come to be understood as bearing a more complicated relationship to society than had initially been thought),[3] sexually graphic animation does more than simply reflect or uphold the dominant power relations of Japanese society.

Part of the reason for pornography's complex role in Japan has to do with the complexity of the genre itself. While I am calling it "pornography," for the sake of brevity, and also in order not to minimize its very high sexual content, the genre might more appropriately be described as "science fiction and occult animation with explicitly sexualized imagery and themes."[4] Often these images and themes are indeed "hard core," but they appear in narratives that are far more imaginative and engrossing than those of mainstream live-action pornography in either the West or Japan. Often pornographic situations are integrated into occult, science fiction, or fantastic narratives that can be genuinely engrossing. Within these nonsexual frameworks the sexual situations that occur bring up not only obvious questions of gender construction and interaction but less obvious ones as well, such as the relation of gendered power and control to technology, tradition, and transition.

Another aspect of the genre's complexity that is directly related to the representation of the body is the general fascination in Japanese animation with the process of metamorphosis, in particular, the metamorphosing body. If the definition of animation is "to give life to inert materials," then Japanese animation plays on this process in a myriad of ways to create a memorable variety of fantasy bodies, consistently depicted in the process of transformation. This is particularly true of the pornographic genre, where the metamorphosing fantasy body is often the narrative and imagistic high point of each film.

It should be noted that within the pornographic genre the term *fantasy body* occupies two sites of meaning. The first is of course as the object of fantasy (presumably male fantasy, although this assumption will be explored further later). As fantasy object, the body in pornographic *anime* tends to be beautiful and voluptuous, if female, and, if male, is usually seen as impressive and powerful. All of this is unsurprising and not dissimilar to much live-action erotica in both Japan and the West.

What is genuinely surprising and far more intriguing, however, is the other form of fantasy body, the "fantastic body." Liberated from the constraints of realism by both the medium of animation and the challenges of the occult and fantastic genres, the fantastic body is the body in magical metamorphosis. Ranging across an extraordinarily wide continuum, from the grotesque to the marvelous, the fantastic body in pornography, particularly the female one,[5] offers a dizzying variety of representations, forcing us to look more deeply into our notions of how pornography represents not only the female but the male as well. Ultimately, the body in this fantastic mode interrogates the dominant constructions of male and female identity in contemporary Japanese society and also suggests how profoundly that society is changing.

Belying the stereotype of women in pornography as being fixed sexualized victims of men, Japanese pornographic animation tends to depict the female body in an often contradictory variety of ways. Most frequently, the female body is indeed an object, to be viewed, violated, and tortured, but the very same narrative will contain other scenes showing women's bodies as awesomely powerful, almost unstoppable forces of nature. For example, in *La Blue Girl* the female *ninja* who has been hideously tortured throughout much of the film, ends up conquering her demonic opponents by aligning her powers with both natural forces and her own ancestors. As is obvious in the preceding example, these two visions of woman as victim and as powerful force can coexist in the same film. Even more intriguingly, they can further be interspersed with scenes in which the female body is shown as an equal partner in joyful, even loving, conventional sexual intercourse, as seen in *La Blue Girl* and *Wicked City.*

Furthermore, while the female body inevitably remains an object of the male gaze, even the most violent pornography frequently represents it as active and capable of intimidating powers of transformation. The 1987 *Wicked City's* opening scene, in which a woman turns into a spider equipped with *vagina dentata,* is one of the most justifiably famous, but such powerful metamorphoses are, as I have argued, among the most important parts of *anime's* repertoire. Although I would not go so far as to suggest that such metamorphoses necessarily represent female empowerment, they clearly figure the female characters as something far beyond the passive objects of male domination that critics have tended to see.

In important contrast, the male body, at least in pornography, is far more restricted in terms of transformation. In fact, in most pornographic *anime* the male characters can be limited to two highly constricting types. The first I have called the "comic voyeur." This type tends to be related to humorous *manga* and *anime* images of shrunken men or boys with grotesquely distended eyes. Far from powerful, the voyeur is reduced to an infantile, largely passive status. The second type I have dubbed the "demonic phallus incarnate." This type is characterized by his nonhumanness (he is, often literally, a demon), his powerful muscular body, and, of course, a huge penis.

Needless to say, these fantastic and often clearly nonhuman bodies are a far cry from the realities of contemporary life. Are they simply compensation for the frustrations of living in a modern society? No doubt the answer is yes, but the issue is more complex than that.

THE FEMALE BODY: UNDER CONTROL?

I would like to discuss these body images in relation to three representative pornographic films, *Wicked City, Twin Dolls,* (1995), and *La Blue Girl* (1992–94), and, compare those images with a fourth, the more soft-core, science-fiction-style *Cutey Honey* (1994).[6] Of the first three, *Wicked City* is by far the most artistically edifying, a genuine horror masterpiece (given four stars by *Imagi-Movies* and described as a "future-goth noir thriller"[7]), but it is also genuinely hard-core pornography, replete with scenes of stomach-churning violence of the sexual torturing of women. *Twin Dolls* and *La Blue Girl* are far less sophisticated than

Wicked City, although they too share surprisingly complicated and even reasonably engrossing plots.

All three narratives revolve around the notion of demonic interaction with the "real world," although *Wicked City's* version is the most richly detailed. *Wicked City* posits a parallel world, called the "Black World," which has knowingly coexisted with humans for at least 500 years. The film's narrative tension involves the signing of a peace treaty between the human world and the Black World and the need to protect the one human representative who can deal with the Black World, an elderly man with the Italian-sounding name of Giuseppe, who turns out to be a massively endowed old lecher. A handsome government agent named Taki Reizaburo and a beautiful Black World agent named Makie are assigned to protect Giuseppe before the treaty signing.

The plot takes off when Giuseppe escapes to a house of prostitution that turns out to be controlled by resistance fighters from the Black World who are determined to destroy the peace negotiations. A Black World woman, posing as a prostitute, almost succeeds in killing Giuseppe in a vivid sequence in which he melts into her dissolving body, a literal return to the womb that is as grotesque as it is memorable. Taki and Makie manage to save the ungrateful Giuseppe at the last minute, however, but only at the cost of sacrificing Makie to the evil Black World resistance that kidnaps her and proceed to sexually torture her in a series of lengthy and graphically sadistic sequences.

Taki determines to rescue her and goes into the demonic other world to do battle in a series of memorably violent scenes, especially a visually stunning sequence in which he confronts a Black World woman who is almost literally all vagina and who tries to seduce him. Destroying his female opponent, Taki ultimately rescues Makie, and the two return to the human world, where they learn the truth, not only about Giuseppe, but their own roles as well. It turns out that Giuseppe has actually been sent to protect Taki and Makie, who are uniquely capable of creating a new race combining humans and black-worlders. In a surprisingly tender sequence the two are brought back from the dead and they make love. The ending is an upbeat one in which the pregnant Makie is seen as potentially uniting the two worlds.

In contrast to *Wicked City,* the *Twin Dolls* narrative dispenses with political subplots to concentrate purely on the occult and the sexual. Demons from Hell are trying to take over the world, through the torture and enslavement of women, and the kidnapping of the descendant of one of Japan's greatest gods, Sugawara Michizane. Two high school girls, the Twin Dolls, who are themselves descendants of a heavenly ancestress who bequeathed to them skills in the traditional arts of shrine dancing and magic martial arts, inherit the task of protecting Michizane's descendant. This descendant, named Onimaru, turns out to be a lecherous midget, and much sexual humor is derived from Onimaru's persistent efforts to see the girls naked. Demons provide the nonhumorous sex in the form of kidnapping, torturing, and raping the high school girls and their friends. Although the demons are eventually quelled (at least for the moment), the climax features a lengthy sequence in which the Twin Dolls are tied up and hung over the pit of Hell with their legs splayed open, while the chief demon, an enormous figure with a penis the size of a baseball bat, tortures and taunts them.

The equally violent *La Blue Girl* intermixes a bit of conventional sex within a more complicated hellish/demon-rapist narrative. The film takes place in an isolated mountain village, where two female ninjas go in search of a demonic criminal who is raping young high school girls. The ninjas, Yaku and Miko, are specially trained in "sexual magic arts" and a subplot involves their attempt to recover a family sword that itself has amazing sexual properties. The opening scene sets the tone of sexual violence within a traditional setting as the viewer sees what appears to be a temple interior, in which nude bodies of women are scattered everywhere, their vaginas covered in blood.

The sex in *La Blue Girl* is not always violent, however. Yaku and Miko clearly enjoy sex, and the film actually shows sequences of Yaku enjoying conventional heterosexual sex with one of the local boys, who has been spying on them as they bathe in their traditional Japanese inn. The ending of the film is also somewhat unusual. Although there is the requisite torture-by-demons-sex-scene, Miko ends up destroying the demons with the help of her boy sidekick, a kind of junior ninja named Nin Nin, her traditional *ninja* powers, and the local village boys who ride to the rescue in their souped-up sports cars.

I have detailed the plots of these films at some length, partly in order to demonstrate some of their more obvious similarities, but also to emphasize that pornographic animation in Japan is more than simply a series of bodies coming together. These bodies are embedded within both a narrative and a visual context that is worth examining in greater detail.

One striking aspect of all these films is of course their use of the occult. I will discuss the demonic body later but, for now, it is interesting to ponder the power of the essentially gothic context of setting and theme. Although *Wicked City* is set in a time close to the present, with the usual film-noir venues of bleak, labyrinthine, modern architecture, all three films convey the sense of an occult/gothic other world, paralleling our own.

The gothic is a clearly nostalgic mode and it is perhaps not surprising that in the last two films discussed, this other world is explicitly identified with traditional Japan.[8] The hells depicted in *Twin Dolls* are very similar to the ones shown in medieval Buddhist paintings, complete with lakes of blood and jagged mountains (although the huge phallic-shaped stalagmites are, I suspect, a modern interpolation). Even more significant, much of the "real world" action in both films takes place in such traditional settings as temples, *dojo* (martial arts halls), and a country inn. Even when more modern settings occur, such as the high school where the Twin Dolls study, these are seen mainly as hunting grounds, places from which the demons lure the young students.

The gothic and the occult are often considered female genres, especially in relation to their privileging of dark interior spaces, and fluid, engulfing entities. It is perhaps no accident that traditional Japan is associated with the feminine as well. It makes symbolic sense, therefore, that the twin dolls are shrine dancers, and that Yaku and Miko are ninjas, or even that the agent from the implicitly gothic Black World in *Wicked City* is female. These are female bodies that carry strong cultural resonances.

One of the first nude scenes in *La Blue Girl,* for example, takes place in the old-fashioned wooden bath of their traditional Japanese inn, while the two girls discuss their ninja-enhanced sexual abilities. The full moon rises in a scroll-shaped window behind them as they finger each other's bodies in a scene that, except for the more obvious nudity, would not be out of place in an eighteenth-century Japanese print. Also smacking of tradition is the interpolation of a voyeur, the figure of the inn's aged proprietor who peeps at them through the window.

Even more replete with tradition are several dance sequences in *Twin Dolls* in which the "dolls" cavort in the air, changing from their regular clothes to shrine-maiden costumes, with a quick glimpse of their nudity thrown in. The traditional dance itself is actually quite lovely, a graceful, strangely poignant scene, as the girls weave ribbons woven from the *hagoromo* costume of their heavenly ancestress around themselves as they fly through the air inside their training hall. Liberated from gravity, and apparently unconcerned with any male gaze, the dancers seem both sexual and powerful in their own, uniquely female realm.

Perhaps the most important aspect of the female body is its occult ability to change, a property which has both traditional and contemporary resonances. *Wicked City*, for example, contains four major female metamorphoses, three of which may be considered negative, within the context of the film, as they exemplify woman at her most sexually powerful and therefore threatening. The film's famous opening sequence revolves around the seduction of the human agent Taki Reizaburo by a woman from the Black World, who turns out to possess both spiderlike properties and a literal *vagina dentata*. In the middle of sexual intercourse the woman's black-stockinged and -gartered legs suddenly elongate insect-like around the hapless Taki, binding him to her. Even though he escapes, he and the viewer are afforded a glimpse of her teethed vagina, looking remarkably like a metal trap, and, as she scampers down the building side after him, she manages to appear both intensely sexual and terrifyingly demonic at the same time (see Figure 46).

Giuseppe's humiliation with the black world prostitute mimics Taki's encounter on an even darker level. The prostitute's vagina/womb first dis-

46. Metamorphosis of the fantastic female body; Kawajiri Yoshiaki, *Wicked City* (1987).

solves into flesh-colored ooze and then opens up and enlarges to literally engulf Giuseppe's small body within it. Unlike the teethed vagina of the previous scene, here it is woman's fluidity, her wet, oozing, engulfing flesh, that is emphasized. Even more frightening than the weaponlike vagina of the spider woman that appears strongly sexual and threatens castration, the female body here clearly threatens incorporation, a total transgression of boundaries.

The third negative metamorphosis occurs near the end of *Wicked City* and combines both sexual and maternal attributes: Taki confronts a Black World demoness whose entire torso turns into a huge red vagina spewing liquid as she moves toward him seductively, asking if he is "man enough" for her. The image of the huge vagina is grotesquely terrifying rather than sexually exciting, however, and it is little wonder that Taki easily resists temptation and goes on to destroy her.

Yaku, in *La Blue Girl,* also undergoes a transformation, although this one is somewhat more conventional, as *anime* metamorphoses go. If Yaku has sex without orgasm during a full moon, she transforms into a werewolf. In the film this power comes to her rescue as she is being sexually tortured by her demonic enemy Kugutsumen, who is determined to make her die from pleasure. Instead she turns into a fearsome (yet still feminine) werewolf and chases him away temporarily.

The transformative power of the female body is an important convention in both high and folk culture in Japan. Not only are ghosts in Japan traditionally female, but also there is a very popular genre of stories detailing women who were originally animals and who, when caught, return to animal form. The implicitly sexual nature of these stories is made completely explicit in modern pornography and, if anything, is seen as even more threatening.

The scene of the Twin Dolls dancing in air may also be seen as a kind of transformation scene, although, significantly, this is not sexual. The light, floating movements of the dance still exude a sense of feminine power, however. In all of these examples of transformation, we can see how strongly Japanese pornography goes beyond simple fantasies of male dominance and female submission. Women's bodies in these scenes are clearly powerful, more powerful than those of the male, in fact. These *anime* depict the female body as being in touch with intense, even magical forces, capable of overwhelming male-dominated reality.

It must be admitted, however, that the potential for female power is deeply undercut in other ways. The most powerful women in *Wicked City*, for example, are all evil, and ultimately destroyed by the stalwart Taki. Makie is initially positioned as stronger, a better fighter, and a generally more powerful agent than Taki, but is soon refigured into a sacrificial victim, giving her body for the sake of her duty to the egregious Giuseppe, and finally being saved by Taki, rather than through her own abilities. No longer a powerful figure in her own right, she has become a means of restoring Taki's ego, after his embarrassing encounter with the spider succubus. Her final transformation, the fourth female metamorphosis I mentioned, is away from the sexual to the maternal as she becomes pregnant with Taki's child.

Wicked City thus uses the image of female metamorphosis to inscribe itself back into the patriarchal order. Despite the film's brilliant transformation sequences, its underlying message is that of what Rosemary Jackson describes as conservative fantasy.[9] The collectivity is threatened by a series of fantastic others, but ultimately order is restored and chaos is controlled by the reassuring image of Makie's beautiful body now serving its most traditional function.

Women's sexuality itself is turned back on them in *La Blue Girl*. While Yaku is having sex with one of the village boys, Miko wanders off in sexual frustration. She encounters Kugutsumen in disguise, wielding an extraordinary instrument, which might be described as an air-powered dildo, whose puffs excite her in spite of herself. Although Miko seems to be receiving only pleasure in this scene, there is a clear sadistic subtext. The dildo's real purpose is to attach a kind of homing device into her womb that will allow the demon to control her. As the demon explains, "The womb is the source of all energy and life for a female ninja. If you control the womb, you control the woman."

In the case of Miko, this is literally so, as the device compels her to betray Yaku, thus leading to the two girls' sexual subjugation by Kugutsumen. The womb is thus seen as both a contested territory and one that ultimately can betray the female, even a magical female ninja.

But the film's final message is contradictory. Miko's "sexual ninja arts" have kept her womb trained enough to ultimately expel the controlling device. Awakening from her trance with the help of the village boys, her sidekick Nin Nin, and the spectral images of her grandmother, mother, and father, she goes on to destroy the demon using the "Blue Whirlwind technique," another traditional ninja power. *La Blue Girl* thus shows the woman's body in two antinomic ways: the first is as an object of control and violence by the male, and uncontrollable by the female (hence Yaku's transformation into a werewolf); the second is as an active vessel of triumphant resistance, although this triumph is aided by tradition (Miko's ninja arts and her dead relatives), and the timely arrival of the village boys.

Wicked City's message is also somewhat contradictory, although, surprisingly, more conventional than that of *La Blue Girl.* Women can be powerful, but the most powerful ones are clearly evil and their evil is concentrated in their sexuality; all three Black World women are represented as essentially vagina dentata or else all-devouring wombs, and they are all destroyed in lengthy scenes of graphic violence. Makie seems initially to be a more emancipated figure since she is depicted in nonsexual terms (she has short hair and in the opening scenes she wears a black, masculine-looking suit), as an intelligent and effective agent. But Makie's body also becomes subject to violence, although not through her sexual appetite, but through another womanly attribute, her willingness to sacrifice herself for another.

The protagonists of *Twin Dolls* also come across as more self-sacrificing than sexual since it is their devotion to duty that leads to their being tortured by the head demon. The other girl students at their high school, however, are shown as far more sexual beings. One girl, in particular, jealous of the twin dolls' abilities and attractiveness, ends up being seduced by the head demon and becoming his slave, sexual and otherwise. Interestingly, she is shown craving sex with the mammoth chief demon while the twin dolls are shown as resisting it till the end. In what may be a subtextual underscoring of the purity of tradition versus the degradedness of the contemporary period, the film pits the evil sluttish female (still wearing her high school student uniform), against the virginal twin dolls in their shrine-maiden robes. Also intriguingly, the "dolls," although tortured, are never depicted as having conventional intercourse with the demon. At the film's end they are still, both technically and symbolically, "virgins."[10]

The eponymous heroine of the science fiction film *Cutey Honey* makes an interesting comparison to the women in the three occult *anime.* Less violent or overtly sexual, the film relies on graphic nudity, rather than on scenes of intercourse or torture, for its sexual content.

Furthermore, Honey, initially at least, seems generally more in control than any of the female characters in the other films. A denizen of a near future dystopia, Honey is a crusader for good who takes on many disguises in her fight against (inevitably demonic) evildoers. As she herself sums it up, "Sometimes I'm an entertainment reporter, sometimes I'm a Chinese Fighter (martial arts master), sometimes I'm a rock and roll singer but always there is Honey Flash."

The term "Honey Flash" refers to her transformation sequence (see Figure 47). Each film in the series contains scenes of Honey metamorphosing into a variety of identities (usually preceded by her announcing, "I'm going to change!"), each of which carries with it the appropriately attractive accoutrement such as clothing and hairstyles. But this is more than simply fashion change; in general, these guises are of competent, powerful females. Or, as Honey's young male sidekick explains, "Honey's really great. She can do *anything!*"

Two factors subvert this empowering message, however. The first is the fact that Honey is not human. As we discover at the end of *Cutey Honey 2,* she is actually an android. Her superhuman competence is precisely that, *super*human. Not only is she not a real woman, at the end of *Cutey*

47. Honey Flash; *Cutey Honey* (1984).

Honey 2, her body is temporarily destroyed and she returns as a literal angel, complete with white robe and huge enfolding wings.

For a soft-core pornographic fantasy, this transcendent ending is certainly a pleasant change from the usual demonic violence set against hellish backdrops. But it is clear that Honey achieves this appealing metamorphosis through self-sacrifice, "dying" in order to save her friends. What might have been a message of female empowerment instead ends up sending decidedly mixed signals: the best kind of woman is one with an android's body that she is willing to sacrifice.

The other factor undercutting any message of empowerment is found in Honey's frequent transformation sequences. As Honey metamorphoses into whatever new guise she is going to adopt, the viewer is treated to a set sequence in which her clothes are stripped off her as her nude body rotates, apparently in the air. Next, her new outfit wriggles onto her, ending usually with the strings of her halter top tying themselves around her ample breasts. The entire process almost gives the impression that the viewer is first disrobing and then dressing her, in a ritual series of gestures choreographed to a set piece of music.

The transformation from regular person to superhero is of course a staple of science fiction and comic books but, for anyone who remembers Clark Kent's modest concern to about finding a private place in which to change from his secret identity, the public, celebratory, and clearly erotic nature of Honey's metamorphosis is startling, to say the least. The viewer is now able to participate in a way that I would argue is both voyeuristic and erotic, not simply in the viewing of Honey's nude body or even in the mental disrobing and clothing of it, but in the sense of being able to take part in an almost ecstatic process, the transformation of the body itself. I call this process "the frenzy of metamorphosis," with a nod to Linda Williams's description of pornography as the "frenzy of the visible."

Metamorphosis, power, and control of the female body are intimately linked in all four of the films. The twin dolls rotate in air, transforming for a time into powerful shrine virgins who dance, warrior style, brandishing their white ribbons. The film's torture sequence subverts that very transformation process, however, as the two are again shown in the air, but this time are hung suspended on ropes, their legs being pulled apart by the head demon's tentacular hair. The dance/metamorphosis scenes of lightness and autonomy are now replaced by images of imprisonment and victimization. The girls are now able to move only at the male's behest, with his hair being an obvious phallic substitute.

The female ninja in *La Blue Girl* are clearly punished, both for their sexuality and their metamorphic abilities. Yaku is unable to transform into a werewolf of her own accord, she is a victim of her sexual appetites. Miko, her womb taken over due to her own concupiscence, ends up betraying both of them in a torture scene similar to that in *Twin Dolls* where the girls are rendered immobile and tortured, only this time with a phallic sword rather than with the demon's hair.

Aside from the evil women of *Wicked City,* it is only the android Cutey Honey, whose slogan is "I'm going to change," who seems able to glory in metamorphosis for its own sake. But her transformation, as I have said, has obvious voyeuristic implications. On the purely sexual side, the presumably male viewer is invited in, to participate in the unclothing and clothing of her nude body, while both male and female viewer alike are allowed the vicarious participation in the ecstatic transformation process. Interestingly, Honey's final transformation into an angel is not shown, perhaps because of the overtly erotic nature of the transformations until that point. Presumably, a sexual angel would be too disturbing.

As with the other three films, it is safest to say that *Cutey Honey* sends mixed messages. Despite the regressive and voyeuristic aspects of her characterization, she is still clearly the film's hero, one worthy of admiration and emulation. Although the viewer is invited to enjoy her body, she is never shown being tortured and in the film's several violent scenes she more than holds her own. It is perhaps significant that *Cutey Honey*'s futuristic world, while certainly noir, is more generic science fiction than Japanese gothic. As an android in a non-Japanese environment, Honey is more liberated than the women still trapped in tradition.[11]

Overall, the female body in these four animated films seems to be far more than simply an object of sexual desire. The body is seen as capable of being powerful, mysterious, and frightening, controllable only by demons, and only temporarily by them. In the women's frightening potential for change, they reflect some of the serious dislocations Japanese society has undergone over the last decade or so, in which women's roles have changed enormously. In the 1980s and 1990s women have grown more independent, both financially and socially, taking on far more varied identities than the "good wife/wise mother" stereotype of Meiji Japan. Like Cutey Honey, women in the theater of the real Japan are "going to change."

In the theater of anime, women's changes are displayed, explored, and interrogated. Most obviously in *Wicked City* and in the werewolf sequence in *La Blue Girl,* these changes take on nightmarish proportions. Change is not always negative, however. In *Wicked City* the fearsome metamorphoses of the demon women are matched with the more soothing transformation on Makie's part, from powerful agent, to sacrifice, to mother. Ultimately, the patriarchal hierarchy is reinscribed.

Cutey Honey and the end of *La Blue Girl* seem at least potentially more genuinely subversive toward the notion of male dominance. Honey revels in her many identities even if at the end, her most permanent one is that of sacrificial angel. Miko on the other hand, uses her transformative powers to save herself and her friend, metamorphosing from victim to victor. The film's ending is problematic, however: Miko watches in lonely envy as Yaku goes off with one of the village boys. As she turns away, Nin Nin, the lecherous junior ninja, grasps her leg and peers beneath her skirt, telling her that he will "always be there."

THE MALE BODY: DEMONIC DOMINANCE AND COMIC FRUSTRATION

The image of a woman shackled by a small male, who attaches himself to her leg, is an interesting way to end a pornographic film and it brings me to my second topic of exploration, the male body. Surprisingly, it is in the depiction of the male body in pornographic animation that we may find portrayals more potentially subversive to patriarchal culture. While the female body's changes are manifold, ranging from glamorous to frightening to traditional, male bodies are largely fixed, and their frozen identities are far from the attractive range of the female ones. The male body in pornography does vary, as is clear in the films discussed previously, but the variations are usually ones that are hardly empowering.

While the female body in pornography is almost always young, beautiful, tall, the male body ranges over a variety of types from the grotesquely demonic to the humorously childlike. It is possible, however, to divide the male body into two general types, the comic and the demonic. The first might be called the comic voyeur, a shrunken, often childlike body, with emphasis on the head, especially such expressive features as mouth and eyes. Giuseppe, Nin Nin, and Onimaru are all examples of this type, whose chief function seems to be to watch longingly.

This emphasis on voyeurism rather than on sexual action is an important part of Japanese pornography, both in *manga* comics and in *anime.* Anne Allison has explored the scopophilia endemic in *manga,* suggesting that the strong emphasis on the male gaze positions males "to be masterful viewers," put in the positions of "voyeur and consumer,"[12] an assertion that is underscored by the depiction of the male body in general. Even the strongly hard-core *anime,* such as *La Blue Girl* or *Twin Dolls,* emphasize voyeurism as much as intercourse and we are as likely to see close-ups of male faces as we are of genitalia.

The comic faces, diminutive bodies, and passive positions of so many of the male actants are intriguing in the notion of male identity that they project. Allison performs an interesting analysis of the dynamic of the male gaze in the popular television *anime Machiko Sensei,* in which the male gaze first "stops" the woman, making her "an object or image of male viewing,"[13] but then goes on to make the male immobile. In the films discussed here, however, the male is not so much immobile as active but frustrated. Much of the comedy revolves around their comic attempts to see, touch, and, ultimately, to have sex with women, although they are usually unsuccessful.

It is this body image of the ever-ready, usually frustrated, grotesquely comic male that I find so intriguing. While the male gaze itself may have power, many of the males depicted in pornographic animation are virtually powerless. Onimaru in *Twin Dolls* is perhaps the most exemplary representative here. An eighteen-year-old in the body of a six-year-old, Onimaru's sexual adventures are relegated to such apparently frustrating activities as peeping from afar, trying to climb up girls' legs, and trying to lift up their skirts. Inevitably, he ends up being beaten by the girls and carried off by his guardian servant for his pains. Although the viewer sees his massive erections (through his trousers) and his slavering expressions of lust, he is never shown ameliorating his frustrations through masturbation or actual intercourse.

Similarly, Nin Nin, the diminutive ninja sidekick in *La Blue Girl,* although often shown as wild with lust, never actually has intercourse. He does perform cunnilingus on Kugutsumen's female accomplice but is caught and punished by the demonic male. In an interesting variation of the bugged-out-eyes image, Nin Nin always wears a blue ninja mask but his sexual excitement is shown both through erections and his eye holes changing color.

Giuseppe, while portrayed in a constant state of arousal, is also never shown performing active sex. Our most memorable image of him is when Taki and Makie have to literally drag him out of the huge oozing womb/vagina of the Black World prostitute into whom he is in the process of dissolving. This arresting scene highlights not only Giuseppe's concupiscence but also his vulnerability; his aging little body, almost engulfed by the cavernous stomach/womb/vagina of the demonic female, looks pathetic and helpless as compared to her powerful torso.

From an American perspective, scenes of continual sexual frustration in what is certainly hard-core sexual fantasy may be somewhat puzzling. Why should hard-core pornography of all genres privilege delayed or displaced gratification? There are a number of possible explanations. The first relates to the important position of the voyeur in Japanese erotic culture. Although voyeurism is important in the West as well, it is one of the most significant aspects of sexual fantasy in Japan, from at least the time of the tenth-century *Tale of Genji* and *The Tales of Ise,* where virtually all erotic encounters were presaged by the hidden hero first peeping at the woman who excites his interest.

Perhaps most important, we have the complex relationship of viewer and *anime* that I suspect leads to the heart of the matter. The comic infantile or aged male body is an inherently unthreatening one. The viewer can both identify with Nin Nin's, Onimaru's, and Giuseppe's lust and at the same time feel superior to them. Indeed, it may be that he may also identify, and be comfortably familiar with, their perennial frustration, a frustration which can become a form of erotic activity in itself (perhaps related to the traditional emphasis on voyeurism).[14]

Of course not all sexual activity in *anime* is frustrated, which brings me to the other paradigmatic male body in so much of pornographic animation, the demonic. The demonic body is in many ways the antithesis of the comic male body. Preternaturally huge, covered with rippling muscles, and inevitably equipped with an enormous phallus (and often with phallic tentacles as well), the demon is all action. In important contrast to the comic male, whose chief action is ogling, the demon's main activity is penetration of the female, both through the phallus and through as many phallic substitutes as possible. Thus the opening scene in *Twin*

Dolls shows a crowd of what might be called junior demons, small in stature and genitalia-less, forcing their horns into their female victims.

Even more obvious in its phallic function is Zipangu, the demonic sword in *La Blue Girl.* According to legend, the sword is an ancient one used by a Korean princess for masturbatory pleasure, after she has already used it in its typical normal function for killing her lovers. Eventually, she ends up killing herself in sexual ecstasy by driving the sword up through her vagina into her throat. By this time, however, the sword has taken on a sexual life of its own and the film depicts it, first, enslaving Kugutsumen's female accomplice and then attempting to take over Miko's body in the climactic final scene.

It would seem therefore, that, with the exception of Taki in *Wicked City,* the most powerful male bodies in *anime* are nonhuman ones. The combination of magic, traditional and sexual power in the body of the demon is an intriguing one in comparison to the comic voyeur. Although there are more conventional sexual activities portrayed in Japanese animation (*La Blue Girl,* for example, shows one of the village boys while he is engaged in clearly satisfying intercourse with Yaku), the male body that consistently gains sexual satisfaction in *anime* is one that in origin, iconography, and substance, is clearly Other, demonic, made of steel, bulging with tentacles.

What does this mean? Is it simply an aesthetic coincidence based on the special powers of animation? Or does it suggest something about Japanese male sexual identity?

I would suggest that the answer is "yes" to both. It is important to remember that the animator's art lends itself to fantasy. The development of tentacles, the huge phalluses, the horned heads of the little demons are all features difficult to portray in realistic cinema.[15] At the same time they are extraordinarily memorable in ways that depictions of more conventional sexual intercourse simply are not.

It is impossible to ignore the social or cultural context in which animation takes place, however. The image of a constantly changing female body is surely related to the transformation of the Japanese woman's social and political identity over the last few decades. Confronted with women grown more powerful and more independent, Japanese men have apparently suffered their own form of identity crisis. Jane Condon has pointed to some of the most disturbing sociological phenomena included in this male reaction, especially the growth of sexual interest in very young (i.e., nonthreatening girls),[16] and I would suggest that the violent and demonic depictions of both men and women in *anime* are symptomatic reactions of these social changes as well.

This brings me to another important question: Is it not in the depiction of the male body that we find a potential subversion of patriarchal culture?

I would suggest that, at the very least, the bifurcation of the male body into the immobilized, shrunken voyeur, and the enormous, sexually potent demon, suggests a real despair over the male identity, perhaps not only sexual but in a wider context as well.[17] The male viewer is obviously going to identity, at least at some level, with the sexually active males in the films but his choices are remarkably limited, goggle-eyed infantile voyeurism and demonic sadistic action. It seems that the only way a man can imagine himself as sexually potent is to transmogrify his identity into the demonic. While neither of these choices are unique to Japan, (although the demonic is clearly stressed more in Japan than elsewhere), the truly remarkable lack of conventional sexually active males hints that sexual activity and identity are still not integrated into regular life in Japan.

Furthermore, the notion of otherness is intriguing in relation to the sociocultural context as well. Just as with the female Gothic, the sexually active males belong to another, more traditional world. The demons themselves share numerous iconographical similarities with the demons in medieval art (as well as with eighteenth- and nineteenth-century woodblock prints) and their association with a clearly medieval Japanese hell is important as well. The sword in *La Blue Girl* is of course a traditional medieval sword.

Only Taki in Wicked City is depicted as conventionally sexually successful and attractive. But he too needs magical help (from Giuseppe of all people) to finally mate satisfactorily. Even more interestingly, he is one of the few male characters in any of the *anime* depicted who achieves orgasm, or so we can assume, since he successfully impregnates Makie. The only other example is the village boy in *La Blue Girl* whom we see commenting appreciatively that he "came five times."

In general, however, male orgasm is depicted far less frequently than male frustration on the part of the comic voyeur or simply endless penetration on the part of the phallic demon, perhaps because orgasm would suggest a vulnerable loss of control.[18] The combination of frustration and desperate need for control in the depiction of the sexual male underlines once again the paucity of sexual identities available to the Japanese male. The eternal displacement or delaying of orgasm suggests a truly hellish world in which genuine satisfaction can never be achieved. Always erect, the male body, be it comic or demonic, seems to be continually seeking and never finding fulfillment. In contrast, the female body, in its frenzy of metamorphosis, seems finally and frustratingly unavailable, an elusive will-o'-the-wisp whose transformations only underline the frozen and reductive nature of contemporary male identity.

It is both ironic and significant that one of the most satisfied "males" in any of the films discussed is the sword Zipangu in *La Blue Girl.* Animated only by sexual desire, it is shown enveloping the demonic female Kamiri, who seems in total ecstasy as a result. But Zipangu is actually an androgyne. As "he" explains, "the lust (of the princess) survives in me." This most literally phallic of weapons, then, is actually an instrument of female desire. Perhaps because of this uncanny combination of the sexes, the ninjas perceive the sword as being the most dangerous to them, and at the end of the film, Miko's "Blue Whirlwind Attack" rends it into fragments. The image of the fragmented male/female phallic substitute makes a memorable ending for the film, suggesting the ultimate impossibility of any male/female connection.

This essay has attempted to describe some of the most important ways in which both female and male bodies appear in animated pornography. I have tried to demonstrate that, despite the stereotype of Japanese pornography as always depicting men in dominant positions over women,[19] the reality is actually far more diverse, if perhaps equally disturbing. The male-female relationships in these films are unquestionably problematic but they are also varied and complicated. Pornographic animation in Japan may want to show women in positions of abjection and submission. What it in fact shows is a much more intricate series of contesting hierarchical relations in which men do not always come out on top and women's bodies, in their frenzy of metamorphoses, suggest new kinds of power.

NOTES

1. For a discussion of the connections between horror and pornography, see Carol J. Clover's "Her Body, Himself," in which she points out that "[h]orror and pornography are the only two genres specifically devoted to the arousal

of bodily sensation." (Irons, ed., *Gender, Language, and Myth: Essays on Popular Narrative,* 255). It is surely no accident that three of the four films discussed in this essay can be considered members of the horror genre.

2. Douglas Kellner, *Media Culture* (London: Routledge, 1995), 111.
3. For a comprehensive and ground-breaking discussion of the complexities of pornographic film in the West, see Linda Williams, *Hard Core: Power, Pleasure, and the Frenzy of the Visible* (Berkeley: University of California Press, 1989).
4. Interestingly, while the erotic has a long tradition in Japanese culture, the nude body does not. The woodblock prints of the Edo period (1600–1867), which many see as the precursors of both *manga* and *anime,* highlighted an actor's poses or the sweep of a courtesan's robe, but seldom dwelled on the unclothed body as a whole. Even the ubiquitous and often very graphic *shunga,* or erotic prints, tended to morselize the body into a courtesan's nipple or a customer's exaggeratedly large genitalia, while covering most of the human figure in flowing and evocative robes. Besides costume itself, the accoutrement of fashion or sex, such as sashes, dildoes, pipes, and swords, remained far more important than the human figure. The arrival of Western art, Western morals, and Western technology at the end of the nineteenth century brought the body into focus in a variety of ways. Western-style painters began to paint the nude at the same time as authorities started closing down mixed public bathhouses, fearing Western censure. This clash of the aesthetic and the moral meant that the nude, which had been taken for granted in premodern Japan, now became a problematic issue, subject to both aesthetic and erotic celebration and censorship. An even more intriguing variation on this development occurred after World War II when censorship was relaxed in some areas but remained uniquely powerful in others. Most notable was the government's ban on the depiction of genitalia or pubic hair, within explicitly sexual scenes. This unique form of censorship led to much creativity on the part of pornographic artists, who resorted to depictions of phallic and female genital substitutes such as pipes, guns, clams, etc., in effect harking back to the essence of Edo period eroticism. For a fascinating discussion of the use of genital substitutes in *manga* art see Sandra Buckley, "Penguin in Bondage: A Graphic Tale of Japanese Comic Books," in Constance Penley and Andrew Ross, eds., *Technoculture* (Minneapolis: University of Minnesota Press, 1991), 163–96.
5. Although, as I argue in this essay, the male body in animated pornography is usually more limited in comparison to the transforming female body, male bodies in other *anime* genres may be seen in a wide variety of metamorphoses. The cyberpunk masterpiece *Akira,* for example, contains an extraordinary and lengthy metamorphosis sequence that is the film's imagistic and narrative climax. The fantasy comedy *Ranma 1/2* revolves around the male title character's enforced transformation into a female every time he encounters cold water. The whole premise of the entire *mecha* genre (science fiction anime involving "hard" technology) is based on male and female characters transforming into cyborgs. In fact, it is the very protean quality of the charac-

ters in so much of *anime* that makes the relative fixity of the male characters in pornography so intriguing.

6. With the exception of *Wicked City,* all the films mentioned are parts of series and all four films are actually OVAs (original video animations), which means that they were not shown on television or in cinemas before distribution. For reference material in English on Japanese animation, see Ledoux and Ranney, *The Complete Anime Guide* (Issaquah, Wash.: Tiger Mountain Press, 1997).
7. *Imagi-Movies,* 2, no. 4 (summer 1995): 36.
8. But the gothic has increasingly taken on a contemporary resonance as well, and not only in Japan. A recent exhibition of contemporary Gothic art at the Institute of Contemporary Art in Boston describes what it calls the "full-blown revival of a "Gothic sensibility'" in our culture in the following intriguing terms: "The desire to be entertained and shocked through intense and stimulating sensations produced by the encounter with emotional extremes from delight to terror has seldom been more pronounced than today. An obsession with the paranormal and fantastic, with evil and distorted deeds, occupies once again a central place in the popular imagination. 'Gothic' has become the ubiquitous keyword to describe the somber and disturbing moods, sites, events and cultural byproducts prevalent at the end of the millennium. . .

   "The Gothic in contemporary art speaks of the subjects that transgress society's vague definitions of normality, discreetly peeling away the pretenses of outmoded conventions and blurring the amorphous border between good and evil, sanity and madness, erotic desire and repulsion, disinterested and visual offensiveness. . .

   "The old Gothic themes of the uncanny, the fantastic and pathological, and the tension between the artificial and organic are infused in contemporary art with new potency as they address concerns about the body, disease, voyeurism, and power" (Institute of Contemporary Art Brochure, Boston, 1997).

   Although I question the ICA's assertion that our period is uniquely suited to the Gothic, I do agree that an obsession with a variety of "Gothic" elements is a trend that seems to categorize some of the most interesting cultural products in contemporary industrialized societies. Indeed, what is so fascinating about occult animation is how so many of the visual tropes, such as demons, darkness, and the grotesque, are both peculiarly Japanese but completely recognizable to Westerners as well.
9. Rosemary Jackson, *Fantasy: The Literature of Subversion* (London: Methuen, 1981), 6.
10. This paradigm of the "bad girl" enjoying, even craving, sex while the "good girls" resist it, is one that is not confined to Japan. As Williams points out in her analysis of American sadomasochistic pornography, the "good" female victim is allowed to survive and even receive (supposedly against her will) some sexual pleasure, although she cannot acknowledge it. Williams suggests that the survival of the good girls is dependent partly on the viewer's

bisexual identification with them as victims. The viewer can enjoy the sadistic sex forced on the female victims, while at the same time identifying with them in their victim and "good girl" status. She states, "But, unlike the slasher film, where the sexual 'bad' women do not survive as female victim/heroes with whom male viewers identify, in sadomasochistic pornography these identificatory victim/heroes *do* survive – though they are punished for their sexual pleasures." *Hard Core,* 209. In *Twin Dolls* we have both "good" and "bad" girls, thus allowing the viewer to participate in an array of identifications without finally troubling his own sexual identity too strongly. The twin dolls are "punished," after all, even though they ultimately triumph.

11. In fact, I was interested to learn from a young Japanese woman (April 1997) that Cutey Honey was her "idol" when she was in junior high school, and the idol of her female friends as well. Less interested in the erotic nature of Honey's metamorphoses, the young Japanese girls were impressed by Honey's power and abilities.
12. Anne Allison, "A Male Gaze in Japanese Children's Cartoons or Are Naked Female Bodies Always Sexual?," Working Papers in Asian/Pacific Studies (Durham: Duke University, 1993) 33.
13. Ibid., 22.
14. The question of viewer identification is a crucial one in pornography, especially in violent pornography. In her seminal study of slasher films, *Men, Women, and Chain Saws* (Princeton: Princeton University Press, 1992), Carol Clover suggests that there is a strong confusion in gendered identity, perhaps especially beginning in the 1980s which allows the male viewer to identify with the last female victim in the slasher films, the only one who is usually left standing at the end of the movie. Although I would hesitate to say that a similar process goes on in Japanese pornography/horror, I would at least suggest that the desiring but helpless male figure is a way of working through a host of sexual uncertainties in a nonthreatening way. The demon, on the other hand, displaces the anxieties of the "normal" viewer, allowing him to enjoy vicarious sexual satisfaction without the need to identify on a deep level with his demonic substitute.
15. The fascination with phallic substitutes is hardly limited to *anime.* Sandra Buckley has done extensive work on what she calls "the graphics of representation through nonrepresentation" (186) noting its roots in censorship, but also reading it as an attempted "reinsertion of phallic order" (187), an interpretation that seems to support my reading of *anime* as suggesting a fundamental lack of power on the part of the would-be sexual male.
16. Jane Condon, *A Half Step Behind: Japanese Women Today* (Tokyo: Tuttle, 1985), 75–76.
17. The sublimation and displacement of male fear and anger through pornography is of course not restricted to Japan. Williams summarizes Soble on this theme, suggesting that "the contemporary increase in pornographic consumption can be accounted for by male loss of power in the wake of feminism and women's new unwillingness to accommodate their pleasures to those of men. Men who develop a dependence on pornography have . . .

given up the struggle for power in reality. Recourse to pornography would be an escape into a nostalgic past where rape, ravishment and abuse of women was without censure" (Williams, 163–64).

18. It is also possible to assume that the lack of depiction of male orgasm in Japanese animation (a major difference from Western pornographic film) is also related to the strict censorship of depictions of genitalia that was active until the early 1990s.
19. See, for example, Kinko Ito, "Sexism in Japanese Weekly Comic Magazines for Men" in John Lent, ed., *Asian Popular Culture* (Boulder: Westview Press, 1995), in which she suggests that in *manga* comic books, at least, "Men are always depicted in full control, seeking the ultimate pleasure from women" (122). Although this may be more the case in *manga,* in *anime,* as we have seen, control often ends up in the *woman*'s hands.

Selected Bibliography of Articles and Books in English

Anderson, Joseph. "Japanese Film Periodicals." *The Quarterly Review of Film, Radio, and Television* 9.4 (Summer 1955).

———. "Japanese Swordfighters and American Gunfighters." *Cinema Journal* 12 (spring 1973).

———. "Spoken Silents in the Japanese Cinema: Essay on the Necessity of Katsuben." *Journal of Film and Video* 9.1 (winter 1988).

———. "The Spaces Between: American Criticism of Japanese Films." *Wide Angle* 1.4 (1977).

Anderson, Joseph, and Donald Richie "Traditional Theater and Film in Japan." *Film Quarterly.* 12.1 (fall 1958).

———. "Kenji Mizoguchi." *Sight and Sound* 25.2 (autumn 1955).

———. "The Films of Heinosuke Gosho." *Sight and Sound* 26 (autumn 1956).

———. *The Japanese Film: Art and Industry.* Princeton: Princeton University Press, 1982.

Asanuma, Keiji. "A Theory of the Cinema and Traditional Aesthetic Thought in Japan". *Iconics.* 16 (spring 1993).

Bernardi, Joanne. "Tanizaki Jun'ichiro's `The Present and Future of the Moving Pictures.'" In *Currents in Japanese Culture: Translations and Transformations,* ed. Amy Vladeck Heinrich. New York: Columbia University Press, 1997.

———. "The Literary Link: Tanizaki and the Pure Film Movement." In *A Tanizaki Feast: The International Symposium in Venice,* ed. Adriana Boscaro and Anthony Hood Chambers. Ann Arbor: Center for Japanese Studies, University of Michigan, 1998.

———. "The Pure Film Movement and the Contemporary Drama Genre in Japan." In *Film and the First World War,* ed. Karel Dibbets and Bert Hogenkamp. Amsterdam: Amsterdam University Press, 1995.

Bock, Audie. "Ozu Reconsidered." *Film Criticism* 8.1 (fall 1983).

———. *Japanese Film Directors.* Tokyo: Kodansha International, 1980.

Bordwell, David, and Kristin Thompson. *Film Art, An Introduction.* New York: Alfred A. Knopf, 1986.

Bordwell, David. "Mizoguchi and the Evolution of Film Language." *Cinema and Language,* ed. Stephen Heath and Patricia Mellencamp. Frederick Md.: University Publications of America, 1983.

———. "Our Dream-Cinema: Western Historiography and the Japanese Film." *Film Reader* 4 (1979).

———. *Narration in the Fiction Film.* Madison: University of Wisconsin Press, 1985.

———. Ozu and the Poetics of Cinema. Princeton: Princeton University Press, 1988.

Bornoff, Nicholas. *Pink Samurai: Love, Marraige and Sex in Contemporary Japan* New York: Pocket Books, 1991.

Boyers, Robert. "Secular Vision, Transcendental Style: The Art of Yasujiro Ozu." *Georgia Review* 32 (spring 1978).

Broderick, Mick, ed. *Hibakusha Cinema: Hiroshima, Nagasaki and the Nuclear Image in Japanese Film.* New York: Kegan Paul International, 1996.

Buehrer, Beverly. *Japanese Films: A Bibliography and Commentary.* Jefferson, N.C.: McFarland & Co., 1990.

Burch, Noel. "Oshima Nagisa and Japanese Cinema in the 60s." *Cinema: A Critical Dictionary, Vol. 2,* ed. Richard Roud. London: Martin Secker and Warburg, 1980.

———. *To the Distant Observer: Form and Meaning in the Japanese Cinema.* Berkeley: University of California Press, 1979.

Buruma, Ian. *Behind the Mask: On Sexual Demons, Sacred Mothers, Transvestites, Gangsters, Drifters and Other Japanese Cultural Heroes.* New York: Pantheon, 1984.

Cameron, Ian. *Second Wave.* New York: Praeger, 1970.

Casebier, Allen. "Images of Irrationality in Modern Japan: The Films of Shohei Imamura." *Film Criticism* 8.1 (fall 1983).

———. "Oshima in Contemporary Theoretical Perspective." *Wide Angle* 11.2 (1985).

Ching, Leo. "Imaginings in the Empires of the Sun: Japanese Mass Culture in Asia." *Asia/Pacific as Space of Cultural Production,* ed. Rob Wilson and Arif Dirlik. Durham, N.C.: Duke University Press, 1995.

Cohen, Robert. "Mizoguchi and Modernism: Structure, Culture, Points of View." *Sight and Sound* 47.2 (spring 1978).

———. "Teinosuke Kinugasa: A Japanese Romantic." *Sight and Sound* 45 (summer 1976).

Danly, Robert. *In the Shade of Spring Leaves: The Life and Writings of Higuchi Ichiyô.* New Haven: Yale University Press, 1981.

Davies, Anthony. *Filming Shakespeare's Plays: The Adaptations of Laurence Olivier, Orson Welles, Peter Brook, and Akira Kurosawa.* New York: Cambridge University Press, 1988.

Davis, Darrell William. *Picturing Japaneseness: Monumental Style, National Identity, Japanese Film.* New York: Columbia University Press, 1996.

Desser, David, ed., *Ozu's Tokyo Story.* New York: Cambridge University Press, 1997.

Desser, David. Eros Plus Massacre: An Introduction to the Japanese New Wave Cinema. Bloomington: Indiana University Press, 1988.

———. *The Samurai Films of Akira Kurosawa.* Ann Arbor: UMI Research Press Studies Center, 1983.

———. "From the Opium War to the Pacific War: Japanese Propaganda Films of World War II." *Film History* 7.1 (1995).

Dower, John W. *Embracing Defeat: Japan in the Wake of World War II.* New York: W. W. Norton/New Press, 1999.

———. *War Without Mercy: Race and Power in the Pacific War.* New York: Pantheon, 1986.

Ehrlich, Linda C., and David Desser, eds., *Cinematic Landscapes.* Austin: University of Texas Press, 1994.

Ehrlich, Linda. "Internationalization and Orientalism in Japanese Cinema." *Synthesis* 2.1 (1995).

Fowler, Edward. *The Rhetoric of Confession: Shishôsetsu in Early Twentieth-Century Japanese Fiction.* Berkeley: University of California Press, 1988.

Freiberg, Freda. *Women in Mizoguchi Films.* Melbourne: Japanese Studies Center, 1981.

Fujii, James. *Complicit Fictions: The Subject In The Modern Japanese Prose Narrative.* Berkeley: University of California Press, 1993.

Galbraith, Stuart, IV. *The Japanese Filmography: A Complete Reference To 209 Filmmakers and the Over 1,250 Films Released In The United States; 1900 through 1994.* Jefferson, N.C.: McFarland & Co., 1996.

Gerow, A. A. "The Benshi's New Face: Defining Cinema in Taisho Japan." *Iconics.* 3 (1994).

Gillett, John, and David Wilson. *Yasujiro Ozu: A Critical Anthology,* ed. London: British Film Institute, 1976.

Grilli, Peter. *Japan in Film: A Comprehensive Annotated Catalogue of Documentary and Theatrical Film in Japan Available in the U.S.* New York: Japan Society, 1984.

Hauser, William B. "Women and War: The Japanese Film Image." In *Recreating Japanese Women, 1600–1945.* ed. Gail Lee Bernstein (Berkeley: University of California Press, 1991).

Hirano, Kyoko. *Mr. Smith goes to Tokyo: the Japanese cinema under the American occupation, 1945–1952.* Washington, D.C.: Smithsonian Institution, 1992.

Holthof, Marc. "Ozu's Reactionary Cinema." *Jump Cut* 18 (August 1978).

Iwamoto, Kenji. "Japanese Cinema Until 1930: A Consideration of its Formal Aspects." *Iris* 16 (spring 1993).

Izbicki, Joanne. "The Shape of Freedom: The Female Body in Post-Surrender Japanese Cinema." *U.S.-Japan Women's Journal* 12 (1997).

Johnson, William. "The Splitting Image: The Contrary Canon of Heinosuke Gosho." *Film Comment* 27.1 (January, February 1991).

Karatani, Kojin. *Origins of Modern Japanese Literature.* Durham, N.C.: Duke University Press, 1993.

Kasza, Gregory J. *The State and the Mass Media in Japan, 1918–1945.* Berkeley: University of California Press, 1988.

Kirihara, Donald. "Kabuki, Cinema and Mizoguchi Kenji." *Cinema and Language,* ed. Stephen Heath and Patricia Mellencamp. Frederick, Md.: University Publications of America, 1983.

———. "Reconstructing Japanese Film." In *Post-Theory: Reconstructing Film Studies,* ed. David Bordwell and Noel Carroll. Madison: University of Wisconsin Press, 1996.

———. "Critical Polarities and the Study of Japanese Film Style." *Journal of Film and Video* 34.1 (winter 1987).

———. *Patterns of Time: Mizoguchi and the 1930s.* Madison: University of Wisconsin Press, 1992.

Kondo, Masaki. "The Impersonalization of the Self in the Image Society." *Iris* 16 (spring 1993).

Konshak, Dennis J. "Space and Narrative in Tokyo Story." *Film Criticism* 4.3 (spring 1980).

Lehman, Peter. "The Act of Making Films: An Interview with Oshima Nagisa." *Wide Angle.* 4.2 (1980).

———. "The Mysterious Orient, the Crystal Clear Orient, the Non-existent Orient: Dilemmas of Western Scholars of Japanese Film." *Journal of Film and Video* 39 (winter 1987).

McDonald, Keiko. *Cinema East: A Critical Study of Major Japanese Films.* Rutherford, N.J.: Fairleigh Dickinson University Press, 1983.

———. *Japanese Classical Theater in Films.* London: Fairleigh Dickinson University Press, 1994.

———. *Kenji Mizoguchi.* Boston: Twayne Publishers, 1984.

———. "Form and Function in Osaka Elegy." *Film Criticism* 6.2 (winter 1982).

McWilliams, Dean. "The Ritual Cinema of Yukio Mishima." *Wide Angle* 4 (1977).

Mellen, Joan. *Waves at Genji's Door: Japan Through its Cinema.* (New York: Pantheon, 1976).

———. *Voices from the Japanese Cinema.* New York: Liveright, 1975.

Nada, Hisashi. "The Little Cinema Movement in the 1920s and the Introduction of Avant-Garde Cinema in Japan." Iconics 3 (1994).

Nolletti, Arthur, Jr., and David Desser, eds. *Reframing Japanese Cinema: Authorship, Genre, History.* Bloomington: Indiana University Press, 1992.

Nolletti, Arthur, Jr. "Mitsuo Yanagimachi's *Himatsuri:* An Analysis." *Film Criticism* 10.3 (spring 1986).

Nornes, Abe Markus, and Fukushima Yukio, eds. *Japan/America Film Wars: WWII Propaganda and its Cultural Contexts.* New York: Harwood, 1994.

Nornes, Abe Markus. "Context and The Makioka Sisters." *East-West Film Journal* (spring 1991).

Nygren, Scott. "Reconsidering Modernism: Japanese Film and the Post-Modern Context." *Wide Angle* 11.3 (July 89).

Peterson, James. "A War of Utter Rebellion: Kinugasa's Page of Madness and the Japanese Avant-Garde of the 1920's." *Cinema Journal* 29.1 (fall 1989).

Prince, Stephen. *The Warrior's Camera: The Cinema of Akira Kurosawa.* (Princeton: Princeton University Press, 1991).

Raine, Michael, and Dudley Andrew. "Japanese Image Culture." *Iconics* 16 (spring 1993).

Richie, Donald, and Anderson Joseph L., "Kenji Mizoguchi." *Sight and Sound* 2 (autumn 1955).

Richie, Donald. *Japanese Cinema: An Introduction.* (New York: Oxford University Press, 1990).

———. *Japanese Cinema: Film Style and National Character.* New York: Anchor, 1971.

———. *Ozu.* Berkeley: University of California Press, 1974.

———. *The Films of Akira Kurosawa.* Berkeley: University of California Press, 1984.

———. *The Japanese Movie.* Tokyo: Kodansha, 1982.

Sato, Tadao. "Oshima: Sex, Militarism and Empire." *American Film* 8.10 (September 1983).

———. "Benshi – The Japanese Tradition of Accompanying Silent Films." *Retrospective of the Japanese Short Film 1955–1991,* ed. Stadt Oberhausen, International Short Film Festival Oberhausen: Neue Bucherstube Laufen, 1994.

———. *Currents in Japanese Cinema.* Trans. Gregory Barrett. Tokyo: Kodansha International, 1982.

Schilling, Mark. "Into the Heartland with Tora-san." *Japan Quarterly* 40.2 (April-June 1993).

Schrader, Paul. *Transcendental Style in Film: Ozu, Bresson, Dreyer.* Berkeley: University of California Press, 1972.

Sewell, Dorita. "Japanese Film as a Storytelling". *Wide Angle* 5.1 (1983).

Silver, Alain. *The Samurai Film.* Woodstock, N.Y.: Overlook, 1983.

Stanbrook, Alan. "On the Track of Hiroshi Shimizu." *Sight and Sound* 52.2 (spring 1988).

Suzuki, Shirouyasu. "From the Summit of the 'Body' and Beyond: The Meaning Behind Personal Films." In *Japanese Experimental Film & Video 1955–1994,* ed. Image Forum. Osaka: Kirin Plaza Osaka, 1994.

Suzuki, Tomi. *Narrating the Self: Fictions of Japanese Modernity.* Stanford: Stanford University Press, 1996.

Thompson, Kristin, and David Bordwell. "Space and Narrative in the Films of Ozu." *Screen* (summer, 1976).

Tucker, Richard. *Japan: Film Image* London: Studio Vista, 1973.

Turim, Maureen. "Rituals, Desire, Death in Oshima's Ceremonies." *Enclitic.* 5.2/6.1 (fall 1981 – spring 1982).

———. *The Films of Oshima Nagisa: Images of Japanese Iconoclast.* Berkeley: University of California Press, 1998.

Vasey, Ruth. "Ozu and the Nô." *Australian Journal of Screen Theory* 7 (1980).

Wakeman, John, ed. *World Film Directors Vol. I: 1890–1945.* New York: H. W. Wilson, 1987.

Walker, Janet. *The Japanese Novel of the Meiji Period and the Ideal of Individualism.* Princeton: Princeton University Press, 1979.

Washburn, Dennis C. *The Dilemma of the Modern in Japanese Fiction.* New Haven: Yale University Press, 1995.

Yamamoto, Kikuo. "Ozu and Kabuki." *Iconics* 1 (1987).

Yoshimoto, Mitsuhiro. "Melodrama, Postmodernism, and the Japanese Cinema." *East-West Film Journal* 5.1 (January 1991).

———. "The Difficulty of Being Radical: The Discipline of Film Studies and the Postcolonial World Order." In *Japan in the World,* ed. Masao Miyoshi and H. D. Harootunian. Durham: Duke University Press, 1993.

———. "The Postmodern and Mass Images in Japan." *Public Culture* 1:2 (1989).

Index

LaVergne, TN USA
04 May 2010
181535LV00002B/2/P

9 780521 777414